Western Civilization
A Brief History

Other Books by Marvin Perry

An Intellectual History of Modern Europe

Sources of the Western Tradition
Fourth Edition
Perry/Peden/Von Laue

- Two-Volume Paperback
  Volume I: From Ancient Times to the Enlightenment
  Volume II: From the Renaissance to the Present

Western Civilization: Ideas, Politics, and Society
Sixth Edition
Perry/Chase/Jacob/Jacob/Von Laue

- One-Volume Paperback
  Complete (Chapters 1–34)

- Two-Volume Paperback
  Volume I: To 1789 (Chapters 1–18)
  Volume II: From the 1600s (Chapters 16–34)

- One-Volume Paperback
  From the 1400s (Chapters 13–34)

Sources of Twentieth-Century Europe
Perry/Berg/Krukones

- One-Volume Paperback
  Complete (Chapters 1–9)

VOLUME I: TO 1789

Western Civilization

A Brief History

FOURTH EDITION

MARVIN PERRY

Baruch College
City University of New York

George W. Bock, *Editorial Associate*

Houghton Mifflin Company   BOSTON   NEW YORK

Editor-in-Chief: Jean Woy
Senior Sponsoring Editor: Nancy Blaine
Associate Editor: Julie Dunn
Project Editor: Gabrielle Stone
Production/Design Coordinator: Jodi O'Rourke
Senior Manufacturing Coordinator: Priscilla Bailey
Senior Marketing Manager: Sandra McGuire

Cover Image: *St. Augustine in His Study* by Sandro Botticelli (1444–1510). Fresco.
Credit: Chiesa di Ognissanti/Art Resource, NY.
Cover Design: Deborah Azerrad Savona

Printed in the U.S.A.

Library of Congress Catalog Card Number: 00–131417

ISBN: 0-618-04422-1

23456789–CRS–04 03 02 01 00

❖ Contents

❖ Maps

❖ Chronologies

❖ Preface

Western civilization is a grand but tragic drama. The West has forged the instruments of reason that make possible a rational comprehension of physical nature and human culture, conceived the idea of political liberty, and recognized the intrinsic worth of the individual. But the modern West, though it has unravelled nature's mysteries, has been less successful at finding rational solutions to social ills and conflicts between nations. Science, a great achievement of the Western intellect, while improving conditions of life, has also produced weapons of mass destruction. Though the West has pioneered in the protection of human rights, it has also produced totalitarian regimes that have trampled on individual freedom and human dignity. And although the West has demonstrated a commitment to human equality, it has also practiced brutal racism.

Western Civilization: A Brief History, Fourth Edition, is an abridged version of *Western Civilization: Ideas, Politics, and Society,* Sixth Edition. Like the longer text, this volume examines the Western tradition—those unique patterns of thought and systems of values that constitute the Western heritage. While focusing on key ideas and broad themes, the text also provides economic, political, and social history for students in Western civilization courses.

The text is written with the conviction that history is not a meaningless tale. Without a knowledge of history, men and women cannot fully know themselves, for all human beings have been shaped by institutions and values inherited from the past. Without an awareness of the historical evolution of reason and freedom, the dominant ideals of Western civilization, commitment to these ideals will diminish. Without a knowledge of history, the West cannot fully comprehend or adequately cope with the problems that burden its civilization and the world.

In attempting to make sense out of the past, the author has been careful to avoid superficial generalizations that oversimplify historical events and forces and arrange history into too neat a structure. But the text does strive to interpret and synthesize in order to provide students with a frame of reference with which to comprehend the principal events and eras in Western history.

Changes in the Fourth Edition

For the fourth edition, most chapters have been reworked to some extent. The numerous carefully selected modifications and additions significantly enhance the text. Some changes deepen the book's conceptual character; others provide useful and illustrative historical details. The concluding essays in several chapters have been enlarged and improved. Several chapters treating intellectual history have been expanded, and the art essays have been reorganized.

Specific changes in Chapter 1, "The Ancient Near East," include expanded treatments of prehistory, Hammurabi's Code, and the end-piece, "The Religious Orientation of the Ancient Near East." In Chapter 2, "The Hebrews," the end-piece, "The Legacy of the Jews," has been broadened. In Chapter 3, "The Greeks," we have deepened the analysis of Greek politics, the role of Greek women, and Thucydides' thought. Chapter 4, "Rome," contains new material on Roman expansion and culture. In Chapter 5, "Early Christianity," the discussion of Judaism at the time of Jesus has been deepened. Also deepened is the end section, "Christianity and Classical Humanism: Alternative World Views." The most significant changes in the chapters on the Middle Ages are broader discussions of Christian-Jewish relations and medieval attitudes toward women. Chapter 10, "Intellectual Transformation," includes richer treatments of Galileo, Locke, Hobbes, Motesquieu, Voltaire, and the end-piece, "The Enlightenment and the Modern Mentality." In Chapter 11, "The Era of the French Revolution," the end-piece, "The Meaning of the French Revolution," has been revised. Also revised is the treatment of nationalism in Chapter 13, "Thought and Culture in the Early Nineteenth Century." In Chapter 15, "Thought and Culture in the Mid-Nineteenth Century," more attention has been given to Social Darwinism. The section, "Russia: Tsarist Autocracy," has been moved to Chapter 16, "Europe in the Late Nineteenth Century"; in that same chapter, the treatment of racial nationalism and anti-Semitism has been expanded. In Chapter 17, "Modern Consciousness," we have sharpened the discussion of irrationalism, improved the treatment of pivotal thinkers, particularly Nietzsche and Freud, and upgraded the end-piece, "The Enlightenment Tradition in Disarray." The section on the Russian Revolution has been relocated in Chapter 18, "World War I," which also includes a fuller treatment of soldiering in the trenches, and a new section, "The Question of Responsibility." The material on the Soviet Union has been incorporated in a new Chapter 19, "An Era of Totalitarianism," which also contains an analysis of the nature and meaning of totalitarianism. Underlying reasons for the Russian victory on the Eastern front and additional material on the Holocaust has been added to Chapter 20, "World War II." The concluding chapter, Chapter 21, "The West in a Global Age," has been significantly restructured and updated.

Distinctive Features

This brief edition was prepared for Western Civilization courses that run for one term only, for instructors who like to supplement the main text with primary source readers, novels, or monographs, and for humanities courses in which additional works on literature and art will be assigned. In abbreviating the longer text by about a third, the number of chapters has been reduced from 34 to 21. The emphasis on the history of ideas and culture has been retained, but the amount of detail has of necessity been reduced.

The text contains several pedagogical features. Chapter introductions provide comprehensive overviews of key themes and give a sense of direction and coherence to the flow of history. Chronologies at the beginning of most chapters show the sequence of important events discussed in the chapter. Many chapters contain concluding essays that treat the larger meaning of the material. Facts have been carefully selected to illustrate key relationships and concepts and to avoid overwhelming students with unrelated and disconnected data. Each chapter concludes with an annotated bibliography and review questions. The questions refer students to principal points and aim at eliciting thoughtful answers.

This text is published in both single-volume and two-volume editions. Volume I treats the period from the first civilizations in the Near East through the age of Enlightenment in the eighteenth century (Chapters 1–10). Volume II covers the period from the Renaissance and the Reformation to the contemporary age (Chapters 8–21), and incorporates the last three chapters in Volume I: "Transition to the Modern Age: Renaissance and Reformation," "Political and Economic Transformation: National States, Overseas Expansion, Commercial Revolution," and "Intellectual Transformation: The Scientific Revolution and the Age of Enlightenment." Volume II also contains a comprehensive introduction that surveys the ancient world and the Middle Ages; the introduction is designed particularly for students who have not taken the first half of the course.

Ancillaries

Learning and teaching ancillaries, including a *Study Guide, Instructor's Manual with Test Items, Computerized Test Items,* and *Map Transparencies,* also contribute to the text's usefulness. The *Study Guide* has been prepared by Professor Lyle E. Linville of Prince George's Community College. For each text chapter, the *Study Guide* contains an introduction, learning objectives, words to know, identifications, a map study exercise, chronological/relational exercises, multiple-choice and essay questions, and a "transition," which reflects back on the chapter and looks forward to the next chapter's topic. The map study has outline maps, and students are asked to locate geographical features on them. A duplicate set of maps appears at the back of the book and may be removed for use in class quizzes.

The *Instructor's Manual with Test Items* was prepared for the brief edition by Professor Diane Moczar of Northern Virginia Community

College. The *Manual* contains chapter outlines, learning objectives, lecture topics, a film/video bibliography, essay and discussion questions, identifications, and multiple-choice questions and answers. The test questions are also available on computer disk (for Macintosh, IBM and IBM-compatible computers). In addition, a set of map transparencies is available on adoption.

Acknowledgments

In preparing this abridgment, I have made extensive use of the chapters written by my colleagues for *Western Civilization: Ideas, Politics, and Society*. Chapter 8, "Transition to the Modern Age: Renaissance and Reformation," and Chapter 9, "Political and Economic Transformation: National States, Overseas Expansion, Commercial Revolution," are based largely on James R. Jacob's and Margaret C. Jacob's chapters in the longer volume. Parts of Chapter 12, "The Industrial Revolution: The Transformation of Society," and of Chapter 16, "Europe in the Late Nineteenth Century: Modernization, Nationalism, Imperialism," are drawn from Myrna Chase's chapters. Material on tsarist Russia and the Soviet Union and the concluding chapter, "The West in a Global Age," are based very much on Theodore H. Von Laue's contribution to the larger text. To a lesser or greater extent, my colleagues' material has been abridged, restructured, and rewritten to meet the needs of this volume. Therefore, I alone am responsible for all interpretations and any errors. I wish to thank my colleagues for their gracious permission to use their words and thoughts.

I wish to thank the following instructors for their critical reading of sections of the manuscript:

Lester J. Bartson, University of Massachusetts, Boston; Judith G. Coffin, University of Texas, Austin; Gary Cross, Pennsylvania State University; Maureen C. Miller, George Mason University; and John Nicols, University of Oregon.

I am also grateful to the staff of Houghton Mifflin Company who lent their considerable talents to the project. In particular, I wish to thank Gabrielle Stone, project editor, for her careful attention to detail, Alice Manning, whose copyediting skills are reflected in the final manuscript, and Julie Dunn, developmental editor, who supervised the project. I am especially grateful to my friend George Bock who read the manuscript with an eye for organization, major concepts, and essential relationships. As ever, I am grateful to my wife Phyllis G. Perry for her encouragement.

M. P.

Geography of Europe

The map on the following pages shows the continent of Europe and the countries around the Mediterranean Sea. It gives the names and countries and their capitals and indicates the physical features of the land, such as major rivers and other bodies of water, mountains, and changes in elevation. A knowledge of the geography of this area will help give a sense of the connection between geography and history: of how the characteristics of the terrain and the availability of rivers and other bodies of water affected the movement of people and the relationship between people and the environment throughout history.

Europe is the smallest continent in the world with the exception of Australia. The other continents are Africa, Asia, North America, South America, and Antarctica. The continent of Europe, which can be viewed as the western extension of the Asian landmass, is distinctive in its configuration. Peninsulas make up a significant portion of its land area. This feature gives Europe an unusually long coastline, equal in distance to one and a half times around the equator (37,877 miles). Europe's western boundary is the Atlantic Ocean; the Ural Mountains, Ural River, and Caspian Sea—in Russia and Kazakhstan—form its eastern boundary. The European continent extends southward to the Caucasus Mountains, the Black Sea, and the Mediterranean Sea, and northward to the Arctic Ocean. Off the mainland but considered by geographers to be part of Europe are thousands of islands, most notably the British Isles to the northwest.

The small size of the European continent often surprises North Americans. France, for example, covers less geographic area than Texas, and England is similar in size to Alabama. The distance from London to Paris is about the same as from New York to Boston; the distance from Berlin to Moscow is comparable to that from Chicago to Denver. And the entire continent of Europe is about the size of Canada.

Major Peninsulas and Islands   There are five major European peninsulas: the Iberian (Portugal and Spain); the Apennine (Italy); the Balkan (Albania, Bulgaria, Greece, and parts of the former Yugoslavia and Turkey); the Scandinavian (Norway and Sweden); and Jutland (Denmark). Ireland and the United Kingdom of England, Wales, and Scotland make up the British Isles. Major islands of the Mediterranean Sea include the Balearic Islands, Corsica, Sardinia, Sicily, Crete, and Cyprus.

Seas, Lakes, and Rivers   Europe's irregular coastline divides large areas of the surrounding waters into bays, gulfs, and seas. Located in the Mediterranean Sea are, from west to east, the Tyrrhenian Sea (bordered by Italy, Sicily, Sardinia, and Corsica), the Adriatic Sea (between Italy and the former Yugoslavia), the Ionian Sea (between Italy and Greece), and the Aegean Sea (between Greece and Turkey).

The Baltic Sea, in the north, is bordered by Finland, Estonia, Latvia, Lithuania, Poland, Germany, and Sweden. Narrow channels connect it to the North Sea, which lies between Great Britain and the countries of the northwestern mainland. The English Channel separates England and France, and the Bay of Biscay is bounded by the west coast of France and the north coast of Spain. The Black Sea, on the southern border of Russia and the Ukraine, is linked by water passages to the Aegean Sea. The Caspian Sea, which lies partly in Russia and Kazakhstan, and partly in Asia, is the world's largest saltwater lake. At ninety-two feet below sea level, it is also the lowest point in Europe.

Elevation

Meters	Feet
4,000	13,120
2,000	6,560
500	1,640
200	656
Sea level	Sea level
Below sea level	Below sea level

✳ National capital
• Other city

NORWAY

SCOTLAND

Oslo ✳

SWEDEN

North Sea

DENMARK

Copenhagen ✳

NORTHERN IRELAND

UNITED

IRELAND

Dublin ✳

KINGDOM

ENGLAND

WALES

Thames

London •

NETHERLANDS

Amsterdam ✳

Berlin ✳

Elbe

ATLANTIC

English Channel

Brussels ✳

GERMANY

BELGIUM

LUXEMBOURG
✳ Luxembourg

OCEAN

Seine

Paris ✳

Prague ✳

CZECHOSLOVAKIA

Loire

Bay
of
Biscay

FRANCE

Bern ✳

Vienna ✳

SWITZERLAND

AUSTRIA

Rhine

A L P S

SLOVENIA

Ljubljana ✳

Zagreb ✳

Po

CROATIA

PORTUGAL

SPAIN

PYRENEES

Ebro

A
P
E
N
N
I
N
E
S

Adriatic

BOSNIA
HERZEG.

Sarajevo •

Lisbon ✳

Madrid ✳

Tiber

Sea

MONTEN.

Corsica

Rome ✳

Tito

ITALY

Balearic Is.

Sardinia

Tyrrhenian

GIBRALTAR
(Gr. Br.)

Sea

Rabat ✳

Algiers ✳

Sicily

Tunis ✳

MALTA

MOROCCO

TUNISIA

Tripoli ✳

ALGERIA

0	100	200	300	400	500 Km.
0	100	200	300	400	500 Mi.

LIBYA

Europe's many rivers have served as transportation routes for thousands of years. Several of the major rivers, including the longest, flow across the Russian plain. The Volga, Europe's longest river (2,194 miles), rises west of Moscow and empties into the Caspian Sea; canals and other river systems link it to the Arctic Ocean and the Baltic Sea. The Dnieper flows south through the agricultural heartland of the Ukraine into the Black Sea.

The second longest river, the Danube (1,777 miles), is the principal waterway in southeastern Europe. Originating in Germany, it flows through Austria, Slovakia, Hungary, the former Yugoslavia, Bulgaria, and Romania and into the Black Sea. The Rhine winds northward from the Alps, through western Germany and the Netherlands, to the North Sea, which is also the destination of the Elbe River in eastern Germany. In France, the Rhône flows south into the Mediterranean, and the Seine and Loire flow west to the English Channel and the Bay of Biscay. Other important waterways are the Po in northern Italy, the Vistula in Poland, and the Thames in England.

The proximity of most areas of the European landmass to the coastline or to major river systems is important to understanding the historical development of European civilization. Trading routes evolved and major cities grew along these waterways, and rivers have served as natural boundaries.

Land Regions Despite its small size, Europe presents a wide range of landforms, from rugged mountains to sweeping plains. These landforms can be separated into four major regions: the Northwest Mountains, the Great European Plain, the Central Uplands, and the Alpine Mountain System. The mountains of the northwest cover most of that region, running through northwestern France, Ireland, Scotland, Norway, Sweden, northern Finland, and the northwestern corner of Russia.

The Great European Plain spreads across almost the entire European part of the former Soviet Union, extending from the Arctic Ocean to the Caucasus Mountains. It stretches westward across Poland, Germany, Belgium, the western portion of France, and southeastern England.

The Central Uplands are a belt of high plateaus, hills, and low mountains. This belt reaches from the central plateau of Portugal, across Spain and the central highlands of France, to the hills and mountains of southern Germany, the Czech Republic, and Slovakia.

The Alpine Mountain System comprises several mountain chains. Within it lie the Pyrenees, between Spain and France; the Alps in southeastern France, northern Italy, Switzerland, and Western Austria, and the Apennine range in Italy. Also included are the mountain ranges of the Balkan Peninsula, the Carpathian Mountains in Slovakia, Poland, and Romania, and the Caucasus Mountains between the Black and Caspian Seas. Throughout history, these mountain ranges have been formidable barriers and boundaries, affecting the movement of people and the relationship of people to each other and to the land.

When studying the map of Europe, it is important to notice the proximity of western regions of Asia—especially those at the eastern end of the Mediterranean Sea—to parts of North Africa. The cultures of these areas have not only interacted with those of Europe, but they have also played a significant role in shaping the history of Western civilization.

Western Civilization
A Brief History

❖ PART ONE

The Ancient World: Foundation of the West

TO A.D. 500

The Acropolis of Athens. (*Robert Harding Picture Library*)

POLITICS AND SOCIETY	THOUGHT AND CULTURE
3000 B.C. Rise of civilization in Sumer (c. 3200) Union of Upper and Lower Egypt (c. 2900) Rise of Minoan civilization (c. 2600)	Cuneiform writing in Sumer; hieroglyphics in Egypt
2000 B.C. Rise of Mycenaean civilization (c. 2000) Hammurabi of Babylon builds an empire (1792–1750)	*Epic of Gilgamesh* (c. 1900) Code of Hammurabi (c. 1790) Amenhotep IV and a movement toward monotheism in Egypt (1369–1353) Moses and the Exodus (1200s)
1000 B.C. Creation of a unified Hebrew monarchy under David (1000–961) Dark Age in Greece (c. 1100–800) Hellenic Age (c. 800–323) Persian conquest of Near East (550–525) Formation of Roman Republic (509)	Homer's *Iliad* and *Odyssey* (700s) Age of classical prophecy: flowering of Hebrew ethical thought (750–430)
500 B.C. Persian Wars (499–479) Peloponnesian War (431–404) Conquest of Greek city-states by Philip of Macedonia (338) Conquests of Alexander the Great (336–323) Hellenistic Age (323–30) Roman conquest of Carthage and Hellenistic kingdoms (264–146)	Law of the Twelve Tables (450) Rise of Greek philosophy: Ionians, Pythagoreans, Parmenides (500s and 400s) Greek dramatists: Aeschylus, Sophocles, Euripides, Aristophanes (400s) Greek philosophers: Socrates, Plato, Aristotle (400s and 300s) Hellenistic philosophies: Epicureanism and Stoicism
100 B.C. Political violence and civil wars in Rome (88–31) Assassination of Julius Caesar (44) Octavian takes the title Augustus and becomes first Roman emperor (27) Pax Romana: height of Roman Empire (27 BC–180 AD)	Roman philosophers during the Republic: Lucretius, Cicero (1st cent.) Rise and spread of Christianity: Jesus (d. 29 AD); Paul's missionary activity (c. 34–64) Gospel of Mark (c. 66–70) Roman historians, poets, and philosophers during the Pax Romana: Livy, Tacitus, Virgil, Horace, Ovid, Juvenal, Seneca, Marcus Aurelius
200 A.D. Military anarchy in Rome (235–285) Goths defeat Romans at Adrianople (378) End of Roman Empire in the West (476)	Church fathers; Jerome, Ambrose, Augustine (300s and 400s)

❖ CHAPTER I

The Ancient Near East: The First Civilizations

*C*ivilization was not inevitable; it was an act of human creativity. The first civilizations emerged some five thousand years ago in the river valleys of Mesopotamia and Egypt. There, human beings established cities and states, invented writing, developed organized religion, and constructed large-scale buildings and monuments — all characteristics of civilized life. Humanity's rise to civilization was long and arduous. Some 99 percent of human history took place before the creation of civilization, in the vast ages of prehistory. ❖

Prehistory

The period called the Paleolithic Age, or Old Stone Age, began with the earliest primitive toolmaking human beings who inhabited East Africa nearly three million years ago. It ended about ten thousand years ago in parts of the Near East when people discovered how to farm. Our Paleolithic ancestors lived as hunters and food gatherers. Because they had not learned how to farm, they never established permanent villages. When their food supplies ran short, they abandoned their caves or tentlike structures of branches and searched for new dwelling places.

Human social development was shaped by this three-million-year experience of hunting and food gathering. For survival, groups of families formed bands consisting of around thirty people; members learned how to plan, organize, cooperate, trust, and share. Hunters assisted one another in tracking and killing game, finding cooperative efforts more successful than individual forays. By sharing their kill and bringing some back to their camp for the rest of the group, they reinforced the social bond. So, too, did women, who gathered nuts, seeds, and fruit for the group. Bands that did not cooperate in the hunt, in food gathering, or in food distribution were unlikely to survive.

Although human progress was very slow during the long centuries of the Paleolithic Age, developments occurred that influenced the future enormously. Paleolithic people developed spoken language and learned how to make and use tools of bone, wood, and stone. With these simple tools, they dug up roots; peeled the bark off trees; trapped, killed, and skinned animals;

Chronology 1.1 ❖ The Near East

3200 B.C.*	Rise of civilization in Sumer
2900	Union of Upper and Lower Egypt
2686–2181	Old Kingdom: essential forms of Egyptian civilization take shape
2180	Downfall of Akkadian empire
1792–1750	Hammurabi of Babylon brings Akkad and Sumer under his control and fashions a code of laws
1570	Egyptians drive out Hyksos and embark on empire
1369–1353	Reign of Amenhotep IV: a movement toward monotheism
1200	Fall of Hittite empire
612	Fall of Assyrian empire
604–562	Reign of Nebuchadnezzar: height of Chaldean empire
550–525 B.C.	Persian conquests form a world empire

*Most dates are approximations.

made clothing; and fashioned fishnets. They also discovered how to control fire, which allowed them to cook their meat and provided warmth and protection.

Like toolmaking and the control of fire, language was a great human achievement. Language enabled individuals to acquire and share with one another knowledge, experiences, and feelings. Thus, language was the decisive factor in the development of culture and its transmission from one generation to the next.

Most likely, our Paleolithic ancestors developed mythic-religious beliefs to explain the mysteries of nature, birth, sickness, and death. They felt that living powers operated within and beyond the world they experienced, and they sought to establish friendly relations with these powers. To Paleolithic people, the elements — sun, rain, wind, thunder, and lightning — were alive. The natural elements were spirits; they could feel and act with a purpose. To appease them, Paleolithic people made offerings. Gradually, there emerged shamans, medicine men, and witch doctors, who, through rituals, trances, and chants, seemed able to communicate with these spirits. Paleolithic people also began the practice of burying their dead, sometimes with offerings, which suggests belief in life after death.

Between thirty thousand and twelve thousand years ago, Paleolithic people sought out the dark and silent interior of caves, which they probably viewed

Paleolithic Cave Painting from Lascaux, France.   Produced as part of magical religious rites of hunting, these early paintings display considerable artistic skills. (*French Government Tourist Office*)

as sanctuaries, and, with only torches for light, they painted remarkably skillful and perceptive pictures of animals on the cave walls. When these prehistoric artists drew an animal with a spear in its side, they probably believed that this act would make them successful in hunting; when they drew a herd of animals, they probably hoped that this would cause game to be plentiful.

Some ten thousand years ago, the New Stone Age, or Neolithic Age, began in the Near East. During the Neolithic Age, human beings discovered farming, domesticated animals, established villages, polished stone tools, made pottery, and wove cloth. So important were these achievements that they are referred to as the Neolithic Revolution.

Agriculture and the domestication of animals revolutionized life. Whereas Paleolithic hunters and food gatherers had been forced to use whatever nature made available to them, Neolithic farmers altered their environment to satisfy human needs. Instead of spending their time searching for grains, roots, and berries, women and children grew crops near their homes; instead of tracking animals over great distances, men could slaughter domesticated goats or sheep nearby. Farming made possible a new kind of community. Since farmers had to live near their fields and could store food for the future, farming led to the rise of permanent settlements.

Villages changed the patterns of life. A food surplus freed some people to devote part of their time to sharpening their skills as basket weavers or tool-makers. The demand for raw materials and the creations of skilled artisans fostered trade, sometimes across long distances, and spurred the formation of trading settlements. An awareness of private property emerged. Hunters had accumulated few possessions, since belongings presented a burden when moving from place to place. Villagers, however, acquired property and were determined to protect it from one another and from outsiders, nomadic horsemen, who might raid the village. Hunting bands were egalitarian; generally, no one member had more possessions or more power than another. In farming villages, a ruling elite emerged that possessed wealth and wielded power.

No doubt farming also affected emotional development. Human beings who had evolved as hunters and foragers, enjoying considerable leisure, personal freedom, independence, and equality, were now forced to adjust to a different tempo of life — unending toil, stifling routine, and the need to obey the commands of the elite. Scholars ponder the psychological dimensions of this shift from the hunter's way of life to sedentary farming.

Neolithic people made great strides in technology. By shaping and baking clay, they made pottery containers for cooking and for storing food and water. The invention of the potter's wheel enabled them to form bowls and plates more quickly and precisely. Stone tools were sharpened by grinding them on rock. The discoveries of the wheel and the sail improved transportation and promoted trade, and the development of the plow and the ox yoke made tilling the soil easier for farmers.

The Neolithic period also marked the beginning of the use of metals. The first to be used was copper, which was easily fashioned into tools and weapons. Copper implements lasted longer than those of stone and flint, and they could be recast and reshaped if broken. In time, artisans discovered how to make bronze by combining copper and tin in the proper ratio. Bronze was harder than copper, which made a sharper cutting edge possible.

During the Neolithic Age, the food supply became more reliable, village life expanded, and the population increased. Families that acquired wealth gained a higher social status and became village leaders. Religion grew more formal and structured; nature spirits evolved into deities, each with specific powers over nature or human life. Altars were erected in their honor, and ceremonies were conducted by priests, whose power and wealth increased as people gave offerings to the gods. Neolithic society was growing more organized and complex; it was on the threshold of civilization.

The Rise to Civilization

What we call *civilization* arose some five thousand years ago in the Near East (in Mesopotamia and Egypt) and then later in East Asia (in India and China). The first civilizations began in cities that were larger, more populated, and more complex in their political, economic, and social structure than Neolithic villages. Because the cities depended on the inhabitants of adjacent villages for their food, farming techniques must have been sufficiently developed to produce food surpluses. Increased production provided food for urban inhabitants, who engaged in nonagricultural occupations; they became merchants, craftsmen, bureaucrats, and priests.

The invention of writing enabled the first civilizations to preserve, organize, and expand knowledge and to pass it on to future generations. It also allowed government officials and priests to conduct their affairs more efficiently. Moreover, civilized societies possessed organized governments, which issued laws and defined the boundary lines of their states. On a scale much larger than Neolithic communities, the inhabitants erected buildings and monuments, engaged in trade and manufacturing, and used specialized labor for different projects. Religious life grew more organized and complex, and a powerful and wealthy priesthood emerged. These developments — cities, specialization of labor, writing, organized government, monumental architecture, and a complex religious structure — differentiate the first civilizations from prehistoric cultures.

Religion was the central force in these primary civilizations. It provided satisfying explanations for the workings of nature, helped ease the fear of death, and justified traditional rules of morality. Law was considered sacred, a commandment of the gods. Religion united people in the common enterprises needed for survival — for example, the construction and maintenance of irrigation works and the storage of food. Religion also promoted creative achievements in art, literature, and science. In addition, the power of rulers, who were regarded either as gods or as agents of the gods, derived from religion.

The emergence of civilization was a great creative act and not merely the inevitable development of agricultural societies. Many communities had learned how to farm, but only a handful made the leap to civilization. How was it possible for Sumerians and Egyptians, the creators of the earliest civilizations, to make this breakthrough? Most scholars stress the relationship between civilizations and river valleys. Rivers deposited fertile silt on adjoining fields, provided water for crops, and served as avenues for trade. But environmental factors alone do not adequately explain the emergence of civilization. What cannot be omitted is the human contribution: capacity for thought and cooperative activity. Before these rivers could be of any value in producing crops, swamps around them had to be drained; jungles had to be cleared; and dikes, reservoirs, and canals had to be built. To construct and maintain irrigation works required the cooperation of large numbers of people, a necessary condition for civilization.

In the process of constructing and maintaining irrigation networks, people learned to formulate and obey rules and developed administrative, engineering, and mathematical skills. The need to keep records stimulated the invention of writing. These creative responses to the challenges posed by nature spurred the early inhabitants of Sumer and Egypt to make the breakthrough to civilization, thereby altering the course of human destiny.

Civilization also had its dark side. Epidemic disease thrived in urban centers, where people lived close together in unsanitary conditions, drinking contaminated water and surrounded by rotting garbage. The authority wielded by rulers and their officials and the habits of discipline acquired by the community's members made possible the construction of irrigation works, but they were also harnessed for destructive conflicts between states. Such warfare was far more lethal than the sporadic and disorganized acts of violence that had occurred in Neolithic times. And warfare fascinated the people who created the first civilizations. Scribes recounted battle after battle, warrior-kings boasted of their military conquests, and military heroes were held in the highest esteem.

Mesopotamian Civilization

Mesopotamia is the Greek word for "land between the rivers." It was here, in the valleys of the Tigris and Euphrates Rivers, that the first civilization began. The first people to develop an urban civilization in Mesopotamia (modern-day Iraq) were the Sumerians, who colonized the marshlands of the lower Euphrates, which, along with the Tigris, flows into the Persian Gulf.

Through constant toil and imagination, the Sumerians transformed the swamps into fields of barley and groves of date palms. Around 3000 B.C., their hut settlements gradually evolved into twelve independent city-states, each consisting of a city and its surrounding countryside. Among the impressive achievements of the Sumerians were a system of symbol writing in which pictures for objects and marks for numbers were engraved on clay tablets with a reed stylus (*cuneiform*) to represent ideas; elaborate brick houses, palaces, and temples; bronze tools and weapons; irrigation works; trade with other peoples; an early form of money; religious and political institutions; schools; religious and secular literature; varied art forms; codes of law; medicinal drugs; and a lunar calendar.

The history of Mesopotamia is marked by a succession of conquests. To the north of Sumer lay a Semitic* city called Akkad. About 2350 B.C., the people of Akkad, led by Sargon the Great, the warrior-king, conquered the Sumerian cities. Sargon built the world's first empire, which extended from the Persian Gulf to the Mediterranean Sea. Establishing a pattern that future despotic rulers would emulate, Sargon stationed garrisons in conquered lands and appointed governors and officials to administer the territories, as well as additional bureaucrats to register and parcel out the precious metals, horses, grain, and other commodities exacted from conquered peoples. He also retained a large standing army to quell revolts and to launch new imperialistic ventures. The Akkadians adopted Sumerian cultural forms, including

*Semites included Akkadians, Hebrews, Babylonians, Phoenicians, Canaanites, Assyrians, and Aramaeans. Hebrew and Arabic are Semitic languages.

cuneiform, and spread them beyond the boundaries of Mesopotamia with their conquests. Mesopotamian religion became a blend of Sumerian and Akkadian elements.

In succeeding centuries, the Sumerian cities were incorporated into various kingdoms and empires. The Sumerian language, replaced by a Semitic tongue, became an obscure language known only to priests, and the Sumerians gradually disappeared as a distinct people. But their cultural achievements endured. Akkadians, Babylonians, Elamites, and others adopted Sumerian religious, legal, literary, and art forms. The Sumerian legacy served as the basis for a Mesopotamian civilization, which maintained a distinct style for three thousand years.

Religion: The Basis of Mesopotamian Civilization

Religion lay at the center of Mesopotamian life. Every human activity — political, military, social, legal, literary, or artistic — was generally subordinated to an overriding religious purpose. Religion was the Mesopotamians' frame of reference for understanding nature, society, and themselves; it dominated and inspired all other cultural expressions and human activities. Wars between cities, for instance, were interpreted as conflicts between the gods of those cities, and victory ultimately depended on divine favor, not on human effort. Myths — narratives about the activities of the gods — explained the origins of the human species. According to the earliest Sumerian myths, the first human beings issued forth from the earth like plant life, or were shaped from clay by divine craftsmen and granted a heart by the goddess Nammu, or were formed from the blood of two gods sacrificed for that purpose.

The Mesopotamians believed that people were given life so that they could execute on earth the will of the gods in heaven. No important decisions were made by kings or priests without first consulting the gods. To discover the wishes of the gods, priests sacrificed animals and then examined their entrails; or the priests might find their answers in the stars or in dreams.

The cities of Mesopotamia were sacred communities dedicated to serving divine masters, and people hoped that appeasing the gods would bring security and prosperity to their cities. Each city belonged to a particular god, who was the real owner of the land and the real ruler of the city; often a vast complex of temples was built for the god and the god's family.

Supervised by priests, the temple was the heart of the city's life. The temple probably owned most of the land in its city; temple priests collected rents, operated businesses, and received contributions for festivals. Most inhabitants of the city worked for the temple priests as tenant farmers, agricultural laborers, or servants. Anxious to curry favor with the gods and goddesses who watched over the fields, peasants surrendered part of their crops to the temples. Priests coordinated the city's economic activity, supervising the distribution of land, overseeing the irrigation works, and storing food for emergencies. Temple scribes kept records of expenditures and receipts. By serving as stewards of

Wooden Soundbox of a Sumerian Harp, Ur, c. 2600 B.C.   The top panel features a heroic figure embracing two man-faced bulls made from shells inlaid in bitumen. Beneath are three panels with various animals carrying food or drink and musical instruments. The theme may depict a fable of some festive celebration or ritual myth. (*University Museum, University of Pennsylvania, Negative #S8–22097*)

the city's deities and managing their earthly estates, the priests sustained civilized life.

The Mesopotamians believed that the gods controlled the entire universe and everything in it. The moon, the sun, and the storm, the city, the irrigation works, and the fields — each was directed by a god. The Mesopotamians saw gods and demons everywhere in nature. There was a god in the fire and another in the river; evil demons stirred up sandstorms, caused disease, and endangered women in childbirth. To protect themselves from hostile powers,

Mesopotamians wore charms and begged their gods for help. When misfortune befell them, they attributed it to the gods. Even success was not due to their own efforts, but to the intervention of a god who had taken a special interest in them. Compared with the gods, an individual was an insignificant and lowly creature.

Uncertainty and danger filled life in Mesopotamia. Sometimes, the unpredictable waters of the rivers broke through the dikes, flooding fields, ruining crops, and damaging cities. At other times, an insufficient overflow deprived the land of water, causing crops to fail. Mesopotamia had no natural barriers to invasion. Feeling themselves surrounded by incomprehensible and often hostile forces, Mesopotamians lived in an atmosphere of anxiety, which permeated their civilization.

Contributing to this sense of insecurity was the belief that the gods behaved capriciously, malevolently, and vindictively. What do the gods demand of me? Is it ever possible to please them? To these questions Mesopotamians had no reassuring answers, for the gods' behavior was a mystery to mere human beings.

A mood of uncertainty and anxiety, an awareness of the cosmos as unfathomable and mysterious, a feeling of dread about the fragility of human existence and the impermanence of human achievement — these attitudes are as old as the first civilization. The *Epic of Gilgamesh*, the finest work of Mesopotamian literature, masterfully depicts this mood of pessimism and despair. The *Gilgamesh* deals with a profound theme: the human protest against death. Confronted with the reality of his own death, Gilgamesh yearns for eternal life. But he learns that when the gods created human beings, they made death part of their lot. "Where is the man who can clamber to heaven? Only the gods live forever . . . but as for us men, our days are numbered, our occupations are a breath of wind."[1] And in contrast to the Egyptians (see page 16), the Mesopotamians had little to look forward to after death. They believed that they would either be confined to a dreary underworld whose rulers would inflict pain on them or be transformed into spirits, flying about and tormenting the living.

Government, Law, and Economy

Kingship, bestowed on a man by the gods, was the central institution in Mesopotamian society. Unlike Egyptian pharaohs, Mesopotamian kings did not see themselves as gods, but rather as great men selected by the gods to represent them on earth. Gods governed through the kings, who reported to the gods about conditions in their land (which was the gods' property) and petitioned the gods for advice.

The king administered the laws, which came from the gods. The principal collection of laws in ancient Mesopotamia was the famous code of Hammurabi (c. 1792–c. 1750 B.C.), the Babylonian ruler. Unearthed by French archaeologists in 1901–1902, the code has provided invaluable insights into Mesopotamian society. In typical Mesopotamian fashion, Hammurabi claimed that his code rested on the authority of the gods; to violate it was to contravene the divine order.

The code reveals social status and mores in that area and time. Women were subservient to men, although efforts were made to protect women and children from abuse. By making death the penalty for adultery, the code probably sought to preserve family life. Punishments were generally severe — "an eye for an eye and a tooth for a tooth." The code prescribed death for housebreaking, kidnapping, aiding the escape of slaves, receiving stolen goods, and bearing false witness, but being forgiven by the wronged party could mitigate the penalty. For example, a wife who committed adultery could be spared execution if she was pardoned by her husband. Class distinctions were expressed in the code. For example, a person received more severe punishment for harming a noble than for harming a commoner. Government officials who engaged in extortion or bribery were harshly punished. The code's many provisions relating to business transactions underscore the importance of trade to Mesopotamian life.

The economy of Mesopotamian cities depended heavily on foreign and domestic trade. To safeguard it, governments instituted regulations to prevent fraud, and business transactions had to be recorded in writing. Enterprising businessmen set up trading outposts in distant lands, making the Mesopotamians pioneers in international trade.

Mathematics, Astronomy, and Medicine

The Mesopotamians made some impressive advances in mathematics. They devised multiplication and division tables, including even cubes and cube roots. They determined the area of right-angle triangles and rectangles, divided a circle into 360 degrees, and had some understanding of the principles that centuries later would be developed into the Pythagorean theorem and quadratic equations. But the Babylonians, who made the chief contribution in mathematics, barely advanced to the level of devising theories; they did not formulate general principles or furnish proofs for their mathematical operations.

By carefully observing and accurately recording the positions of planets and constellations of stars, Babylonian sky watchers took the first steps in developing the science of astronomy, and they devised a calendar based on the cycles of the moon. As in mathematics, however, they did not form theories to coordinate and illuminate their data. They believed that the position of the stars and planets revealed the will of the gods. Astronomers did not examine the heavens to find what we call cause and effect connections between the phenomena. Rather, they sought to discover what the gods wanted. With this knowledge, people could organize their political, social, and moral lives in accordance with divine commands, and they could escape the terrible consequences that they believed resulted from ignoring the gods' wishes.

Consistent with their religious world-view, the Mesopotamians believed that gods or demons caused disease. To cure a patient, priest-physicians

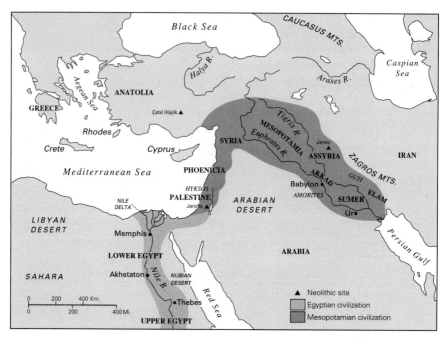

Map 1.1   Mesopotamian and Egyptian Civilizations

resorted to magic; through prayers and sacrifices, they attempted to appease the gods and eject the demons from the sick body. Nevertheless, in identifying illnesses and prescribing appropriate remedies, Mesopotamians demonstrated some accurate knowledge of medicine and pharmacology.

Egyptian Civilization

During the early period of Mesopotamian civilization, the Egyptians developed their civilization in the fertile valley of the Nile. Without this mighty river, which flows more than four thousand miles from central Africa northward to the Mediterranean, virtually all Egypt would be a desert. When the Nile overflowed its banks, as it did reliably and predictably, the floodwaters deposited a layer of fertile black earth, which, when cultivated, provided abundant food to support Egyptian civilization. The Egyptians learned how to control the river — a feat that required cooperative effort and ingenuity, as well as engineering and administrative skills. In addition to water and fertile land, the Nile provided an excellent transportation link between Upper (southern) and Lower (northern) Egypt. Natural barriers — mountains, deserts, cataracts (rapids) in the Nile, and the Mediterranean — protected

Egypt from attack, allowing the inhabitants to enjoy long periods of peace and prosperity. Thus, unlike Mesopotamians, Egyptians derived a sense of security from their environment.

From the Old Kingdom to the Middle Kingdom

About 2900 B.C., a ruler of Upper Egypt known as Narmer, or Menes, conquered the Nile Delta and Lower Egypt. By 2686 B.C., centralized rule had been firmly established, and great pyramids, which were tombs for the pharaohs, were being constructed. The pyramids required rigorous central planning to coordinate the tens of thousands of laborers drafted to build these immense monuments. During this Pyramid Age, or Old Kingdom (2686–2181 B.C.), the essential forms of Egyptian civilization crystallized.

The Egyptians believed the pharaoh to be both a man and a god, the earthly embodiment of the deity Horus. He was an absolute ruler who kept the irrigation works in order, maintained justice in the land, and expressed the will of heaven. In time, the nobles who served as district governors gained in status and wealth and gradually came to undermine the divine king's authority. The nobles' growing power and the enormous expenditure of Egypt's human and material resources on building pyramids led to the decline of the Old Kingdom. From 2181 to 2040 B.C., a span of time called the First Intermediate Period, rival families competed for the throne, destroying the unity of the kingdom. The civil wars and the collapse of central authority required to maintain the irrigation system cast a pall over the land.

During what is called the Middle Kingdom (2040–1786 B.C.), strong kings reasserted pharaonic rule and reunited the state. The restoration of political stability reinvigorated cultural life, and economic activity revived. Pharaohs extended Egyptian control south over the land of Nubia (modern Sudan), which became a principal source of gold. A profitable trade was carried on with Palestine, Syria, and Crete.

Around 1800 B.C., central authority again weakened. In the era known as the Second Intermediate Period (1786–1570 B.C.), the nobles regained some of their power, the Nubians broke away from Egyptian control, and the Hyksos (a mixture of Semites and Indo-Europeans) invaded Egypt. The Hyksos dominated Egypt for about a hundred years, until the Egyptians drove them out in 1570 B.C. The period of empire building known as the New Kingdom (1570–1085 B.C.) then began.

The basic features of Egyptian civilization had been forged during the Old and Middle Kingdoms. Egyptians looked to the past, convinced that the ways of their ancestors were best. For almost three thousand years, Egyptian civilization sought to retain a harmony with the order of nature instituted at creation. Believing in a changeless universe, the Egyptians did not value change or development — what we call progress — but venerated the institutions, traditions, and authority that embodied permanence.

Religion: The Basis of Egyptian Civilization

Religion was omnipresent in Egyptian life and accounted for the outstanding achievements of Egyptian civilization. Religious beliefs were the basis of Egyptian art, medicine, astronomy, literature, and government. The great pyramids, which took decades to finish, were tombs for the pharaohs, man-gods. Magical utterances pervaded medical practices, for disease was attributed to the gods. Astronomy evolved to determine the correct time for performing religious rites and sacrifices. The earliest examples of literature dealt wholly with religious themes. A sacrosanct monarch, the pharaoh served as an intermediary between the gods and human beings. The Egyptians developed an ethical code, which they believed the gods had approved.

Egyptian polytheism took many forms, including the worship of animals, for the people believed that gods manifested themselves in both human and animal shapes. The Egyptians also believed the great powers in nature — sky, sun, earth, the Nile — to be gods. Thus, the universe was teeming with divinities, and human lives were tied to the movements of the sun and the moon and to the rhythm of the seasons. In the heavens alive with gods, the Egyptians found answers to the great problems of human existence.

A crucial feature of Egyptian religion was the afterlife. Through pyramid-tombs, mummification to preserve the dead, and funerary art, the Egyptians showed their yearning for eternity and their desire to overcome death. Mortuary priests recited incantations to ensure the preservation of the dead body and the continuity of existence. Inscribed on the pyramids' interior walls were "pyramid texts," written in *hieroglyphics* — a form of picture writing in which figures, such as crocodiles, sails, eyes, and so forth, represented words or sounds that would be combined to form words. The texts contained fragments from myths, historical annals, and magical lore and provided spells to assist the king in ascending to heaven. To the Egyptians, the other world offered the same pleasures as those enjoyed on earth: friends, servants, fishing, hunting, paddling a canoe, picnicking with family members, entertainment by musicians and dancers, and good food. But since earthly existence was not fundamentally unhappy, Egyptians did not long for death.

Divine Kingship

Divine kingship was the basic institution of Egyptian civilization. The Egyptians saw rule by a god-king as the only acceptable political arrangement: it was in harmony with the order of the universe, and it brought justice and security to the nation.

The pharaoh's power extended to all sectors of society. Peasants were drafted to serve in labor corps as miners or construction workers. Foreign trade was a state monopoly, conducted according to the kingdom's needs. As the supreme overlord, the pharaoh oversaw an army of government officials, who collected taxes, supervised construction projects, checked the irrigation works, surveyed the land, kept records, conducted foreign trade,

**Pharaoh Mycerinus and His Queen,
c. 2525 B.C.** Swelling chests and
hips idealize the royal couple's humanity, but the cubic feeling of the
sculpture and the rigid confidence of
the pose proclaim their unquestioned
divinity. (*Harvard MFA Expedition.
Courtesy, Museum of Fine Arts,
Boston*)

and supervised government warehouses, where grain was stored as insurance against a bad harvest. All Egyptians were subservient to the pharaoh,
whose word was regarded as a divine ordinance. Most pharaohs took their
responsibilities seriously and tried to govern as benevolent protectors of the
people.

The pharaoh was seen as ruling in accordance with Ma'at, which means
justice, law, right, and truth. To oppose the pharaoh was to violate the universal and divinely ordained order of Ma'at and to bring disorder to society.
Because the Egyptians regarded Ma'at, which was established with the creation of the universe, as the right order of nature, they believed that its preservation must be the object of human activity — the guiding norm of the state
and the standard by which individuals conducted their lives. Those who did
Ma'at and spoke Ma'at would be justly rewarded. Could anything be more

The Eighteenth Dynasty King Akhenaton. His religious revolution has intrigued historians. Here he is depicted with his wife, Nefertiti, and their daughter, seated on her lap. The sun disk, representing the sole god Aton, looms above. (*Egyptian Museum Berlin/Bildarchiv Preussischer Kulturbesitz*)

reassuring than this belief that divine truth was represented in the person of the pharaoh, who guaranteed and defended the sacred order of the universe?

Science and Mathematics

Like the Mesopotamians, the Egyptians made practical advances in the sciences. They demonstrated superb engineering skills in building pyramids and fashioned an effective system of mathematics, including geometry for measurements, which enabled them to solve relatively simple problems. The Egyptians' solar calendar, which allowed them to predict when the Nile would overflow, was more accurate than the Babylonians' lunar calendar.

In the area of medicine, Egyptian doctors were more capable than their Mesopotamian counterparts. They could identify illnessess and recognized that uncleanliness encouraged contagion. They also had some knowledge of anatomy and performed operations: circumcision and perhaps the draining of abscessed teeth. But their knowledge of medicine, like that of the Mesopotamians, was handicapped by their belief that spiritual forces caused illnesses.

The New Kingdom and the Decline of Egyptian Civilization

The New Kingdom began in 1570 B.C. with the war of liberation against the Hyksos. This war gave rise to an intense militancy, which found expression in empire building. Aggressive pharaohs conquered territory that extended as far east as the Euphrates River. From its subject states, Egypt acquired tribute and slaves. Conquests led to the expansion of the bureaucracy, the development of a professional army, and the increased power of priests, whose temples shared in the spoils. The formation of the empire ended Egyptian isolation and accelerated commercial and cultural intercourse with other peoples. During this period, Egyptian art, for example, showed the influence of foreign forms.

A growing cosmopolitanism was paralleled by a movement toward monotheism during the reign of Pharaoh Amenhotep IV (c. 1369–1353 B.C.). Amenhotep sought to replace traditional polytheism with the worship of Aton, a single god of all people, who was represented as the sun disk. Amenhotep took the name Akhenaton ("It is well with Aton") and moved the capital from Thebes to a newly constructed holy city called Akhataten (near modern Tell el Amarna). The city had palaces, administrative centers, and a temple complex honoring Aton. Akhenaton and his wife, Nefertiti, who played a prominent role in his court, dedicated themselves to Aton — the creator of the world, the sustainer of life, and the god of love, justice, and peace. Akhenaton also ordered his officials to chisel out the names of other gods from inscriptions on temples and monuments. With awe, Akhenaton glorified Aton:

> *How manifold are thy works!*
> *They are hidden from man's sight.*
> *O sole god, like whom there is no other.*
> *Thou hast made the earth according to thy desire.*[2]

Akhenaton's "monotheism" had little impact on the masses of Egyptians, who retained their ancient beliefs, and was resisted by priests, who resented his changes. After Akhenaton's death, a new pharaoh had the monuments to Aton destroyed, along with records and inscriptions bearing Akhenaton's name.

The most significant historical questions about Akhenaton are these two: was his religion genuine monotheism, which pushed religious thought in a new direction? And if so, did it influence Moses, who led the Israelites out of Egypt about a century later? These questions have aroused controversy among historians. The principal limitation on the monotheistic character of Atonism is that there were really two gods in Akhenaton's religion: Aton and the pharaoh himself, who was still worshiped as a deity. Nor is there any evidence that Akhenaton influenced the monotheism of Moses. Moreover, the Hebrews never identified God with the sun or any other object in nature.

Late in the thirteenth century B.C., Libyans, probably seeking to settle in the more fertile land of Egypt, attacked from the west, and the Peoples of the Sea, as unsettled raiders from the Aegean Sea area and Asia Minor were called, launched a series of strikes at Egypt. A weakened Egypt abandoned its empire. In the succeeding centuries, Egypt came under the rule of Libyans, Nubians, Assyrians, Persians, and finally Greeks, to whom Egypt lost its independence in the fourth century B.C.

Egyptian civilization had flourished for nearly two thousand years before it experienced an almost one-thousand-year descent into stagnation, decline, and collapse. During its long history, the Egyptians tried to preserve the ancient forms of their civilization, revealed to them by their ancestors and representing for all time those unchanging values that they believed were the way of happiness.

Empire Builders

The rise of an Egyptian empire during the New Kingdom was part of a wider development in Near Eastern history after 1500 B.C. — the emergence of international empires. Empire building led to the intermingling of peoples and cultural traditions and to the extension of civilization well beyond the river valleys.

One reason for the growth of empires was the migration of peoples known as Indo-Europeans. Originally from a wide area ranging from southeastern Europe to the region beyond the Caspian Sea, Indo-Europeans embarked, around 2000 B.C., on a series of migrations that eventually brought them into Italy, Greece, Asia Minor, Mesopotamia, Persia, and India. From a core Indo-European tongue emerged the Greek, Latin, Germanic, Slavic, Persian, and Sanskrit languages.

Hittites

Several peoples established strong states in the Near East around 1500 B.C. — the Hurrians in northern Mesopotamia, the Kassites in southern Mesopotamia, and the Hittites in Asia Minor. The Hittites wanted to control the trade routes that ran along the Euphrates River into Syria. In the 1300s, the Hittite empire reached its peak. Its leaders ruled Asia Minor and northern Syria, raided Babylon, and challenged Egypt for control of Syria and Palestine.

The Hittites borrowed several features of Mesopotamian civilization, including cuneiform, legal principles, and literary and art forms. Hittite religion blended the beliefs and practices of Indo-Europeans, native inhabitants of Asia Minor, and Mesopotamians. The Hittites were probably the first people to develop a substantial iron industry. Initially, they apparently used iron only for ceremonial and ritual objects, and not for tools and weapons. However, because iron ore was more readily available than copper or tin (needed for bronze), after 1200 B.C. iron weapons and tools spread throughout the Near East, although bronze implements were still used. Around 1200 B.C., the Hittite empire fell, most likely to Indo-European invaders from the north.

Small Nations

During the twelfth century B.C., there was a temporary lull in empire building, and this permitted a number of small nations in Syria and Palestine to assert their sovereignty. Three of these peoples — the Phoenicians, the Aramaeans, and the Hebrews* — were originally Semitic desert nomads. The Phoenicians

---

* The Hebrews are discussed in Chapter 2.

were descendants of the Canaanites, a Semitic people who had settled Palestine around 3000 B.C. The Canaanites who had migrated northwest into what is now Lebanon were called Phoenicians.

Settling in the coastal Mediterranean cities of Tyre, Byblos, Berytus (Beirut), and Sidon, the Phoenicians were naturally drawn to the sea. These daring explorers established towns along the coast of North Africa, on the islands of the Western Mediterranean, and in Spain; they became the greatest sea traders of the ancient world. The Phoenicians (or their Canaanite forebears) devised the first alphabet, which was a monumental contribution to writing. Since all words could be represented by combinations of letters, it saved memorizing thousands of diagrams and aided the Phoenicians in transmitting the civilizations of the Near East to the Western Mediterranean. Adopted by the Greeks, who added vowels, the phonetic alphabet became a crucial component of European languages.

The Aramaeans, who settled in Syria, Palestine, and northern Mesopotamia, performed a role similar to that of the Phoenicians. As great caravan traders, they carried both goods and cultural patterns to various parts of the Near East. The Hebrews and the Persians, for example, acquired the Phoenician alphabet from the Aramaeans.

Assyria

In the ninth century B.C., empire building resumed with the Assyrians, a Semitic people from the region around the upper Tigris River. Although they had made forays of expansion in 1200 and 1100 B.C., the Assyrians begain their march to "world" empire three centuries later. In the eighth and seventh centuries, they became a ruthless fighting machine that stormed through Mesopotamia — including Armenia and Babylonia — as well as Syria, Palestine, and Egypt.

The Assyrian king, who was the representative and high priest of the god Ashur, governed absolutely. Nobles appointed by the king kept order in the provinces and collected tribute. The Assyrians improved roads, established messenger services, and engaged in large-scale irrigation projects to facilitate effective administration of their conquered lands and to promote prosperity. They exacted obedience by resorting to terror and by deporting troublemakers from their home territories.

Despite an almost all-consuming concern for war, the Assyrians preserved and spread the culture of the past. They copied and edited the literary works of Babylonia, adopted the old Sumerian gods, and used Mesopotamian art forms. The Assyrian king Ashurbanipal (669–626 B.C.) maintained a great library that housed thousands of clay tablets. After a period of wars and revolts by oppressed subjects weakened Assyria, a coalition of Medes from Iran and Chaldeans, or Neo-Babylonians, sacked the Assyrian capital of Nineveh in 612 B.C., destroying Assyrian power.

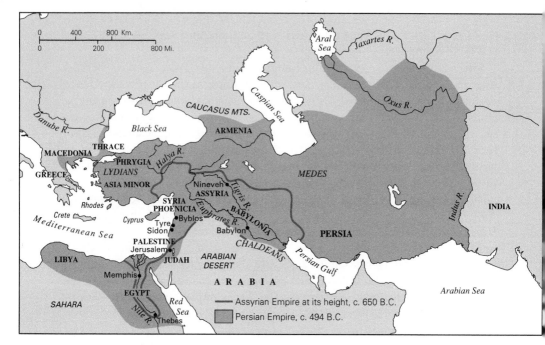

Map 1.2   The Assyrian and Persian Empires

Persia: Unifier of the Near East

The destruction of the Assyrian empire made possible the rise of a Chaldean empire that included Babylonia, Assyria, Syria, and Palestine. Under Nebuchadnezzar, who ruled from 604 to 562 B.C., the Chaldean, or Neo-Babylonian, empire reached its height. After Nebuchadnezzar's death, the empire was torn by civil war and threatened by a new power: the Persians, an Indo-European people who had settled in southern Iran. Under Cyrus the Great and his son and successor, Cambyses, the Persians conquered all lands between the Nile in Egypt and the Indus River in India. This conquest took twenty-five years, from 550 to 525 B.C.

The Near Eastern conception of absolute monarchy justified by religion reached its culminating expression in the person of the Persian king, who, with divine approval, ruled a vast empire, "the four quarters of the earth." Persian kings developed an effective system of administration — based in part on an Assyrian model — that gave stability and a degree of unity to their extensive territories. The Persian empire was divided into twenty provinces (*satrapies*), each one administered by a governor (*satrap*) responsible to the emperor. To guard against subversion, the king employed special agents — "the eyes and ears of the emperor" — who supervised the activities of the governors. Persian kings allowed the provincials a large measure of self-rule.

They also respected local traditions, particularly in matters of religion, as long as subjects paid their taxes, served in the royal army, and refrained from rebellion.

The empire was bound together by a uniform language, Aramaic (the language of the Aramaeans of Syria), used by government officials and merchants. Aramaic was written in letters based on the Phoenician alphabet. By making Aramaic a universal language, the Persians facilitated written and oral communication within the empire. The empire was further unified by an elaborate network of roads, an efficient postal system, a common system of weights and measures, and an empirewide coinage based on an invention of the Lydians from Western Asia Minor.

Besides providing impressive political and administrative unity, the Persians fused and perpetuated the various cultural traditions of the Near East. Persian palaces, for example, boasted the terraces of Babylon, the colonnades of Egypt, the winged bulls that decorated Assyrian palace gates, and the craftsmanship of Median goldsmiths.

The political and cultural universalism of the Persian empire had its counterpart in the emergence of a higher religion, Zoroastrianism, which contained both monotheistic and dualistic elements and emphasized the individual's capacity to choose between good and evil. Named for its founder, the Persian prophet Zoroaster, who probably lived in the sixth century B.C. (although some scholars place him much earlier), this religion taught belief in Ahura Mazda — the Wise Lord — god of light, justice, wisdom, goodness, and immortality. In addition to Ahura Mazda, however, there existed Ahriman, the spirit of darkness, who was evil and destructive; Ahriman was in conflict with the ultimately triumphant Ahura Mazda. People were free to choose whom they would follow. To serve Ahura Mazda, one had to speak the truth and be good to others; the reward for such behavior was life eternal in paradise, the realm of light and goodness. Followers of the evil spirit could be cast into a realm of darkness and torment. In contrast to the traditional religions of the Near East, Zoroastrianism rejected magic, polytheism, and blood sacrifices. Instead, it stressed ethics.

Persia unified the nations of the Near East into a world-state, headed by a divinely appointed king. It also synthesized the region's cultural traditions. Soon it would confront the city-states of Greece, whose political system and cultural orientation differed from those of the Near East.

The Religious Orientation of the Ancient Near East

Religion dominated, suffused, and inspired all features of Near Eastern society: law, kingship, art, and science. It was the source of the vitality and creativity of Mesopotamian and Egyptian civilizations. Priest-kings or god-kings, their power sanctioned by divine forces, furnished the necessary authority to organize large numbers of people in cooperative ventures. Religion also encouraged and justified wars — including enslavements and massacres — which were seen as conflicts between the gods.

A Myth-Making World-View

A religious, or mythopoeic (myth-making), view of the world gives Near Eastern civilization its distinctive form and allows us to see it as an organic whole. Mesopotamians and Egyptians inherited from their prehistoric ancestors a great variety of communally produced imagery, rituals, and tales accounting for the origin of the world and human life. With unrestrained imagination, they altered the old myths and elaborated new ones to resolve questions that today we try to answer with science. Myth-making was humanity's first way of thinking; it was the earliest attempt to explain the beginnings of the universe and human history, to make nature and life comprehensible. Appealing primarily to the imagination and emotions, rather than to reason, mythical thinking, as expressed in language, art, poetry, and social organization, has been a fundamental formative element of human culture.

Originating in sacred rites, ritual dances, feasts, and ceremonies, myths depicted the deeds of gods, who, in some remote past, had brought forth the world and human beings. Holding that human destiny was determined by the gods, Near Eastern people interpreted their experiences through myths. Myths also enabled Mesopotamians and Egyptians to make sense out of nature, to explain the world of phenomena. Through myths, the Near Eastern mind sought to give coherence to the universe and make it intelligible. These myths gave Near Eastern people a framework with which to pattern their experiences into a meaningful order, justify their rules of conduct, and try to overcome the uncertainty of existence.

The civilizations of the ancient Near East were based on a way of thinking fundamentally different from the modern scientific outlook. The difference between scientific and mythical thinking is profound. The scientific mind views physical nature as an *it* — inanimate, impersonal, and governed by universal law. The myth-making mind of the Near East saw every object in nature as a *thou* — personified, alive, with an individual will. It saw gods or demons manipulating things. The world was enchanted, imbued with mysterious spirits. The sun and stars, the rivers and mountains, the wind and lightning were either gods or the dwelling places of gods. An Egyptian or a Mesopotamian experienced natural phenomena — a falling rock, a thunderclap, a rampaging river — as life facing life. If a river flooded the region, destroying crops, it was because it wanted to; the river or the gods desired to punish the people.

> *In other words, the ancients told myths instead of presenting an analysis or conclusions. We would explain, for instance, that certain atmospheric changes broke a drought and brought about rain. The Babylonians observed the same facts but experienced them as the in-*

tervention of the gigantic bird Imdugud which came to their rescue. It covered the sky with the black storm clouds of its wings and devoured the Bull of Heaven, whose hot breath had scorched the crops.[3]

The Egyptians believed that Nut, the sky goddess, gave birth to the sun, a deity who sailed west across the celestial sea before descending into his mother's womb to be reborn again in the morning. For the Egyptians, the rising and setting of the sun were not natural occurrences — a celestial body obeying an impersonal law — but a religious drama.

The scientific mind holds that natural objects obey universal rules; hence, the location of planets, the speed of objects, and the onset of a hurricane can be predicted. The myth-making mind of the ancient Near East was not troubled by contradictions. It did not seek logical consistency and had no awareness of repetitive laws inherent in nature. Rather, it attributed all occurrences to the actions of gods, whose behavior was often erratic and unpredictable. Shamans employed magic to protect people from evil supernatural forces that surrounded them. The scientific mind appeals to reason: it analyzes nature logically and systematically and searches for general principles that govern phenomena. The myth-making mind appeals to the imagination and feelings and proclaims a truth that is emotionally satisfying, not one that has been arrived at through intellectual analysis and synthesis. Mythical explanations of nature and human experience enrich perception and feeling. Thus, they made life seem less overwhelming and death less frightening.

Of course, Near Eastern people did engage in rational forms of thought and behavior. They certainly employed reason in building irrigation works, in preparing a calendar, and in performing mathematical operations. Moreover, in their daily life, men and women were often driven by purely pragmatic concerns. Fields had to be planted, goods sold, and household chores attended to. In dealing with these concerns, people did what had to be done in commonsense ways. They planned and prepared; they weighed actions as either beneficial or harmful and behaved accordingly. However, because rational, or logical, thought remained subordinate to a mythic-religious orientation, they did not arrive at a *consistently* and *self-consciously* rational method of inquiring into physical nature and human culture.

Thus, Near Eastern civilization reached the first level in the development of science: observing nature, recording data, and improving technology in mining, metallurgy, and architecture. But it did not advance to the level of self-conscious philosophical and scientific thought — that is, logically deduced abstractions, hypotheses, and generalizations. Mesopotamians and Egyptians did not fashion a body of philosophical and scientific ideas that were logically structured, discussed, and debated. They had no awareness of general laws that govern particular events. These later developments were the singular achievement of Greek philosophy. It gave a "rational interpretation to natural occurrences which had previously been explained by ancient mythologies. . . .

With the study of nature set free from the control of mythological fancy, the way was opened for the development of science as an intellectual system."[4]

Near Eastern Achievements

The Sumerians and the Egyptians demonstrated enormous creativity and intelligence. They built irrigation works and cities, organized governments, charted the course of heavenly bodies, performed mathematical operations, constructed large-scale monuments, engaged in international trade, established bureaucracies and schools, and considerably advanced the level of technology. Without the Sumerian invention of writing — one of the great creative acts in history — what we mean by *civilization* could not have emerged.

Many elements of ancient Near Eastern civilization were passed on to the West. The wheeled vehicle, the plow, and the phonetic alphabet — all important to the development of civilization — derive from the Near East. In the realm of medicine, the Egyptians knew the value of certain drugs, such as castor oil; they also knew how to use splints and bandages. The innovative divisions that gave 360 degrees to a circle and 60 minutes to an hour originated in Mesopotamia. Egyptian geometry and Babylonian astronomy were utilized by the Greeks and became a part of Western knowledge. The belief that a king's power issued from a heavenly source, a key idea in Western political thought, also derived from the Near East. In Christian art, too, one finds connections to Mesopotamian art forms — for example, the Assyrians depicted winged angel-like beings.

Both the Hebrews and the Greeks borrowed Mesopotamian literary themes. For instance, some biblical stories — the Flood, the quarrel between Cain and Abel, and the Tower of Babel — stem from Mesopotamian antecedents. A similar link exists between the Greek and the earlier Mesopotamian mythologies.

Thus, many achievements of the Egyptians and the Mesopotamians were inherited and assimilated by both the Greeks and the Hebrews. Even more important for an understanding of the essential meaning of Western civilization are the ways in which the Greeks and the Hebrews rejected or transformed elements of the older Near Eastern traditions to create new points of departure for the human mind.

Notes

1. *Epic of Gilgamesh*, with an introduction by N. K. Sandars (Baltimore: Penguin Books, 1960), pp. 69, 104.
2. Quoted in John A. Wilson, *The Culture of Ancient Egypt* (Chicago: University of Chicago Press, Phoenix Books, 1951), p. 227.
3. Henri Frankfort, et al., *Before Philosophy* (Baltimore: Penguin Books, 1949), p. 15.
4. Samuel Sambursky, *The Physical World of the Greeks* (New York: Collier Books, 1962), pp. 18–19.

Suggested Reading

Campbell, Bernard G., *Humankind Emerging* (1982). The world of prehistory.

David, Rosalie A., *The Ancient Egyptians* (1982). Focuses on religious beliefs and practices.

Frankfort, Henri, et al., *The Intellectual Adventure of Ancient Man* (1946); paperback edition is entitled *Before Philosophy*. Brilliant discussions of the role of myth in the ancient Near East by distinguished scholars.

Gowlett, John, *Ascent to Civilization* (1984). An up-to-date study, with excellent graphics.

Hallo, W. W., and W. K. Simpson, *The Ancient Near East* (1971). An authoritative survey of the political history of the Near East.

Kuhrt, Amélie, *The Ancient Near East* (1995). An authoritative two-volume history.

Moscati, Sabatino, *The Face of the Ancient Orient* (1962). An illuminating survey of the various peoples of the ancient Near East.

Oppenheim, A. L., *Ancient Mesopotamia* (1964). Stresses social and economic history.

Saggs, H. W. F., *Civilization Before Greece and Rome* (1989). Focuses on culture and society.

———, *The Might That Was Assyria* (1984). Survey of Assyrian history and culture.

Silverman, David P., ed., *Ancient Egypt* (1997). Clearly written accounts by experts on all phases of ancient Egyptian society.

Strouhal, Eugen, *Life of the Ancient Egyptians* (1992). Daily life of Egyptians; lavishly illustrated.

Tyldesley, Joyce, *Hatchepsut* (1996). A study of the female pharaoh.

von Soden, Wolfram, *The Ancient Orient* (1994). A thematic treatment of ancient Mesopotamian civilization.

Wilson, John A., *The Culture of Ancient Egypt* (1951). An interpretation by a distinguished Egyptologist.

Review Questions

1. Why is the development of the Neolithic Age referred to as the Neolithic Revolution?
2. What is meant by civilization? Under what conditions did it emerge?
3. How did religion influence Mesopotamian civilization?
4. What did the Mesopotamians achieve in trade, mathematics, and science?
5. How did the Egyptians' religious beliefs affect their civilization?
6. What is the historical significance of Akhenaton?
7. How did the Persians give unity to the Near East?
8. What is myth? How does mythical thought differ from scientific thought?
9. What advances in science were made by Near Eastern civilization? How did a myth-making view of nature limit science?
10. What were the accomplishments of the civilizations of the Near East? What elements of Near Eastern civilizations were passed on to Western civilization?

❖ CHAPTER 2

The Hebrews: A New View of God and the Individual

*A*ncient Mesopotamia and Egypt, the birthplace of the first civilizations, are not the spiritual ancestors of the West; for the origins of the Western tradition we must turn to the Hebrews (Jews) and the Greeks. Both Greeks and Hebrews, of course, absorbed elements of the civilizations of Mesopotamia and Egypt, but what is more significant is how they transformed this inheritance and shaped worldviews that differed markedly from the outlooks of these first civilizations. As Egyptologist John A. Wilson writes,

> *The Children of Israel built a nation and a religion on the rejection of things Egyptian. Not only did they see God as one, but they ascribed to him consistency of concern for man and consistency of justice to man. . . . Like the Greeks, the Hebrews took forms from their great neighbors; like the Greeks, they used those forms for very different purposes.*[1]

In this chapter, we examine one source of the Western tradition, the Hebrews, whose conception of God broke with the outlook of the Near East and whose ethical teachings helped to fashion the Western idea of the dignity of the individual. ❖

Early Hebrew History

The Hebrews originated in Mesopotamia and migrated to Canaan, a portion of which was later called Palestine. The Hebrew patriarchs — Abraham, Isaac, and Jacob, so prominently depicted in the Old Testament — were chieftains of seminomadic clans that roamed Palestine and occasionally journeyed to Mesopotamia and Egypt. The early Hebrews absorbed some features of Mesopotamian civilization. For example, there are parallels between biblical law and the Mesopotamian legal tradition. Several biblical stories — the Creation, the Flood, the Garden of Eden — derive from Mesopotamian sources.

Some Hebrews journeyed from Canaan to Egypt to be herdsmen and farmers, but they eventually became forced laborers for the Egyptians. Fearful of turning into permanent slaves of the pharaoh, the Hebrews yearned for an opportunity to escape. In the thirteenth century B.C., an extraordinary leader rose among them, called Moses, who was accepted by his people as a messenger of God. Leading the Hebrews in their exodus from Egypt, Moses transformed them during their wanderings in the wilderness of Sinai into a nation, united and uplifted by a belief in Yahweh, the one God.

The wandering Hebrews returned to Canaan to rejoin other Hebrew tribes that had not migrated to Egypt. The conquest and colonization of Canaan was a gradual process that took many generations. Threatened by the Philistines (originally from the islands of the Aegean Sea and the coast of Asia Minor), the twelve Hebrew tribes united under the leadership of Saul, a charismatic hero, whom they acclaimed as their first king. Under Saul's successor, David, a gifted warrior and poet, the Hebrews (or Israelites) broke the back of Philistine power and subdued neighboring peoples.

David's son Solomon built a royal palace in Jerusalem and beside it a magnificent temple honoring God. Under Solomon, ancient Israel was at the height of its political power and prosperity, but opposition to Solomon's tax policies and his favored treatment of the region of Judah in the south led to the division of the kingdom after his death in 922 B.C. The tribes loyal to Solomon's son belonged to the Kingdom of Judah, whereas the other tribes organized the northern Kingdom of Israel.

In 722 B.C., Israel fell to the Assyrians, who deported many Hebrews to other parts of the Assyrian empire. These transplanted Hebrews merged with neighboring peoples and lost their identity as the people of the one God. In 586 B.C., the Chaldeans conquered Judah, destroyed Solomon's temple, devastated the land, and deported several thousand Hebrews to Babylon. This was the darkest moment in the history of the Hebrews. Their state was gone, and neighboring peoples had overrun their land; their holy temple, built during the reign of King Solomon, was in ruins; thousands had died in battle or had been executed or had fled to Egypt and other lands; and thousands more were in exile in Babylon. This exile is known as the Babylonian Captivity.

Still, the Hebrews, now commonly called Jews, survived as a people — a fact that is a marvel of history. Although many of the exiles in Babylon assimilated Babylonian ways, some remained faithful to their God, Yahweh, and to the Law of Moses, and they longed to return to their homeland. Thus, their faith enabled them to endure conquest and exile. When the Persians conquered Babylon, King Cyrus, in 538 B.C., permitted the exiles to return to Judah, now a Persian province, and to rebuild the temple.

The Jews regained their independence in the second century B.C.; however, in the next century their land fell within the Roman orbit. After failed revolutions in the first and second centuries A.D., they became a dispersed people. But they never relinquished their commitment to God and his Law as recorded in the Hebrew Scriptures. Called *Tanak* by Jews (and Old Testament by Christians), these Scriptures consist of thirty-nine books* by several authors who lived in different centuries. Jews call the first five books — Genesis,

---

*In ancient times, the number of books was usually given as twenty-four. Certain books are now divided into two parts, and the twelve works by the minor prophets are now counted as individual books.

Chronology 2.1 ❖ The Hebrews

1250 B.C.*	Hebrew exodus from Egypt
1024–1000	Reign of Saul, Israel's first king
1000–961	Creation of a united monarchy under David
961–922	Reign of Solomon; construction of the first temple
750–430	Age of classical prophecy
722	Kingdom of Israel falls to Assyrians
586	Kingdom of Judah falls to Chaldeans; the temple is destroyed
586–539	Babylonian exile
538	Cyrus of Persia allows exiles to return to Judah
515 B.C.	Second temple is dedicated

*Most dates are approximations.

Exodus, Leviticus, Numbers, and Deuteronomy — the Torah (which originally meant "teaching" or "instruction"). Often the Torah is referred to as the Pentateuch, a Greek word meaning "five books."

The Hebrew Scriptures represent Jewish written and oral tradition dating from about 1250 to 150 B.C. The record of more than a thousand years of ancient Jewish life, they include Jewish laws, wisdom, hopes, legends, and literary expressions. In describing an ancient people's efforts to comprehend the ways of God, the Scriptures emphasize and value the human experience; their heroes are not demigods but human beings. The Scriptures depict human strength as well as weakness. Some passages exhibit cruelty and unseemly revenge against the enemies of Israel, but others express the highest ethical values.

Compiled by religious devotees, not research historians, the Hebrew Scriptures understandably contain factual errors, imprecisions, and discrepancies. However, they also offer passages of reliable history, and historians find these Scriptures an indispensable source for studying the ancient Near East. Students of literature explore the Old Testament for its poetry, legends, and themes, all of which are an integral part of the Western literary tradition. But it is as a work of religious inspiration that the Hebrew Bible attains its profoundest importance. As set forth there, the Hebrew idea of God and his relationship to human beings is one of the foundations of the Western tradition.

God: One, Sovereign, Transcendent, Good

Monotheism, the belief in one God, became the central force in the life of the Hebrews, and marked a profound break with Near Eastern religious thought.

A Dead Sea Scroll, Judea, Second Century B.C. The sacredness of the biblical texts and the authority of the recorded word of God remain a unifying factor in modern Jewish society. Many ancient Hebrew scrolls were found in caves near the west bank of the Dead Sea beginning in the late 1940s. The scroll depicted here contains the earliest existing copy of a complete Hebrew text of the book of the prophet Isaiah. It barely differs from more modern manuscripts. (© *John C. Trevor, 1970*)

Near Eastern gods were not truly free; their power was not without limits. Unlike Yahweh, Near Eastern gods were not eternal, but were born or created; they issued from some prior realm. They were also subject to biological conditions, requiring food, drink, sleep, and sexual gratification. Sometimes they became ill or grew old or died. When they behaved wickedly, they had to answer to fate, which demanded punishment as retribution; even the gods were subject to fate's power.

The Hebrews regarded God as *fully sovereign.* He ruled all and was subject to nothing. Yahweh's existence and power did not derive from a preexisting realm, as was the case with the gods of other peoples. The Hebrews believed that no realm of being preceded God in time or surpassed him in power. They saw God as eternal, the source of all in the universe, and as having a supreme will.

Whereas Near Eastern divinities dwelt within nature, the Hebrew God was *transcendent,* above nature and not a part of it. Yahweh was not identified with any natural force and did not dwell in a particular place in heaven or on earth. Since God was the creator and ruler of nature, there was no place for a sun god, a moon god, a god in the river, or a demon in the storm. Nature was God's creation but was not itself divine. Therefore, when the Hebrews confronted natural phenomena, they experienced God's magnificent handiwork, not objects with wills of their own. All natural phenomena — rivers, mountains, storms, stars — were divested of any supernatural quality. The stars and planets were creations of Yahweh, not divinities or the abodes of divinities. The Hebrews neither regarded them with awe nor worshiped them.

The removal of the gods from nature — the demythicizing of nature — is a necessary prerequisite for scientific thought. But concerned with religion and morality, the Hebrews did not create theoretical science. As testimony to God's greatness, nature inspired them to sing the praises of the Lord; it invoked worship of God, not scientific curiosity. When they gazed at the heavens, they did not seek to discover mathematical relationships but admired God's handiwork. They did not view nature as a system governed by self-operating physical principles or natural law. Rather, they saw the rising sun, spring rain, summer heat, and winter cold as God intervening in an orderly manner in his creation. The Hebrews, unlike the Greeks, were not philosophical or scientific thinkers. They were concerned with God's will, not the human intellect; with the feelings of the heart, not the power of the mind; with righteous behavior, not abstract thought.

Unlike the Greeks, the Hebrews did not speculate about the origins of all things and the operations of nature; they knew that God had created everything. For the Hebrews, God's existence was based on religious conviction, not on rational inquiry; on revelation, not reason. It was the Greeks, not the Hebrews, who originated self-conscious, systematic, rational thought. But Christianity, born of Judaism, retained the Hebrew view of a transcendent God and the orderliness of his creation: concepts that could accommodate Greek science.

The Hebrews also did not speculate about God's nature. They knew only that he was *good* and that he made ethical demands on his people. Unlike Near Eastern gods, Yahweh was not driven by lust or motivated by evil but was "merciful and gracious, long-suffering, and abundant in goodness and truth . . . forgiving inequity and transgression and sin" (Psalm 145:8).[2] In contrast to pagan gods, who were indifferent to human beings, Yahweh was attentive to human needs. By asserting that God was *one, sovereign, transcendent,* and *good,* the Hebrews effected a religious revolution that separated them entirely from the world-view held by the other peoples of the ancient Near East.

The Individual and Moral Autonomy

This new conception of God made possible a new awareness of the individual. In confronting God, the Hebrews developed an awareness of *self,* or *I:* the individual became conscious of his or her own person, moral autonomy, and personal worth. The Hebrews believed that God, who possessed total freedom, had bestowed on people moral freedom — the capacity to choose between good and evil.

Fundamental to Hebrew belief was the insistence that God did not create people to be his slaves. The Hebrews regarded God with awe and humility, with respect and fear, but they did not believe that God wanted people to grovel before him; rather, he wanted them to fulfill their moral potential by freely making the choice to follow or not to follow God's Law. Thus, in creating men and women in his own image, God made them autonomous and sovereign. In God's plan for the universe, human beings were the highest creation, subordinate only to God. Of all his creations, only they had been given the freedom to choose between righteousness and wickedness, between "life and good, and death and evil" (Deuteronomy 30:15). But having the power to choose freely, men and women must bear the responsibility for their choice.

God demanded that the Hebrews have no other gods and that they make no images "nor any manner of likeness, of any thing that is in heaven above, or that is in the earth beneath, . . . thou shalt not bow down unto them nor serve them" (Exodus 20:4–5). The Hebrews believed that the worship of idols deprived people of their freedom and dignity; people cannot be fully human if they surrender themselves to a lifeless idol. Hence, the Hebrews rejected images and all other forms of idolatry. A crucial element of Near Eastern religion was the use of images — art forms that depicted divinities — but the Hebrews believed that God, the Supreme Being, could not be represented by pictures or sculpture fashioned by human hands. The Hebrews rejected entirely the belief that an image possessed divine powers, which could be manipulated for human advantage. Ethical considerations, not myth or magic, were central to Hebrew religious life.

By making God the center of life, Hebrews could become free moral agents; no person, no human institution, and no human tradition could claim their souls. Because God alone was the supreme value in the universe, only he was worthy of worship. Thus, to give ultimate loyalty to a king or a general violated God's stern warning against the worship of false gods. The first concern of the Hebrews was righteousness, not power, fame, or riches, which were only idols and would impoverish a person spiritually and morally.

There was, however, a condition to freedom. For the Hebrews, people were not free to create their own moral precepts or their own standards of right and wrong. Freedom meant voluntary obedience to commands that originated with God. Evil and suffering were not caused by blind fate, malevolent demons, or arbitrary gods; they resulted from people's disregard of God's commandments. The dilemma is that in possessing freedom of choice, human beings are also free to disobey God, to commit a sin, which leads to suffering and death. Thus, in the Genesis story, Adam and Eve were punished for disobeying God in the Garden of Eden.

For the Hebrews, to know God was not to comprehend him intellectually, to define him, or to prove his existence; to know God was to be righteous and loving, merciful and just. When men and women loved God, the Hebrews believed, they were uplifted and improved. Gradually, they learned to overcome the worst elements of human nature and to treat people with respect and compassion. The Jews came to interpret the belief that man was created in God's image to mean that each human being has a divine spark in him or her, giving every person a unique dignity that cannot be taken away.

Through their devotion to God, the Hebrews asserted the value and autonomy of human beings. Thus, the Hebrews conceived the idea of moral freedom: that each individual is responsible for his or her own actions. These concepts of human dignity and moral autonomy, which Christianity inherited, are at the core of the Western tradition.

The Covenant and the Law

Central to Hebrew religious thought and decisive in Hebrew history was the covenant, God's special agreement with the Hebrew people: if they obeyed his commands, they would "be unto Me a kingdom of priests, and a holy nation" (Exodus 19:6). By this act, the Israelites as a nation accepted God's lordship. Justice was the central theme of Old Testament ethics. The Israelites, liberated from slavery by a righteous and compassionate God, had a moral responsibility to overcome injustice, to care for the poor, the weak, and the oppressed.

The Hebrews came to see themselves as a unique nation, a "chosen people," for God had given them a special honor, a profound opportunity, and (as they could never forget) an awesome responsibility. The Hebrews did not claim that God had selected them because they were better than other peoples or because they had done anything special to deserve God's election. They believed that God had selected them to receive the Law so that their nation would set an example of righteous behavior and ultimately make God and the Law known to the other nations.

This responsibility to be the moral teachers of humanity weighed heavily on the Hebrews. They believed that God had revealed his Law — including the moral code known as the Ten Commandments — to the Hebrew people as a whole, and obedience to the Law became the overriding obligation of each Hebrew.

Israelite law incorporated many elements from Near Eastern legal codes and oral traditions. But by making people more important than property, by expressing mercy toward the oppressed, and by rejecting the idea that law should treat the poor and the rich differently, Israelite law demonstrated a greater ethical awareness and a more humane spirit than other legal codes of the Near East. Thus, there were laws to protect the poor, widows, orphans, resident aliens, hired laborers, and slaves:

> *Ye shall not steal; neither shall ye deal falsely, nor lie to one another. . . . Thou shalt not oppress thy neighbour nor rob him. . . . Ye shall do no unrighteousness in judgment; thou shalt not [be partial to] respect the person of the poor, nor favour the person of the*

Wall Painting from the Synagogue in Dura-Europos.   Some time after 1050 B.C. the Israelites engaged the Philistines, formidable warriors who dominated Canaanite cities, in battle near Aphek. The Israelites brought the Ark of the Covenant into their camp, hoping that God's presence would produce victory. However, the Philistines decimated the Israelites and captured the ark. These events are described in 1 Samuel, Chapter 4. This painting from a third-century synagogue in Roman Syria depicts the ark's capture. (*Yale University Art Gallery, Dura-Europos Collection*)

> *mighty; but in righteousness shalt thou judge thy neighbor. . . . And if a stranger sojourn with thee in your land, ye shall not do him wrong. The stranger that sojourneth with you shall be unto you as the home born among you, and thou shalt love him as thyself. (Leviticus 19:11, 13, 15, 33, 34)*[3]

Like other Near Eastern societies, the Jews placed women in a subordinate position. The husband was considered his wife's master, and she often addressed him as a servant or subject would speak to a superior. A husband could divorce his wife, but she could not divorce him. Only when there was no male heir could a wife inherit property from her husband or a daughter inherit from her father. Outside the home, women were not regarded as competent witnesses in court and played a lesser role than men in organized worship.

On the other hand, the Jews also showed respect for women. Wise women and prophetesses like Judith and Deborah were esteemed by the community and consulted by its leaders. Prophets compared God's love for the Hebrews with a husband's love for his wife. Jewish law regarded the woman as a person, not as property. Even female captives taken in war were not to be abused or humiliated. The law required a husband to respect and support his wife and never to strike her. One of the Ten Commandments called for honoring both father and mother.

The Hebrew Idea of History

Their idea of God made the Hebrews aware of the crucial importance of historical time. Holidays commemorating such specific historical events as the Exodus from Egypt, the receiving of the Ten Commandments on Mount Sinai, and the destruction of Solomon's temple kept the past alive and vital. Egyptians and Mesopotamians did not have a similar awareness of the uniqueness of a given event; to them, today's events were repetitions of events experienced by their ancestors. To the Jews, the Exodus and the covenant at Mount Sinai were singular, nonrepetitive occurrences, decisive in shaping their national history. This historical uniqueness and importance of events derived from the idea of a universal God who is profoundly involved in human affairs — a God who cares, teaches, and punishes.

The Jews valued the future as well as the past. Regarding human history as a process leading to a goal, they envisioned a great day when God would establish on earth a glorious age of peace, prosperity, happiness, and human brotherhood. This utopian notion has become deeply embedded in Western thought.

The Hebrews saw history as the work of God; it was a divine drama filled with sacred meaning and moral significance. Historical events revealed the clash of human will with God's commands. Through history's specific events, God's presence was disclosed and his purpose made known. When the Hebrews suffered conquest and exile, they interpreted these events as divine retribution for violating God's Law and as punishment for their stubbornness, sinfulness, and rebelliousness. For the Hebrews, history also revealed God's compassion and concern. Thus, the Lord liberated Moses and the Israelites at the Red Sea and appointed prophets to plead for the poor and the oppressed. Because historical events revealed God's attitude toward human beings, these events possessed spiritual meaning and therefore were worth recording, evaluating, and remembering.

The Prophets

Jewish history was marked by the emergence of spiritually inspired persons called *prophets,* who felt compelled to act as God's messengers. The flowering of the prophetic movement — the age of classical, or literary, prophecy — began in the eighth century B.C. Among the prophets were Amos, a shepherd

Wall Painting from the Synagogue in Dura-Europos, Roman Syria, Early Third Century A.D. This painting shows a Hebrew prophet reading from an open scroll. (*Yale University Art Gallery, Dura-Europos Collection*)

from Judea in the south; his younger contemporary, Hosea, from Israel in the north; Isaiah of Jerusalem; and Jeremiah, who witnessed the siege of Jerusalem in the early sixth century B.C. The prophets cared nothing for money or possessions, feared no one, and preached without invitation. Often emerging in times of social distress and moral confusion, they pleaded for a return to the covenant and the Law. They exhorted the entire nation and taught that when people forgot God and made themselves the center of all things, they would bring disaster on themselves and their community. The prophets saw national misfortune as an opportunity for penitence and reform. They were remarkably courageous individuals who did not quake before the powerful.

In attacking oppression, cruelty, greed, and exploitation, the classical prophets added a new dimension to Israel's religious development. These prophets were responding to problems emanating from Israel's changed social structure. A tribal society generally lacks class distinctions, but this situation had been altered by the rise of Hebrew kings, the expansion of commerce, and the growth of cities. By the eighth century, there was a significant disparity between the wealthy and the poor. Small farmers in debt to moneylenders faced the loss of their land or even bondage; the poor were often dispossessed by the greedy wealthy. To the prophets, these social evils were religious sins that would bring ruin to Israel. In the name of God, they denounced the hypocrisy and pomp of the heartless rich and demanded justice. God is compassionate, they insisted. He cares for all, especially the poor, the unfortunate, the suffering, and the defenseless. God's injunctions, declared Isaiah, were to

> *Put away the evil of your doings*
> *From before mine eyes,*
> *Cease to do evil;*
> *Learn to do well;*
> *Seek justice, relieve the oppressed,*
> *Judge [defend] the fatherless, plead for the widow.*
> (Isaiah 1:16–17)[4]

Prophets stressed the direct spiritual-ethical encounter between the individual and God. The inner person concerned them more than the outer forms of religious activity. Holding that the essence of the covenant was universal righteousness, the prophets criticized priests whose commitment to rites and rituals was not supported by a deeper spiritual insight or a zeal for morality in daily life. To the prophets, an ethical sin was far worse than a ritual omission. Above all, said the prophets, God demands righteousness, living justly before God. To live unjustly, to mistreat one's neighbors, to act without compassion — these actions violated God's Law and endangered the entire social order.

The prophets thus helped shape a social conscience that has become part of the Western tradition. They held out the hope that life on earth could be improved, that poverty and injustice need not be accepted as part of an unalterable natural order, and that the individual was capable of elevating himself or herself morally and could respect the dignity of others.

Two tendencies were present in Hebrew thought: parochialism and universalism. Parochial-mindedness stressed the special nature, destiny, and needs of the chosen people, a nation set apart from others. This narrow, tribal outlook was offset by universalism: a concern for all humanity, which found expression in those prophets who envisioned the unity of all people under God. All people were equally precious to God.

The prophets were not pacifists, particularly if a war was being waged against the enemies of Yahweh. But some prophets denounced war as obscene and looked forward to its elimination. They maintained that when people glorify force, they dehumanize their opponents, brutalize themselves, and dishonor God. When violence rules, there can be no love of God and no regard for the individual.

The prophets' universalism was accompanied by an equally profound awareness of the individual and his or her intrinsic worth. Before the prophets, virtually all religious tradition had been produced communally and anonymously. The prophets, however, spoke as fearless individuals who, by affixing their signatures to their thoughts, fully bore the responsibility for their religious inspiration and conviction.

The prophets emphasized the individual's responsibility for his or her own actions. In coming to regard God's Law as a *command to conscience, an appeal to the inner person,* the prophets heightened the awareness of the human personality. They indicated that the individual could not know God by simply following edicts and performing rituals; the individual must experience God. Precisely this *I-Thou* relationship could make the individual fully conscious of self and could deepen and enrich his or her own personality. During the Exodus, the Hebrews were a tribal people who obeyed the Law largely out of awe and group compulsion. By the prophets' time, the Jews appeared to be autonomous individuals who heeded the Law because of a deliberate, conscious inner commitment.

The ideals proclaimed by the prophets helped sustain the Jews throughout their long and often painful historical odyssey, and they remain a vital force for Jews today. Incorporated into the teachings of Jesus, these ideals, as part of Christianity, are embedded in the Western tradition.

The Legacy of the Ancient Jews

For the Jews, monotheism had initiated a process of self-discovery and self-realization unmatched by other peoples of the Near East. The great value that westerners place on the individual derives in part from the ancient Hebrews, who held that man and woman were created in God's image and possessed free will and a conscience answerable to God.

Christianity, the essential religion of Western civilization, emerged from ancient Judaism, and the links between the two, including monotheism, moral autonomy, prophetic values, and the Hebrew Scriptures as the Word of God, are numerous and strong. The historical Jesus cannot be understood without examining his Jewish background, and his followers appealed to the Hebrew Scriptures in order to demonstrate the validity of their beliefs. For these reasons, we talk of a Judeo-Christian tradition as an essential component of Western civilization.

The Hebrew vision of a future messianic age, a golden age of peace and social justice, is at the root of the Western idea of progress — that people can build a more just society, that there is a reason to be hopeful about the future. This way of perceiving the world has greatly influenced modern reform movements.

In seeking to comprehend their relationship to God, the writers of the Hebrew Scriptures produced a treasury of themes, stories, and models of literary style and craftsmanship that have been a source of inspiration for Western religious thinkers, novelists, poets, and artists to the present day. Historians and archaeologists find the Hebrew Scriptures a valuable source in their efforts to reconstruct Near Eastern history.

Notes

1. John A. Wilson, "Egypt — the Kingdom of the 'Two Lands,'" in *At the Dawn of Civilization*, ed. E. A. Speiser (New Brunswick, N.J.: Rutgers University Press, 1964), pp. 267–268. Vol. I in *The World History of the Jewish People*.
2. The scriptural quotations in this chapter come from *The Holy Scriptures* (Philadelphia: The Jewish Publication Society of America, 1917), and are used with the permission of The Jewish Publication Society of America.
3. *From The Tanakh: The New JPS Translation According to the Traditional Hebrew Text.* Copyright © 1985 by the Jewish Publication Society. Used by permission.
4. Ibid.

Suggested Reading

Anderson, Bernhard, *Understanding the Old Testament,* 2nd ed. (1966). An excellent survey of the Old Testament in its historical setting.

Armstrong, Karen, *A History of God* (1994). Changing views of God from the ancient Hebrews until today.

Boadt, Lawrence, *Reading the Old Testament* (1984). A study of ancient Israel's religious experience by a sympathetic Catholic scholar.

Bright, John, *A History of Israel* (1972). A thoughtful, clearly written survey; the best of its kind.

Grant, Michael, *The History of Ancient Israel* (1984). A lucid account.

Heschel, Abraham, *The Prophets,* 2 vols. (1962). A penetrating analysis of the nature of prophetic inspiration.

Kaufmann, Yehezkel, *The Religion of Israel* (1960). An abridgment and translation of Kaufmann's classic multivolume work.

Kuntz, Kenneth J., *The People of Ancient Israel* (1974). A useful introduction to Old Testament literature, history, and thought.

Metzger, Bruce M. and Michael D. Coogan, eds., *The Oxford Companion to the Bible* (1993). A valuable reference work.

Zeitlin, Irving M., *Ancient Judaism* (1984). A sociologist examines the history and thought of ancient Israel.

Review Questions

1. How did the Hebrew view of God mark a revolutionary break with Near Eastern religious thought?
2. How did Hebrew religious thought promote the idea of moral autonomy?
3. Provide examples showing that Hebrew law expressed a concern for human dignity.
4. Why did the Hebrews consider history to be important, and how did they demonstrate its importance?
5. What role did the prophets play in Hebrew history? What is the enduring significance of their achievements?
6. Why are the Hebrews regarded as one source of Western civilization?

❖ CHAPTER 3

The Greeks: From Myth to Reason

*T*he Hebrew conception of ethical monotheism, with its stress on human dignity, is one principal source of the Western tradition. The second major source is ancient Greece. Both Hebrews and Greeks absorbed the achievements of Near Eastern civilizations, but they also developed their own distinctive viewpoints and styles of thought, which set them apart from the Mesopotamians and Egyptians. The great achievements of the Hebrews lay in the sphere of religious-ethical thought; those of the Greeks lay in the development of philosophical and scientific thought.

The Greeks conceived of nature as following general rules, not acting according to the whims of gods or demons. They saw human beings as having a capacity for rational thought, a need for freedom, and a worth as individuals. Although the Greeks never dispensed with the gods, they increasingly stressed the importance of human reason and human decisions; they came to assert that reason is the avenue to knowledge and that people — not the gods — are responsible for their own behavior. In this shift of attention from the gods to human beings, the Greeks broke with the myth-making orientation of the Near East and created the rational humanist outlook that is a distinctive feature of Western civilization. ❖

Early Aegean Civilizations

Until the latter part of the nineteenth century, historians placed the beginning of Greek (or Hellenic) history in the eighth century B.C. Now it is known that two civilizations preceded Hellenic Greece: the Minoan and the Mycenaean. Although the ancient Greek poet Homer had spoken of an earlier Greek civilization in his works, historians had believed that Homer's epics dealt solely with myths and legends, not with a historical past. In 1871, however, a successful German businessman, Heinrich Schliemann, began a search for earliest Greece. In excavating several sites mentioned by Homer, Schliemann discovered tombs, pottery, ornaments, and the remains of palaces of what hitherto had been a lost Greek civilization. The ancient civilization was named after Mycenae, the most important city of the time.

Chronology 3.1 ❖ The Greeks

1700–1450 B.C.*	Height of Minoan civilization
1400–1230	Height of Mycenaean civilization
1100–800	Dark Age
c. 700	Homer
750–550	Age of Colonization
594	Solon is given power to institute reforms
507	Cleisthenes broadens democratic institutions
480	Xerxes of Persia invades Greece; Greek naval victory at Salamis
479	Spartans defeat Persians at Plataea, ending Persian Wars
431	Start of Peloponnesian War
404	Athens surrenders to Sparta, ending Peloponnesian War
387	Plato founds a school, the Academy
359	Philip II becomes king of Macedonia
338	Battle of Chaeronea: Greek city-states fall under dominion of Macedonia
335	Aristotle founds a school, the Lyceum
323 B.C.	Death of Alexander the Great

*Some dates are approximations.

In 1900, Arthur Evans, a British archaeologist, excavating on the island of Crete, southeast of the Greek mainland, unearthed a civilization even older than that of the Mycenaean Greeks. The Cretans, or Minoans, were not Greeks and did not speak a Greek language, but their influence on mainland Greece was considerable and enduring. Minoan civilization lasted about 1,350 years (2600–1250 B.C.) and reached its height during the period from 1700 to 1450 B.C.

The centers of Minoan civilization were magnificent palace complexes, whose construction attested to the wealth and power of Minoan kings. The palaces housed royal families, priests, and government officials and contained workshops that produced decorated silver vessels, daggers, and pottery for local use and for export.

Judging by the archaeological evidence, the Minoans were peaceful. Minoan art generally did not depict military scenes, and Minoan palaces, unlike the Mycenaean ones, had no defensive walls or fortifications. Thus, the Minoans were vulnerable to the warlike Mycenaean Greeks, whose invasion contributed to the decline of Minoan civilization.

Who were these Mycenaeans? Around 2000 B.C., Greek-speaking tribes moved southward into the Greek peninsula, where, together with the pre-Greek population, they fashioned the Mycenaean civilization. In the Peloponnesus, in southern Greece, the Mycenaeans built palaces that were based in part on Cretan models. In these palaces, Mycenaean kings conducted affairs of state, and priests and priestesses performed religious ceremonies. Potters, smiths, tailors, and chariot builders practiced their crafts in the numerous workshops, much like their Minoan counterparts. Mycenaean arts and crafts owed a considerable debt to Crete. A script that permitted record keeping probably also came from Crete.

Mycenaean civilization, which consisted of several small states, each with its own ruling dynasty, reached its height in the period from 1400 to 1230 B.C. Following that, constant warfare among the Mycenaean kingdoms (and perhaps foreign invasions) led to the destruction of the palaces and the abrupt disintegration of Mycenaean civilization about 1100 B.C. But to the later Greek civilization, the Mycenaeans left a legacy of religious forms, pottery making, metallurgy, agriculture, language, a warrior culture and code of honor immortalized in the Homeric epics, and myths and legends that offered themes for Greek drama.

Evolution of the City-States

From 1100 to 800 B.C., the Greek world passed through the Dark Age, an era of transition between a dead Mycenaean civilization and a still unborn Hellenic civilization. The Dark Age saw the migration of Greek tribes from the barren mountainous regions of Greece to more fertile plains, and from the mainland to Aegean islands and the coast of Asia Minor. During this period, the Greeks experienced insecurity, warfare, poverty, and isolation.

After 800 B.C., however, town life revived. Writing again became part of the Greek culture, this time with the more efficient Phoenician script. The population increased dramatically, there was a spectacular rise in the use of metals, and overseas trade expanded. Gradually, Greek cities founded settlements on the islands of the Aegean, along the coast of Asia Minor and the Black Sea, and to the west in Sicily and southern Italy. These colonies, established to relieve overpopulation and land hunger, were independent, self-governing city-states, not possessions of the homeland city-states. During these two hundred years of colonization (750–550 B.C.), trade and industry expanded and the pace of urbanization quickened.

Homer: Shaper of the Greek Spirit

The poet Homer lived during the eighth century B.C., just after the Dark Age. His great epics, the *Iliad* and the *Odyssey,* helped shape the Greek spirit and

Greek religion. Homer was the earliest molder of the Greek outlook and character. For centuries, Greek youngsters grew up reciting the Homeric epics and admiring the Homeric heroes, who strove for honor and faced suffering and death with courage.

Homer was a poetic genius who could reveal a human being's deepest thoughts, feelings, and conflicts in a few brilliant lines. His characters, complex in their motives and expressing powerful human emotions — wrath, vengeance, guilt, remorse, compassion, and love — would intrigue and inspire Western writers down into the twentieth century.

The *Iliad* deals in poetic form with a small segment of the last year of the Trojan War, which had taken place centuries before Homer's time, during the Mycenaean period. Homer's theme is the wrath of Achilles. In depriving "the swift and excellent" Achilles of his rightful war prize (the captive young woman Briseis), King Agamemnon has insulted Achilles' honor and has violated the solemn rule that warrior heroes treat each other with respect. His pride wounded, Achilles refuses to rejoin Agamemnon in battle against Troy. Achilles plans to affirm his honor by demonstrating that the Greeks need his valor and military prowess. Not until many brave men have been slain, including his dearest friend Patroclus, does Achilles set aside his quarrel with Agamemnon and enter the battle.

Homer employs a *particular* event, the quarrel between an arrogant Agamemnon and a revengeful Achilles, to demonstrate a *universal* principle: that "wicked arrogance" and "ruinous wrath" will cause much suffering and death. Homer grasps that there is an internal logic to existence. For Homer, says British classicist H. D. F. Kitto, "actions must have their consequences; ill-judged actions must have uncomfortable results."[1] People, and even the gods, operate within a certain unalterable framework; their deeds are subject to the demands of fate, or necessity. With a poet's insight, Homer sensed what would become a fundamental attitude of the Greek mind: there is a universal order to things. Later Greeks would formulate it in scientific and philosophical terms.

In Homer, we also see the origin of the Greek ideal of *areté*, excellence. The Homeric warrior expresses a passionate desire to assert himself, to demonstrate his worth, to gain the glory that poets would immortalize in their songs. In the warrior-aristocrat world of Homer, *excellence* was principally interpreted as bravery and skill in battle. Homer's portrayal also bears the embryo of a larger conception of human excellence, one that combines thought with action. A man of true worth, says the wise Phoenix to the stubborn Achilles, is both "a speaker of words and a doer of deeds." In this passage, we find the earliest statement of the Greek educational ideal: the molding of a man who, says classicist Werner Jaeger, "united nobility of action with nobility of mind," who realized "the whole of human potentialities."[2] Thus, in Homer we find the beginnings of Greek humanism — a concern with man and his achievements.

Essentially, Homer's works are an expression of the poetic imagination and mythical thought. However, his view of the eternal order of the world and his

Athenian Daily Life. Athenian vase paintings provide insights into daily life. This painting shows two women holding cloth that they had made from yarn. (*The Metropolitan Museum of Art, Fletcher Fund*)

conception of the individual striving for excellence form the foundations of the Greek outlook.

Although Homer did not intend his poetry to have any theological significance, his treatment of the gods had important religious implications for the Greeks. In time, his epics formed the basis of the Olympian religion accepted throughout Greece. The principal gods were said to reside on Mount Olympus, and on its highest peak was the palace of Zeus, the chief deity. Religion pervaded daily life, but in time, traditional religion was challenged and undermined by a growing secular and rational spirit.

The Break with Theocratic Politics

From 750 B.C. to the death of Alexander the Great in 323 B.C., Greek society comprised many independent city-states. The city-state based on tribal allegiances was generally the first political association during the early stages of civilization. Moreover, Greece's many mountains, bays, and islands — natural barriers to political unity — favored this type of political arrangement.

The scale of the city-state, or *polis,* was small; most city-states had fewer than 5,000 male citizens. Athens, which was a large city-state, had some 35,000 to 40,000 adult male citizens at its height in the fifth century B.C.; the rest of its population of 350,000 consisted of women, children, resident aliens, and slaves, none of whom could participate in lawmaking. The polis gave individuals a sense of belonging, for its citizens were intimately involved in the political and cultural life of the community.

In the fifth century B.C., at its maturity, the Greeks viewed their polis as the only avenue to the good life — "the only framework within which man could realize his spiritual, moral, and intellectual capacities," in Kitto's words.[3] The mature polis was a self-governing community that expressed the will of free citizens, not the desires of gods, hereditary kings, or priests. In the Near East, religion dominated political activity, and to abide by the mandates of the gods was the ruler's first responsibility. The Greek polis also had begun as a religious institution, in which the citizens sought to maintain an alliance with their deities. Gradually, however, the citizens de-emphasized the gods' role in political life and based government not on the magic powers of divine rulers, but on human intelligence as expressed through the community. The great innovation that the Greeks introduced into politics and social theory was the principle that law did not derive from gods or divine kings, but from the human community.

The emergence of rational attitudes did not, of course, spell the end of religion, particularly for the peasants, who retained their devotion to their ancient cults, gods, and shrines. Worshiping the god of the city remained a required act of patriotism, to which Greeks unfailingly adhered. Thus, the religious-mythical tradition never died in Greece but existed side by side with a growing rationalism, becoming weaker as time passed. When Athenian democracy reached its height in the middle of the fifth century B.C., religion was no longer the dominant factor in politics. Athenians had consciously come to rely on human reason, not divine guidance, in their political and intellectual life.

What made Greek political life different from that of earlier Near Eastern civilizations, and also gave it enduring significance, was the Greeks' gradual realization that community problems are caused by human beings and require human solutions. The Greeks also valued free citizenship. An absolute king, a tyrant who ruled arbitrarily and by decree and who was above the law, was abhorrent to them.

The ideals of political freedom are best exemplified by Athens. But before turning to Athens, let us examine another Greek city, which followed a different political course.

Sparta: A Garrison State

Situated on the Peloponnesian peninsula, Sparta conquered its neighbors, including Messenia, in the eighth century B.C. Instead of selling the Messenians abroad, the traditional Greek way of treating a defeated foe, the Spartans kept them as state serfs, or *helots.* Helots were owned by the state rather than by individual Spartans. Enraged by their enforced servitude, the Messenians, also a Greek people, desperately tried to regain their freedom. After a bloody uprising was suppressed, the fear of a helot revolt became indelibly stamped on Spartan consciousness.

To maintain their dominion over the Messenians, who outnumbered them ten to one, the Spartans — with extraordinary single-mindedness, discipline, and loyalty — transformed their own society into an armed camp. Agricultural labor was performed by helots; trade and crafts were left to the *perioikoi*, conquered Greeks who were free but who had no political rights. The Spartans learned only one craft, soldiering, and were inculcated with only one conception of excellence: fighting bravely for their city, and if needed, dying for it.

The Spartans were trained in the arts of war and indoctrinated to serve the state. Military training for Spartan boys began at age seven; they exercised, drilled, competed, and endured physical hardships. Other Greeks admired the Spartans for their courage, obedience to law, and achievement in molding themselves according to an ideal. Spartan soldiers were better trained and disciplined and were more physically fit than other Greeks. But the Spartans were also criticized for having a limited conception of areté.

Athens: The Rise of Democracy

The contrast between the city-states of Athens and Sparta is striking. Whereas Sparta was a land power and exclusively agricultural, Athens was located on the peninsula of Attica near the coast, possessed a great navy, and was the commercial leader among the Greeks. To the Spartans, freedom meant preserving the independence of their fatherland; this overriding consideration demanded order, discipline, and regimentation. The Athenians also were determined to protect their city from enemies, but, unlike the Spartans, they valued political freedom and sought the full development and enrichment of the human personality. Thus, while authoritarian and militaristic Sparta turned culturally sterile, the relatively free and open society of Athens became the cultural leader of Hellenic civilization.

Greek city-states generally moved through four stages: rule by a king (monarchy), rule by landowning aristocrats (oligarchy), rule by one man who seized power (tyranny), and rule by the people (democracy). During the first stage, monarchy, the king, who derived his power from the gods, commanded the army and judged civil cases.

Oligarchy, the second stage, was instituted in Athens during the eighth century B.C. when aristocrats (*aristocracy* is a Greek word meaning "rule of the best") usurped power from hereditary kings. In the next century, aristocratic regimes experienced a social crisis. Peasants who borrowed from the aristocracy, pledging their lands as security, lost their property and even became enslaved for nonpayment of their debts. Merchants and peasants also protested that the law, which was based on oral tradition and administered exclusively by aristrocrats, was unjust. In Athens, the embittered and restless middle and lower classes were granted one concession. In 621 B.C., the aristocrats appointed Draco to draw up a code of law. Although Draco's code let the poor know what the law was and reduced the possibility that aristocratic judges would behave arbitrarily, penalties were extremely severe, and the code provided no relief for the peasants' economic woes. As the poor began to

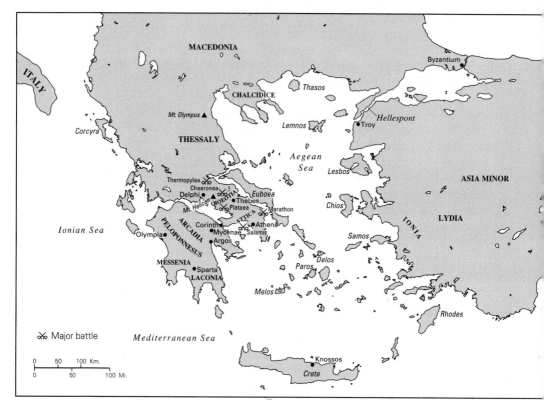

Map 3.1   The Aegean Basin

organize and press for the cancellation of their debts and the redistribution of land, Athens was moving toward civil war.

Solon, the Reformer   In 594 B.C., Solon (c. 640–559 B.C.), a traveler and poet with a reputation for wisdom, was elected chief executive. He maintained that the wealthy landowners, through their greed, had disrupted community life and brought Athens to the brink of civil war. Solon initiated a rational approach to the problems of society by de-emphasizing the gods' role in human affairs and attributing the city's ills to the specific behavior of individuals; he sought practical remedies for these ills; and he held that written law should be in harmony with *Diké*, the principle of justice that underlies the human community. At the same time, he wanted to instill in Athenians of all classes a sense of working for the common good of the city.

Solon aimed at restoring a sick Athenian society to health by restraining the nobles and improving the lot of the poor. To achieve this goal, he canceled debts, freed Athenians enslaved for debt, and brought back to Athens those who had been sold abroad; however, he refused to confiscate and redistribute the nobles' land as the extremists demanded. He permitted all classes of free men, even the poorest, to sit in the Assembly, which elected magistrates and accepted or rejected legislation proposed by a new Council of Four Hundred. He also opened the highest offices in the state to wealthy commoners, who had previously been excluded from these positions because they lacked noble birth. Thus, Solon undermined the traditional rights of the hereditary aristocracy and initiated the transformation of Athens from an aristocratic oligarchy into a democracy.

Solon also instituted ingenious economic reforms. Recognizing that the poor soil of Attica was not conducive to growing grain, he urged the cultivation of grapes for wine and the growing of olives, whose oil could be exported. To encourage industrial expansion, he ordered that all fathers teach their sons a trade and granted citizenship to foreign craftsmen who were willing to migrate to Athens. These measures and the fine quality of the native reddish-brown clay allowed Athens to become the leading producer and exporter of pottery. Solon's economic policies transformed Athens into a great commercial center. However, Solon's reforms did not eliminate factional disputes among the aristocratic clans or relieve all the discontent of the poor.

Pisistratus, the Tyrant   In 546 B.C., Pisistratus (c. 605–527 B.C.), an aristocrat, took advantage of the general instability to become a one-man ruler, driving into exile those who had opposed him. Tyranny thus replaced oligarchy. Tyranny occurred frequently in the Greek city-states. Almost always aristocrats themselves, tyrants generally posed as champions of the poor in their struggle against the aristocracy. Pisistratus sought popular support by having conduits constructed to increase the Athenian water supply; like tyrants in other city-states, he gave to peasants land confiscated from exiled aristocrats and granted state loans to small farmers.

Pisistratus' great achievement was the promotion of cultural life. He initiated grand architectural projects, encouraged sculptors and painters, arranged for public recitals of the Homeric epics, and founded festivals, which included dramatic performances. In all these ways, he made culture, formerly the province of the aristocracy, available to commoners. Pisistratus thus launched a policy that eventually led Athens to emerge as the cultural capital of the Greeks.

Cleisthenes, the Democrat   Shortly after Pisistratus' death, a faction headed by Cleisthenes, an aristocrat sympathetic to democracy, assumed leadership. By an ingenious method of redistricting the city, Cleisthenes ended the aristocratic clans' traditional jockeying for the chief state positions, which had caused much divisiveness and bitterness in Athens. Cleisthenes replaced this practice, rooted in tradition and authority, with a new system, rationally planned to ensure that historic allegiance to tribe or clan would be superseded by loyalty to the city as a whole.

Cleisthenes hoped to make democracy the permanent form of government for Athens. To safeguard the city against tyranny, he introduced the practice of *ostracism*. Once a year, Athenians were given the opportunity to inscribe on a fragment of pottery (*ostracon*) the name of anyone who, they felt, endangered the state. An individual against whom enough votes were cast was ostracized, that is, forced to leave Athens for ten years.

Cleisthenes firmly secured democratic government in Athens. The Assembly, which Solon had opened to all male citizens, was in the process of becoming the supreme authority in the state. But the period of Athenian greatness lay in the future; the Athenians first had to fight a war of survival against the Persian Empire.

The Persian Wars

In 499 B.C., the Ionian Greeks of Asia Minor rebelled against their Persian overlord. Sympathetic to the Ionian cause, Athens sent twenty ships to aid the revolt. Bent on revenge, Darius I, king of Persia, sent a small detachment to Attica. In 490 B.C., on the plains of Marathon, the citizen army of Athens defeated the Persians — for the Athenians, one of the finest moments in their history. Ten years later, Xerxes, Darius' son, organized a huge invasion force — some 250,000 men and more than 500 ships — with the aim of reducing Greece to a Persian province. Setting aside their separatist instincts, many of the city-states united to defend their independence and their liberty.

The Persians crossed the waters of the Hellespont (Dardanelles) and made their way into northern Greece. Herodotus describes their encounter at the mountain pass of Thermopylae with three hundred Spartans, who, true to their training and ideal of areté, "resisted to the last with their swords if they had them, and if not, with their hands and teeth, until the Persians, coming on from the front over the ruins of the wall and closing in from behind, finally overwhelmed them."[4] Northern Greece fell to the Persians, who continued south, burning a deserted Athens.

When it appeared that the Greeks' spirit had been broken, the Athenian statesman and general Themistocles (c. 527–460 B.C.), demonstrating in military affairs the same rationality that Cleisthenes had shown in political life, lured the Persian fleet into the narrows of the Bay of Salamis. Unable to deploy its more numerous ships in this cramped space, the Persian armada was destroyed by Greek ships. In 479 B.C., a year after the Athenian naval victory at Salamis, the Spartans defeated the Persians in the land battle of Plataea. The inventive intelligence with which the Greeks had planned their military operations and a fierce desire to preserve their freedom — which, the war made them realize, was their distinguishing attribute — had enabled them to defeat the greatest military power the Mediterranean world had yet seen.

The Persian Wars were decisive in the history of the West. The confidence and pride that came with victory propelled Athens into a golden age, whose achievements were pivotal in the shaping of European culture. But the conflict also roused the Athenian urge for dominance in Greece. The Persian Wars ushered in an era of Athenian imperialism, which had drastic consequences for the future. Immediately after the wars, more than 150 city-states organized a confederation, the Delian League (named after its treasury on the island of Delos), to protect themselves against a renewed confrontation with Persia. Because of its wealth, its powerful fleet, and the restless energy of its citizens, Athens assumed leadership of the Delian League. Athenians consciously and rapaciously manipulated the league for their own economic advantage, seeing no contradiction between imperialism and democracy. Athens forbade member states to withdraw, stationed garrisons on the territory of confederate states, and used the league's treasury to finance public works in Athens. Although member states did receive protection from both pirates and Persians, were not overtaxed, and enjoyed increased trade, they resented Athenian domination.

The Mature Athenian Democracy

Athenian imperialism was one consequence of the Persian Wars; another was the flowering of Athenian democracy and culture. The Athenian state was a direct democracy, in which the citizens themselves, not elected representatives, made the laws. In the Assembly, which was open to all adult male citizens and which met some forty times a year, Athenians debated and voted on key issues of state: they declared war, signed treaties, and spent public funds. The lowliest cobbler, as well as the wealthiest aristocrat, had the opportunity to express his opinion in the Assembly, to vote, to speak before and submit motions to the Assembly, to hold the highest public positions, and to receive equal treatment before the law. By the middle of the fifth century, the will of the people, as expressed in the Assembly, was supreme.

The Council of Five Hundred (which had been established by Cleisthenes to replace Solon's Council of Four Hundred) managed the ports, military installations, and other state properties and prepared the agenda for the Assembly. Because its members were chosen annually by lot and could not serve more than twice in a lifetime, the Council could never supersede the Assembly. Chosen at random, its membership could not become a cabal of the most powerful and ambitious citizens. Some 350 magistrates, also chosen by lot, performed administrative tasks: collecting fines, policing the city, repairing streets, inspecting markets, and so forth. In view of the special competence that their posts required, the ten generals who led the army were not chosen by lot but were elected by the Assembly.

Athens has been aptly described as a government of amateurs: there were no professional civil servants, no professional soldiers and sailors, no state judges, and no elected lawmakers. Ordinary citizens performed the duties of government. Such a system rested on the assumption that the average citizen was capable of participating intelligently in the affairs of state and that he would, in a spirit of civic patriotism, carry out his responsibilities to his city. In Athens of the fifth century B.C., excellence was equated with good citizenship — a concern for the good of the community that outweighs personal aspirations. Indeed, to a surprisingly large number of Athenians, politics was an overriding concern, and they devoted considerable time and thought to civic affairs. Those who allowed private matters to take precedence over the needs of the community were denounced as useless people living purposeless lives.

Athenian democracy achieved its height in the middle of the fifth century B.C. under the leadership of Pericles (c. 495–429 B.C.), a gifted statesman, orator, and military commander. In the opening stage of the monumental clash with Sparta, the Peloponnesian War (431–404 B.C.), Pericles delivered an oration in honor of the Athenian war casualties. The oration, as reported by Thucydides, the great Athenian historian of the fifth century B.C., contains a glowing description of the Athenian democratic ideal:

> *We are called a democracy, for the administration is in the hands of the many and not of the few. But while the law secures equal justice to all alike in their private disputes, the claim of excellence is also recognized; and when a citizen is any way distinguished, he is [selected for] public service . . . as the reward of merit. Neither is poverty a bar, but a man may benefit his country whatever may be the obscurity of his condition. . . . There is no exclusiveness in our public life, and in our private intercourse we are not suspicious of one another, nor angry with our neighbor if he does what he likes; we do not put on sour looks at him which though harmless are unpleasant. . . . a spirit of reverence pervades our public acts; we are prevented from doing wrong by respect for authority and for the laws. . . .*[5]

Athenian democracy undoubtedly had its limitations and weaknesses. Modern critics point out that resident aliens were almost totally barred from citizenship and therefore from political participation. Slaves, who constituted about one-fourth of the Athenian population, enjoyed none of the freedoms that Athenians considered so precious. The Greeks regarded slavery as a necessary precondition for civilized life; for some to be free and prosperous, they believed, others had to be enslaved. Slaves were generally prisoners of war or captives of pirates. In Athens, some slaves were Greeks, but most were foreigners. Slaves usually did the same work as Athenian citizens: farming, commerce, manufacturing, and domestic chores. However, those slaves, including preadolescent children, who toiled in the mines suffered a grim fate.

Athenian women were another group denied legal or political rights. Most Greeks, no doubt, agreed with Aristotle, who said: "The male is by nature superior, and the female inferior, and . . . the one rules and the other is ruled." A girl usually was married at fourteen, to a man twice her age, and the marriage was arranged by a male relative. The wedding day might be the first time that the young bride saw her future husband. Although either spouse could obtain a divorce, the children remained with the father after the marriage was dissolved. Wives did not dine with their husbands and spent much of their time in the women's quarters.

Athenian women were barred from holding public office and generally could not appear in court without a male representative. They could not act in plays, and, when they attended the theater, they sat in the rear, away from the men. Greek women received no formal education, although some young women learned to read and write at home. Training in household skills was considered the only education a woman needed. Since it was believed that a woman could not act independently, she was required to have a guardian — normally her father or her husband — who controlled her property and supervised her behavior. Convinced that financial dealings were too difficult for women and that they needed to be protected from strangers, men, not women, did the marketing. When a woman left the house, she was usually accompanied by a male. The Athenian wife was treated as a minor; in effect, she was her husband's ward.

The flaws in Athenian democracy should not cause us to undervalue its extraordinary achievement. The idea that the state represents a community of free, self-governing citizens remains a crucial principle of Western civilization. Athenian democracy embodied the principle of the legal state — a government based not on force, but on laws debated, devised, altered, and obeyed by free citizens.

This idea of the legal state could have arisen only in a society that was aware of and respected the rational mind. Just as the Greeks demythicized nature, so too they removed myth from the sphere of politics. Holding that government was something that people create to satisfy human needs, the Athenians regarded their leaders neither as gods nor as priests, but as men who had demonstrated a capacity for statesmanship.

Both democratic politics and systematic political thought originated in Greece. There, people first asked questions about the nature and purpose of the state, rationally analyzed political institutions, speculated about human nature and justice, and discussed the merits of various forms of government. It is to Greece that we ultimately trace the idea of democracy and all that accompanies it: citizenship, constitutions, equality before the law, government by law, reasoned debate, respect for the individual, and confidence in human intelligence.

The Decline of the City-States

Although the Greeks shared a common language and culture, they remained divided politically. A determination to preserve city-state sovereignty prevented the Greeks from forming a larger political grouping, which might have prevented the intercity warfare that ultimately cost the city-state its vitality and independence. But the creation of a Pan-Hellenic union would have required a radical transformation of the Greek character, which for hundreds of years had regarded the independent city-state as the only suitable political system.

The Peloponnesian War

Athenian control of the Delian League frightened the Spartans and their allies in the Peloponnesian League. Sparta and the Peloponnesian states decided on war because they saw a dynamic and imperialistic Athens as a threat to their independence. At stake for Athens was control over the Delian League, which gave Athens political power and contributed to its economic prosperity. Neither Athens nor Sparta anticipated the catastrophic consequences that the war would have for Greek civilization.

The war began in 431 B.C. and ended in 404 B.C. When a besieged Athens, with a decimated navy and a dwindling food supply, surrendered, Sparta

Attic Black-Figure Hydria, c. 510 B.C. This hydria, or water jug, showing women drawing water from a fountainhouse dates from the sixth century B.C. These trips to the fountainhouse provided one of few opportunities for women to socialize outside of the home. (*William Francis Warden Fund. Courtesy, Museum of Fine Arts, Boston*)

dissolved the Delian League, left Athens with only a handful of ships, and forced the city to pull down its long walls — ramparts designed to protect it against siege weapons.

The Peloponnesian War shattered the spiritual foundations of Hellenic society. During its course, men became brutalized, selfish individualism triumphed over civic duty, moderation gave way to extremism, and in several cities, including Athens, politics degenerated into civil war between oligarchs and democrats. Oligarchs, generally from the wealthier segments of Athenian society, wanted to concentrate power in their own hands by depriving the lower classes of political rights. Democrats, generally from the poorer segment of society, sought to preserve the political rights of all adult male citizens. Strife between oligarchs and democrats was quite common in the Greek city-states even before the Peloponnesian War.

The Fourth Century

The Peloponnesian War was the great crisis of Hellenic history. The city-states never recovered from their self-inflicted spiritual wounds. The civic loyalty and confidence that had marked the fifth century waned, and the fourth century was dominated by a new mentality that the leaders of the Age of Pericles would have abhorred. A concern for private affairs superseded devotion to the general good of the polis. Increasingly, professionals, rather than ordinary citizens, administered the tasks of government, and mercenaries began to replace citizen soldiers.

In the fourth century, the quarrelsome city-states formed new systems of alliances and persisted in their ruinous conflicts. While the Greek cities battered one another in fratricidal warfare, a new power was rising in the north — Macedonia. To the Greeks, the Macedonians, a wild mountain people who spoke a Greek dialect and had acquired a sprinkling of Hellenic culture, differed little from other non-Greeks, whom they called barbarians. In 359 B.C., at the age of twenty-three, Philip II (382–336 B.C.) ascended the Macedonian throne. Converting Macedonia into a first-rate military power, he began a drive to become master of the Greeks.

Incorrectly assessing Philip's strength, the Greeks were slow to organize a coalition against Macedonia. In 338 B.C., at Chaeronea, Philip's forces decisively defeated the Greeks, and all of Greece was his. The city-states still existed, but they had lost their independence. The world of the small, independent, and self-sufficient polis was drawing to a close, and Greek civilization was taking a different shape.

The Dilemma of Greek Politics

Philip's conquest of the city-states points to a fundamental weakness of Greek politics. Despite internal crisis and persistent warfare, the Greeks were unable to fashion any political framework other than the polis. The city-state was fast becoming an anachronism, but the Greeks were unable to see that, in a world moving toward larger states and empires, the small city-state could not compete. An unallied city-state, with its small citizen army, could not withstand the powerful military machine that Philip had created. A challenge confronted the city-states: the need to shape some form of political union, a Pan-Hellenic federation, that would end the suicidal internecine warfare, promote economic well-being, and protect the Greek world from hostile states. Because they could not respond creatively to this challenge, the city-states ultimately lost their independence to foreign conquerors.

The waning of civic responsibility among the citizens was another reason for the decline of the city-states. The vitality of the city-state depended on the willingness of its citizens to put aside private concerns for the good of the community. The Periclean ideal of citizenship dissipated as Athenians neglected the community in order to concentrate on private affairs or sought to derive personal profit from public office. The decline in civic responsibility could be seen in the hiring of mercenaries to replace citizen soldiers and in the indifference and hesitancy with which Athenians confronted Philip.

Greek political life demonstrated both the best and the worst features of freedom. On the one hand, as Pericles boasted, freedom encouraged active citizenship, reasoned debate, and government by law. On the other, as Thucydides lamented, freedom could degenerate into factionalism, demagoguery, unbridled self-interest, and civil war.

Greek politics also revealed both the capabilities and the limitations of reason. Originally, the polis was conceived as a divine institution, in which the citizen had a religious obligation to obey the law. As the rational and secular outlook became more pervasive, the gods lost their authority. When people no longer regarded law as an expression of sacred traditions ordained by the gods but saw it as a merely human contrivance, respect for the law diminished, weakening the foundations of the society. The results were party conflicts, politicians who scrambled for personal power, and moral uncertainty. Although the Greeks originated the lofty ideal that human beings could regulate their political life according to reason, their history, marred by intercity warfare and internal violence, demonstrates the extreme difficulties involved in creating and maintaining a rational society.

Philosophy in the Hellenic Age

The Greeks broke with the mythopoeic outlook of the Near East and conceived a new way of viewing nature and human society that is the basis of the Western scientific and philosophical tradition. By the fifth century B.C., the Greeks had emancipated thought from myth and gradually applied reason to the physical world and to all human activities. This emphasis on reason marks a turning point for human civilization.

The development of rational thought in Greece was a process, a trend, not a finished achievement. The process began when some thinkers rejected mythical explanations for natural phenomena. The nonphilosophical majority of the people never entirely eliminated the language, attitudes, and beliefs of myth from their life and thought. For them, the world remained controlled by divine forces, which were appeased through cultic practices. Even in the mature philosophy of Plato and Aristotle, mythical modes of thought persisted. What is of immense historical importance, however, is not the degree to which the Greeks successfully integrated the norm of reason, but the fact that they originated this norm, defined it, and applied it to their intellectual development and social and political life.

The first theoretical philosophers in human history emerged in the sixth century B.C., in the Greek cities of Ionia in Asia Minor. Curious about the essential composition of nature and dissatisfied with earlier creation legends, the Ionians sought physical, rather than mythic-religious, explanations for natural occurrences. In the process, they arrived at a new concept of nature and a new method of inquiry. They maintained that nature was not manipulated by arbitrary and willful gods, nor was it governed by blind chance. As the Ionians saw it, underlying the seeming chaos of nature were principles of order — general laws ascertainable by the human mind. This discovery marks the beginning of scientific thought. The early Greek thinkers are called cosmologists, because they were concerned with the nature of the universe, or Pre-Socratics, because they came before Socrates, a pivotal figure in the evolution of Greek thought.

The Cosmologists: A Rational Inquiry into Nature

The cosmologists sought to discover the underlying principles of the universe: how nature came to be the way it was. They held that some single, eternal, and imperishable substance, which underwent various modifications, gave rise to all phenomena in nature.

Ionian philosophy began with Thales (c. 624–548 B.C.) of Miletus, a city in Ionia. He was a contemporary of Solon of Athens and concerned himself with understanding the order of nature. Thales said that water was the basic element, the underlying substratum of nature, and that through some natural process — similar to the formation of ice or steam — water gave rise to everything else in the world.

Thales revolutionized thought because he omitted the gods from his account of the origins of nature and searched for a natural explanation of how all things came to be. Thales also broke with the commonly held belief that earthquakes were caused by Poseidon, god of the sea, and offered instead a naturalistic explanation for these disturbances: that the earth floated on water, and when the water experienced turbulent waves, the earth was rocked by earthquakes.

Anaximander (c. 611–547 B.C.), another sixth-century Ionian, rejected Thales' theory that water was the original substance. He rejected any specific substance and suggested that an indefinite substance, which he called the Boundless, was the source of all things. He believed that from this primary mass, which contained the powers of heat and cold, there gradually emerged a nucleus, the seed of the world. He said that the cold and wet condensed to form the earth and its cloud cover, while the hot and dry formed the rings of fire that we see as the moon, the sun, and the stars. The heat from the fire in the sky dried the earth and shrank the seas. From the warm slime on earth arose life, and from the first sea creatures there evolved land animals, including human beings. Anaximander's account of the origins of the universe and nature understandably contained fantastic elements. Nevertheless, by offering a natural explanation for the origin of nature and life and by holding that nature was lawful, it surpassed the creation myths.

Like his fellow Ionians, Anaximenes, who died about 525 B.C., made the transition from myth to reason. He also maintained that a primary substance, air, underlay reality and accounted for the orderliness of nature. Air that was rarefied became fire, whereas wind and clouds were formed from condensed air. If the process of condensation continued, it produced water, earth, and eventually stones. Anaximenes also rejected the old belief that a rainbow was the goddess Iris; instead, he said that the rainbow was caused by the sun's rays falling on dense air.

The Ionians have been called "matter philosophers" because they held that everything issued from a particular material substance. Other thinkers of the sixth century B.C. tried a different approach. Pythagoras (c. 580–507 B.C.) and his followers, who lived in the Greek cities in southern Italy, did not find the nature of things in a particular substance, but rather in mathematical relationships. The Pythagoreans discovered that the intervals in the musical scale can be expressed mathematically. Extending this principle of proportion found in sound to the universe at large, they concluded that the cosmos also contained an inherent mathematical order. Thus, the Pythagoreans shifted the emphasis from matter to form, from the world of sense perception to the logic of mathematics. The Pythagoreans were also religious mystics who believed in the immortality and transmigration of souls. Consequently, they refused to eat animal flesh, fearing that it contained former human souls.

Parmenides (c. 515–450 B.C.), a native of the Greek city of Elea in southern Italy, challenged the fundamental view of the Ionians that all things emerged from one original substance. In developing his position, Parmenides applied to philosophical argument the logic used by the Pythagoreans in mathematical thinking. In putting forth the proposition that an argument must be consistent and contain no contradictions, Parmenides became the founder of formal logic. Despite appearances, asserted Parmenides, reality — the cosmos and all that is within it — is one, eternal, and unchanging. It is made known not through the senses, which are misleading, but through the mind; not through experience, but through reason. Truth is reached through abstract thought alone. Parmenides' concept of an unchanging reality apprehended by thought alone influenced Plato and is the foundation of metaphysics.

Democritus (c. 460–370 B.C.), from the Greek mainland, renewed the Ionians' concern with the world of matter and reaffirmed their confidence in knowledge derived from sense perception. But he also retained Parmenides' reverence for reason. His model of the universe consisted of two fundamental realities: empty space and an infinite number of atoms. Eternal, indivisible, and imperceptible, these atoms moved in the void. All things consisted of atoms, and combinations of atoms accounted for all change in nature. In a world of colliding atoms, everything behaved according to mechanical principles.

Concepts essential to scientific thought thus emerged in embryonic form with the early Greek philosophers: natural explanations for physical occurrences (Ionians), the mathematical order of nature (Pythagoras), logical proof (Parmenides), and the mechanical structure of the universe (Democritus). By giving to nature a rational, rather than a mythical, foundation and by holding that theories should be grounded in evidence and that one should be able to defend them, the early Greek philosophers pushed thought in a new direction. This new approach made possible theoretical thought and the systematization of knowledge — as distinct from the mere observation and collection of data.

This systematization of knowledge extended into several areas. Greek mathematicians, for example, organized the Egyptians' practical experience with land measurements into the logical and coherent science of geometry. They established mathematics as an ordered system based on fundamental premises and necessary connections, and they developed logical procedures for arriving at mathematical proofs. Both Babylonians and Egyptians had performed fairly complex mathematical operations, but unlike the Greeks, they made no attempt to prove underlying mathematical principles. In another area, Babylonian priests had observed the heavens for religious reasons, believing that the stars revealed the wishes of the gods. The Greeks used the data collected by the Babylonians, but not for a religious purpose; they sought to discover the geometrical laws that govern the motions of heavenly bodies.

A parallel development occurred in medicine. No Near Eastern medical text explicitly attacked magical beliefs and practices. In contrast, Greek doctors

The Parthenon, Athens, 447–432 B.C. A masterpiece of the Doric style, the great temple dedicated to Athena Parthenos (the Maiden), the patron goddess of the city, was constructed through the efforts of Pericles. Its cult statue and sculptural reliefs under its roof line were designed by the outstanding sculptor of the age, Phidias. In post-Hellenistic times, it served as a Christian church and subsequently an Islamic mosque, until it was destroyed by an explosion in 1687. Between 1801 and 1812, the marble reliefs were removed by the English Lord Elgin and now reside in the British Museum, in London. (*Hirmer Verlag GmbH*)

associated with the medical school of Hippocrates (c. 460–c. 377 B.C.) asserted that diseases have a natural, not a supernatural, cause. The following tract on epilepsy, which was considered a sacred disease, illustrates the development of a scientific approach to medicine:

> *I am about to discuss the disease called "sacred." It is not, in my opinion, any more divine or sacred than any other disease, but has a natural cause, and its supposed divine origin is due to men's inexperience, and to their wonder at its peculiar character. Now . . . men continue to believe in its divine origin because they are at a loss to understand it. . . . My own view is that those who first attributed a sacred character to this malady were like the magicians, purifiers, charlatans, and quacks of our own day; men who claim great piety and*

superior knowledge. Being at a loss, and having no treatment which would help, they concealed and sheltered themselves behind superstition, and called this illness sacred, in order that their utter ignorance might not be manifest.[6]

The Sophists: A Rational Investigation of Human Culture

In their effort to understand the external world, the cosmologists had created the tools of reason. Greek thinkers then turned away from the world of nature and attempted a rational investigation of people and society. The Sophists exemplified this shift in focus. They were professional teachers who wandered from city to city teaching rhetoric, grammar, poetry, gymnastics, mathematics, and music. The Sophists insisted that it was futile to speculate about the first principles of the universe, for such knowledge was beyond the grasp of the human mind. Instead, they urged that individuals improve themselves and their cities by applying reason to the tasks of citizenship and statesmanship.

The Sophists answered a practical need in Athens, which had been transformed into a wealthy and dynamic imperial state after the Persian Wars. Because the Sophists claimed that they could teach *political* areté — the skill to formulate the right laws and policies for cities and the art of eloquence and persuasion — they were sought as tutors by politically ambitious young men, especially in Athens. The Western humanist tradition owes much to the Sophists, who examined political and ethical problems, cultivated the minds of their students, and invented formal secular education.

The Sophists were philosophical relativists; that is, they held that no truth is universally valid. Protagoras, a fifth-century Sophist, said that "man is the measure of all things." By this he meant that good and evil, truth and falsehood are matters of individual judgment; there are no universal standards that apply to all people at all times.

In applying reason critically to human affairs, the Sophists attacked the traditional religious and moral values of Athenian society. Some Sophists taught that speculation about the divine was useless; others went further and asserted that religion was just a human invention to ensure obedience to traditions and laws.

The Sophists also applied reason to law, with the same effect: the undermining of traditional authority. The laws of a given city, they asserted, did not derive from the gods; nor were they based on any objective, universal, and timeless standards of justice and good, for such standards did not exist. The more radical Sophists argued that law was merely something made by the most powerful citizens for their own benefit. This view had dangerous implications: since law rested on no higher principle than might, it need not be obeyed.

Some Sophists combined this assault on law with an attack on the ancient Athenian idea of *sophrosyne* — moderation and self-discipline — because it denied human instincts. Instead of moderation, they urged that people should maximize pleasure and trample underfoot those traditions that restricted them from fully expressing their desires.

In subjecting traditions to the critique of reason, the radical Sophists provoked an intellectual and spiritual crisis. Their doctrines encouraged disobedience to law, neglect of civic duty, and selfish individualism. These attitudes became widespread during and after the Peloponnesian War, dangerously weakening community bonds. Conservatives sought to restore the authority of law and a respect for moral values by renewing allegiance to those sacred traditions undermined by the Sophists.

Socrates: Shaping The Rational Individual

Socrates (c. 469–399 B.C.), one of the most extraordinary figures in the history of Western civilization, took a different approach. He attacked the Sophists' relativism, holding that people should regulate their behavior in accordance with universal values. While he recognized that the Sophists taught skills, he felt that they had no insights into questions that really mattered: What is the purpose of life? What are the values by which man should live? How does man perfect his character? Here the Sophists failed, said Socrates; they taught the ambitious to succeed in politics, but persuasive oratory and clever reasoning do not instruct a man in the art of living. According to Socrates, the Sophists had attacked the old system of beliefs but had not provided the individual with a constructive replacement.

Socrates' central concern was the perfection of individual human character, the achievement of moral excellence. For Socrates, moral values did not derive from a transcendent God, as they did for the Hebrews. Individuals attained them by regulating their lives according to objective standards arrived at through rational reflection, that is, by making reason the formative, guiding, and ruling agency of the soul. For Socrates, true education meant the shaping of character according to values discovered through the active and critical use of reason.

Socrates wanted to subject all human beliefs and behavior to the scrutiny of reason and in this way remove ethics from the realm of authority, tradition, dogma, superstition, and myth. He believed that reason was the only proper guide to the most crucial problem of human existence — the question of good and evil.

Dialectics   In urging Athenians to think rationally about the problems of human existence, Socrates offered no systematic ethical theory and no list of ethical precepts. What he did supply was a method of inquiry called *dialectics,* or logical discussion. As Socrates used it, a dialectical exchange between individuals or with oneself, a *dialogue,* was the essential source of knowledge. It forced people out of their apathy and smugness and compelled them to examine their thoughts critically; to confront illogical, inconsistent, dogmatic, and imprecise assertions; and to express their ideas in clearly defined terms.

Dialectics demonstrated that the acquisition of knowledge was a creative act. The human mind could not be coerced into knowing; it was not a passive vessel into which a teacher poured knowledge. The dialogue compelled the individual to play an active role in acquiring the ideals and values by which to live. In a dialogue, individuals became thinking participants in a search for knowledge. Through relentless cross-examination, Socrates induced the persons with whom he spoke to explain and justify their opinions rationally, for only thus did knowledge become a part of one's being.

Dialogue implied that reason was meant to be used in relations between human beings and that they could learn from each other, help each other, teach each other, and improve each other. It implied further that the human mind could and should make rational choices. To deal rationally with oneself and others is the distinctive mark of being human.

The Execution of Socrates   Socrates devoted much of his life to the mission of persuading his fellow Athenians to think critically about how they lived their lives. Through probing questions, he tried to stir people out of their complacency and make them realize how directionless and purposeless their lives were.

For many years, Socrates challenged Athenians without suffering harm, for Athens was generally distinguished by its freedom of speech and thought. However, in the uncertain times during and immediately after the Peloponnesian War, Socrates made enemies. When he was seventy, he was accused of corrupting the youth of the city and of not believing in the city's gods but in other, new divinities. Underlying these accusations was the fear that Socrates was a troublemaker, a subversive who threatened the state by subjecting its ancient and sacred values to the critique of thought.

Socrates denied the charges and conducted himself with great dignity at his trial, refusing to grovel and beg forgiveness. Instead, he defined his creed:

> *If you think that a man of any worth at all ought to . . . think of anything but whether he is acting justly or unjustly, and as a good or a bad man would act, you are mistaken. . . . If you were therefore to say to me, "Socrates, we will not listen to [your accuser]. We will let you go, but on the condition that you give up this investigation of yours, and philosophy. If you are found following these pursuits again you shall die." I say, if you offered to let me go on these terms, I should reply: . . . As long as I have breath and strength I will not give up philosophy and exhorting you and declaring the truth to every one of you whom I meet, saying, as I am accustomed, "My good friend, you are a citizen of Athens . . . are you not ashamed of caring so much for making of money and for fame and prestige, when you neither think nor care about wisdom and truth and the improvement of your soul?"*[7]

Convicted by an Athenian court, Socrates was ordered to drink poison. Had he attempted to appease the jurors, he probably would have been given a light punishment, but he would not disobey the commands of his conscience and alter his principles even under threat of death.

Socrates did not write down his philosophy and beliefs. We are able to construct a coherent account of his life and ideals largely through the works of his most important disciple, Plato.

Plato: The Rational Society

Plato (c. 429–347 B.C.) used his master's teachings to create a comprehensive system of philosophy that embraced both the world of nature and the social world. Virtually all the problems discussed by Western philosophers for the past two millennia were raised by Plato. We focus on two of his principal concerns, the theory of Ideas and that of the just state.

Theory of Ideas Socrates had taught that universal standards of right and justice exist and are arrived at through thought. Building on the insights of his teacher, Plato postulated the existence of a higher world of reality, independent of the world of things that we experience every day. This higher reality, he said, is the realm of Ideas, or Forms — unchanging, eternal, absolute, and universal standards of beauty, goodness, justice, and truth.

Truth resides in this world of Forms and not in the world made known through the senses. For example, a person can never draw a perfect square, but the properties of a perfect square exist in the world of Forms. Similarly, the ordinary person derives an opinion of what beauty is only from observing beautiful things; the philosopher, aspiring to true knowledge, goes beyond what he sees and tries to grasp with his mind the Idea of beauty. The ordinary individual lacks a true conception of justice or goodness; such knowledge is available only to the philosopher, whose mind can leap from worldly particulars to an ideal world beyond space and time. Thus, true wisdom is obtained through knowledge of the Ideas and not through the imperfect reflections of the Ideas that the senses perceive.

A champion of reason, Plato aspired to study human life and arrange it according to universally valid standards. In contrast to sophistic relativism, he maintained that objective and eternal standards do exist.

The Just State In adapting the rational legacy of Greek philosophy to politics, Plato constructed a comprehensive political theory. What the Greeks had achieved in practice — the movement away from mythic and theocratic politics — Plato accomplished on the level of thought: the fashioning of a rational model of the state.

Like Socrates, Plato attempted to resolve the problem caused by the radical Sophists: the undermining of traditional values. Socrates had tried to dispel this spiritual crisis through a moral transformation of the individual, based on reason, whereas Plato wanted the entire community to conform to rational principles. Plato said that if human beings are to live an ethical life, they must do so as citizens of a just and rational state. In an unjust state, people cannot achieve Socratic wisdom, for their souls will mirror the state's wickedness.

Plato had experienced the ruinous Peloponnesian War and witnessed Socrates' trial and execution. Disillusioned by the corruption of Athenian morality and democratic politics, he concluded that under the Athenian constitution neither the morality of the individual Athenian nor the good of the state could be enhanced. He became convinced that Athens required moral and political reform founded on Socratic philosophy.

In his great dialogue, *The Republic,* Plato devised an ideal state based on standards that would rescue his native Athens from the evils that had befallen it. For Plato, the just state could not be founded on tradition (for inherited attitudes did not derive from rational standards) or on the doctrine of might being right (a principle taught by radical Sophists and practiced by Athenian statesmen). A just state, in his view, had to conform to universally valid principles and aim at the moral improvement of its citizens, not at increasing its power and wealth. Such a state required leaders distinguished by their wisdom and virtue rather than by sophistic cleverness and eloquence.

Fundamental to Plato's political theory as formulated in *The Republic* was his criticism of Athenian democracy. An aristocrat by birth and temperament, Plato believed that it was foolish to expect the common man to think intelligently about foreign policy, economics, or other vital matters of state. Yet the common man was permitted to speak in the Assembly and to vote, and he could also be selected, by lot, for executive office. A second weakness of democracy for Plato was that leaders were chosen and followed for nonessential reasons, such as persuasive speech, good looks, wealth, and family background.

A third danger of democracy was that it could degenerate into anarchy, said Plato. Intoxicated by liberty, the citizens of a democracy could lose all sense of balance, self-discipline, and respect for law: "The citizens become so sensitive that they resent the slightest application of control as intolerable tyranny, and in their resolve to have no master they end up by disregarding even the law, written or unwritten."[8]

As the democratic city falls into disorder, a fourth weakness of democracy will become evident. A demagogue will be able to gain power by promising to plunder the rich to benefit the poor. To retain his hold over the state, the tyrant "begins by stirring up one war after another, in order that the people may feel their need of a leader."[9] Because of these inherent weaknesses of democracy, Plato insisted that Athens would be governed properly only when the wisest people, the philosophers, attained power.

Plato rejected the fundamental principle of Athenian democracy: that the ordinary citizen is capable of participating sensibly in public affairs. People would not entrust the care of a sick person to just anyone, said Plato, nor would they allow a novice to guide a ship during a storm. Yet, in a democracy, amateurs were permitted to run the government and to supervise the education of the young; no wonder Athenian society was disintegrating. Plato believed that these duties should be performed only by the best people in the city, the philosophers, who would approach human problems with reason and wisdom derived from knowledge of the world of unchanging and perfect Ideas. He asserted that only these possessors of truth would be competent to rule.

Plato divided people into three groups: those who demonstrated philosophical ability should be rulers; those whose natural bent revealed exceptional courage should be soldiers; and those driven by desire, the great masses, should be producers (tradespeople, artisans, or farmers). In *The Republic,* the philosophers were selected by a rigorous system of education that was open to all children. Those not demonstrating sufficient intelligence or strength of character were to be weeded out to become workers or warriors, depending on their natural aptitudes. After many years of education and practical military and administrative experience, the philosophers were to be entrusted with political power. If they had been properly educated, the philosopher-rulers would not seek personal wealth or personal power; they would be concerned with pursuing justice and serving the community. The philosophers were to be absolute rulers. Although the people would have lost their right to participate in political decisions, they would have gained a well-governed state, whose leaders, distinguished by their wisdom, integrity, and sense of responsibility, sought only the common good. Only thus, said Plato, could the individual and the community achieve well-being.

Aristotle: Synthesis of Greek Thought

Aristotle (384–322 B.C.) stands at the apex of Greek thought because he achieved a creative synthesis of the knowledge and theories of earlier thinkers. The range of Aristotle's interests and intellect is extraordinary. He was the leading expert of his time in every field of knowledge, with the possible exception of mathematics.

Aristotle undertook the monumental task of organizing and systematizing the thought of the Pre-Socratics, Socrates, and Plato. He shared with the natural philosophers a desire to understand the physical universe; he shared with Socrates and Plato the belief that reason was a person's highest faculty and that the polis was the primary formative institution of Greek life.

Critique of Plato's Theory of Ideas   To the practical and empirically minded Aristotle, the Platonic notion of an independent and separate world of Forms beyond space and time seemed contrary to common sense. To comprehend reality, said Aristotle, one should not escape into another world. For him, Plato's two-world philosophy suffered from too much mystery, mysticism, and poetic fancy; moreover, Plato undervalued the world of facts and objects revealed through sight, hearing, and touch, a world that Aristotle valued. Like Plato, Aristotle desired to comprehend the essence of things and held that understanding universal principles is the ultimate aim of knowledge. But unlike Plato, he did not turn away from the world of things to obtain such knowledge. Possessing a scientist's curiosity to understand nature, Aristotle respected knowledge obtained through the senses.

For Aristotle, the Forms were not located in a higher world outside and beyond phenomena but existed in things themselves. He said that, through human experience with such things as men, horses, and white objects, the essence of man, horse, and whiteness can be discovered through reason; the Form of Man, the Form of Horse, and the Form of Whiteness can be determined. These universals, which apply to all men, all horses, and all white things, were for both Aristotle and Plato the true objects of knowledge. For Plato, these Forms existed independently of particular objects: the Forms for men or horses or whiteness or triangles or temples existed, whether or not representations of these Ideas in the form of material objects were made known to the senses. For Aristotle, however, universal Ideas could not be determined without examination of particular things. Whereas Plato's use of reason tended to stress otherworldliness, Aristotle brought philosophy back to earth.

By holding that certainty in knowledge comes from reason alone and not from the senses, Plato was predisposed toward mathematics and metaphysics — pure thought that transcends the world of change and material objects. By stressing the importance of knowledge acquired through the rational examination of sense experience, Aristotle favored the development of empirical sciences — physics, biology, zoology, botany, and other disciplines based on the observation and investigation of nature and the recording of data.

Ethical Thought   Like Socrates and Plato, Aristotle believed that a knowledge of ethics was possible and that it must be based on reason, for this is what distinguishes human beings from other forms of life. In *Nicoamachean Ethics* Aristotle, the good life was the examined life; it meant making intelligent decisions when confronted with specific problems. People could achieve happiness when they exercised the distinctively human trait of reasoning, when they applied their knowledge relevantly to life, and when their behavior was governed by intelligence and not by whim, tradition, or authority.

Aristotle recognized, however, that people are not entirely rational and that the passionate element in the human personality can never be eradicated or ignored. According to Aristotle, surrendering completely to desire meant descending to the level of beasts, but denying the passions and living as an ascetic was a foolish and unreasonable rejection of human nature. Aristotle maintained that by proper training, people could learn to regulate their desires. They could achieve moral well-being, or virtue, when they avoided extremes of behavior and rationally chose the way of moderation. "Nothing in excess" is the key to Aristotle's ethics.

Political Thought   Aristotle's *Politics* complements his *Ethics*. To live the good life, he said, a person must do so as a member of a political community. Only the polis would provide people with an opportunity to lead a rational and moral existence, that is, to fulfill their human potential. With this assertion, Aristotle demonstrated a typically Greek attitude. Also in typically Greek fashion, Aristotle held that enhancing the good of the community is nobler and more virtuous than doing good for oneself, however worthy the act.

Like Plato, Aristotle presumed that political life could be rationally understood and intelligently directed. He emphasized the importance of the rule of law. He placed his trust in law rather than in individuals, for individuals are subject to passions. Aristotle recognized that at times laws should be altered, but he recommended great caution; otherwise, people would lose respect for law and legal procedure.

Tyranny and revolution, Aristotle said, can threaten the rule of law and the well-being of the citizen. To prevent revolution, the state must maintain "the spirit of obedience to law. . . . Men should not think it slavery to live according to the rule of the constitution, for it is their salvation."[10]

Aristotle held "that the best political community is formed by citizens of the middle class [that is, those with a moderate amount of property], and that those states are likely to be well-administered in which the middle class is large and stronger if possible than the other classes [the wealthy and the poor]." Both the rich, who excel in "beauty, strength, birth, [and] wealth," and the poor, who are "very weak or very much disgraced [find it] difficult to follow rational principle. Of these two the one sort grow into violence and great criminals, the other into rogues and petty rascals." The rich are unwilling "to submit to authority . . . for when they are boys, by reason of the luxury in which they are brought up, they never learn even at school, the habit of obedience." Consequently, the wealthy "can only rule despotically." On the other hand, the poor "are too degraded to command and must be ruled like slaves."[11] Middle-class citizens are less afflicted by envy than the poor and are more likely than the rich to view their fellow citizens as equals.

Art

The classical age of Greek art spans the years from the end of the Persian Wars (479 B.C.) to the death of Alexander the Great (323 B.C.). During this period, standards were established that would dominate Western art until the emergence of modern art in the late nineteenth century.

Greek art coincided with Greek achievement in all other areas. Like Greek philosophy and politics, it too applied reason to human experience and made the transition from a mythopoeic-religious world-view to a world perceived as orderly and rational. It gradually transformed the supernatural religious themes with which it was at first preoccupied into secular human themes. Classical art was representational — that is, it strove to imitate reality, to represent the objective world realistically, as it appeared to the human eye.

Artists carefully observed nature and human beings and sought to achieve an exact knowledge of human anatomy; they tried to portray accurately the body at rest and in motion. They knew when muscles should be taut or relaxed, one hip lower than the other, the torso and neck slightly twisted — in other words, they succeeded in transforming marble or bronze into a human likeness that seemed alive. Yet although it was realistic and naturalistic, Greek art was also idealistic, aspiring to a finer, more perfect representation of what was seen and depicting the essence and form of a thing more truly than the way it actually appeared. Thus, a Greek statue resembled no specific individual but revealed a flawless human form, without wrinkles, warts, scars, or other imperfections.

In achieving an accurate representation of objects and in holding that there were rules of beauty that the mind could discover, the Greek artist employed an approach consistent with the new scientific outlook. The Greek temple, for example, is an organized unity, obeying nature's laws of equilibrium and harmony; classical sculpture captures the basic laws that govern life in motion. Such art, based on reason, draws the mind's attention to the clear outlines of the outer world; at the same time, it directs the mind's attention to the mind itself, making human beings the center of an intelligible world and the masters of their own persons.

Greek artists, just like Greek philosophers, proclaimed the importance and creative capacity of the individual. They exemplified the humanist spirit that characterized all aspects of Greek culture. Classical art placed people in their natural environment, made the human form the focal point of attention, and exalted the nobility, dignity, self-assurance, and beauty of the human being.

Poetry and Drama

Like philosophers and artists, Greek poets and dramatists gave expression to the rise of the individual and the emerging humanist values. One of the earliest and best of the Greek poets was Sappho; she lived around 600 B.C., on the island of Lesbos. Sappho established a school to teach music and singing to well-to-do girls and to prepare them for marriage. With great tenderness, Sappho wrote poems of friendship and love.

Pindar (c. 518–438 B.C.) was another Greek lyric poet. In his poem of praise for a victorious athlete, Pindar expressed the aristocratic view of excellence. Although life is essentially tragic — triumphs are short-lived, misfortunes are many, and ultimately death overtakes all — man must still demonstrate his worth by striving for excellence.

The high point of Greek poetry is drama, an art form that originated in Greece. In portraying the sufferings, weaknesses, and triumphs of individuals, Greek dramatists shifted attention from the gods to human beings. Greek drama evolved as a continuous striving toward humanization and individualization. Just as a Greek sculptor shaped a clear visual image of the human form, so a Greek dramatist brought the inner life of human beings, their fears and hopes, into sharp focus and tried to find the deeper meaning of human experience. Thus, both art and drama evidenced the growing self-awareness of the individual.

Drama originated in the religious festivals honoring Dionysus, the god of wine and agricultural fertility. A profound innovation in these sacred performances, which included choral songs and dances, occurred in the last part of the sixth century B.C.: Thespis, the first actor known to history, stepped out of the chorus and engaged it in dialogue. By separating himself from the choral group, Thespis demonstrated a new awareness of the individual.

With only one actor and a chorus, however, the possibilities for dramatic action and human conflicts were limited. Then Aeschylus introduced a second actor in his dramas, and Sophocles a third. Dialogue between individuals thus

Floor Mosaic Depicting Dionysus, the Patron God of the Theater.   The panther's snarl, claws, and craning neck convey a fierceness that vividly contrasts with Dionysus' serene manner. (*Archaeological Receipts Fund, Athens*)

became possible. The Greek actors wore masks, and by changing them, each actor could play several roles in the same performance. This flexibility allowed the dramatists to depict the clash and interplay of human wills and passions on a greater scale. By the middle of the fifth century B.C., tragedies were performed regularly as civic festivals.

A development parallel to Socratic dialectics — dialogue between thinking individuals — occurred in Greek drama. By setting characters in conflict against each other, dramatists showed individuals as active subjects, responsible for their behavior and decisions.

Like the natural philosophers, Greek dramatists saw an inner logic to the universe; they called this logic Fate or Destiny. Both physical and social worlds obeyed laws. People paid a price for being stubborn, narrow-minded, arrogant, or immoderate; the order in the universe required it. In being free to make decisions, the dramatists said, individuals have the potential for greatness, but in choosing wrongly, unintelligently, they bring disaster to themselves and others.

Also like philosophy, Greek tragedy entailed rational reflection. Tragic heroes were not passive victims of fate. They were thinking human beings who felt a need to comprehend their position, explain the reasons for their actions, analyze their feelings, and respond to their fate with insight.

The essence of Greek tragedy lies in the tragic heroes' struggle against cosmic forces and insurmountable obstacles, which eventually crush them. But what impressed the Greek audience (and impresses us today) was not the vulnerability or weaknesses of human beings, but their courage and determination in the face of these forces.

The three great Athenian tragedians were Aeschylus (525–456 B.C.), Sophocles (c. 496–406 B.C.), and Euripides (c. 485–406 B.C.). Aeschylus believed that the world was governed by divine justice, which could not be violated with impunity; when individuals evinced *hubris* (overweening pride or arrogance), which led them to overstep the bounds of moderation, they had to be punished. Another principal theme was that through suffering people acquired knowledge: the terrible consequences of sins against the divine order should remind all to think and act with moderation and caution.

Sophocles maintained that individuals should shape their character in the way a sculptor shapes a form: according to laws of proportion. In his view, when the principles of harmony were violated by immoderate behavior, a person's character would be thrown off balance and misfortune would strike.

The rationalist spirit of Greek philosophy permeated the tragedies of Euripides. Like the Sophists, Euripides subjected the problems of human life to critical analysis and challenged human conventions. His plays carefully scrutinized the role of the gods, women's conflicts, the horrors of war, the power of passion, and the prevalence of human suffering and weakness. Euripides blended a poet's insight with the psychologist's probing to reveal the tangled world of human passions and souls in torment.

Greek dramatists also wrote comedies. Aristophanes (c. 448–c. 380 B.C.), the greatest of the Greek comic playwrights, lampooned Athenian statesmen and intellectuals and censured government policies. Behind Aristophanes' sharp wit lay a deadly seriousness; he sought an end to the ruinous Peloponnesian War and a reaffirmation of traditional values, which the Sophists had undermined.

History

The Mesopotamians and the Egyptians kept annals that purported to narrate the deeds of gods and their human agents, the priest-kings or god-kings. The Hebrews valued history, but, believing that God acted in human affairs, they did not remove historical events from the realm of religious-mythical thought.

The Greeks initiated a different approach to the study of history. For them, history was not a narrative about the deeds of gods, as it was for the Egyptians and Mesopotamians, or the record of God's wrath or benevolence, as it was for the Hebrews; instead, it dealt with the actions of human beings.

As the gods were eliminated from the nature philosophers' explanations for the origins of things in the natural world, mythical elements were also removed from the writing of history. Greek historians asked themselves questions about the deeds of people, based their answers on available evidence, and wrote in prose, the language of rational thought. They not only narrated events but also examined causes.

Herodotus

Often called the "father of history," Herodotus (c. 484–c. 424 B.C.) wrote a history of the Persian Wars. The central theme of this book, entitled *The Histories,* is the contrast between Near Eastern despotism and Greek freedom and the subsequent clash of these two world-views in the wars. Though Herodotus found much to praise in the Persian Empire, he was struck by a lack of freedom and by what he considered barbarity. He emphasized that the mentality of the free citizen was foreign to the East, where men were trained to obey the ruler's commands absolutely. Not the rule of law but the whim of despots prevailed in the East.

Another theme evident in Herodotus' work was punishment for hubris. In seeking to become king of both Asia and Europe, Xerxes had acted arrogantly; although he behaved as if he were superhuman, "he too was human, and was sure to be disappointed of his great expectations."[12] Like the Greek tragedians, Herodotus drew universal moral principles from human behavior.

In several ways, Herodotus was a historian rather than a teller of tales. First, he asked questions about the past, instead of merely repeating ancient legends; he tried to discover what had happened and the motivations behind the actions. Second, he demonstrated at times a cautious and critical attitude toward his sources of information. Third, although the gods appeared in his narrative, they played a far less important role than they did in Greek popular mythology. Nevertheless, by retaining a belief in the significance of dreams, omens, and oracles and by allowing divine intervention, Herodotus fell short of being a thoroughgoing rationalist. His writings contain the embryo of rational history. Thucydides brought it to maturity.

Thucydides

Thucydides (c. 460–c. 400 B.C.) also concentrated on a great political crisis confronting the Hellenic world: the Peloponnesian War. Living in Periclean Athens, whose lifeblood was politics, Thucydides regarded the motives of statesmen and the acts of government as the essence of history. He did not just catalogue facts, but sought those general concepts and principles that the facts illustrated. His history was the work of an intelligent mind trying to make sense of his times.

Thucydides applied to the sphere of political history a rationalist empiricism worthy of the Ionian natural philosophers. He searched for the truth underlying historical events and attempted to present it objectively. From the Sophists, Thucydides learned that the motives and reactions of human beings follow patterns. Therefore, a proper analysis of the events of the Peloponnesian War would reveal general principles that govern human behavior. He intended his history to be a source of enlightenment for future ages, a possession for all time, because the kinds of behavior that caused the conflict between Sparta and Athens would recur regularly through history.

In Thucydides' history, there was no place for myths, for legends, for the fabulous — all hindrances to historical truth. He recognized that a work of history was a creation of the rational mind and not an expression of the poetic imagination. The historian seeks to learn and to enlighten, not to entertain.

Rejecting the notion that the gods interfere in history, Thucydides looked for the social forces and human decisions behind events. Undoubtedly, he was influenced by Hippocratic doctors, who frowned on divine explanations for disease and distinguished between the symptoms of a disease and its causes. Where Herodotus occasionally lapsed into supernatural explanations, Thucydides wrote history in which the gods were absent, and he denied their intervention in human affairs. For Thucydides, history was the work of human beings. And the driving force in history was men's will to power and domination.

In addition to being a historian, Thucydides was also an astute and innovative political thinker with a specific view of government, statesmen, and international relations. He warned against the dangers of extremism unleashed by the strains of war, and he believed that when reason was forsaken, the state's plight would worsen. He had contempt for statesmen who waged war lightly, acting from impulse, reckless daring, and an insatiable appetite for territory. Although Thucydides admired Athens for its democratic institutions, rule of law, sense of civic duty, and cultural achievements, he recognized an inherent danger in democracy: the emergence of demagogues, who rise to power by stirring up the populace.

Political scientists, historians, and statesmen still turn to Thucydides for insights into the realities of power politics, the dangers of political fanaticism, the nature of imperialism, the methods of demagogues, and the effects of war on democratic politics.

The Hellenistic Age: The Second Stage of Greek Civilization

Greek civilization, or Hellenism, passed through three distinct stages: the Hellenic Age, the Hellenistic Age, and the Greco-Roman Age. The Hellenic Age began around 800 B.C. with the early city-states, reached its height in the fifth century B.C., and endured until the death of Alexander the Great in 323 B.C. At that time, the ancient world entered the Hellenistic Age, which ended in 30 B.C. when Egypt, the last major Hellenistic state, fell to Rome. The Greco-Roman Age lasted five hundred years, encompassing the period of the Roman Empire up to the collapse of the Empire's western half in the last part of the fifth century A.D.

Although the Hellenistic Age absorbed the heritage of classical (Hellenic) Greece, its style of civilization changed. During the first phase of Hellenism, the polis had been the center of political life. The polis had given Greeks an identity, and only within the polis could a Greek live a good and civilized life. With the coming of the Hellenistic Age, this situation changed. Kingdoms and empires eclipsed the city-state in power and importance. Even though cities retained a large measure of autonomy in domestic affairs, they had lost their freedom of action in foreign affairs. No longer were they the self-sufficient and independent communities of the Hellenic period. Unable to stand up to kingdoms, the city-state had become an outmoded institution. The bonds between the individual and the city loosened. People had to deal with the feelings of isolation and insecurity produced by the decline of the polis.

As a result of Alexander the Great's conquests of the lands between Greece and India, tens of thousands of Greek soldiers, merchants, and administrators settled in eastern lands. This mixing of Greek and Near Eastern peoples and cultures defines the Hellenistic Age.

In the Hellenic Age, Greek philosophers had a limited conception of humanity, dividing the world into Greek and barbarian. In the Hellenistic Age, the intermingling of Greeks and peoples of the Near East caused a shift in focus from the city to the *oikoumene* (the inhabited world); parochialism gave way to cosmopolitanism and universalism as people began to think of themselves as members of a world community. Philosophers came to regard the civilized world as one city, the city of humanity.

Alexander the Great

After the assassination of Philip of Macedon in 336 B.C., his twenty-year-old son, Alexander, succeeded to the throne. Alexander inherited a proud and fiery temperament from his mother. From his tutor Aristotle, Alexander gained an appreciation for Greek culture, particularly the Homeric epics. Undoubtedly, the young Alexander was stirred by these stories of legendary heroes, especially Achilles, and their striving for personal glory. Alexander acquired military skills and qualities of leadership from his father.

Alexander inherited from Philip an overriding policy of state: the invasion of Persia. With an army of thirty-five thousand men, Macedonians and Greeks combined, he crossed into Asia Minor in 334 B.C. and eventually advanced all the way to India. In these campaigns, Alexander proved himself to be a superb strategist and leader of men. Winning every battle, his army carved an empire that stretched from Greece to India.

The world after Alexander differed sharply from the one that existed before he took up the sword. Alexander's conquests brought West and East closer together, marking a new epoch. Alexander himself helped to implement this transformation. He took a Persian bride, arranged for eighty of his officers and ten thousand of his soldiers to marry Near Eastern women, and planned to incorporate thirty thousand Persian youths into his army. Alexander founded Greek-style cities in Asia, where Greek settlers mixed with the native population.

As Greeks acquired greater knowledge of the Near East, the parochialism of the polis gave way to a world outlook. As trade and travel between West and East expanded, as Greek merchants and soldiers settled in Asiatic lands, and as Greek culture spread to non-Greeks, the distinctions between barbarian and Greek lessened. Although Alexander never united all the peoples in a world-state, his career pushed the world in a new direction, toward a fusion of disparate peoples and the intermingling of cultural traditions.

The Competing Dynasties

In 323 B.C., Alexander, not yet thirty-three years old, died after a sickness that followed a drinking party. After his premature death, his generals engaged in a long and bitter struggle to see who would succeed the conqueror. Since none of the generals or their heirs had enough power to hold together Alexander's vast empire, the wars of succession ended in a stalemate. By 275 B.C., the empire was fractured into three dynasties: the Ptolemies in Egypt, the Seleucids in Asia, and the Antigonids in Macedonia. Macedonia, Alexander's native country, continued to dominate the Greek cities, which periodically tried to break its hold. Later, the kingdom of Pergamum in Western Asia Minor emerged as the fourth Hellenistic monarchy.

In the third century B.C., Ptolemaic Egypt was the foremost power in the Hellenistic world. The Seleucid Empire, which stretched from the Mediterranean to the frontiers of India and encompassed many different peoples, attempted to extend its power in the west but was resisted by the Ptolemies. Finally, the Seleucid ruler Antiochus III (223–187 B.C.) defeated the Ptolemaic forces and established Seleucid control over Phoenicia and Palestine. Taking advantage of Egypt's defeat, Macedonia seized several of Egypt's territories.

Rome, a new power, became increasingly drawn into the affairs of the quarrelsome Hellenistic kingdoms. By the middle of the second century B.C., it had imposed its will upon them. From that time on, the political fortunes of the Western and Eastern Mediterranean were inextricably linked.

Cosmopolitanism

Hellenistic society was characterized by a mingling of peoples and an interchange of cultures. Greek traditions spread to the Near East, and Mesopotamian, Egyptian, Hebrew, and Persian traditions — particularly religious beliefs — moved westward. A growing cosmopolitanism replaced the parochialism of the city-state. Although the rulers of the Hellenistic kingdoms

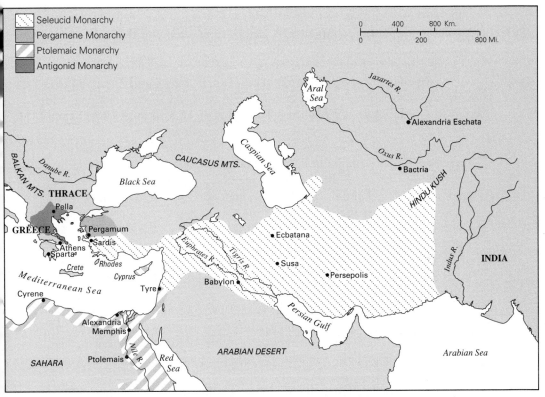

Map 3.2   The Division of Alexander's Empire and the Spread of Hellenism

were Macedonians and their high officials and generals were Greeks, the style of government was modeled after that of the ancient oriental kingdoms. In the Hellenic Age, the law had expressed the will of the community, but in this new age of monarchy, the kings were the law. The Macedonian rulers encouraged the oriental practice of worshiping the king as a god or as a representative of the gods. In Egypt, for example, the priests conferred on the Macedonian king the same divine powers and titles traditionally held by Egyptian pharaohs; in accordance with ancient tradition, statues of the divine king were installed in Egyptian temples.

Following Alexander's lead, the Seleucids founded cities in the east patterned after the city-states of Greece. The cities, which were often founded to protect trade routes and as fortresses against hostile tribes, adopted the political institutions of Hellenic Greece, including a popular assembly and a council. Hellenistic kings generally did not intervene in the cities' local affairs. Thousands of Greeks settled in these cities, which were Greek in architecture and contained Greek schools, temples, theaters (where performances of classical plays were staged), and gymnasia. Gymnasia were essentially places to exercise, train in sports, and converse, but some had libraries and halls where public lectures and competitions of orators and poets were held. Hellenistic kings brought books, paintings, and statues from Greece to their cities. Hellenistic cities, inhabited by tens of thousands of people from many lands and dominated by a Hellenized upper class, served as centers and agents of Hellenism, which non-Greeks adopted. The cities in Egypt and Syria saw the emergence of a native elite who spoke Greek, wore Greek-style clothing, and adopted Greek customs. *Koine* (or shared language), a form of Greek, came to be spoken throughout much of the Mediterranean world.

The greatest city of the time and the one most representative of the Hellenistic Age was Alexandria in Egypt, founded by Alexander the Great. Strategically located at one of the mouths of the Nile, Alexandria became a center of commerce and culture. The most populous city of the Mediterranean world, Alexandria at the beginning of the Christian era contained perhaps a million people: Egyptians, Persians, Macedonians, Greeks, Jews, Syrians, and Arabs. The city was an unrivaled commercial center; goods from the Mediterranean world, East Africa, Arabia, and India circulated in its marketplaces. This cosmopolitan center also attracted poets, philosophers, physicians, astronomers, and mathematicians.

All phases of cultural life were permeated by cultural exchange. Sculpture showed the influence of many lands. Historians wrote world histories, not just local ones. Greek astronomers worked with data collected over the centuries by the Babylonians. The Hebrew Scriptures were translated into Greek for use by Greek-speaking Jews, and some Jewish thinkers, admiring Greek learning, expressed Jewish religious ideas in philosophical terms: God was identified with reason and Moses' Law with the rational order of the universe. Greeks increasingly demonstrated a fascination with oriental religious cults. Philosophers helped to break down the barriers between peoples by asserting that all inhabit a single fatherland.

The spread of Greek civilization from the Aegean to the Indus River gave the Hellenistic world a cultural common denominator, but Hellenization did not transform the East and make it one with the West. Hellenization was limited almost entirely to the cities, and in many urban centers it was often only a thin veneer. Many Egyptians in Alexandria learned Greek, and some assumed Greek names, but for most, Hellenization did not go much deeper. In the countryside, there was not even the veneer of Greek culture. Retaining traditional attitudes, the countryside in the East resisted Greek ways. In the villages, local and traditional law, local languages, and family customs remained unchanged; religion, the most important ingredient of the civilizations of the Near East, also kept its traditional character.

Hellenistic Thought and Culture

Hellenistic culture rested on a Hellenic foundation, but it also revealed new trends: a heightened universalism and a growing individualism.

History

The leading historian of the Hellenistic Age was Polybius (c. 200–118 B.C.), whose history of the rise of Rome is one of the great works of historical literature. Reflecting the universal tendencies of the Hellenistic Age, Polybius endeavored to explain how Rome had progressed from a city-state to a world conqueror. As a disciple of Thucydides, Polybius sought rational explanations for human events. Like Thucydides, he relied on eyewitness accounts (including his own personal experiences), checked sources, and strove for objectivity.

Art

Hellenistic art, like Hellenistic philosophy, expressed a heightened awareness of the individual. Whereas Hellenic sculpture aimed to depict ideal beauty — the perfect body and face — Hellenistic sculpture, moving from idealism to realism, captured individual character and expression, often of ordinary people. Scenes of daily life were realistically depicted.

Science

During the Hellenistic Age, Greek scientific achievement reached its height. When Alexander invaded Asia Minor, the former student of Aristotle brought along surveyors, engineers, scientists, and historians, who continued with him into Asia. The vast amount of data on botany, zoology, geography, and astronomy collected by Alexander's staff stimulated an outburst of activity. Hellenistic science, says historian Benjamin Farrington, stood "on the threshold of the modern world. When modern science began in the sixteenth century, it took up where the Greeks left off."[13]

Because of its state-supported museum, Alexandria attracted leading scholars and superseded Athens in scientific investigation. The museum contained a library of more than half a million volumes, as well as botanical gardens and an observatory. It was really a research institute, in which some of the best minds of the day studied and worked.

Alexandrian doctors advanced medical skills. They improved surgical instruments and techniques and, by dissecting bodies, added to anatomical knowledge. Through their research, they discovered organs of the body not known until then, made the distinction between arteries and veins, divided nerves into those constituting the motor and the sensory systems, and identified the brain as the source of intelligence. Their investigations brought knowledge of anatomy and physiology to a level that was not significantly improved until the sixteenth century A.D.

Knowledge in the fields of astronomy and mathematics also increased. Eighteen centuries before Copernicus, the Alexandrian astronomer Aristarchus (310–230 B.C.) said that the sun was the center of the universe, that the planets revolved around it, and that the stars were situated at great distances from the earth. But these revolutionary ideas were not accepted, and

Nike, the Goddess of Victory, on a Gold Earring, Hellenistic Period.   The calm, timeless, idealized forms of classical period sculpture gave way to a new style — the Hellenistic, marked by more dynamic, emotion-laden realism. This new aesthetic form reflected the cosmopolitan character of the Greek culture that emerged from Alexander's conquests. (*H. L. Pierce Fund. Courtesy Museum of Fine Arts, Boston*)

the belief in an earth-centered universe persisted. In geometry, Euclid, an Alexandrian mathematician who lived around 300 B.C., creatively synthesized earlier developments. Euclid's hundreds of geometric proofs, derived from reasoning alone, are a profound witness to the power of the rational mind.

Eratosthenes (c. 275–194 B.C.), an Alexandrian geographer, sought a scientific understanding of the enlarged world. He divided the planet into climatic zones, declared that the oceans are joined, and, with extraordinary ingenuity and accuracy, measured the earth's circumference. Archimedes of Syracuse (287–212 B.C.), who studied at Alexandria, was a mathematician, a physicist, and an ingenious inventor. His mechanical inventions, including war engines, dazzled his contemporaries. However, in typically Greek fashion, Archimedes dismissed his practical inventions, preferring to be remembered as a theoretician.

Philosophy

Hellenistic thinkers preserved the rational tradition of Greek philosophy, but they also transformed it, for they had to adapt their thought to the requirements of a cosmopolitan society. In the Hellenic Age, the starting point of philosophy was the citizen's relationship to the city; in the Hellenistic Age, the point of departure was the solitary individual's relationship to humanity, the individual's destiny in a complex world. Philosophy tried to deal with the feeling of alienation resulting from the weakening of the individual's attachment to the polis and sought a conception of community that corresponded to the social realities of a world grown larger. It aspired to make people ethically independent so that they could achieve happiness in a hostile and competitive world. In striving for tranquillity of mind and relief from conflict, Hellenistic thinkers reflected the general anxiety that pervaded their society.

Epicureanism   Two principal schools of philosophy arose in the Hellenistic world: Epicureanism and Stoicism. In the tradition of Plato and Aristotle, Epicurus (342–270 B.C.) founded a school in Athens at the end of the fourth century B.C. Epicurus broke with the attitude of the Hellenic Age in significant ways. Unlike classical Greek philosophers, Epicurus, reflecting the Greeks' changing relationship to the city, taught the value of passivity and withdrawal from civic life. To him, citizenship was not a prerequisite for individual happiness. Wise persons, said Epicurus, would refrain from engaging in public affairs, for politics could deprive them of their self-sufficiency, their freedom to choose and to act. Nor would wise individuals pursue wealth, power, or fame, as the pursuit would only provoke anxiety. For the same reason, wise persons would not surrender to hate or love, desires that distress the soul. They would also try to live justly, because those who behave unjustly are burdened with troubles. Nor could people find happiness if they worried about dying or pleasing the gods.

To Epicurus, dread that the gods interfered in human life and could inflict suffering after death was the principal cause of anxiety. To remove this source of human anguish, he favored a theory of nature that had no place for supernatural intervention in nature or in people's lives. Therefore, he adopted the physics of Democritus, which taught that all things consist of atoms in motion. In a universe of colliding atoms, there could be no higher intelligence ordering things; there was no room for divine activity. Epicurus taught that the gods probably did exist, but that they did not influence human affairs; consequently, individuals could order their own lives.

People could achieve happiness, said Epicurus, when their bodies were "free from pain" and their minds "released from worry and fear." Although Epicurus wanted to increase pleasure for the individual, he rejected unbridled hedonism. Because he believed that happiness must be pursued rationally, he urged avoidance of the merely sensuous pleasures that have unpleasant after-effects (such as overeating and excessive drinking). In general, Epicurus espoused the traditional Greek view of moderation and prudence. By opening his philosophy to men and women, slave and free, Greek and barbarian, and by separating ethics from politics, Epicurus fashioned a philosophy adapted to the post-Alexandrian world of kingdoms and universal culture.

Stoicism   Around the time when Epicurus founded his school, Zeno (335–263 B.C.) also opened a school in Athens. Zeno's teachings, called Stoicism (because his school was located in the *stoa*, or colonnade), became the most important philosophy in the Hellenistic world. By teaching that the world constituted a single society, Stoicism gave theoretical expression to the world-mindedness of the age. Through its concept of a world-state, the

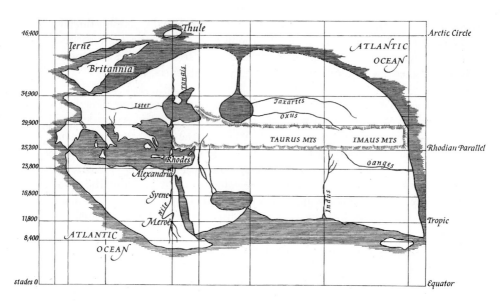

Reconstruction of the Map of the World by Eratosthenes (c. 275–194 B.C.).   Geographical knowledge expanded enormously among the Hellenistic Greeks. The first systematic scientific books on geography were credited to Eratosthenes, head of the Alexandrian Library, the greatest scientific and humanistic research center in the Hellenistic world. Eratosthenes estimated the circumference of the earth with remarkable accuracy for his time. His map illustrates the limits of the world known to the Greeks. (*From John Onians,* Art and Thought in the Hellenistic Age [*Thames and Hudson,* 1979]. *Reprinted by permission of Thames and Hudson Ltd.*)

city of humanity, Stoicism offered an answer to the problem of community and alienation posed by the decline of the city-state. By stressing inner strength in dealing with life's misfortunes, it opened an avenue to individual happiness in a world fraught with uncertainty.

At the core of Stoicism was the belief that the universe contained a principle of order, variously called the Divine Fire, God — more the fundamental force of the universe than a living person — and Divine Reason (*Logos*). This ruling principle underlay reality and permeated all things; it accounted for the orderliness of nature. The Stoics reasoned that, being part of the universe, people too shared in the Logos that operated throughout the cosmos. The Logos was implanted in every human soul; it enabled people to act intelligently and to comprehend the principles of order that governed nature. Since reason was common to all, human beings were essentially brothers and fundamentally equal. Reason gave individuals dignity and enabled them to recognize and respect the dignity of others. To the Stoics, all people — Greek and barbarian, free and slave, rich and poor — were fellow human beings, and one law, the law of nature, applied to everyone. Thus, the Stoics, like the Hebrews, arrived at the idea of the oneness of humanity.

Like Socrates, the Stoics believed that a person's distinctive quality was the ability to reason and that happiness came from the disciplining of emotions by the rational part of the soul. Also like Socrates, the Stoics maintained that individuals should progress morally, should perfect their character. In the Stoic view, wise persons ordered their lives according to the natural law, the law of reason, that underlay the cosmos. This harmony with the Logos would give them the inner strength to resist the torments inflicted by others, by fate, and by their own passionate natures. Self-mastery and inner peace, or happiness, would follow. Such individuals would remain undisturbed by life's misfortunes, for their souls would be their own. Even slaves were not denied this inner freedom; although their bodies were subjected to the power of their masters, their minds still remained independent and free.

Stoicism had an enduring influence on the Western mind. To some Roman political theorists, the Empire fulfilled the Stoic ideal of a world community, in which people of different nationalities held citizenship and were governed by a worldwide law that accorded with the law of reason, or natural law, operating throughout the universe. Stoic beliefs — that by nature we are all members of one family, that each person is significant, that distinctions of rank and race are of no account, and that human law should not conflict with natural law — were incorporated into Roman jurisprudence, Christian thought, and modern liberalism. There is continuity between the Stoic idea of natural law — a moral order that underlies nature — and the principle of inalienable rights stated in the American Declaration of Independence.

The Greek Achievement: Reason, Freedom, Humanism

Like other ancient peoples, the Greeks warred, massacred, and enslaved; they could be cruel, arrogant, contentious, and superstitious; and they often violated their own ideals. But their achievement was unquestionably of profound historical significance. Western thought essentially begins with the Greeks, who first defined the individual by the capacity to reason. It was the great achievement of the Greek spirit to rise above magic, miracles, mystery, authority, and custom and to discover the procedures and terminology that permit a rational understanding of nature and society. Every aspect of Greek civilization — science, philosophy, art, drama, literature, politics, historical writing — showed a growing reliance on human reason and a diminishing dependence on the gods and mythical thinking.

In Mesopotamia and Egypt, people had no clear conception of their individual worth and no understanding of political liberty. They were not citizens, but subjects marching to the command of a ruler whose power originated with the gods. Such royal power was not imposed on an unwilling population; it was religiously accepted and obeyed.

In contrast, the Greeks created both civic politics and political freedom. They saw the state as a community of free citizens who made laws in their own interest; the citizens had no master other than themselves. The Greeks held that men are capable of governing themselves, and they valued active citizenship. For the Greeks, the state was a civilizing agent, permitting people to live the good life. Greek political thinkers arrived at a conception of the rational, or legal, state: a state in which law was an expression of reason, not of whim or divine commands; of justice, not of might; of the general good of the community, not of self-interest.

The Greeks also gave to Western civilization a conception of inner, or ethical, freedom. People were free to choose between shame and honor, cowardice and duty, moderation and excess. The heroes of Greek tragedy suffered not because they were puppets being manipulated by higher powers, but because they possessed the freedom of decision. The idea of ethical freedom reached its highest point with Socrates, who shifted the focus of thought from cosmology to the human being and the moral life. To shape oneself according to ideals known to the mind — to develop into an autonomous and self-directed person — became for the Greeks the highest form of freedom.

During the Hellenistic Age, the Greeks, like the Hebrews earlier, arrived at the idea of universalism, the oneness of humanity. Stoic philosophers taught that all people, because of their ability to reason, are fundamentally alike and can be governed by the same laws. This idea is at the root of the modern principle of natural, or human, rights, which are the birthright of each individual.

Underlying everything accomplished by the Greeks was a humanist attitude toward life. The Greeks expressed a belief in the worth, significance, and dignity of the individual. They called for the maximum cultivation of human talent, the full development of human personality, and the deliberate pursuit of excellence. In valuing the human personality, the Greek humanists did not approve of living without restraints; they aimed at creating a higher type of man. Such a man would mold himself according to worthy standards and make his life as harmonious and flawless as a work of art. This aspiration required effort, discipline, and intelligence. Fundamental to the Greek humanist outlook was the belief that human beings could master themselves. Although people could not alter the course of nature, for there was an order to the universe over which neither they nor the gods had control, the humanist believed that people could control their own lives.

By discovering theoretical reason, by defining political freedom, and by affirming the worth and potential of human personality, the Greeks broke with the past and founded the rational and humanist tradition of the West. "Had Greek civilization never existed," says the poet W. H. Auden, "we would never have become fully conscious, which is to say that we would never have become, for better or worse, fully human."[14]

Notes

1. H. D. F. Kitto, *The Greeks* (Baltimore: Penguin Books, 1957), p. 60.

2. Werner Jaeger, *Paideia: The Ideals of Greek Culture*, trans. Gilbert

Highet (New York: Oxford
University Press, 1945), 1:8.
3. Kitto, *The Greeks*, p. 78.
4. Herodotus, *The Histories*, trans.
Aubrey de Sélincourt (Baltimore:
Penguin Books, 1954), p. 493.
5. Thucydides, *The Peloponnesian
War*, trans. B. Jowett (Oxford:
Clarendon Press, 1881), bk. 2, chap.
37.
6. Quoted in George Sarton, *A History
of Science*, vol. 1 (Cambridge,
Mass.: Harvard University Press,
1952), pp. 355–356.
7. Plato, *Apology*, trans. F. J. Church,
rev. R. D. Cummings (Indianapolis:
Bobbs-Merrill, 1956), secs. 16–17.

8. Plato, *The Republic*, trans. F. M.
Cornford (New York: Oxford
University Press, 1945), p. 289.
9. Ibid., p. 293.
10. *Politics*, in *Basic Works of Aristotle*,
ed. Richard McKeon (New York:
Random House, 1941), pp. 1246,
1251.
11. Ibid., pp. 1220–21.
12. Herodotus, *The Histories*, p. 485.
13. Benjamin Farrington, *Greek Science*
(Baltimore: Penguin Books, 1961),
p. 301.
14. W. H. Auden, ed., *The Portable
Greek Reader* (New York: Viking,
1952), p. 38.

Suggested Reading

Boardman, John, et al., *The Oxford
History of the Classical World* (1986).
Essays on all facets of Greek culture.
Copleston, Frederick, *A History of
Philosophy*, vol. 1 (1962). An excellent
analysis of Greek philosophy.
Cornford, F. M., *Before and After
Socrates* (1968). The essential meaning
of Greek philosophy clearly presented.
Ferguson, John, *The Heritage of
Hellenism* (1973). A good introduction
to Hellenistic culture.
Fine, John V. A., *The Ancient Greeks*
(1983). An up-to-date, reliable analysis
of Greek history.
Finley, M. I., ed., *The Legacy of Greece*
(1981). Essays on all phases of Greek
culture.
Frost, Frank J., *Greek Society* (1987).
Social and economic life in ancient
Greece.
Grant, Michael, *A Social History of
Greece and Rome* (1992). Essays on
the rich, the poor, women, slaves, and
freedmen and freedwomen.
———, *From Alexander to Cleopatra*
(1982). A fine survey of all phases of
Hellenistic society and culture.
Guthrie, W. K. C., *The Greek
Philosophers from Thales to Aristotle*
(1960). A short, reliable survey of
Greek philosophy.

Hooper, Finley, *Greek Realities* (1978).
A literate and sensitive presentation of
Greek society and culture.
Jaeger, Werner, *Paideia: The Ideals of
Greek Culture* (1939–1944). A three-
volume work on Greek culture by a
distinguished classicist. The treatment
of Homer, the early Greek
philosophers, and the Sophists in
volume 1 is masterful.
Jones, W. T., *A History of Western
Philosophy*, vol. 1 (1962). Clearly
written; contains useful passages from
original sources.
Kitto, H. D. F., *The Greeks* (1957). A
stimulating survey of Greek life and
thought.
Levi, Peter, *The Pelican History of Greek
Literature* (1985). Sound insights into
Greek writers.
Meier, Christian, *The Greek Discovery
of Politics* (1990). Answers the
question: How was it that Greek
civilization, unlike all others
preceding it, gave birth to
democracies?
Murray, Oswyn, *Early Greece* (1980).
Good on relations with the Near East
and lifestyles of the aristocracy.
Powell, Anton, ed., *The Greek World*
(1995). Essays by authorities on all
phases of Greek life.

Stockton, David, *The Classical Athenian Democracy* (1990). The evolution and nature of Greek democracy.

Taylor, A. E., *Socrates* (1951). A discussion of the man and his thought.

Vernant, Jean-Pierre, *The Origins of Greek Thought* (1982). The movement from myth to reason.

Wallbank, F. W., *The Hellenistic World* (1982). A survey of the Hellenistic world; makes judicious use of quotations from original sources.

Webster, T. B. L., *Athenian Culture and Society* (1973). Discusses Athenian religion, crafts, art, drama, education, and so on.

Review Questions

1. Why is Homer called "the shaper of Greek civilization"?
2. How did the Greek polis break with the theocratic politics of the Near East?
3. Describe the basic features and the limitations of Athenian democracy.
4. What were the causes of the Peloponnesian War? What was the impact of this war on the Greek world?
5. Explain how Greek political life demonstrated both the best and the worst features of freedom and both the capabilities and the limitations of reason.
6. What was the achievement of the Ionian natural philosophers?
7. How did the Sophists advance the tradition of reason initiated by the natural philosophers? How did they contribute to a spiritual crisis in Athens?
8. What was Socrates' answer to the problems posed by the Sophists?
9. Describe the essential features of Plato's *Republic* and discuss the reasons that led him to write it.
10. How did Aristotle both criticize and accept Plato's theory of Ideas? What do Aristotle's political thought and ethical thought have in common?
11. Greek art was realistic, idealistic, and humanistic. Explain.
12. Why do the Greek plays have perennial appeal?
13. What were the basic differences between the Hellenic and Hellenistic ages?
14. How did Alexander the Great contribute to the shaping of the Hellenistic Age?
15. Hellenistic science stood on the threshold of the modern world. Explain.
16. What problems concerned Hellenistic philosophers?
17. What was the enduring significance of Stoicism?
18. The Greeks broke with the mythopoeic outlook of the ancient Near East and conceived a world-view that is the foundation of Western civilization. Discuss.

❖ CHAPTER 4

Rome: From City-State to World Empire

$\mathcal{R}$ ome's great achievement was to transcend the narrow political orientation of the city-state and to create a world-state that unified the different nations of the Mediterranean world. Regarding the polis as the only means to the good life, the Greeks had not desired a larger political unit and had almost totally excluded foreigners from citizenship. Although Hellenistic philosophers had conceived the possibility of a world community, Hellenistic politics could not shape one. But Rome overcame the limitations of the city-state mentality and developed an empirewide system of law and citizenship. The Hebrews were distinguished by their prophets and the Greeks by their philosophers; Rome's genius found expression in law and government.

Historians divide Roman history into two broad periods. The period of the Republic began in 509 B.C. with the overthrow of the Etruscan monarchy; that of the Empire started in 27 B.C., when Octavian (Augustus) became in effect the first Roman emperor, ending almost five hundred years of republican self-government. By conquering the Mediterranean world and extending its law and, in some instances, citizenship to different nationalities, the Roman Republic transcended the parochialism typical of the city-state. The Republic initiated the trend toward political and legal universalism, which reached fruition in the second phase of Roman history, the Empire. ❖

Evolution of the Roman Constitution

By the eighth century B.C., peasant communities existed on some of Rome's seven hills near the Tiber River in central Italy. To the north stood Etruscan cities, and to the south, Greek cities. The more advanced civilizations of both Etruscans and Greeks were gradually absorbed by the Romans.

The origin of the Etruscans remains a mystery, although some scholars believe that they came from Asia Minor and settled in northern Italy. From them, Romans acquired architectural styles and skills in road construction, sanitation, hydraulic engineering (including underground conduits), metallurgy,

Chronology 4.1 ❖ Rome

509 B.C.	Expulsion of the Etruscan monarch
287	The end of the Struggle of the Orders
264–241	First Punic War: Rome acquires provinces
218–201	Second Punic War: Hannibal is defeated
133–122	Land reforms by the Gracchi brothers; they are murdered by the Senate
88–83	Conflict between Sulla and the forces of Marius; Sulla emerges as dictator
49–44	Caesar is dictator of Rome
27 B.C.	Octavian assumes the title *Augustus* and becomes, in effect, the first Roman emperor; start of the Pax Romana
A.D. 180	Marcus Aurelius dies; end of the Pax Romana
212	Roman citizenship is granted to virtually all free inhabitants of Roman provinces
235–285	Military anarchy; Germanic incursions
285–305	Diocletian tries to deal with the crisis by creating a regimented state
378	Battle of Adrianople: Visigoths defeat the Roman legions
406	Borders collapse, Germanic tribes move into the Empire
476	End of the Roman Empire in the West

ceramics, and portrait sculpture. Etruscan words and names entered the Latin language, and Roman religion absorbed Etruscan gods.

The Etruscans had expanded their territory in Italy during the seventh and sixth centuries B.C., and they controlled the monarchy in Rome. Defeated by Celts, Greeks, and finally Romans, by the third century B.C. the Etruscans ceased to exercise any political power in Italy.

Rome became a republic at the end of the sixth century B.C. — the traditional date is 509 B.C. — when the landowning aristocrats, or patricians, overthrew the Etruscan king. As in the Greek cities, the transition from theocratic monarchy to republic offered possibilities for political and legal growth. In the opening phase of republican history, religion governed the people, dictated the law, and legitimized the rule of the patricians, who regarded themselves as the preservers of sacred traditions. Gradually, the Romans loosened the ties between religion and politics and hammered out a constitutional

Etruscan Couple. In Etruscan funerary art, the deceased were sometimes represented in full length on the lid of the coffin. Here a husband and wife are shown side by side smiling. (*Museo Nazionale di Villa Giulia/AKG, London*)

system that paralleled the Greek achievement of rationalizing and secularizing politics and law. In time, the Romans, like the Greeks, came to view law as an expression of the public will and not as the creation of god-kings, priest-kings, or a priestly caste.

The impetus for the growth of the Roman constitution came from a conflict — known as the Struggle of the Orders — between the patricians and the commoners, or plebeians. At the beginning of the fifth century B.C., the patrician-dominated government consisted of two elected executives, called consuls, the Centuriate Assembly, and the Senate. Patricians owned most of the land and controlled the army. The executive heads of government were the two annually elected consuls, who came from the nobility; they commanded the army, served as judges, and initiated legislation.

The Centuriate Assembly was a popular assembly, but because of voting procedures, it was controlled by the nobility. The Assembly elected consuls and other magistrates and made the laws, which also needed Senate approval. The Senate advised the Assembly but did not itself enact laws; it controlled public finances and foreign policy. Senators either were appointed for life terms by the consuls or were former magistrates. The Senate was the principal organ of patrician power.

The tension between patricians and commoners stemmed from plebeian grievances, which included enslavement for debt, discrimination in the courts, prevention of intermarriage with patricians, lack of political representation, and the absence of a written code of laws. Resenting their inferior status and eager for economic relief, the plebeians organized and waged a struggle for political, legal, and social equality.

The plebeians had one decisive weapon: their threat to secede from Rome, that is, not to pay taxes, work, or serve in the army. Realizing that Rome, which was constantly involved in warfare on the Italian peninsula, could not endure without plebeian help, the pragmatic patricians grudgingly made concessions. Thus, the plebeians slowly gained legal equality.

Early in the fifth century, the plebeians won the right to form their own assembly (the Plebeian Assembly, which was later enlarged and called the Tribal Assembly). This Assembly could elect tribunes, officials who were empowered to protect plebeian rights. As a result of plebeian pressure, in around 450 B.C. the first Roman code of laws was written. Called the Twelve Tables, the code gave plebeians some degree of protection against unfair and oppressive patrician officials, who could interpret customary law in an arbitrary way. Other concessions gained later by the plebeians included the right to intermarry with patricians, access to the highest political, judicial, and religious offices in the state, and the elimination of slavery as payment for debt. In 287 B.C., a date generally recognized as the termination of the plebeian-patrician struggle, laws passed by the Tribal Assembly no longer required the Senate's approval.

Although the plebeians had gained legal equality and the right to sit in the Senate and to hold high offices, Rome was still ruled by an upper class. The oligarchy that held power now consisted of patricians and influential plebeians who had joined forces with the old nobility. Marriages between patricians and politically powerful plebeians strengthened this alliance. Since generally only wealthy plebeians became tribunes, they tended to side with the old nobility rather than defend the interests of poor plebeians. By using bribes, the ruling oligarchy maintained control over the Assembly, and the Senate remained a bastion of aristocratic power. Deeming themselves Rome's finest citizens, the ruling oligarchy led Rome during its period of expansion and demonstrated a sense of responsibility and a talent for statesmanship.

During the two-hundred-year Struggle of the Orders, the Romans forged a constitutional system based on civic needs rather than on religious mystery. The essential duty of government ceased to be the regular performance of religious rituals and became the maintenance of order at home and the preservation of Roman might and dignity in international relations. Although the Romans retained the ceremonies and practices of their ancestral religion, public interest, not religious tradition or the prospect of divine punishment, determined the content of law. Public interest was also the standard by which all the important acts of the city were judged. In the opening stage of republican history, law was priestly and sacred, spoken only by priests and known only to men of religious families. Gradually, as law was written, debated, and altered, it became disentangled from religion. Another step in this process of secularization and rationalization occurred when the study and interpretation of law passed from the hands of priests to a class of professional jurists, who analyzed, classified, and systematized it and sought commonsense solutions to legal problems.

The Roman constitution was not a product of abstract thought, nor was it the gift of a great lawmaker, such as the Athenian Solon. Rather, like the unwritten English constitution, the Roman constitution evolved gradually and empirically in response to specific needs. The Romans, unlike the Greeks, were distinguished by practicality and common sense, not by a love of abstract thought. In their pragmatic and empirical fashion, they gradually developed the procedures of public politics and the legal state.

Roman Expansion to 146 B.C.

At the time of the Struggle of the Orders, Rome was also extending its power over the Italian peninsula. Without the civic harmony and stability gained by patrician concessions, it could not have achieved expansion. By 146 B.C., it had become the dominant power in the Mediterranean world.

Roman expansion occurred in three main stages: the uniting of the Italian peninsula, which gave Rome the manpower that transformed it from a city state into a great power; the collision with Carthage, from which Rome emerged as ruler of the Western Mediterranean; and the subjugation of the Hellenistic states, which brought Romans in close contact with Greek civilization. As Rome expanded territorially, its leaders enlarged their vision. Instead of restricting citizenship to people having ethnic kinship, Rome assimilated other peoples into its political community. As law had grown to cope with the earlier grievances of the plebeians, so too it adjusted to the new situations resulting from the creation of a multinational empire. The city of Rome was evolving into the city of humanity — the cosmopolis envisioned by the Stoics.

The Uniting of Italy

During the first stage of expansion, Rome extended its hegemony over Italy, subduing in the process neighboring Latin kinsmen, semicivilized Italian tribes, the once-dominant Etruscans, and Greek city-states in southern Italy. Rome's conquest of Italy stemmed in part from superior military organization and discipline. Copying the Greeks, the Romans organized their soldiers into battle formations; in contrast, their opponents often fought as disorganized hordes, which were prone to panic and flight. Romans also willingly made sacrifices so that Rome might endure. In conquering Italy, they were united by a moral and religious devotion to their city strong enough to overcome social conflict, factional disputes, and personal ambition. Also fueling Roman expansion was an aristocratic ethos that placed the highest value on glory. Demonstrating prowess in war, aristocrats believed, was the finest way to win the esteem of fellow Romans, bring honor to their family, and enhance their political career.

Despite its army's strength, Rome could not have mastered Italy without the cooperation of other Italian peoples. Like other ancient peoples, Rome plundered, enslaved, and brutalized, at times with great ferocity. But it also endeavored, through generous treatment, to gain the loyalty of conquered people. Some defeated communities retained a measure of self-government but turned the conduct of foreign affairs over to Rome and contributed contingents to the army when Rome went to war. Other conquered people received partial or full citizenship. In extending its dominion over Italy, Rome displayed a remarkable talent for converting former enemies into allies and eventually into Roman citizens. No Greek city had ever envisaged integrating nonnatives into its political community.

The Conquest of the Mediterranean World

When Rome finished unifying Italy, there were five great powers in the Mediterranean area: the Seleucid monarchy in the Near East, the Ptolemaic monarchy in Egypt, the kingdom of Macedonia, Carthage in the Western Mediterranean, and the Roman-dominated Italian Confederation. One hundred twenty years later — in 146 B.C. — Rome had subjected these states to its dominion.

Roman expansion beyond Italy did not proceed according to a set plan. Indeed, some Roman leaders considered involvement in foreign adventures a threat to both Rome's security and its traditional way of life. However, as its interests grew, Rome was drawn into conflicts and, without planning it, acquired an overseas empire.

Shortly after asserting supremacy in Italy, Rome engaged Carthage, the other great power in the Western Mediterranean, in a prolonged conflict, the First Punic War (264–241 B.C.). Founded about 800 B.C. by Phoenicians, the North African city of Carthage had become a prosperous commercial center. The Carthaginians had acquired an empire comprising North Africa and coastal regions of southern Spain, Sardinia, Corsica, and Western Sicily.

War between the two great powers began because Rome feared Carthage's designs on the northern Sicilian city of Messana. Rome was apprehensive about the southern Italian city-states that were its allies, fearing that Carthage would use Messana either to attack them or to interfere with their trade. Rome decided that the security of its allies required intervention in Sicily. Although Rome suffered severe losses — including the annihilation of an army that had invaded North Africa and the destruction of hundreds of ships in battle and storms — the Romans never considered anything but a victor's peace. Drawing manpower from loyal allies throughout Italy, Rome finally prevailed over Carthage, which had to surrender Sicily to Rome. Three years later, Rome seized the islands of Corsica and Sardinia from a weakened Carthage. With the acquisition of these territories beyond Italy, which were made into provinces, Rome had the beginnings of an empire.

Carthaginian expansion in Spain precipitated the Second Punic War (218–201 B.C.). Coming from Spain, the Carthaginian army was commanded by Hannibal (247–183 B.C.), whose military genius astounded the ancients. Hannibal led a seasoned army, complete with war elephants for charging enemy lines, across mountain passes so steep and icy that men and animals sometimes lost their footing and fell to their deaths. Some twenty-six thousand men survived the crossing into Italy; fifteen thousand more were recruited from Gallic tribesmen of the Po Valley. At the battle of Cannae (216 B.C.), Hannibal's army completely destroyed a Roman army of sixty thousand soldiers — the largest single force Rome had ever put into the field.

These were the Republic's worst days. Nevertheless, says the Roman historian Livy, the Romans did not breathe a word of peace. Hannibal could not follow up his victory at Cannae with a finishing blow, for Rome wisely would

Cast Made from Trajan's Column.   Emperor Trajan (98–117 A.D.) constructed a column to commemorate his campaigns. One of the reliefs depicts a Roman fleet landing at the port of Acona. During the First Punic War, Rome had become a naval power able to counter Carthage's fleet. (*Alinari/Art Resource, NY*)

not allow its army to be lured into another major engagement. Nor did Hannibal possess the manpower to capture the city itself. Rome invaded North Africa, threatening Carthage and forcing Hannibal to withdraw his troops from Italy in order to defend his homeland. Hannibal, who had won every battle in Italy, was defeated by Scipio Africanus at the battle of Zama in North Africa in 202 B.C., forcing Carthage to sue for peace. Carthage was compelled to surrender Spain and to give up its elephants and its navy.

The Second Punic War left Rome as the sole great power in the Western Mediterranean; it also hastened Rome's entry into the politics of the Hellenistic world. In the year after Cannae, during Rome's darkest ordeal, Philip V of Macedonia entered into an alliance with Hannibal. Fearing that the Macedonian ruler might invade Italy, Rome initiated the First Macedonian War and won it in 205 B.C. To end Macedonian influence in Greece, which Rome increasingly viewed as a Roman protectorate, the Romans fought two other wars with Macedonia. Finally, in 148 B.C., Rome created the province of Macedonia.

Intervention in Greece led to Roman involvement in the Hellenistic kingdoms of the Near East and Asia Minor: Seleucia, Egypt, and Pergamum. The Hellenistic states became client kingdoms of Rome and consequently lost their freedom of action in foreign affairs.

In 146 B.C., the same year that Rome's hegemony over the Hellenistic world was assured, Rome concluded an unnecessary Third Punic War with Carthage. Rome had launched this war of annihilation against Carthage in 149 B.C. even though Carthage was by then a second-rate power and no longer a threat to Rome's security. The Romans were driven by old hatreds and the traumatic memory of Hannibal's near-conquest. Rome sold Carthaginian survivors into slavery, obliterated the city, and turned the territory into the Roman province of Africa. Rome's savage and irrational behavior toward a helpless Carthage was an early sign of the deterioration of senatorial leadership; there would be others.

Rome had not yet reached the limits of its expansion, but there was no doubt that by 146 B.C. the Mediterranean world had been subjected to its will. No power could stand up to Rome.

The Consequences of Expansion

Expansion had important consequences for Rome and the Mediterranean world. Thousands of Greeks, many of them educated persons who had been enslaved as a result of Rome's eastern conquests, came to Rome. This influx accelerated the process of Hellenization that had begun earlier through Rome's contact with the Greek cities of southern Italy.

A crucial consequence of expansion was Roman contact with the legal experience of other peoples, including the Greeks. Demonstrating the Roman virtues of pragmatism and common sense, Roman jurists selectively incorporated into Roman law elements of the legal codes and traditions of these nations. Thus, Roman jurists gradually and empirically fashioned the *jus gentium*, the law of nations, or peoples, which eventually was applied throughout the Empire.

Roman conquerors transported to Italy hundreds of thousands of war captives, including Greeks, from all over the Empire. It is estimated that between 80 and 8 B.C., more than two million enslaved aliens were transported to

Map 4.1   The Growth of Rome: From Republic to Empire   ▶

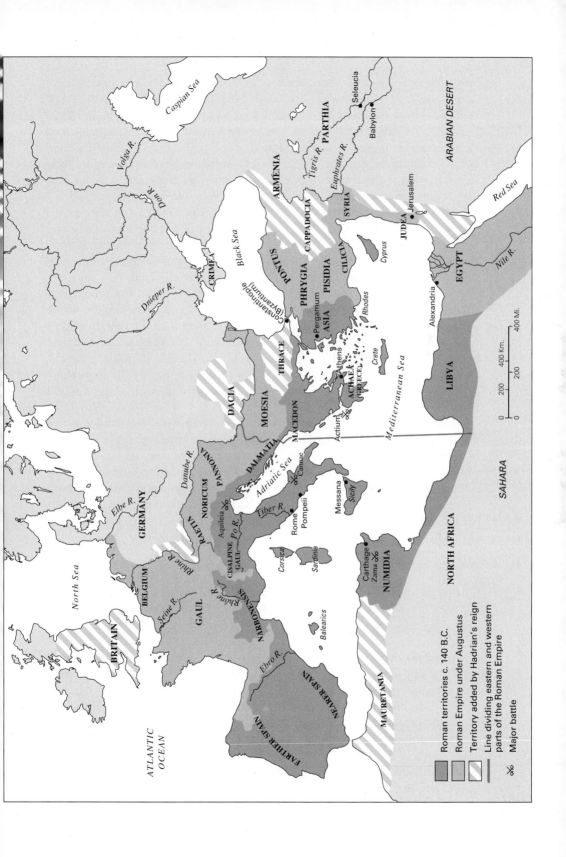

Roman territories c. 140 B.C.

Roman Empire under Augustus

Territory added by Hadrian's reign

Line dividing eastern and western parts of the Roman Empire

Major battle

Italy. By the middle of that century, slaves constituted about one-third of Italy's population, compared with about 10 percent before the Second Punic War. The more fortunate slaves worked as craftsmen and servants; the luckless and more numerous toiled on the growing number of plantations or died early laboring in mines under inhuman conditions. Roman masters often treated their slaves brutally. Although slave uprisings were not common, their ferocity terrified the Romans. In 135 B.C., slaves in Sicily revolted and captured some key towns, defeating Roman forces before being subdued. In 73 B.C., gladiators, led by Spartacus, broke out of their barracks and were joined by tens of thousands of runaways. Spartacus aimed to escape into Gaul and Thrace, the homelands of many slaves. His slave army defeated Roman armies and devastated southern Italy before the superior might of Rome prevailed. Some six thousand of the defeated slaves were crucified.

Roman governors, lesser officials, and businessmen found the provinces a source of quick wealth; they were generally unrestrained by the Senate, which was responsible for administering the overseas territories. Exploitation, corruption, looting, and extortion soon ran rampant. "No administration in history has ever devoted itself so whole-heartedly to fleecing its subjects for the private benefit of its ruling class as Rome of the last age of the Republic," concludes E. Badian.[1] The Roman nobility proved unfit to manage a world empire.

Despite numerous examples of misrule in the provinces, Roman administration had many positive features. Rome generally allowed its subjects a large measure of self-government and did not interfere with religion and local customs. Usually, the Roman taxes worked out to be no higher, and in some instances were lower, than those under previous regimes. Most important, Rome reduced the endemic warfare that had plagued these regions.

Culture in the Republic

One of the chief consequences of expansion was greater contact with Greek culture. During the third century B.C., Greek civilization started to exercise an increasing and fruitful influence on the Roman mind. Greek teachers, both slave and free, came to Rome and introduced Romans to Hellenic cultural achievements. As they conquered the Eastern Mediterranean, Roman generals began to ship libraries and works of art from Greek cities to Rome. Roman sculpture and painting imitated Greek prototypes. In time, Romans acquired from Greece knowledge of scientific thought, philosophy, medicine, and geography. Roman writers and orators used Greek history, poetry, and oratory as models. Adopting the humanist outlook of the Greeks, the Romans came to value human intelligence and eloquent and graceful prose and poetry. Wealthy Romans retained Greek tutors, poets, and philosophers in their households and sent their sons to Athens to study. Thus, Rome creatively assimilated the Greek achievement and transmitted it to others, thereby extending the orbit of Hellenism. To be sure, some conservative Romans were hostile to the Greek influence, which they felt threatened traditional Roman values. Cato the Censor (234–149 B.C.) denounced Socrates for undermining respect for Athenian law and warned that Greek philosophy might lure Roman youth into similar subversive behavior.

Plautus (c. 254–184 B.C.), Rome's greatest playwright, adopted features of fourth- and third-century Greek comedy. His plays had Greek characters and took place in Greek settings; the actors wore the Greek style of dress. But the plays also contained familiar elements that appealed to Roman audiences: scenes of gluttony, drunkenness, womanizing, and the pains of love.

Another playwright, Terence (c. 185–159 B.C.), was originally from North Africa and had been brought to Rome as a slave. His owner, a Roman senator, provided the talented youth with an education and freed him. Terence's humor, restrained and refined, lacked the boisterousness of Plautus that Romans liked, but his style was technically superior.

Catullus (c. 84–c. 54 B.C.), a native of northern Italy, is generally regarded as one of the world's great lyric poets. His father provided him with a gentleman's education. Tormented by an ill-fated love, Catullus wrote memorable poems dealing with passion and its anguish.

The leading Roman Epicurean philosopher, Lucretius (c. 96–c. 55 B.C.), was influenced by the conflict fostered by two generals, Marius and Sulla, which is discussed later in this chapter. Distraught by the seemingly endless strife, Lucretius yearned for philosophical tranquillity. In his work *On the Nature of Things*, Lucretius expressed his appreciation of Epicurus. Like his mentor, Lucretius denounced superstition and religion for fostering psychological distress and advanced a materialistic conception of nature, one that left no room for the activity of gods — mechanical laws, not the gods, governed all physical happenings. To dispel the fear of punishment after death, Lucretius marshaled arguments to prove that the soul perishes with the body. He proposed that the simple life, devoid of political involvement and excessive passion, was the highest good and the path that would lead from emotional turmoil to peace of mind.

Cicero (106–43 B.C.), a leading Roman statesman, was also a distinguished orator, an unsurpassed Latin stylist, and a student of Greek philosophy. His letters, more than eight hundred of which have survived, provide modern historians with valuable insights into the politics of the late Republic. His Senate speeches have served as models of refined rhetoric for all students of Latin. Dedicated to republicanism, Cicero sought to prevent one-man rule. He admired the Stoic goal of the self-sufficient sage who sought to accord his life with standards of virtue inherent in nature. He adopted the Stoic belief that natural law governs the universe and applies to all, that all belong to a common humanity, and that reason is the individual's noblest faculty. Stoicism was the most influential philosophy in Rome. Its stress on virtuous conduct and performance of duty coincided with Roman ideals, and its doctrine of a natural law that applies to all nations harmonized with the requirements of a world empire.

The Collapse of the Republic

In 146 B.C., Roman might spanned the Mediterranean world. After that year, the principal concerns of the Republic were no longer foreign invasions but adjusting city-state institutions to the demands of empire and overcoming critical social and political problems at home. The Republic proved unequal to either challenge. Instead of developing a professional civil service to administer the conquered lands, Roman leaders attempted to govern an empire with city-state institutions, which had evolved for a different purpose. The established Roman administration proved unable to govern the Mediterranean world. In addition, Rome's ruling elite showed little concern for the welfare of its subjects. Provincial rule worsened as governors, tax collectors, and soldiers shamelessly exploited the provincials.

During Rome's march to empire, all its classes had demonstrated a magnificent civic spirit in fighting foreign wars. With Carthage and Macedonia no longer threatening Rome, this cooperation deteriorated. Internal dissension tore Rome apart as the ferocious drive for domination formerly directed against foreign enemies turned inward, against fellow Romans. Civil war replaced foreign war.

Neither the Senate nor its opponents could rejuvenate the Republic. Eventually it collapsed, a victim of class tensions, poor leadership, power-hungry demagogues, and civil war. Underlying all these conditions was the breakdown of social harmony and the deterioration of civic patriotism. The Republic had conquered an empire, only to see the spiritual qualities of its citizens decay. In a high moral tone, the historian Sallust (c. 86–34 B.C.) condemned the breakdown of republican values:

> Growing love of money, and the lust for power which followed it, engendered every kind of evil. Avarice destroyed honor, integrity, and every other virtue, and instead taught men to be proud and cruel, to neglect religion, and to hold nothing too sacred to sell. Ambition tempted many to be false. . . . At first these vices grew slowly and sometimes met with punishments; later on, when the disease had spread like a plague, Rome changed: her government, once so just and admirable, became harsh and unendurable.[2]

The Gracchian Revolution

The downhill slide of the Republic began with an agricultural crisis. During the long war with Hannibal in Italy, farms were devastated, and with many Roman soldier-farmers serving in the army for long periods, fields lay neglected. Returning veterans lacked the money to restore their land. They were forced to sell their farms to wealthy landowners at low prices.

Another factor that helped to squeeze out the small farm owners was the importation of hundreds of thousands of slaves to work on large plantations, called *latifundia*. Farmers who had formerly increased meager incomes by working for wages on neighboring large estates were no longer needed. Sinking ever deeper into poverty and debt, they gave up their lands and went to Rome to seek work. The dispossessed peasantry found little to do in Rome, where there was not enough industry to provide them with employment and where much of the work was done by slaves. The once sturdy and independent Roman farmer, who had done all that his country had asked of him, was becoming part of a vast urban underclass, poor, embittered, and alienated.

In 133 B.C., Tiberius Gracchus (163–133 B.C.), who came from one of Rome's most honored families, was elected tribune. Distressed by the injustice done to the peasantry and recognizing that the Roman army depended on the loyalty of small landowners, Tiberius made himself the spokesman for land reform. He proposed a simple and moderate solution for the problem of the landless peasants: he would revive an old law barring any Roman from using more than 312 acres of the state-owned land obtained in the process of uniting Italy. For many years, the upper class had ignored this law, occupying vast tracts of public land as squatters and treating this land as their own. By enforcing the law, Tiberius hoped to free land for distribution to landless citizens.

Rome's leading families viewed Tiberius as a revolutionary who threatened their property and political authority. They also feared that he was seeking to stir up the poor in order to gain political power for himself. To preserve the status quo, with wealth and power concentrated in the hands of a few hundred families, senatorial extremists killed Tiberius and some three hundred of his followers, dumping their bodies into the Tiber.

The cause of land reform was next taken up by Gaius Gracchus (153–121 B.C.), a younger brother of Tiberius, who was elected tribune in 123 B.C. Gaius aided the poor by reintroducing his brother's plan for land distribution and by enabling them to buy grain from the state at less than half the market price. But like his brother, Gaius aroused the anger of the senatorial class. A brief civil war raged in Rome, during which Gaius Gracchus (who may have committed suicide) and three thousand of his followers perished. By killing the Gracchi, the Senate had substituted violence for reason and made murder a means of coping with troublesome opposition.

Soon the club and the dagger became common weapons in Roman politics, hurling Rome into an era of political violence that ended with the destruction of the Republic. Although the Senate considered itself the guardian of republican liberty, in reality it was expressing the determination of a few hundred families to retain their control over the state. It is a classic example of a once creative minority clinging tenaciously to power long after it had ceased to govern effectively or to inspire allegiance. In the century after the Gracchi, Roman politics was bedeviled by intrigues, rivalries, personal ambition, and political violence. The Senate behaved like a decadent oligarchy, and the Tribal Assembly, which had become the voice of the urban mob, demonstrated a weakness for demagogues, an openness to bribery, and an abundance of deceit and incompetence. The Roman Republic had passed the peak of its greatness.

Rival Generals

Marius (157–86 B.C.), who became consul in 107 B.C., adopted a military policy that eventually contributed to the wrecking of the Republic. Short of troops for a campaign in Numidia in North Africa, Marius disposed of the traditional property requirement for entrance into the army and filled his legions with volunteers from the urban poor, a dangerous precedent. These new soldiers, disillusioned with Rome, served only because Marius held out the promise of pay, loot, and land grants after discharge. They gave their loyalty not to Rome but to Marius, and they remained loyal to their commander only as long as he fulfilled his promises.

Other ambitious commanders followed the example set by Marius. They saw that a general could use his army to advance his political career — that by retaining the confidence of his soldiers, he could cow the Senate and dictate Roman policy. No longer an instrument of government, the army became a private possession of generals. Seeing its authority undermined by generals appointed by the Assembly, the Senate was forced to seek army commanders who would champion the cause of senatorial rule. In time, Rome would be engulfed in civil wars, as rival generals used their troops to further their own ambitions or strengthen their political affiliations.

Meanwhile, the Senate continued to deal ineffectively with Rome's problems. When Rome's Italian allies pressed for citizenship, the Senate refused to make concessions. The Senate's shortsightedness plunged Italy into a terrible war, known as the Social War (91–88 B.C.). As war ravaged the peninsula, the Romans reversed their policy and conferred citizenship on the Italians. The unnecessary and ruinous rebellion petered out.

A conflict between Marius and Sulla (138–78 B.C.), who had distinguished himself in the Social War, over who would command an army in the east led to a prolonged civil war. Sulla won the first round, capturing the capital. But then Marius and his troops retook Rome and, in a frenzy, lashed out at Sulla's supporters. The killing lasted for five days and nights. Marius died shortly afterward. Sulla quickly subdued Marius's supporters on his return and instituted a terror that far surpassed Marius's violence.

Sulla believed that only rule by an aristocratic oligarchy could protect Rome from future military adventurers and assure domestic peace. Consequently, he restored the Senate's right to veto acts of the Assembly, limited the power of the tribunes and the Assembly, and, to prevent any march on Rome, reduced the military authority of provincial governors. To make the Senate less oligarchic, he increased its membership to six hundred. Having put through these reforms, Sulla retired.

Julius Caesar

The Senate, however, failed to wield its restored authority effectively. The Republic was still menaced by military commanders who used their troops for their own political advantage, and underlying problems remained unsolved.

In 60 B.C., a triumvirate (a ruling group of three) consisting of Julius Caesar (c. 100–44 B.C.), a politician, Pompey, a general, and Crassus, a wealthy banker, conspired to take over Rome. The ablest of the three was Caesar.

Recognizing the importance of a military command as a prerequisite for political prominence, Caesar gained command of the legions in Gaul in 59 B.C. The following year he began the conquest of the part of Gaul outside of Roman control, bringing the future France into the orbit of Greco-Roman culture. The successful Gallic campaigns and invasion of Britain revealed Caesar's exceptional talent for generalship. Indeed, his victories alarmed the Senate, which feared that Caesar would use his devoted troops and soaring reputation to seize control of the state.

Meanwhile, the triumvirate had fallen apart. In 53 B.C., Crassus had perished with his army in a disastrous campaign against the Parthians in the East. Pompey, who was jealous of Caesar's success and eager to expand his own power, drew closer to the Senate. Supported by Pompey, the Senate ordered Caesar to relinquish his command. Caesar, realizing that without his troops he would be defenseless, decided instead to march on Rome. After he crossed the Rubicon River into Italy in 49 B.C., civil war again ravaged the Republic. Pompey proved no match for so talented a general; the Senate acknowledged Caesar's victory and appointed him to be dictator, a legal office, for ten years.

Caesar realized that republican institutions no longer operated effectively and that only strong and enlightened leadership could permanently end the civil warfare destroying Rome. He fought exploitation in the provinces and generously extended citizenship to more provincials. To aid the poor in Rome, he began a public works program, which provided employment and beautified the city. He also relocated more than a hundred thousand veterans and members of Rome's lower class to the provinces, where he gave them land.

In February 44 B.C., Rome's ruling class, jealous of Caesar's success and power and afraid of his ambition, became thoroughly alarmed when his temporary dictatorship was converted into a lifelong office. The aristocracy saw this event as the end of senatorial government and their rule, which they equated with liberty, and as the beginning of a Hellenistic type of monarchy. On March 15, a group of aristocrats, regarding themselves as defenders of republican traditions more than four and a half centuries old, assassinated Caesar.

The Republic's Last Years

The assassination of Julius Caesar did not restore republican liberty; it plunged Rome into renewed civil war. Two of Caesar's trusted lieutenants, Mark Antony and Lepidus, joined with Octavian, Caesar's adopted son, and defeated the armies of Brutus and Cassius, conspirators in the plot against Caesar. After Lepidus was forced into political obscurity, Antony and Octavian fought each other, with control of Rome as the prize. In 31 B.C., at the naval battle of Actium, in Western Greece, Octavian crushed the forces of

Antony and his wife, Egypt's Queen Cleopatra. Octavian emerged as master of Rome and four years later became, in effect, the first Roman emperor.

The Roman Republic, which had amassed power to a degree hitherto unknown in the ancient world, was wrecked not by foreign invasion but by internal weaknesses: the degeneration of senatorial leadership and the willingness of politicians to use violence; the formation of private armies, in which soldiers gave their loyalty to their commander rather than to Rome; the transformation of a self-reliant peasantry into an impoverished and demoralized city rabble; and the deterioration of the ancient virtues that had been the source of the state's vitality. Before 146 B.C., the threat posed by foreign enemies, particularly Carthage, forced Romans to work together for the benefit of the state. This social cohesion broke down when foreign danger had been reduced.

Augustus and the Foundations of the Roman Empire

After Octavian's forces defeated those of Antony and Cleopatra at the battle of Actium, no opponents could stand up to him. The century of civil war, political murder, corruption, and mismanagement had exhausted the Mediterranean world, which longed for order. Like Caesar before him, Octavian recognized that only a strong monarchy could rescue Rome from civil war and anarchy. But, learning from Caesar's assassination, he also knew that republican ideals were far from dead. To exercise autocratic power openly, like a Hellenistic monarch, would have aroused the hostility of the Roman ruling class, whose assistance and good will Octavian desired.

Octavian demonstrated his political genius by reconciling his military monarchy with republican institutions: he held absolute power without abruptly breaking with a republican past. Magistrates were still elected, and assemblies still met; the Senate administered certain provinces, retained its treasury, and was invited to advise Octavian. With some truth, Octavian could claim that he ruled in partnership with the Senate. By maintaining the facade of the Republic, Octavian camouflaged his absolute power and contained senatorial opposition, which had already been weakened by the deaths of leading nobles in battle or in the purges that Octavian had instituted against his enemies.

In 27 B.C., Octavian shrewdly offered to surrender his power, knowing that the Senate, purged of opposition, would demand that he continue to lead the state. By this act, Octavian could claim to be a legitimate constitutional ruler leading a government of law, not one of lawless despotism, which was hateful to the Roman mentality. In keeping with his policy of maintaining the appearance of traditional republican government, Octavian refused to be called king or even, like Caesar, dictator. Instead, he cleverly disguised his autocratic rule by taking the inoffensive title *princeps* (first citizen); the rule of Octavian and his successors is referred to as the *principate*. The Senate also conferred on him the semireligious and revered name of *Augustus*.

The reign of Augustus signified the end of the Roman Republic and the beginning of the Roman Empire — the termination of aristocratic politics and the emergence of one-man rule. Despite his introduction of autocratic rule, however, Augustus was by no means a self-seeking tyrant, but a creative statesman. Heir to the Roman tradition of civic duty, he regarded his power as a public trust, delegated to him by the Roman people. He was faithful to the classical ideal that the state should promote the good life by protecting civilization from barbarism and ignorance, and he sought to rescue a dying Roman world.

Augustus instituted reforms and improvements throughout the Empire. He reformed the army to guard against the reemergence of ambitious generals like those whose rivalries and private armies had wrecked the Republic. He maintained the loyalty of his soldiers by ensuring that veterans, on discharge, would receive substantial bonuses and land in Italy or in the provinces. For the city of Rome, Augustus had aqueducts and water mains built, bringing water to most Roman homes. He created a fire brigade, which reduced the danger of great conflagrations in crowded tenement districts, and he organized a police force to contain violence. He improved the distribution of free grain to the impoverished proletariat, and he financed the popular gladiatorial combats out of his own funds.

In Italy, Augustus had roads repaired, fostered public works, and arranged for Italians to play a more important role in the administration of the Empire. He earned the gratitude of the provincials by correcting tax abuses and fighting corruption and extortion, as well as by improving the quality of governors and enabling aggrieved provincials to bring charges against Roman officials. An imperial bureaucracy, which enabled talented and dedicated men to serve the state, gradually evolved.

The Pax Romana

The brilliant statesmanship of Augustus inaugurated Rome's greatest age. For the next two hundred years, the Mediterranean world enjoyed the blessings of the *Pax Romana,* the Roman peace. The ancient world had never experienced such a long period of peace, order, efficient administration, and prosperity. Although both proficient and inept rulers succeeded Augustus, the essential features of the Pax Romana persisted.

The Successors of Augustus

The first four emperors who succeeded Augustus were related either to him or to his third wife, Livia. They constituted the Julio-Claudian dynasty, which ruled from A.D. 14 to 68. Although their reigns were marked by conspiracies, summary executions, and assassinations, the great achievements of Augustus were preserved.

Onyx Cameo of Roma and Augustus, First Century A.D.   The Emperor Augustus sits with the goddess Roma and is crowned with the laurel wreath of victory. At his foot is an eagle, emblem of the god Jupiter and totem of the Roman armies. To the left is a triumphal chariot with Nike, the goddess of Victory. The other figures are believed to be members of the imperial family. (*Kunsthistorisches Museum, Vienna*)

The Julio-Claudian dynasty came to an end when the emperor Nero committed suicide in A.D. 68. Nero had grown increasingly tyrannical and had lost the confidence of the people, the senatorial class, and the generals, who rose in revolt. In the year following his death, anarchy reigned as military leaders competed for the throne. After a bloody civil war, the execution of two emperors, and the suicide of another, Vespasian gained the principate. His reign (A.D. 69–79) marked the beginning of the Flavian dynasty. By having the great Colosseum of Rome constructed for gladiatorial contests, Vespasian earned the gratitude of the city's inhabitants. He also had nationalist uprisings put down in Gaul and Judea.

In Judea, Roman rule clashed with Jewish religious-national sentiments. Recognizing the tenaciousness with which Jews clung to their faith, the Roman leaders deliberately refrained from interfering with Hebraic religious beliefs and practices. Numerous privileges, such as exemption from emperor worship because it conflicted with the requirements of strict monotheism, were extended to Jews not only in Judea, but throughout the Empire. Sometimes, however, the Romans engaged in activities that outraged the Jews. For example, the emperor Caligula (A.D. 37–41) ordered that a golden statue of himself be placed in Jerusalem's temple, the central site and focus of Jewish religious life. To the Jews, this display of a pagan idol in their midst was an abomination. The order was rescinded when the Jews demonstrated their readiness to resist.

Relations between the Jews of Judea and the Roman authorities deteriorated progressively in succeeding decades. Militant Jews, who rejected Roman rule as a threat to the purity of Jewish life, urged their people to take up arms. Feeling a religious obligation to reestablish an independent kingdom in their ancient homeland and unable to reconcile themselves to Roman rule, the Jews launched a full-scale war of liberation in A.D. 66. In A.D. 70, after a five-month siege had inflicted terrible punishment on the Jews, Roman armies captured Jerusalem and destroyed the temple.

Vespasian was succeeded by his sons Titus (A.D. 79–81) and Domitian (A.D. 81–96). The reign of Titus was made memorable by the eruption of Mount Vesuvius, which devastated the towns of Pompeii and Herculaneum. After Titus's brief time as emperor, his younger brother Domitian became ruler. Upon crushing a revolt led by the Roman commander in Upper Germany, a frightened Domitian executed many leading Romans. These actions led to his assassination in A.D. 96, ending the Flavian dynasty.

The Senate selected one of its own, Nerva, to succeed the murdered Domitian. Nerva's reign (A.D. 96–98) was brief and uneventful. But he introduced a wise practice that would endure until A.D. 180: he adopted as his son and designated as his heir a man with proven ability, Trajan, the governor of Upper Germany. This adoptive system assured a succession of competent rulers.

During his rule (A.D. 98–117), Trajan eased the burden of taxation in the provinces, provided for the needs of poor children, and had public works built. With his enlarged army, he conquered Dacia (parts of Romania and Hungary), where he seized vast quantities of gold and silver. He made the territory into a Roman province, adding to the large frontier Rome had to protect. The settlement of the region by many of Trajan's veterans led to its Romanization.

Trajan's successor, Hadrian (A.D. 117–138), strengthened border defenses in Britain and fought the second Hebrew revolt in Judea (A.D. 132–135). After initial successes, including the liberation of Jerusalem, the Jews were again defeated by superior Roman might. The majority of Palestinian Jews were killed, sold as slaves, or forced to seek refuge in other lands. The Romans renamed the province Syria Palestina; they forbade Jews to enter Jerusalem, except once a year; and they encouraged non-Jews to settle the land. Although the Jews continued to maintain a presence in Palestine, they had become a dispossessed and dispersed people.

After Hadrian came another ruler who had a long reign, Antoninus Pius (A.D. 138–161). He introduced humane and just reforms: limits on the right of masters to torture their slaves to obtain evidence and the establishment of the principle that an accused person be considered innocent until proven guilty. During his reign, the Empire remained peaceful and prosperous.

Marcus Aurelius (A.D. 161–180), the next emperor, was also a philosopher; his *Meditations* eloquently expressed Stoic thought. His reign was marked by renewed conflict in the East, with the kingdom of Parthia. The Roman legions were victorious in this campaign but brought back from the East an epidemic that decimated the population of the Empire.

From the accession of Nerva in A.D. 96 to the death of Marcus Aurelius in A.D. 180, the Roman Empire was ruled by the "Five Good Emperors." During this period, the Empire was at the height of its power and prosperity, and nearly all its peoples benefited. The four emperors preceding Marcus Aurelius had no living sons, so they resorted to the adoptive system in selecting successors, which served Rome effectively. But Marcus Aurelius chose his own son, Commodus, to succeed him. With the accession of Commodus, a misfit and a megalomaniac, in A.D. 180, the Pax Romana came to an end.

The "Time of Happiness"

The Romans called the Pax Romana the "Time of Happiness." This period was the fulfillment of Rome's mission: the creation of a world-state that provided peace, security, ordered civilization, and the rule of law. Roman legions defended the Rhine-Danube river frontiers from incursions by German tribesmen, held the Parthians at bay in the east, and subdued the few uprisings that occurred. Nerva's adoptive system of selecting emperors provided Rome with internal stability and a succession of exceptionally able emperors. These Roman emperors did not use military force needlessly but fought for sensible political goals. Generals did not wage war recklessly; instead, they tried to limit casualties, avoid risks, and deter conflicts by a show of force.

Constructive Rule   Roman rule was constructive. The Romans built roads — some fifty-three thousand miles of roads, from Scotland to the Euphrates — improved harbors, cleared forests, drained swamps, irrigated deserts, and cultivated undeveloped lands. The aqueducts they constructed brought fresh water for drinking and bathing to large numbers of people, and the effective sewage systems enhanced the quality of life. Goods were transported over roads made safe by Roman soldiers and across a Mediterranean Sea swept clear of pirates. A wide variety of goods circulated throughout the Empire. A stable currency, generally not subject to depreciation, contributed to the economic well-being of the Mediterranean world.

Scores of new cities sprang up, and old ones grew larger and wealthier. Although these municipalities had lost their power to wage war and had to bow to the will of the emperors, they retained considerable freedom of action in local matters. Imperial troops guarded against civil wars within the cities and prevented warfare between cities — two traditional weaknesses of city life in the ancient world. The municipalities served as centers of Greco-Roman civilization, which spread to the farthest reaches of the Mediterranean, continuing a process initiated during the Hellenistic Age. Citizenship, generously granted, was finally extended to virtually all free men by an edict of A.D. 212.

Improved Conditions for Slaves and Women   Conditions improved for those at the bottom of society, the slaves. At the time of Augustus, slaves may have accounted for a quarter of the population of Italy. But their numbers declined as Rome engaged in fewer wars of conquest. The freeing of slaves also became more common during the Empire. Freed slaves gained citizenship, with most of the rights and privileges of other citizens; their children suffered no legal disabilities whatsoever. During the Republic, slaves had been terribly abused; they were often mutilated, thrown to wild beasts, crucified, or burned alive. Several emperors issued decrees protecting slaves from cruel masters.

The status of women gradually improved during the Republic. In the early days of the Republic, a woman lived under the absolute authority first of her father and then of her husband. By the time of the Empire, a woman could own property and, if divorced, keep her dowry. A father could no longer force his daughter to marry against her will. Women could make business arrangements and draw up wills without the consent of their husbands. Unlike their Greek counterparts, Roman women were not secluded in their homes but could come and go as they pleased. Upper-class women of Rome also had far greater opportunities for education than those of Greece. The history of the Empire — indeed, Roman history in general — is filled with talented and influential women. Cornelia, the mother of Tiberius and Gaius Gracchus, influenced Roman politics through her sons. Livia, the dynamic wife of Augustus, was often consulted on important matters of state, and during the third century there were times when women controlled the throne.

World Community   From Britain to the Arabian Desert, from the Danube River to the sands of the Sahara, some seventy million people with differing native languages, customs, and histories were united by Roman rule into a world community. Unlike officials of the Republic, when corruption and exploitation in the provinces were notorious, officials of the Empire felt a high sense of responsibility to preserve the Roman peace, institute Roman justice, and spread Roman civilization.

In creating a stable and orderly political community with an expansive conception of citizenship, Rome resolved the problems posed by the limitations of the Greek city-state: civil war, intercity warfare, and a parochial attitude that divided people into Greek and non-Greek. Rome also brought to fruition an ideal of the Greek city-state: the protection and promotion of civilized life. By constructing a world community that broke down barriers between nations, by preserving and spreading Greco-Roman civilization, and by developing a rational system of law that applied to all humanity, Rome completed the trend toward universalism and cosmopolitanism that had emerged in the Hellenistic Age.

Roman Culture and Law During the Pax Romana

During the late Roman Republic, Rome had acquired Greek scientific thought, philosophy, medicine, and geography. Roman writers used Greek models; sharing in the humanist outlook of the Greeks, they valued human intelligence and achievement and expressed themselves in a graceful and eloquent style.

Literature and History   Roman cultural life reached its high point during the reign of Augustus, when Rome experienced the golden age of Latin literature. At the request of Augustus, who wanted a literary epic to glorify the Empire and his role in founding it, Virgil (70–19 B.C.) wrote the *Aeneid*, a

Basalt Bust of Livia.   Octavian's third wife Livia (58 B.C.–29 A.D.) was admired for her wisdom and dignity, and the emperor valued her counsel. (*Alinari/Art Resource, NY*)

masterpiece of world literature. The *Aeneid* is a literary epic of national glory. The profoundest ideas and feelings expressed in the poem are Roman virtues — patriotism, devotion to the family, duty to the state, and a strong sense of religion. Virgil ascribed to Rome a divine mission to bring peace and civilized life to the world, and he praised Augustus as a divinely appointed ruler who had fulfilled Rome's mission. The Greeks might be better sculptors, orators, and thinkers, said Virgil, but only the Romans knew how to govern an empire.

> *For other peoples will, I do not doubt,*
> *still cast their bronze to breathe with softer features,*
> *or draw out of the marble living lines, plead causes better,*
> *trace the ways of heaven with wands and tell the rising*
> *constellations; but yours will be the rulership of nations,*
> *remember, Roman, these will be your arts:*
> *to teach the ways of peace to those you conquer, to spare*
> *defeated peoples, to tame the proud.*[3]

In his *History of Rome,* Livy (59 B.C.–A.D. 17) also glorified Roman character, customs, and deeds. He praised Augustus for attempting to revive traditional Roman morality, to which Livy felt a strong attachment. Although Livy was a lesser historian than Thucydides or Polybius, his work was still a major achievement, particularly in its depiction of the Roman character, which helped make Rome great.

Roman writers who excelled in poetry include Horace (65–8 B.C.), the son of a freed slave. He broadened his education by studying literature and philosophy in Athens, and his writings reflect Greek ideals. Horace enjoyed the luxury of country estates, banquets, fine clothes, and courtesans, along with the simple pleasures of mountain streams and clear skies. His poetry touched on many themes — the joy of good wine, the value of moderation, and the beauty of friendship. Unlike Horace, Virgil, or Livy, Ovid (43 B.C.–A.D. 17) did not experience the civil wars during his adult years. Consequently, he was less inclined to praise the Augustan peace. His poetry showed a preference for romance and humor, and he is best remembered for his advice to lovers.

The writers who lived after the Augustan age were mostly of a lesser quality than their predecessors. The historian Tacitus (A.D. 55–c. 118) was an exception. Sympathetic to republican institutions, Tacitus denounced Roman emperors and the imperial system in his *Histories* and *Annals.* In *Germania,* he turned his sights on the habits of the Germanic peoples, describing the Germans as undisciplined but heroic, with a strong love of freedom. Another outstanding writer was the satirist Juvenal (A.D. c. 55–138). His works attacked evils of Roman society, such as the misconduct of emperors, the haughtiness of the wealthy, the barbaric tastes of commoners, the failures of parents, and the noise, congestion, and poverty of the capital.

Philosophy   Stoicism was the principal philosophy of the Pax Romana, and its leading exponents were Seneca (4 B.C.–A.D. 65), Epictetus (A.D. c. 60–c. 117), and Marcus Aurelius. Perpetuating the rational tradition of Greek philosophy, Rome's early Stoics saw the universe as governed by reason, and they esteemed the human intellect. Like Socrates, they sought the highest good in this world, not in an afterlife, and they envisioned no power above human reason. Moral values were obtained from reason alone. The individual was self-sufficient and depended entirely on rational faculties for knowing and doing good. Stoics valued self-sufficient persons who attained virtue and wisdom by exercising rational control over their lives. The Stoic doctrine that all people, because of their capacity to reason, belong to a common humanity coincided with the requirements of the multinational Roman Empire.

The Stoic conception of God underwent a gradual transformation, reflecting the religious yearnings of the times. For the early Stoics, God was an intellectual necessity, an impersonal principle that gave order to the universe. For later Roman Stoics, God had become a moral necessity, comforting and reassuring people. While maintaining the traditional Stoic belief that the individual can attain virtue through unaided reason, Epictetus and Marcus Aurelius came close to seeking God's help to live properly. And Seneca showed an uncommon compassion for slaves and a revulsion for gladiatorial combat. The gap between Greek philosophy and Christianity was narrowing.

Science   The two most prominent scientists during the Greco-Roman Age were Ptolemy, a mathematician, geographer, and astronomer who worked at Alexandria in the second century A.D., and Galen (A.D. c. 130–c. 201), who investigated medicine and anatomy. Ptolemy's thirteen-volume work, *Mathematical Composition* — more commonly known as the *Almagest,* a Greek-Arabic term meaning "the greatest" — summed up antiquity's knowledge of astronomy and became the authoritative text during the Middle Ages. In the Ptolemaic system, a motionless, round earth stood in the center of the universe; the moon, sun, and planets moved about the earth in circles or in combinations of circles. The Ptolemaic system was built on a faulty premise, as modern astronomy eventually showed. However, it did work — that is, it provided a model of the universe that adequately accounted for most observed phenomena. The Ptolemaic system was not challenged until the middle of the sixteenth century.

Just as Ptolemy's system dominated astronomy, so the theories of Galen dominated medicine down to modern times. By dissecting both dead and living animals, Galen attempted a rational investigation of the body's working parts. Although his work contains many errors, he made essential contributions to the knowledge of anatomy. Thanks to Arab physicians who preserved his writings during the Middle Ages, Galen's influence continued in the West into early modern times.

Art and Architecture   The Romans borrowed art forms from other peoples, particularly the Greeks, but they borrowed creatively, transforming and enhancing their inheritance. Roman portraiture continued trends initiated during the Hellenistic Age. Imitating Hellenistic models, Roman sculptors realistically carved every detail of a subject's face: unruly hair, prominent nose, lines and wrinkles, a jaw that showed weakness or strength. Sculpture also gave expression to the imperial ideal. Statues of emperors conveyed nobility and authority; reliefs commemorating victories glorified Roman might and grandeur.

The Romans most creatively transformed the Greek inheritance in architecture. The Greek temple was intended to be viewed from the outside; the focus was exclusively on the superbly balanced exterior. By using arches, vaults, and domes, the Romans built structures with large, magnificent interiors. The vast interior, massive walls, and overarching dome of the famous Pantheon, a temple built in the early second century A.D., during the reign of Hadrian, symbolize the power and majesty of the Roman world-state.

Engineering   The Romans excelled at engineering. In addition to amphitheaters and public baths, they built the finest roads in the ancient world. Roman engineers carefully selected routes, with an eye for minimizing natural barriers and drainage problems. The great embanked roads constructed during the

Empire were designed by military engineers. Stone bridges across rivers, as well as aqueducts, which carried water to Roman cities, still survive.

Law   Expressing the Roman yearning for order and justice, law was Rome's great legacy to Western civilization. Roman law passed through two essential stages: the formation of civil law (*jus civile*) and the formation of the law of nations (*jus gentium*). The basic features of the civil law evolved during the two-hundred-year Struggle of the Orders, at the same time as Rome was extending its dominion over Italy. The Twelve Tables, drawn up in the early days of the patrician-plebeian struggle, established written rules of criminal and civil law for the Roman state that applied to all citizens. Over the centuries, the civil law was expanded through statutes enacted by the assemblies and through the legal decisions of jurisdictional magistrates, the rulings of emperors, and the commentaries of professional jurists, who, aided by familiarity with Greek logic, engaged in systematic legal analysis.

During the period of the Republic's expansion outside Italy, contact with the Greeks and other peoples led to the development of the second branch of Roman law, jus gentium, which combined Roman civil law with principles selectively drawn from the legal tradition of Greeks and other peoples. Roman jurists identified the jus gentium with the natural law (*jus naturale*) of the Stoics. The jurists said that a law should accord with rational principles inherent in nature: uniform and universally valid standards that can be discerned by rational people. Serving to bind different peoples together, the law of nations harmonized with the requirements of a world empire and with Stoic ideals. As Cicero pointed out,

> *True law is right reason in agreement with nature; it is of universal application, unchanging and everlasting. And there will not be different laws at Rome and at Athens or different laws now and in the future, but one eternal and unchangeable law will be valid for all nations and all times.*[4]

The law of nations came to be applied throughout the Empire, although it never entirely supplanted local law. In the eyes of the law, a citizen — and by A.D. 212, virtually all free people had been granted citizenship — was not a Syrian or a Briton or a Spaniard, but a Roman.

After the fall of the Western Roman Empire, Roman law fell into disuse in Western Europe. Gradually reintroduced in the twelfth century, it came to form the basis of the common law in all Western lands except Britain and its dependencies. Some provisions of Roman law are readily recognizable in modern legal systems, as the following excerpts illustrate:

> *Justice is a constant, unfailing disposition to give everyone his legal due.*
>
> *No one is compelled to defend a cause against his will.*
>
> *No one suffers a penalty for what he thinks.*

Aqueduct at Pont du Gard, Nîmes, France, 19 B.C.   The discovery and use of concrete allowed the Romans to carry out a vast program of public works — roads, bridges, aqueducts, harbor facilities, and fortifications. Without such aqueducts to bring clean water from distant sources, the Roman style of urban life would have been impossible. (*Foto Marburg/Art Resource*)

> *In the case of major offenses it makes a difference whether something is committed purposefully or accidentally.*
>
> *In inflicting penalties, the age . . . of the guilty party must be taken into account.*[5]

Entertainment   Despite its many achievements, Roman civilization presents a paradox. On the one hand, Roman culture and law evidence high standards of civilization. On the other, the Romans institutionalized barbaric practices: battles to the death between armed gladiators and the tormenting and slaughtering of wild beasts. The major forms of entertainment in both the Republic and the Empire were chariot races, wild-animal shows, and gladiatorial combat. Chariot races were gala events, in which the most skillful riders and the finest and best-trained stallions raced in an atmosphere of rabid excitement. The charioteers, many of them slaves hoping that victory would bring them freedom, became popular heroes.

The Romans craved brutal spectacles. One form of entertainment pitted wild beasts against each other or against men armed with spears. Another consisted of battles, sometimes to the death, between highly trained gladiators. The gladiators, mainly slaves and condemned criminals, learned their craft at schools run by professional trainers. Some gladiators entered the arena armed with a sword; others, with a trident and a net. The spectators were transformed into a frenzied mob that lusted for blood. If they were displeased with a losing gladiator's performance, they would call for his immediate execution. Over the centuries, these spectacles grew more bizarre and brutal. Hundreds of tigers were set against elephants and bulls; wild bulls tore apart men dressed in animal skins; women battled in the arena; dwarfs fought each other. Few Romans questioned these barbarities, which had become a routine part of daily life. Occasionally, however, thoughtful Romans had strong doubts. After watching a public spectacle, the Stoic philosopher Seneca wrote in disgust: "There is nothing more harmful to one's character than attendance at some spectacle, because vices more easily creep into your soul while you are being entertained. When I return from some spectacle, I am greedier, more aggressive and . . . more cruel and inhuman."[6]

Signs of Trouble

The Pax Romana was one of the finest periods in ancient history. But even during the Time of Happiness, signs of trouble appeared, and they grew to crisis proportions in the third century. The Empire's internal stability was always precarious. Unrest in Egypt, Gaul, and Judea demonstrated that not all people at all times welcomed the grand majesty of the Roman peace, that localist and separatist tendencies persisted in a universal empire. In the centuries that followed, as Rome staggered under the weight of economic, political, and military difficulties, these native loyalties reasserted themselves. Increasingly, the masses and even the Romanized elite of the cities withdrew their support from the Roman world-state.

Social and Economic Weaknesses

A healthy world-state required empirewide trade to serve as an economic base for political unity, expanding agricultural production to feed the cities, and growing internal mass markets to stimulate industrial production. But the economy of the Empire during the Pax Romana had serious defects. The means of communication and transportation were slow, which hindered long-distance commerce. Many nobles, considering it unworthy for a gentleman to engage in business, chose to squander their wealth rather than invest it in commercial or industrial enterprises. Lacking the stimulus of capital investment, the economy could not expand.

Ultimately, only a small portion of the population — the middle and upper classes of the cities, that is, landlords, merchants, and administrators —

reaped the benefits of the Roman peace. They basked in luxury, leisure, and culture. These privileged classes bought off the urban poor with bread and circuses, but occasionally mass discontent expressed itself in mob violence. Outside the cities, the peasantry — still the great bulk of the population — was exploited to provide cheap food for the city dwellers. An enormous cultural gap existed between town and countryside.

Such a parasitical, exploitative, and elitist social system might function in periods of peace and tranquillity, but could it survive crises? Would the impoverished people of town and country — the overwhelming majority of the population — remain loyal to a state whose benefits barely extended to them and whose sophisticated culture, which they hardly comprehended, virtually excluded them?

Cultural Stagnation and Transformation

Perhaps the most dangerous sign for the future was the spiritual paralysis that crept over the ordered world of the Pax Romana. A weary and sterile Hellenism underlay the Roman peace. The ancient world was going through a transformation of values that foreshadowed the end of Greco-Roman civilization.

During the second century A.D., Greco-Roman civilization lost its creative energies, and the values of classical humanism were challenged by mythic-religious movements. No longer regarding reason as a satisfying guide to life, the educated elite subordinated the intellect to feelings and an unregulated imagination. No longer finding the affairs of this world to have purpose, people placed their hope in life after death. The Roman world was undergoing a religious revolution and was seeking a new vision of the divine.

The application of reason to nature and society was the great achievement of the Greek mind. Yet despite its many triumphs, Greek rationalism never entirely subdued the mythic-religious mentality, which draws its strength from human emotion. The masses of peasants and slaves remained attracted to religious forms. Ritual, mystery, magic, and ecstasy never lost their hold on the ancient world — nor, indeed, have they lost their hold on our own scientific and technological society. During the Hellenistic Age, the tide of rationalism gradually receded, and the nonrational, an ever-present undercurrent, showed renewed vigor. This resurgence of the mythical mentality could be seen in the popularity of the occult, magic, alchemy, and astrology. Burdened by danger and emotional stress, and fearing fate as fixed in the stars, people turned for deliverance to magicians, astrologers, and exorcists.

They also became devotees of the many Near Eastern religious cults that promised personal salvation. The proliferation of Eastern mystery religions was a clear expression of this transformation of classical values. During the Hellenistic era, slaves, merchants, and soldiers brought many religious cults westward from Persia, Babylon, Syria, Egypt, and Asia Minor. The various mystery cults possessed many common features. Converts underwent initiations and were bound by oath to secrecy. The initiates, in a state of rapture,

Stone Relief of Mithras Sacrificing a Bull.   The spread and popularity of Near Eastern mystery cults in the Western Roman Empire was a sign of the cultural intermingling that prevailed in Roman imperial society. Among the most popular mystery cults, especially among soldiers, was that of Mithras, a Persian warrior deity also associated with the sun and justice. Mithras promised immortality to those who upheld high ethical standards of conduct and underwent cultic initiation rites. (*Cincinnati Art Museum, Gift of Mr. and Mrs. Fletcher E. Nyce, 1968*)

attempted to unite with the deity after first purifying themselves through baptism (sometimes with the blood of a bull), fasting, having their heads shaved, or drinking from a sacred vessel. Communion was achieved by donning the god's robe, eating a sacred meal, or visiting the god's sanctuary. Cultists were certain that their particular savior god would protect them from misfortune and ensure their soul's immortality. More and more people felt that the good life could not be achieved by individuals through their own efforts; they needed outside help.

Like the mystery religions, philosophy reached for something beyond this world in order to edify and comfort the individual. Philosophers eventually sought escape from this world through union with a divine presence greater than human power. In Neo-Platonism, which replaced Stoicism as the dominant school of philosophy in the Late Roman Empire, religious yearnings were transformed into a religious system that transcended reason. Plotinus (A.D. c. 205–c. 270), the most influential spokesman of Neo-Platonism, subordinated philosophy to mysticism. Plato's philosophy, we have seen, contained both a major and a minor key. The major key stressed a rational interpretation of the human community and called for reforming the polis on the basis of knowledge, whereas the minor key urged the soul to rise to a higher world of reality. Although Plotinus retained elements of Platonic rationalism (he viewed the individual as a reasoning being and used rational argument to explain his religious orientation), he was intrigued by Plato's otherworldliness.

What Plotinus desired was union with the One, or the Good, sometimes called God — the source of all existence. Plotinus felt that the intellect could neither describe nor understand the One, which transcended all knowing, and that joining with the One required a mystical leap, a purification of the soul so that it could return to its true eternal home. For Plotinus, philosophy became a religious experience, a contemplation of the eternal. Compared with this union with the divine One, of what value was knowledge of the sensible world or a concern for human affairs? For Plotinus, this world was a sea of tears and troubles from which the individual yearned to escape. Reality was not in this world but beyond it, and the principal goal of life was not comprehension of the natural world or the fulfillment of human potential or the betterment of the human community, but knowledge of the One. Thus, his philosophy broke with the essential meaning of classical humanism.

By the time of the Late Roman Empire, mystery religions intoxicated the masses, and mystical philosophy beguiled the educated elite. Classical civilization was being transformed. Philosophy had become subordinate to religious belief; secular values seemed inferior to religious experience. The earthly city had raised its eyes toward heaven. The culture of the Roman world was moving in a direction in which the quest for the divine was to predominate over all human enterprises.

The Decline of Rome

In the third century A.D., the ordered civilization of the Pax Romana ended. Several elements caused this disruption. The Roman Empire was plunged into military anarchy, raided by Germanic tribes, and burdened by economic dislocations.

Third-Century Crisis

The degeneration of the army was a prime reason for the crisis. During the great peace, the army had remained an excellent fighting force, renowned for its discipline, organization, and loyalty. In the third century, however, there was a marked deterioration in the quality of Roman soldiers. Lacking loyalty to Rome and greedy for spoils, soldiers used their weapons to prey on civilians and to make and unmake emperors. Fearful of being killed by their unruly troops who wanted spoils or of being murdered by a suspicious emperor, generals were driven to seize the throne. Once in power, they had to buy the loyalty of their soldiers and guard against assassination by other generals. From A.D. 235 to 285, military mutiny and civil war raged, as legion fought legion. Many emperors were assassinated. The once stalwart army neglected its duty of defending the borders and disrupted the internal life of the Empire.

Taking advantage of the military anarchy, Germanic tribesmen crossed the Rhine-Danube frontier to loot and destroy. A reborn Persian Empire, led by the Sassanid dynasty, attacked and for a while conquered Roman lands in the east. Some sections of the Empire, notably in Gaul, attempted to break away; these moves reflected an assertion of local patriotism over Roman universalism. The "city of mankind" was crumbling.

These eruptions had severe economic repercussions. Cities were pillaged and destroyed, farmlands ruined, and trade disrupted. To obtain funds and supplies for the military, emperors confiscated goods, exacted forced labor, and debased the coinage, causing inflation. These measures brought ruin to the middle class. Invasions, civil war, rising prices, a debased coinage, declining agricultural production, disrupted transportation, and the excessive demands of the state caused economic havoc and famine in the cities. The urban centers of the ancient world, creators and disseminators of high civilization, were caught in a rhythm of breakdown.

Diocletian and Constantine: The Regimented State

The emperors Diocletian (A.D. 285–305) and Constantine (A.D. 306–337) tried to contain the awesome forces of disintegration. At a time when agricultural production was steadily declining, they had to feed the city poor and an expanded army of more than 500,000, strung out over the Empire. They also had to prevent renewed outbreaks of military anarchy, drive the Germans back across the Danube frontier, and secure the eastern region against renewed agression from Persia. Their solution was to tighten the reins of government and to squeeze more taxes and requisitions out of the citizens. In the process, they transformed Rome into a bureaucratic, regimented, and militarized state.

Cities lost their traditional right of local self-government, consolidating a trend starting earlier. To ensure continuous production of food and goods, as well as the collection of taxes, the state forced unskilled workers and artisans to hold their jobs for life and to pass them on to their children. For the same reasons, peasants were turned into virtual serfs, bound to the land that they cultivated. An army of government agents was formed to hunt down peasants who fled the land to escape crushing taxes and poverty.

Also frozen into their positions were city officials (*curiales*). They often found it necessary to furnish from their own pockets the difference between the state's tax demands and the amount that they could collect from an already overtaxed population. This system of a hereditary class of tax collectors and of crippling taxes to pay for a vastly expanded bureaucracy and military establishment enfeebled urban trade and industry. Such conditions killed the

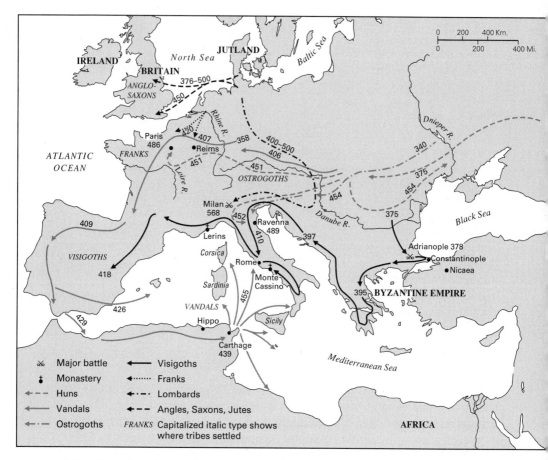

Map 4.2   Migrations and Incursions, c. A.D. 300–500

civic spirit of townspeople, who desperately sought escape. By overburdening urban dwellers with taxes and regulations, Diocletian and Constantine helped to shatter the vitality of city life, on which Roman prosperity and civilization depended.

Rome was now governed by a highly centralized monarchy that regimented the lives of its subjects. Whereas Augustus had upheld the classical ideal that the commonwealth was a means of fostering the good life for the individual, Diocletian adopted the despotic attitude that the individual lives for the state. To guard against military insurrection, he appointed a loyal general as emperor to govern the western provinces of the Empire while he ruled the eastern regions; although both emperors bore the title Augustus, Diocletian remained superior. Constantine furthered this trend of dividing the Empire into eastern and western halves by building an imperial capital, Constantinople, at the Bosporus, a strait where Asia meets Europe.

Tribal Migrations and Invasions

By imposing some order on what had been approaching chaos, Diocletian and Constantine prevented the Empire from collapsing. Rome had been given a reprieve. But in the last part of the fourth century, the problem of guarding the frontier grew more acute.

The Huns, a nomadic people from central Asia, swept across the plains of Russia and with their formidable cavalry put pressure on the Visigoths, a Germanic tribe that had migrated into southeastern Europe. Terrified of the Huns, the Goths sought refuge within the Roman Empire. Hoping to increase his manpower and unable to stop the panic-stricken Germans, the emperor Valens permitted them to cross the Danube frontier. But enraged by their mistreatment at the hands of Roman officials, the Visigoths took up arms. In 378, the Goths defeated the Romans in a historic battle at Adrianople. This battle signified that Rome could no longer defend its borders. The Visigoths were on Roman territory to stay, and they now plundered the Balkans at will. The Germanic tribes increased their pressure on the Empire's borders, which finally collapsed at the very end of 406 as Vandals, Alans, Suebi, and other tribes joined the Goths in devastating and overrunning the Empire's western provinces. In 410, the Visigoths looted Rome.

Economic conditions continued to deteriorate. Cities in Britain, Gaul, Germany, and Spain lay abandoned. Other metropolises saw their populations dwindle and production stagnate. The great network of Roman roads was not maintained, and trade in the West almost disappeared or passed into the hands of Greeks, Syrians, and Jews from the East.

In 451, Attila (c. 406–453), called "the Scourge of God," led his Huns into Gaul, where he was defeated by a coalition of Germans and the remnants of the Roman army. He died two years later, having come within a hairsbreadth of turning Europe into a province of a Mongolian empire. But Rome's misfortunes persisted. In 455, Rome was again looted, this time by the Vandals. Additional regions fell under the control of Germanic chieftains. Germanic soldiers in the pay of Rome gained control of the government and dictated the choice of emperor. In 476, German officers overthrew the Roman emperor Romulus and placed a fellow German, Odoacer, on the throne. This act is traditionally regarded as the end of the Roman Empire in the West.

Reasons for Rome's Decline

What were the underlying causes for the decline and fall of the Roman Empire in the West? Surely no other question has intrigued the historical imagination more than this one. Implicit in the answers suggested by historians and philosophers is a concern for their own civilization. Will it suffer the same fate as Rome?

To analyze so monumental a development as the fall of Rome, some preliminary observations are necessary. First, the fall of Rome was a process lasting hundreds of years; it was not a single event that occurred in A.D. 476.

Second, only the western half of the Empire fell. The eastern half — wealthier, more populous, less afflicted with civil wars, and less exposed to barbarian invasions — survived as the Byzantine Empire until the middle of the fifteenth century. Third, no single explanation suffices to account for Rome's decline; multiple forces operated concurrently to bring about the fall.

The Role of the Germanic Tribes   The pressures exerted by the Germans along an immense frontier aggravated Rome's internal problems. The barbarian attacks left border regions impoverished and depopulated. The Empire imposed high taxes and labor services on its citizens in order to strengthen the armed forces, causing the overburdened middle and lower classes to hate the imperial government that took so much from them.

Spiritual Considerations   The classical mentality, once brimming with confidence about the potentialities of the individual and the power of the intellect, suffered a failure of nerve. The urban upper class, on whom the responsibility for preserving cosmopolitan Greco-Roman culture traditionally rested, became dissolute and apathetic, no longer taking an interest in public life. The aristocrats secluded themselves behind the walls of their fortified country estates; many did not lift a finger to help the Empire. The townspeople demonstrated their disenchantment by avoiding public service and by rarely organizing resistance forces against the barbarian invaders. Hounded by the state and persecuted by the army, many farmers viewed the Germans as liberators. The great bulk of the Roman citizenry, apathetic and indifferent, simply gave up, despite the fact that they overwhelmingly outnumbered the barbarian hordes.

Political and Military Considerations   The Roman government itself contributed to this spiritual malaise through its increasingly autocratic tendencies, which culminated in the regimented rule of Diocletian and Constantine. The insatiable demands and regulations of the state in the Late Roman Empire sapped the initiative and civic spirit of its citizens. The ruined middle and lower classes withdrew their loyalty. For many, the state had become the enemy, and its administration was hated and feared more than the Germans.

In the Late Roman Empire, the quality of Roman soldiers deteriorated, and the legions failed to defend the borders, even though they outnumbered the German invaders. During the third century, the army consisted predominantly of the provincial peasantry. These nonurban, non-Italian, semicivilized soldiers, often the dregs of society, were not committed to Greco-Roman civilization. They had little comprehension of Rome's mission, and at times they used their power to attack the cities and towns. The emperors also recruited large numbers of barbarians into the army to fill its depleted ranks. Ultimately, the army consisted mostly of barbarians, as both legionnaires and officers. Although these Germans made brave soldiers, they too had little loyalty to Greco-Roman civilization and to the Roman state. Moreover, barbarian units serving with the Roman army under their own commanders did not easily submit to traditional discipline or training. This deterioration of the

Roman army occurred because many young citizens evaded conscription. No longer imbued with patriotism, they considered military service a servitude to be shunned.

Economic Considerations   Among the economic factors contributing to the decline of the Roman Empire in the West were a decrease in population, failure to achieve a breakthrough in technology, the heavy burden of taxation, and economic decentralization, which abetted political decentralization.

Largely because of war and epidemics, the population of the Empire may have shrunk from seventy million during the Pax Romana to fifty million in the Late Roman Empire. This decrease adversely affected the Empire in at least three important ways. First, at the same time as the population was declining, the costs of running the Empire were spiraling, which created a terrible burden for taxpayers. Second, fewer workers were available for agriculture, the most important industry of the Empire. Third, population decline reduced the manpower available for the army, forcing emperors to permit the establishment of Germanic colonies within the Empire's borders to serve as feeders for the army. This situation led to the barbarization of the army.

The failure to expand industry and commerce was another economic reason for the Empire's decline. Instead of expanding industry and trade, towns maintained their wealth by exploiting the countryside. The Roman cities were centers of civilized life and opulence, but they lacked industries. They spent, but they did not produce. The towns were dominated by landlords whose estates lay beyond the city and whose income derived from grain, oil, and wine. Manufacturing was rudimentary, confined essentially to textiles, pottery, furniture, and glassware. The methods of production were simple, the market limited, the cost of transportation high, and agricultural productivity low — the labor of perhaps nineteen peasants was required to support one townsman. Such a fundamentally unhealthy economy could not weather the dislocations caused by uninterrupted warfare and the demands of a mushrooming bureaucracy and the military.

With the barbarians pressing on the borders, the increased military expenditures overstrained the Empire's resources. To pay for the food, uniforms, arms, and armor of the soldiers, taxes were raised, growing too heavy for peasants and townspeople. The state also requisitioned wood and grain and demanded that citizens maintain roads and bridges. The government often resorted to force to collect taxes and exact services. Crushed by these demands, many peasants simply abandoned their farms and sought the protection of large landowners or turned to banditry.

The growth of industries on latifundia, the large, fortified estates owned by wealthy aristocrats, also played a part in economic decentralization. Producing exclusively for the local market, these estates contributed to the impoverishment of urban centers by reducing the number of customers available to buy goods made in the cities. As life grew more desperate, urban craftsmen and small farmers, made destitute by the state, sought the protection of these large landlords, whose estates grew in size and importance. The growth of latifundia was accompanied by the decline of cities and the transformation of independent peasants into virtual serfs.

These great estates were also new centers of political power that the imperial government could not curb. A new society was taking shape in the Late Roman Empire. The center of gravity had shifted from the city to the landed estate, from the imperial bureaucrats to the local aristocrats. These developments epitomized the decay of ancient civilization and presaged the Middle Ages.

The Roman Legacy

Rome left the West a rich heritage that has endured for centuries. The idea of a world empire united by a common law and effective government never died. In the centuries following the collapse of Rome, people continued to be attracted to the idea of a unified and peaceful world-state. By preserving and adding to the philosophy, literature, science, and art of ancient Greece, Rome strengthened the foundations of the Western cultural tradition. Latin, the language of Rome, lived on long after Rome perished. The Western church fathers wrote in Latin, and during the Middle Ages, Latin was the language of learning, literature, and law. From Latin came Italian, French, Spanish, Portuguese, and Romanian. Roman law, the quintessential expression of Roman genius, influenced church law and formed the basis of the legal codes of most European states. Finally, Christianity, the core religion of the West, was born within the Roman Empire and was greatly influenced by Roman culture and organization.

Notes

1. E. Badian, *Roman Imperialism in the Late Republic* (Ithaca, N.Y.: Cornell University Press, 1971), p. 87.
2. Sallust, *The Conspiracy of Catiline,* trans. S. A. Handford (Baltimore: Penguin Books, 1963), pp. 181–182.
3. From *The Aeneid of Virgil,* by Allen Mandelbaum. Translation copyright © 1971 by Allen Mandelbaum. Used by permission of Bantam Books, a division of Random House, Inc.
4. Cicero, *De Re Publica,* trans. C. W. Keyes (Cambridge, Mass.: Harvard University Press, Loeb Classical Library, 1928), p. 211.
5. Excerpted in Naphtali Lewis and Meyer Reinhold, eds., *Roman Civilization, Sourcebook II: The Empire* (New York: Harper & Row, 1966), pp. 535, 539, 540, 547, 548.
6. Seneca, *The Epistles,* Trans. Thomas Morell (London: W. Woodfall, 1786), vol. 1, epistle 7.

Suggested Reading

Balsdon, J. P. V. D., *Roman Women* (1962). Describes prominent women and treats various topics — marriage, divorce, concubinage — important to an understanding of the position of women.

Boardman, John, et al., eds., *The Oxford History of the Classical World* (1986). Essays on all facets of Roman culture.

Boren, H. C., *Roman Society* (1977). A social, economic, and cultural history of the Republic and the Empire; written with the student in mind.

Chambers, Mortimer, ed., *The Fall of Rome* (1963). A valuable collection of readings.

Christ, Karl, *The Romans* (1984). A good survey.

Crawford, M., *The Roman Republic* (1982). A reliable survey, with many quotations from original sources.

Dupont, Florence, *Daily Life in Ancient Rome* (1989). Social structure, religion, and notions of time and space.

Errington, R. M., *The Dawn of Empire: Rome's Rise to World Power* (1972). A study of Rome, the reluctant imperialist.

Ferrill, Arthur, *The Fall of the Roman Empire* (1986). A military explanation.

Grant, Michael, *History of Rome* (1978). A synthesis of Roman history by a leading classical scholar; valuable in regard to both the Republic and the Empire.

Grant, Michael. *The Fall of the Roman Empire* (1990). A clearly written synthesis.

Harris, William V., *War and Imperialism in Republican Rome 327–70 B.C.* (1992). The motives behind Roman foreign policy.

Jenkyns, Richard, ed., *The Legacy of Rome* (1992). Essay on Rome's impact on western civilization.

Lewis, Naphtali, and Meyer Reinhold, eds., *Roman Civilization* (1966). A two-volume collection of source readings.

Ogilvie, R. M., *Roman Literature and Society* (1980). An introductory survey of Latin literature.

Southern, Pat, *Augustus* (1998). A recent biography.

Veyne, Paul, ed., *A History of Private Life* (1987). All phases of Roman social life.

Wardman, Alan, *Rome's Debt to Greece* (1976). Roman attitudes toward the Greek world.

White, Lynn, ed., *The Transformation of the Roman World* (1973). A useful collection of essays on the transformation of the ancient world and the emergence of the Middle Ages.

Review Questions

1. What were the causes, results, and significance of the plebeian-patrician controversy?
2. What factors enabled Rome to conquer Italy? What were the consequences of Roman expansion?
3. How was Roman cultural life influenced by Greek civilization?
4. Analyze the reasons for the collapse of the Roman Republic.
5. The Roman world-state completed the trend toward cosmopolitanism and universalism that had emerged during the Hellenistic Age. Discuss this statement.
6. How did Roman law incorporate Stoic principles? What does modern law owe to Roman law?
7. Describe the crisis that afflicted Rome in the third century A.D.
8. How did Diocletian and Constantine try to deal with the Empire's crisis?
9. Discuss the spiritual, military, political, and economic reasons for the decline of the Roman Empire.

❖ CHAPTER 5

Early Christianity: A World Religion

*A*s confidence in human reason and hope for happiness in this world waned in the last centuries of the Roman Empire, a new outlook began to take hold. Evident in philosophy and in the popularity of Near Eastern religions, this viewpoint stressed escape from an oppressive world and communion with a higher reality. Christianity evolved and expanded within this setting of declining classicism and heightening otherworldliness. As one response to a declining Hellenism, Christianity offered a spiritually disillusioned Greco-Roman world a reason for living: the hope of personal immortality. The triumph of Christianity marked a break with classical antiquity and a new stage in the evolution of the West, for there was a fundamental difference between the classical and the Christian concepts of God, the individual, and the purpose of life. ❖

The Origins of Christianity

A Palestinian Jew named Jesus was executed by the Roman authorities during the reign of Tiberius (A.D. 14–37), who had succeeded Augustus. At the time, few people paid much attention to what proved to be one of the most pivotal events in world history. In the quest for the historical Jesus, scholars have stressed the importance of both his Jewishness and the religious ferment that prevailed in Palestine in the first century B.C. Jesus' ethical teachings are rooted in the moral outlook of Old Testament prophets. They must be viewed, says Andrew M. Greeley, a priest and student of religion, as

> *a logical extension of the Hebrew Scriptures . . . a product of the whole religious environment of which Jesus was a part. Jesus defined himself as a Jew, was highly conscious of the Jewishness of his message and would have found it impossible to conceive of himself as anything but Jewish. . . . The teachings of Jesus, then, must be placed squarely in the Jewish religious context of the time.*[1]

Judaism in the First Century B.C.

In the first century B.C., four principal social-religious parties, or sects, existed among the Palestinian Jews: Sadducees, Pharisees, Essenes, and Zealots. The religiously conservative Sadducees, composed of the upper stratum of Jewish society — influential landed gentry and hereditary priests, who controlled the temple in Jerusalem — insisted on a strict interpretation of Mosaic Law and the perpetuation of temple ceremonies. Claiming to be the descendants of Sadok, the high priest of Solomon, Sadducees believed that they were maintaining the ancient Hebrew teachings concerning the Torah, which they interpreted literally. Rejecting the concepts of the resurrection of the dead and of an afterlife, they held that God meted out rewards and punishments on earth. Challenging the Sadducees, the Pharisees adopted a more flexible attitude toward Mosaic Law; they allowed discussion and varying interpretations of the Law and granted authority to oral tradition — an "oral Torah" that was communicated from one generation to another — as well as to written Scripture. The Pharisees had the support of most of the Jewish nation. All later forms of Judaism developed from the Pharisees. The third religious party, the Essenes, founded by a man they referred to as the "Teacher of Righteousness," established a semimonastic community near the Dead Sea. In 1947, leather scrolls in hermetically sealed cylinders were found near the community of Qumran, about fourteen miles from Jerusalem, close to the Dead Sea. Dated from between c. 200 B.C. and A.D. 66–70, "The Dead Sea Scrolls" contain the oldest extant Hebrew manuscripts and also documents that are unique to the sect of the Essenes. The fourth sect, the Zealots, demanded that the Jews neither pay taxes to Rome nor acknowledge the authority of the Roman emperor. Devoted patriots, the Zealots engaged in acts of resistance to Rome, which culminated in the great revolt of A.D. 66–70 (see page 102–103).

The concept of personal immortality is barely mentioned in the Hebrew Scriptures. Unlike the Sadducees, the Pharisees believed in life after death. A later addition to Hebrew religious thought, probably acquired from Persia, the idea had gained wide acceptance by the time of Jesus. The Essenes, too, believed in the physical resurrection of the body but gave this doctrine a more compelling meaning by tying it to the immediate coming of God's kingdom.

Besides the afterlife, another widely recognized idea in the first century B.C. was the belief in the Messiah, a redeemer chosen by God to liberate Israel from foreign rule. In the days of the Messiah, it was predicted, Israel would be free, the exiles would return, and the Jews would be blessed with peace, unity, and prosperity. The Messiah, in contrast to wicked Roman rulers, would govern justly and righteously.

Jesus (c. 4 B.C.–c. A.D. 29) performed his ministry within this context of Jewish religious-national expectations and longings. The hopes of Jesus' early followers stemmed from a lower-class dissatisfaction with the aristocratic Sadducees; the Pharisee emphasis on prophetic ideals and the afterlife; the Essene preoccupation with the end-of-days and belief in the nearness of God and

Portrait of Christ.   Painted on a ceiling in the Catacomb of Domitilla around the second century A.D., this is among the oldest surviving portraits of Jesus. (*Scala/Art Resource, NY*)

the need for repentance; and a conquered people's yearning for the Messiah, who would liberate their land from Roman rule and establish God's reign.

Jesus: Moral Transformation of the Individual

Jesus himself wrote nothing, and nothing was written about him during his lifetime. In the generations following his death, both Roman and Jewish historians paid him scant attention. Consequently, virtually everything we know about Jesus comes from the Bible's New Testament, which was written decades after Jesus' death by devotees seeking to convey a religious truth and to propagate a faith. Modern historians have rigorously and critically analyzed the New Testament; their analyses have provided some insights into Jesus and his beliefs, though much about him remains obscure.

At around the age of thirty, no doubt influenced by John the Baptist, Jesus began to preach the coming of the reign of God and the need for people to repent — to undergo moral transformation so that they could enter God's kingdom. For Jesus, the coming of the kingdom was imminent; the process leading to its establishment on earth had already begun. A new order would soon emerge, in which God would govern his people righteously and mercifully. Hence, the present moment was critical — a time for spiritual preparedness and penitence — because an individual's thoughts, goals, and actions would determine whether he or she would gain entrance into the kingdom. People had to change their lives radically. They had to eliminate base, lustful, hostile, and selfish feelings; stop pursuing wealth and power; purify their hearts; and show their love for God and their fellow human beings.

Chronology 5.1 ❖ Early Christianity

A.D. 29	Crucifixion of Jesus
c. 34–64	Missionary activity of Saint Paul
c. 66–70	Gospel of Mark is written
250–260	Decade of brutal persecution of Christians by the Romans
313	Constantine grants toleration to Christianity
325	Council of Nicaea rules that God and Christ are of the same substance, coequal and coeternal
391–392	Theodosius I prohibits public acts of pagan worship and the public profession of pagan religions; during his reign, Christianity becomes the state religion
430	Death of Saint Augustine
529	Saint Benedict founds monastery at Monte Cassino

Although Jesus did not intend to draw away his fellow Jews from their ancestral religion, he was distressed by the Judaism of his day. The rabbis taught the Golden Rule, as well as God's love and mercy for his children, but it seemed to Jesus that these ethical considerations were being undermined by an exaggerated rabbinical concern with ritual, restrictions, and the fine points of the Law. Jesus believed that the center of Judaism had shifted from prophetic values to obeying the rules and prohibitions regulating the smallest details of daily life. (To Jewish leaders, of course, these detailed regulations governing eating, washing, Sabbath observance, family relations, and so forth were God's commands, intended to sanctify all human activities.) To Jesus, such a rigid view of the Law distorted the meaning of prophetic teachings. Rules dealt only with an individual's visible behavior; they did not penetrate to the person's inner being and lead to a moral transformation based on love, compassion, and selflessness. The inner person concerned Jesus, and it was an inner change that he sought. With the fervor of a prophet, he urged a moral transformation of human character through a direct encounter between the individual and God.

Jewish scribes and priests, guardians of the faith, regarded Jesus as a troublemaker who threatened ancient traditions and undermined respect for the Sabbath. Stated succinctly, Jewish leaders believed that Jesus was setting the authority of his person over Mosaic Law — an unpardonable blasphemy in their eyes. To the Romans who ruled Palestine, Jesus was a political agitator who could ignite Jewish messianic expectations into a revolt against Rome. After Jewish leaders turned Jesus over to the Roman authorities, the Roman procurator, Pontius Pilate, sentenced him to death by crucifixion, a customary punishment for someone guilty of high treason. Jesus' execution was consistent with Roman policy in Judea, for the Romans routinely arrested and executed Jews suspected of inciting unrest against Roman rule.

Believing that Jesus was an inspired prophet or even the long-awaited Messiah, some Jews had become his followers; the chief of these were the Twelve Disciples. But at the time of Jesus' death, Christianity was still just a small Hebrew sect, with dim prospects for survival. What established the Christian movement and gave it strength was the belief of Jesus' followers that he was raised from the dead on the third day after his burial. The doctrine of the Resurrection made possible the belief in Jesus as divine, a savior-god who had come to earth to show people the way to heaven.

In the years immediately following the Crucifixion, the religion of Jesus was confined almost exclusively to Jews, who could more appropriately be called Jewish-Christians. The word *Christian* derives from a name given Jesus: *Christ* (the Lord's Anointed, the Messiah). Before Christianity could realize the universal implications of Jesus' teachings and become a world religion, as distinct from a Jewish sect, it had to extricate itself from Jewish ritual, politics, and culture. This achievement was the work of a Hellenized Jew named Saul — known to the world as Saint Paul.

Saint Paul: From a Jewish Sect to a World Religion

Saint Paul (A.D. c. 5–c. 67) came from the Greek city of Tarsus, in southeastern Asia Minor. He belonged to the Diaspora, or the "Dispersion" — the millions of Jews living outside Palestine. The non-Jews, or *Gentiles* (from Latin *gens,* or "nation"), who came into contact with Jews of the Diaspora were often favorably impressed by Hebrew monotheism, ethics, and family life. Some Gentiles embraced Hebrew monotheism but refused to adhere to provisions of the Law requiring circumcision and dietary regulations. Among these Gentiles and the non-Palestinian Jews who were greatly influenced by the Greco-Roman milieu, Jesus' Apostles would find receptive listeners.

At first, Saul persecuted the followers of Jesus, but then he underwent a spiritual transformation and became a convert to Jesus. Serving as a zealous missionary of Jewish Christianity in the Diaspora, Saint Paul preached to his fellow Jews in synagogues. Recognizing that the Christian message applied to non-Jews as well, Paul urged spreading it to the Gentiles. In the process of his missionary activity — and he traveled extensively throughout the Roman Empire — Paul formulated ideas that represented a fundamental break with Judaism and became the heart of this new religion. He taught that the crucified Messiah had suffered and died for humanity's sins; that through Jesus God had revealed himself to all people, both Jews and Gentiles; and that this revelation supplanted God's earlier revelation to the Jewish people. Alone, one was helpless, possessed by sin, unable to overcome one's wicked nature. Jesus was the only hope, said Paul.

In attempting to reach the Gentiles, Saint Paul had to disentangle Christianity from a Jewish sociocultural context. Thus, he held that neither Gentile nor

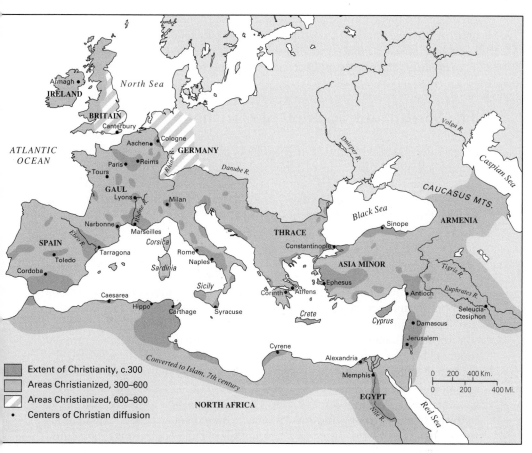

Map 5.1   The Spread of Christianity

Jewish followers of Jesus were bound by the hundreds of rituals and rules that constitute Mosaic Law. As a consequence of Jesus' coming, Paul insisted, Mosaic regulations were obsolete and hindered missionary activity among the Gentiles. To Paul, the new Christian community was the true fulfillment of Judaism. The Jews regarded their faith as a national religion, bound inseparably with the history of their people. Paul held that Jesus fulfilled not only the messianic aspirations of the Jews, but also the spiritual needs and expectations of all peoples. For Paul, the new Christian community was not a nation, but an *oikoumene*, a world community. To this extent, Christianity shared in the universalism of the Hellenistic Age.

In preaching the doctrine of the risen Savior and insisting that Mosaic Law had been superseded, Paul (whatever his intentions) was breaking with his Jewish roots and transforming a Jewish sect into a new religion. Separating Christianity from Judaism enormously increased its appeal for those non-Jews who were attracted to Hebrew ethical monotheism but repelled by circumcision, dietary rules, and other strict requirements of Mosaic Law. Paul built on the personalism and universalism implicit in the teachings of Jesus (and the Hebrew prophets) to create a religion intended not for a people with its own particular history, culture, and land, but for all humanity.

The Spread and Triumph of Christianity

By establishing Christianity's independence from Judaism, Saint Paul made the new religion fit for export to the Greco-Roman world. But its growth was slow. Originating in the first century, Christianity took firm root in the second, grew extensively in the third, and became the official religion of the Roman Empire at the end of the fourth century.

The Appeal of Christianity

The triumph of Christianity was linked to a corresponding decline in the vitality of Hellenism and a shift in cultural emphasis — a movement from reason to emotion and revelation. Offering comforting solutions to the existential problems of life and death, religion demonstrated a greater capacity than reason to stir human hearts. Hellenism had invented the tools of rational thought, but the power of mythical thought was never entirely subdued. By the Late Roman Empire, science and philosophy could not compete with mysticism and myth. Mystery cults, which promised personal salvation, were spreading and gaining followers. Neo-Platonists yearned for a mystical union with the One. Astrology and magic, which offered supernatural explanations for the operations of nature, were also popular. This recoil from rational and worldly values helped prepare the way for Christianity. In a culturally stagnating and spiritually troubled Greco-Roman world, Christianity gave a new meaning to life and a new hope to disillusioned men and women.

The Christian message of a divine Savior and a concerned Father, as well as of brotherly love, inspired men and women who were dissatisfied with the world of the here-and-now — who felt no attachment to city or empire, derived no inspiration from philosophy, and suffered from a profound sense of loneliness. Christianity offered the individual what the city and the Roman world-state could not: an intensely personal relationship with God, an intimate connection with a higher world, and membership in a community of the faithful who cared for one another.

Stressing the intellect and self-reliance, Greco-Roman thought did not provide for the emotional needs of the ordinary person. Christianity addressed itself to this defect in the Greco-Roman outlook. The poor, the oppressed, and the slaves were attracted to the personality, life, death, and resurrection of Jesus, his love for all, and his concern for suffering humanity. They found spiritual sustenance in a religion that offered a hand of love and taught that a person need not be wellborn, rich, educated, or talented to be worthy. To people burdened with misfortune and terrified by death, Christianity held the promise of eternal life, a kingdom of heaven where they would be comforted by God the Father. Thus, Christianity gave the common person what the aristocratic values of Greco-Roman civilization generally did not: hope, a sense of dignity, and inner strength.

Christianity succeeded not only through the appeal of its message, but also through the power of its institution, the Christian church, which grew into a strong organization uniting the faithful. For city dwellers, lonely, alienated, and disillusioned with public affairs — stranded mortals groping for a sense of community — the church that called its members brother and sister filled an elemental need of human beings to belong. The church welcomed women converts, who were often the first to join and brought their menfolk after them. Among the reasons that the church drew women was its command to husbands to treat their wives kindly, remain faithful, and provide for the children. The church won new converts and retained the loyalty of its members by furnishing social services for the poor and infirm, welcoming slaves, criminals, sinners, and other outcasts, and offering a hand of brotherhood and comfort during difficult times.

The ability of an evolving Christianity to assimilate elements from Greek philosophy and even from the mystery religions also contributed in no small measure to its growth. By utilizing Greek philosophy, Christianity was able to present itself in terms intelligible to those versed in Greek learning and thus attract educated people. Converts to Christianity who were trained in philosophy proved to be able defenders of their newly adopted faith. Because some Christian doctrines (the risen Savior-God, the Virgin and child, life after death, communion with the divine), practices (purification through baptism), and holy days (December 25 was the birth date of the god Mithras) either paralleled or were adopted from the mystery religions, it became relatively easy to win converts from these rivals.

Christianity and Rome

Generally tolerant of religions, the Roman government at first did not significantly interfere with the Christian movement. Indeed, Christianity benefited in many ways from its association with the Roman Empire. Christian missionaries traveled throughout the Empire, over roads and across seas made safe by Roman arms. The common Greek dialect, Koine, spoken in most parts of the Empire, facilitated the missionaries' task. Had the Mediterranean world been fractured into separate and competing states, the spread of Christianity might well have faced an insurmountable obstacle. The universalism of the Roman Empire, which made citizenship available to peoples of many nationalities, prepared the way for the universalism of Christianity, which welcomed membership from all nations. Early Christians grafted onto Rome's imperial mission a spiritual evangelical cause: "Go ye therefore and teach all nations." (Matthew 28:19).[2]

As the number of Christians increased, Roman officials began to fear the Christians as subversives who preached allegiance to God and not to Rome.

To many Romans, Christians were enemies of the social order: strange people who would not accept the state gods, would not engage in Roman festivals, scorned gladiator contests, stayed away from public baths, glorified nonviolence, refused to honor deceased emperors as gods, and worshiped a crucified criminal as Lord. Romans ultimately found in Christians a universal scapegoat for the ills burdening the Empire, such as famines, plagues, and military reverses. In an effort to stamp out Christianity, emperors occasionally resorted to persecution. Christians were imprisoned, beaten, starved, burned alive, torn apart by wild beasts in the arena for the amusement of the Roman crowd, and crucified. However, the persecutions did not last long enough to extirpate the new religion. Actually, they strengthened the determination of most of the faithful and won new converts, who were awed by the extraordinary courage of the martyrs willingly dying for their faith.

Unable to crush Christianity by persecution, Roman emperors decided to gain the support of the growing number of Christians within the Empire. In A.D. 313, Constantine, genuinely attracted to Christianity, issued the Edict of Milan, granting toleration to Christians. By A.D. 392, Theodosius I had made Christianity the state religion of the Empire and declared the worship of pagan gods illegal. Persecution did not end, but its target had shifted from Christians to pagans, Jews, and Christians with unorthodox views. Possessing an exclusive attitude toward truth, Christians often viewed nonbelievers as wicked enemies of God who deserved punishment.

Christianity and Greek Philosophy

Christianity synthesized both the Hebrew and the Greco-Roman traditions. Having emerged from Judaism, it assimilated Hebrew monotheism and prophetic morality and retained the Old Testament as the Word of God. As the new religion evolved, it also assimilated elements of Greek philosophy. The ability to combine a historic Judaic monotheism, which had many admirers in the Gentile world, with Greek rational philosophy was a crucial reason for Christianity's triumph in the Roman Empire. But there was a struggle between conservatives, who wanted no dealings with pagan philosophy, and those believers who recognized the value of Greek thought to Christianity.

To conservative church fathers — early Christian writers whose works are accepted as authoritative by the church — classical philosophy was entirely in error because it did not derive from divine revelation. As the final statement of God's truth, Christianity superseded both pagan philosophy and pagan religions. These conservatives feared that studying classical authors would contaminate Christian morality (did not Plato propose a community of wives, and did not the dramatists treat violent passions?) and promote heresy (was not classical literature replete with references to pagan gods?). For these church fathers, there could be no compromise between Greek philosophy and Christian revelation.

Some early church fathers, including several who had a Greek education, defended the value of studying classical literature. They maintained that

Greek philosophy contained a dim glimmer of God's truth, a pre-Christian insight into divine wisdom. Christ had corrected and fulfilled an insight reached by the philosophical mind. Knowledge of Greek philosophy, they also contended, helped Christians explain their beliefs logically and argue intelligently with pagan critics of Christian teachings.

Utilizing the language and categories of Greek philosophy, Christian intellectuals transformed Christianity from a simple ethical creed into a theoretical system, a theology. This effort to express Christian beliefs in terms of Greek rationalism is referred to as the Hellenization of Christianity. Greek philosophy enabled Christians to explain rationally God's existence and revelation.

Christ was depicted as the divine Logos (reason) in human form. The Stoic teaching that all people are fundamentally equal because they share in universal reason could be formulated in Christian terms: that all are united in Christ. Christians could interpret the church to be the true fulfillment of the Stoic idea of a polity embracing the entire world. Stoic ethics, which stressed moderation, self-control, and brotherhood, was compatible with Christianity. Particularly in Platonism, which drew a distinction between a world perceived by the senses and a higher order — a transcendent world that should be the central concern of human existence — Christian thinkers found a congenial vehicle for expressing Christian beliefs. The perfect and universal Forms, or Ideas, which Plato maintained were the true goal of knowledge and the source of ethical standards, were held by Christians to exist in God's mind.

That Greek philosophy exerted an influence on church doctrine is of immense importance: it meant that rational thought, the priceless achievement of the Greek mind, was not lost. However, the Hellenization of Christianity did not mean the triumph of classicism over Christianity, but rather the reverse: Christianity triumphed over Hellenism. Greek philosophy had to sacrifice its essential autonomy to the requirements of Christian revelation; that is, reason had to fit into a Christian framework. Although Christianity made use of Greek philosophy, Christian truth ultimately rested on faith, not reason.

Development of Christian Organization, Doctrine, and Attitudes

Early in its history, the church developed along hierarchical lines. Those members of the Christian community who had the authority to preside over the celebration of the Mass — breaking bread and offering wine as Christ had done at the Last Supper — were called either priests or bishops. Gradually, the designation *bishop* was reserved for the one clergyman in the community with the authority to resolve disputes over doctrines and practices. Regarded as the successors to Christ's Twelve Disciples, bishops supervised religious activities within their regions. In creating a diocese that was supervised by a bishop and had its center in a leading city, the church adapted Roman administrative techniques.

The Antioch Chalice: Roman Syria, Sixth Century. This richly ornamented silver chalice may have been used to hold the wine that Christians believed became the blood of Christ during the Eucharistic liturgy. (*The Metropolitan Museum of Art, The Cloisters Collection, 1950*)

The Primacy of the Bishop of Rome

The bishop of Rome, later to be called the pope, claimed primacy over the other bishops. In developing the case for their supremacy over the church organization, bishops of Rome increasingly referred to the famous New Testament passage in which Jesus says to his disciple Simon (also called Peter): "'And I tell you, you are Peter, and on this rock I will build my church'" (Matthew 16:18). Because *Peter* in Greek means "rock" (petra), it was argued that Christ had chosen Peter to succeed him as ruler of the universal church. Since it was commonly accepted that Saint Peter had established a church in Rome and was martyred there, it was argued further that the Roman bishop inherited the power that Christ had passed on to Peter.

The Rise of Monasticism

Some devout Christians committed to living a perfect Christian life were distressed by the wickedness of the world about them, including the moral laxity of those clergy who chased after wealth and pomp. Seeking to escape from the agonies and corruptions of this world, some ardent Christians withdrew to deserts and mountains in search of spiritual renewal. In their zeal for holiness, they sometimes practiced extreme forms of asceticism: self-flogging, wearing spiked corsets, eating only herbs, or living for years on a column high above the ground. Gradually, colonies of these hermits sprang up, particularly in Egypt;

in time, the leaders of these monastic communities drew up written rules that required monks to refrain from bodily abuses and to engage in manual labor.

The monastic ideal spread from east to west. The principal figure in the shaping of monasticism in the West was Saint Benedict (c. 480–c. 543), who founded a monastery at Monte Cassino, Italy, in 529. The Rule of Saint Benedict called for the monks to live in poverty and to study, labor, and obey the abbot, the head of the monastery. Monks were required to pray often, work hard, talk little, and surrender private property. In imposing discipline and regulations, Benedict eliminated the excessive and eccentric individualism of the early monks; he socialized and institutionalized the spiritual impulse that led monks to withdraw from the world. Benedict demonstrated the same genius for administration that the Romans had shown in organizing and governing their Empire. His rule became the standard for monasteries in Western Europe.

The Scriptural Tradition and Doctrinal Disputes

The earliest surviving Christian writings are Paul's Epistles, written some twenty-five to thirty years after the death of Jesus. Jesus' sayings and deeds were preserved by word of mouth. Sometime around A.D. 66–70, about forty years after the Crucifixion, Saint Mark formulated the Christian message from this oral tradition and perhaps from some material that had been put in writing earlier. Later, Saint Matthew and Saint Luke, relying heavily on Mark's account, wrote somewhat longer Gospels. The Gospels of Mark, Matthew, and Luke are called *synoptic* because their approach to Jesus is very similar. The remaining Gospel, written by Saint John around A.D. 110, varies significantly from the synoptic Gospels. The synoptic Gospels, the Gospel of Saint John, Acts of the Apostles, the twenty-one Epistles, including those written by Saint Paul, and Revelation constitute the twenty-seven books of the Christian New Testament. Christians also accepted the Hebrews' Old Testament as God's Word.

The early Christians had a Bible and a clergy to teach it. But the Holy Writ could be interpreted differently by equally sincere believers, and controversies over doctrine threatened the unity of the early church. The most important controversy concerned how people viewed the relationship between God and Christ. Arius (A.D. 250–336), a Greek priest in Alexandria, led one faction. He denied the complete divinity of Christ, one of the basic tenets of the church. To Arius, Christ was more than man but less than God; there was no permanent union between God and Christ; the Father alone was eternal and truly God.

The Council of Nicaea (A.D. 325), the first assembly of bishops from all parts of the Roman world, was called to settle the controversy. The council condemned Arius and ruled that God and Christ were of the same substance, coequal and coeternal. The position adopted at Nicaea became the basis of the Nicene Creed, which remains the official doctrine of the church. Although Arianism, the name given the heresy of Arius, won converts for a time, it eventually died out.

Christianity and Society

Although salvation was their ultimate aim, Christians still had to dwell within the world and deal with its imperfections. In the process, Christian thinkers challenged some of the mores of Greco-Roman society and formulated attitudes that would endure for centuries. Influenced by passages in the New Testament that condemned acts of revenge and the shedding of blood, some early Christians refused military service. Others, however, held that in a sinful world, defense of the state was necessary and, without concealment or apology, served in the army. After Roman emperors professed Christianity, Christians began to serve the government more often. With the barbarians menacing the borders, these Christian officials could not advocate nonviolence. Christian theorists began to argue that under certain circumstances — to punish injustice or to restore peace — war was just. But even such wars must not entail unnecessary violence.

Sharing in the patriarchal tradition of Jewish society, Saint Paul subjected the wife to her husband's authority. "Wives, be subject to your husbands, as to the Lord. For the husband is the head of the wife as Christ is the head of the church" (Ephesians 5:22–23). But Paul also held that all are baptized in Christ: "There is neither Jew nor Greek, there is neither slave nor free, there is neither male nor female; for you are all one in Christ Jesus" (Galatians 3:28). Consequently, both sexes were subject to divine law; both men and women possessed moral autonomy. The early church held to strict standards on sexual matters. It condemned adultery and esteemed virginity pledged for spiritual reasons.

Christians waged no war against slavery, which was widely practiced and universally accepted in the ancient world. Saint Paul commanded slaves to obey their masters, and many Christians were themselves slave owners. However, Christians taught that slaves, too, were children of God, sought their conversion, and urged owners not to treat them harshly. In the modern world, the Christian teaching that all persons are spiritually equal before God would impel some Christians to fight for the abolition of slavery.

Christianity and the Jews

The central theme of the New Testament Gospels is love of both God and fellow human beings. But the Gospels also devote considerable attention to the fallen angel, Satan, and the evil demons that inhabit his kingdom. Increasingly, Christians identified opponents — Jews, pagans, and heretics — with Satan and viewed conflicts in a moral context: a struggle between God's faithful and Satan's servants. Over the centuries, the view that they were participants in a cosmic struggle between good and evil led Christians to demonize adversaries, a practice that exacerbated hatred and justified mistreatment, even massacre. Christian attitudes and behavior toward Jews poignantly illustrate this point.

Numerous links connect early Christianity and Judaism. Jesus himself and his earliest followers, including the Twelve Apostles, were Jews who were faithful to Jewish law. Jesus' message was first spread in synagogues throughout the Roman Empire. Early Christianity's affirmation of the preciousness of the human being, created in God's image, its belief that God rules history, its awareness of human sinfulness, its call for repentance, and its appeal to God for forgiveness are rooted in Judaism. The Christian reference to God as a "merciful Father" derives from Jewish prayer. Also rooted in Judaism are the moral norms proclaimed by Jesus in the Sermon on the Mount and on other occasions. For example, "Thou shalt love thy neighbor as thyself" was the motto of the Jewish sage Hillel, a contemporary of Jesus who founded a school. The great value that the Torah places on charity was inherited by Christianity. Jesus' use of parables to convey his teachings, the concept of the Messiah, respect for the Sabbath, the practice of giving alms to the poor, and congregational worship likewise stem from Judaism. And, of course, Christians viewed the Hebrew Scriptures as God's Word.

Over the years, however, Christians forgot or devalued this relationship to Judaism, and some thinkers began to show hostility toward Judaism and Jews, which had tragic consequences in later centuries. Several factors fueled this anti-Judaism: resentment against Jews for their refusal to accept Jesus; the polemics of the Jewish establishment against the followers of Jesus; the role in Jesus' death ascribed to Jews by the New Testament; resentment against those Christians who Judaized, that is, continued to observe Jewish festivals and the Jewish Sabbath, to regard the synagogue as holy, and to practice circumcision; and anger that Judaism remained a vital religion, for this undermined the conviction that Christianity was the fulfillment of Judaism and the one true faith.

What made Christian anti-Judaism particularly ominous was the effort of some theologians to demonize the Jewish people. The myth emerged that Jews, murderers of the incarnate God who embodied all that was good, were a cursed nation, children of the Devil, whose suffering was intended by God. Thus Origen (c. 185–c. 251) maintained that "the blood of Jesus [falls] not only upon those who lived then but also upon all generations of the Jewish people following afterwards until the end of the world."[3] In the late fourth century, John Chrysostom described Jews as "inveterate murderers, destroyers, men possessed by the Devil." "[T]hey murder their offspring and immolate them to the devil." The synagogue, he said, was "the domicile of the devil as is also the soul of the Jews." Their rites are "criminal and impure," their religion is "a disease." For the "odius assassination of Christ," there is "no expiation possible, . . . no pardon." Jews will live "under the yoke of servitude without end."[4] Since the Devil was very real to early and medieval Christians, the Jew became identified with evil. Christians developed a mindset, concludes the Reverend Robert A. Everett, that was "unable to see anything positive in Judaism. . . . Judaism and the Jewish people came to have no real value for Christians except as a negative contrast to Christianity."[5] Because of this "teaching of contempt" and the "diabolization of the Jew," the Christian ethic of love did not extend to Jews.

> [O]nce it is established that God has cursed the Jews, how can one
> argue that Christians should love them? If Jews have been fated by
> God to have ... a long history of suffering, who are Christians to
> alter their history by doing anything to relieve Jewish suffering? The
> theology of victimization thus precludes Christian love as a basis of
> relating to Jews.[6]

The diabolization of the Jew, which bore no relationship to the actual behavior of Jews or to their highly ethical religion, and the "theology of victimization," which held that the Jews were collectively and eternally cursed for
denying Christ, became powerful myths. Over the centuries, these myths poi-
soned Christians' hearts and minds against Jews, spurring innumerable humil-
iations, persecutions, and massacres. Alongside this hatred of Jews and
antipathy to their suffering, there also evolved the belief that Jews, faithless
and perfidious though they were, should be permitted to survive, for one day
they would see the light and convert to the true faith.

Saint Augustine: The Christian World-View

During the early history of Christianity, many learned men, fathers of the
church, explained and defended church teachings. Most of the leading early
fathers wrote in Greek, but in the middle of the fourth century, three great
Latin writers — Saint Jerome, Saint Ambrose, and Saint Augustine — profoundly influenced the course of Christianity in the West.

Saint Jerome (A.D. c. 340–420) wrote about the lives of the saints and promoted the spread of monasticism. But his greatest achievement was the translation of the Old and New Testaments from Hebrew and Greek into Latin.
Jerome's text, the common, or Vulgate, version of the Bible, became the official edition of the Bible for the western church.

Saint Ambrose (A.D. 340–397), bishop of Milan, Italy, instructed the clergy
to deal humanely with the poor, the old, the sick, and the orphaned. He urged
clerics not to pursue wealth, but to practice humility and avoid favoring the
rich over the poor. Ambrose sought to defend the autonomy of the church
against the power of the state. His dictum that "the Emperor is within the
church, not above it" became a cardinal principle of the medieval church.

The most important Christian theoretician in the Late Roman Empire was
Saint Augustine (A.D. 354–430), bishop of Hippo, in North Africa, and au-
thor of *The City of God*. Augustine became the principal architect of the
Christian outlook that succeeded a dying classicism.

In 410, when Augustine was in his fifties, Visigoths sacked Rome — a dis-
aster for which the classical consciousness was unprepared. Throughout the
Empire, people panicked. Non-Christians blamed the tragedy on Christianity.
Even Christians expressed anxiety. Why were the righteous also suffering?
Where was the kingdom of God on earth that had been prophesied? In *The
City of God*, Augustine maintained that the worldly city could never be the

Saint Augustine in His Studio. Saint Augustine was the most influential Christian theoretician in the Late Roman Empire. This painting of him in his studio depicts him as a serious thinker. (*CORBIS-Bettmann*)

central concern of Christians. The misfortunes of Rome, therefore, should not distress Christians unduly because the true Christian was a citizen of a heavenly city that could not be pillaged by ungodly barbarians but would endure forever. Compared with God's heavenly city, Rome and its decline were unimportant. What really mattered in history, said Augustine, was not the coming to be or the passing away of cities and empires, but the individual's entrance into heaven or hell.

Augustine did not hold that by his death Christ had opened the door to heaven for all. The majority of humanity remained condemned to eternal punishment, said Augustine; only a handful had the gift of faith and the promise of heaven. People could not by their own efforts overcome a sinful nature; a moral and spiritual regeneration stemmed not from human will power, but from God's grace. The small number endowed with God's grace constituted the City of God. These people lived on earth as visitors only, for they awaited deliverance to the Kingdom of Christ. Most inhabitants of the earthly city were destined for eternal punishment in hell. A perpetual conflict existed between the two cities and between their inhabitants: one city stood for sin and corruption; the other, for God's truth and perfection.

For Augustine, the highest good was not of this world. Rather, it consisted of eternal life with God. His distinction between this higher world of perfection and a lower world of corruption remained influential throughout the Middle Ages.

Augustine repudiated the distinguishing feature of classical humanism: the autonomy of reason. For him, ultimate wisdom could not be achieved through rational thought alone; reason had to be guided by faith. Without faith, there could be no true knowledge, no understanding. Philosophy had no validity if it did not first accept as absolutely true the existence of God and the authority of his revelation. Thus, Augustine upheld the primacy of faith. But he did not necessarily regard reason as an enemy of faith, and he did not call for an end to rational speculation. What he denied of the classical view was that reason alone could attain wisdom. The wisdom that Augustine sought was Christian wisdom, God's revelation to humanity. The starting point for this wisdom, he said, was belief in God and the Scriptures. To Augustine, secular knowledge for its own sake was of little value; the true significance of knowledge lay in its role as a tool for comprehending God's will. Augustine adapted the classical intellectual tradition to the requirements of Christian revelation.

With Augustine, the human-centered outlook of classical humanism, which for centuries had been undergoing transformation, gave way to a God-centered world-view. The fulfillment of God's will, not the full development of human capacities, became the chief concern of life.

Christianity and Classical Humanism: Alternative World-Views

Christianity and classical humanism are the two principal components of the Western tradition. The value that modern Western civilization places on the individual derives ultimately from classical humanism and the Judeo-Christian tradition. Classical humanists believed that worth came from the capacity of individuals to reason and to shape their character and their life according to rational standards. Christianity, too, stresses the importance of

The Ascension of Jesus into Heaven: A Miniature Painting, c. A.D. 586. In this illustration from a gospel book written by the monk Rabbula at Saint John's Abbey, Zagba, Mesopotamia, the upper zone of the painting reflects a vision of the prophet Ezekiel (1:3–28). The lower zone shows Jesus' apostles and his mother Mary with two angels as witnesses to Jesus' Ascension into heaven. (Acts 1:7–14). (*Courtesy of Biblioteca Medicea Laurenziana, Florence. Photo by Donato Pineides.*)

the individual. In the Christian view, God cares for each person; he wants people to behave righteously and to enter heaven; Christ died for all because he loves humanity. Christianity espouses active love and genuine concern for fellow human beings. The idea of a Christian conscience, promoted by God and transcending all other loyalties, reinforces respect for all human beings regardless of cultural and national differences.

But Christianity and classical humanism also represent two inherently different world-views. The triumph of the Christian outlook signified a break with the essential meaning of classical humanism; it pointed to the end of the world of antiquity and the beginning of an age of faith, the Middle Ages. With the victory of Christianity, the ultimate goal of life shifted. Life's purpose was no longer to achieve excellence in this world through the full and creative development of human talent, but to attain salvation in a heavenly city. A person's worldly accomplishments amounted to very little if he or she did not accept God and his revelation.

The Christian ideal of the isolated and contemplative monk, who rejected the world in order to serve God, was alien to the spirit of classical humanism, which valued active citizenship. Equally foreign to the Greco-Roman mind was another idea introduced by Christianity: the need to escape from a sinful human nature, a consequence of Adam and Eve's defiance of God. This view of human corruption, particularly in Augustine's formulation, became deeply embedded in the European mind during the Christian centuries — the Middle Ages.

In the classical view, history had no ultimate end, no ultimate significance; periods of happiness and misery repeated themselves endlessly. In the Christian view, history is filled with spiritual meaning. It is the profound drama of individuals struggling to overcome their original sin in order to gain eternal happiness in heaven. History began with Adam and Eve's defiance of God and would end when Christ returns to earth, evil is eradicated, and God's will prevails.

Classicism held that there was no authority above reason: individuals had within themselves, through unaided reason, the ability to understand the world and life. For early Christianity, however, knowledge, without God as the starting point, was formless, purposeless, and prone to error. In classicism, ethical standards were expressions of universal reason, laws of nature, which human reason could discover. Through reason, individuals could discern the norms by which they should regulate their lives. Reason would enable them to govern their desires and will; it would show them where their behavior was wrong and how to correct it. Early Christianity, on the other hand, taught that ethical standards emanated from the personal will of God. Without obedience to God's commands, people would remain wicked forever; the human will, essentially sinful, could not be transformed by the promptings of reason. Only when individuals turned to God for forgiveness and guidance would they find the inner strength to overcome their sinful nature. People could not perfect themselves through scientific knowledge; spiritual insight and belief in God must serve as the first principle of their lives.

Thus, for classicism, the ultimate good came through independent thought and action; for Christianity, it came through knowing, obeying, and loving God. In early Christianity, the good life was identified not with worldly achievement, but with eternal life. Each person must make entrance into God's kingdom the central aim of life. For the next thousand years, this distinction between heaven and earth, this otherworldly, theocentric outlook, would define the Western mentality.

Notes

1. Andrew M. Greeley, "Hippie Hero? Superpatriot? Superstar? A Christmas Biography," *New York Times Magazine*, December 23, 1973, p. 28.

2. The biblical quotations are from the *Holy Bible, Revised Standard Version* (New York: Thomas Nelson & Sons, 1952). The *Revised Standard Version* is the text used for biblical quotations throughout, except where noted otherwise.

3. *"Commentaria in Evagelium secundum Matthaeum,"* in Patrologiae Cursus Completus, Series Graeca Prior, ed. J. P. Migne, trans. Joseph Castora (Paris, 1862), 13: 1775–76.

4. Quoted in Edward H. Flannery, *The Anguish of the Jews* (London: Macmillan, 1965), p. 48.

5. Randolph Braham, ed., *The Origins of the Holocaust: Christian Anti-*

Semitism (Boulder, Colorado: Social Science Monographs and Institute for Holocaust Studies of the City University of New York, 1986), p. 36.

6. Ibid., p. 37.

Suggested Reading

Armstrong, Karen, *A History of God* (1994). Good material on early Christianity.

Benko, Stephen, *Pagan Rome and the Early Christians* (1984). How Romans and Greeks viewed early Christianity.

Chadwick, Henry, *The Early Church* (1967). A survey of early Christianity in its social and ideological context.

Davies, J. G., *The Early Christian Church* (1967). A splendid introduction to the first five centuries of Christianity.

Ferguson, Everett, ed., *Encylopedia of Early Christianity* (1990). Entries on all aspects of early Christianity.

————, *Backgrounds of Early Christianity* (1993). A clear and thorough examination of the milieu in which Christianity was born.

Gager, John G., *The Origins of Anti-Semitism* (1983). Anti-Semitism as essentially a Christian phenomenon.

Grant, Michael, *Jesus* (1977). An examination of the Gospels.

Meeks, Wayne A., *The Moral World of the First Christians* (1986). Continuity and discontinuity between the moral outlook of early Christianity and that pervading Jewish and Greco-Roman thought.

Pelikan, Jaroslav, *The Christian Tradition* (1971), vol. 1, *The Emergence of the Catholic Tradition*. The first of a five-volume series on the history of Christian doctrine.

Perkins, Pheme, *Reading the New Testament* (1978). Introduces the beginning student to the New Testament.

Perry, Marvin, and Frederick M. Schweitzer, eds., *Jewish-Christian Encounters over the Centuries* (1994). Useful essays on Jesus, Paul, the Dead Sea Scrolls, and early Christian anti-Judaism.

Segal, Allan F., *Rebecca's Children* (1986). Judaism and Christianity in the Roman world.

Wilkin, Robert L., *The Christians as the Romans Saw Them* (1984). Pagan reaction to the rise of Christianity.

Review Questions

1. Why does the life of Jesus present a problem to the historian?
2. What were Jesus' basic teachings?
3. What is the relationship of early Christianity to Judaism?
4. How did Saint Paul transform a Jewish sect into a world religion?
5. What factors contributed to the triumph of Christianity in the Roman Empire?
6. Why did some early Christian thinkers object to the study of classical literature? What arguments were advanced by the defenders of classical learning? What was the outcome of this debate? Why was it significant?
7. What factors contributed to the rise of anti-Judaism among early Christians? Define and explain the historical significance of the "diabolization of the Jew," the "teaching of contempt," and the "theology of victimization."
8. How did Saint Augustine view the fall of Rome, the worldly city, humanity, and Greek philosophy?
9. Compare and contrast the world-views of early Christianity and classical humanism.

❖ PART TWO

The Middle Ages: The Christian Centuries

500–1400

Stained Glass in La Sainte Chapelle Cathedral, Paris. (*Nicholas DeVore III/Bruce Coleman*)

POLITICS AND SOCIETY	THOUGHT AND CULTURE
500 Germanic kingdoms established on former Roman lands (5th and 6th cent.) Saint Benedict founds monastery at Monte Cassino (529) Pope Gregory I sends missionaries to convert the Anglo-Saxons (596)	Boethius, *The Consolation of Philosophy* (523) Law Code of Justinian (529) Byzantine church Hagia Sophia (532–537) Cassiodorus establishes a monastic library at Vivarium (540)
600 Spread of Islam (622–732)	The Koran
700 Charles Martel defeats the Muslims at Tours (732)	Bede, *Ecclesiastical History of the English People* (c. 700) Muslim Golden Age (700s and 800s)
800 Charlemagne crowned emperor of Romans Muslim, Magyar, and Viking invasions of Latin Christendom (9th and early 10th cent.) Growth of feudalism (800–1100)	Carolingian Renaissance (768–814) Alfred the Great promotes learning in England (871–899)
900 German king Otto I becomes first Holy Roman Emperor (962)	
1000 Split between the Byzantine and Roman churches (1054) Norman conquest of England (1066) Start of First Crusade (1096)	Romanesque style in architecture (1000s and 1100s)
1100 Philip Augustus expands central authority in France (1180–1223) Development of common law and jury system in England (1100s) Pontificate of Innocent III: height of papal power (1198–1216)	Flowering of medieval culture (12th and 13th cent.): universities, Gothic architecture, scholastic philosophy, revival of Roman law
1200 Magna Carta (1215) Destruction of Baghdad by Mongols (1258)	Aquinas, *Summa Theologica* (1267–1273)
1300 Hundred Years' War (1337–1453) Black Death (1347–1351) Great Schism of papacy (1378–1417)	Dante, *Divine Comedy* (c. 1307–1321) Chaucer, *Canterbury Tales* (c. 1388–1400)

❖ CHAPTER 6

The Rise of Europe: Fusion of Classical, Christian, and Germanic Traditions

*T*he triumph of Christianity and the establishment of Germanic kingdoms on once Roman lands constituted a new phase in Western history: the end of the ancient world and the beginning of the Middle Ages, a period that spanned a thousand years. In the ancient world, the locus of Greco-Roman civilization was the Mediterranean Sea. The heartland of medieval civilization gradually shifted to the north, to regions of Europe that Greco-Roman civilization had barely penetrated. During the Middle Ages, a common European civilization evolved, integrating Christian, Greco-Roman, and Germanic traditions: Christianity was at the center of medieval civilization, Rome was the spiritual capital and Latin the language of intellectual life, and Germanic customs pervaded social and legal relationships. In the Early Middle Ages (500–1050), the new civilization was struggling to take form; in the High Middle Ages (1050–1300), medieval civilization reached its peak. ❖

The Medieval East

Three new civilizations based on religion emerged from the ruins of the Roman Empire: Latin Christendom (western and central Europe) and two Eastern civilizations, Byzantium and Islam.

Byzantium

Although the Roman Empire in the West fell to the German tribes, the eastern provinces survived. They did so because they were richer, more urbanized, and more populous and because the main Germanic and Hunnish invasions were directed at the western regions. In the eastern parts, Byzantine civilization took shape. Its religion was Christianity; its language and culture Greek; and its machinery of administration Roman. The capital, Constantinople, was a fortress city, perfectly situated to resist attacks from land and sea.

144

Chronology 6.1 ❖ The Early and High Middle Ages

496	Clovis adopts Roman Christianity
596	Pope Gregory I sends missionaries to convert the Anglo-Saxons
732	Charles Martel defeats the Muslims at Tours
768	Charlemagne becomes king of the Franks
800	Charlemagne is crowned emperor of the Romans by Pope Leo III
c. 840s	Height of Viking attacks
962	Otto I crowned emperor of the Romans, beginning the Holy Roman Empire
987	Hugh Capet becomes king of France
1054	Split between the Byzantine and Roman churches
1066	Norman conquest of England
1075	Start of the Investiture Controversy
1096	First Crusade begins
1198–1216	Pontificate of Innocent III: height of the church's power

During the Early Middle Ages, Byzantine civilization was economically and culturally far more advanced than that of the Latin West. At a time when few westerners (Latin Christians) could read or write, Byzantine scholars studied the literature, philosophy, science, and law of ancient Greece and Rome. Whereas trade and urban life had greatly declined in the West, Constantinople was a magnificent Byzantine city of schools, libraries, open squares, and bustling markets.

Over the centuries, many differences developed between the Byzantine church and the Roman church. The pope resisted domination by the Byzantine emperor, and the Byzantines would not accept the pope as head of all Christians. The two churches quarreled over ceremonies, holy days, the display of images, and the rights of the clergy. The final break came in 1054: the Christian church split into the Roman Catholic in the West and the Eastern (Greek) Orthodox in the East, a division that still persists.

Political and cultural differences widened the rift between Latin Christendom and Byzantium. In the Byzantine Empire, Greek was the language of religion and intellectual life; in the West, Latin predominated. Latin Christians refused to recognize that the Byzantine emperors were, as they claimed to be, successors to the Roman emperors. Byzantine emperors were absolute rulers who held that God had chosen them to rule and to institute divine will on earth. As successors to the Roman emperors, they claimed to rule all the lands that had once been part of the Roman Empire.

At its height, under Emperor Justinian, who reigned from 527 to 565, the Byzantine Empire included Greece, Asia Minor, Italy, southern Spain, and parts of the Near East, North Africa, and the Balkans. Over the centuries, the Byzantines faced attacks from the Germanic Lombards and Visigoths, Persians, Muslim Arabs, Seljuk Turks, and Latin Christians. The death blow to the empire was dealt by the Ottoman Turks. Originally from central Asia, they had accepted Islam and had begun to build an empire. They drove the Byzantines from Asia Minor and conquered much of the Balkans. By the beginning of the fifteenth century, the Byzantine Empire consisted of only two small territories in Greece and the city of Constantinople. In 1453, the Ottoman Turks broke through Constantinople's great walls and plundered the city. After more than ten centuries, the Byzantine Empire had come to an end.

During its thousand years, Byzantium had a significant impact on world history. First, it prevented the Muslim Arabs from advancing into Eastern Europe. Had the Arabs broken through Byzantine defenses, much of Europe might have been converted to the new faith of Islam. Another far-reaching development was the codification of the laws of ancient Rome under Justinian. This monumental achievement, the *Corpus Juris Civilis,* preserved Roman law's principles of reason and justice. Today's legal codes in much of Europe and Latin America trace their roots to the Roman law recorded by Justinian's lawyers. The Byzantines also preserved the philosophy, science, mathematics, and literature of ancient Greece.

Contacts with Byzantine civilization stimulated learning in both the Islamic world to the east and Latin Christendom to the west. Byzantium also carried its advanced civilization and Orthodox Christianity to some Slavic peoples of Eastern and Southeastern Europe, including the Russians. It gave those Slavs legal principles, art forms, and an alphabet (the Cyrillic, based on the Greek) that enabled them to put their own languages into writing.

Islam

The second civilization to arise after Rome's fall was based on the vital new religion of Islam, which emerged in the seventh century among the Arabs of Arabia. Its founder was Muhammad (c. 570–632), a prosperous merchant in the trading city of Mecca. When Muhammad was about forty, he believed that he was visited in his sleep by the angel Gabriel, who ordered him to "recite in the name of the Lord!" Transformed by this experience, Muhammad came to believe that he had been chosen to serve as a prophet. Although most desert Arabs worshiped tribal gods, many Arabs in the towns and trading centers were familiar with Judaism and Christianity, and some had accepted the idea of one God. Rejecting the many deities of the tribal religions, Muhammad offered the Arabs a new monotheistic faith, Islam, which means "surrender to Allah (God)."

Church of the Holy Wisdom (Hagia Sophia), Constantinople, A.D. 532–537.   The largest church ever built in the Byzantine world, Hagia Sophia was constructed by Emperor Justinian. Its immense dome was decorated with golden mosaics simulating the light of heaven. After the Turkish conquest of Constantinople in A.D. 1453, the mosaics were painted white and the church was converted into a mosque. (*Gary Yeowell/Tony Stone Images*)

Islamic standards of morality and rules governing daily life are set by the Koran, which Muslims believe contains the words of Allah as revealed to Muhammad. Muslims see their religion as the completion and perfection of Judaism and Christianity. They regard the ancient Hebrew prophets as messengers of God and value their message of compassion and the oneness of humanity. They also acknowledge Jesus as a great prophet but do not consider him divine. Muslims view Muhammad as the last and greatest of the prophets and see him as entirely human; they worship only Allah, the creator and ruler of heaven and earth, a single, all-powerful God who is merciful, compassionate, and just. According to the Koran, on the Day of Judgment unbelievers and the wicked will be dragged into a fearful place of "scorching winds and seething water," and "sinners . . . shall eat . . . [bitter] fruit . . . [and] drink boiling water."[1] Faithful Muslims who have lived virtuously are promised paradise, a garden of bodily pleasures and spiritual delights.

In a little more than two decades, Muhammad united the often feuding Arabian tribes into a powerful force dedicated to Allah and the spreading of the Islamic faith. After Muhammad's death in 632, his friend and father-in-law, Abu Bakr, became his successor, or caliph. Regarded as the defender of the faith, whose power derived from Allah, the caliph governed in accordance with Muslim law as defined in the Koran. The Islamic state was a theocracy, in which government and religion were inseparable; there could be no distinction between secular and spiritual authority. Muslims viewed God as the source of all law and political authority and the caliph as his earthly deputy. Divine law regulated all aspects of human relations. The ruler who did not enforce Koranic law failed in his duties. Thus, Islam was more than a religion; it was also a system of government, society, law, and thought that bound its adherents into an all-encompassing community. The idea of a society governed by the Koran remained deeply embedded in the Muslim mind over the centuries and is still a powerful force today.

Christians and Jews who lived in Islamic lands had fewer rights than Muslims — they could not bear arms, were assessed a special tax, and, at times, were barred from testifying in court against a Muslim. Nevertheless, as "people of the book," Jews and Christians were protected communities, and despite instances of loss of property or life, or both, the two groups generally went about their business and practiced their religions free of persecution. In fact, Jews were physically safer in Muslim than in Christian lands, and unlike medieval Christians, Muslims did not demonize Jews as a hateful and cursed people, deserving of divine punishment.

Islam gave the many Arab tribes the unity, discipline, and organization to succeed in their wars of conquest. Under the first four caliphs, who ruled from 632 to 661, the Arabs, with breathtaking speed, overran the Persian Empire, seized some of Byzantium's provinces, and invaded Europe. Muslim warriors believed that they were engaged in a holy war (*jihad*) to spread Islam to nonbelievers and that those who died in the jihad were assured a place in paradise. A desire to escape from the barren Arabian Desert and to exploit the rich Byzantine and Persian lands was another compelling reason for expansion. In the east, Islam's territory eventually extended into India and to the borders of China; in the west, it encompassed North Africa and most of Spain. But the Muslims' northward push lost momentum and was halted in 717 by the Byzantines at Constantinople and in 732 by the Franks at the battle of Tours, in central France.

In the eighth and ninth centuries, under the Abbasid caliphs, Muslim civilization entered its golden age. Islamic civilization creatively integrated Arabic, Byzantine, Persian, and Indian cultural traditions. During the Early Middle Ages, when learning was at a low point in Western Europe, the Muslims forged a high civilization. Muslim science, philosophy, and mathematics rested largely on the achievements of the ancient Greeks. The Muslims acquired Greek learning from the older Persian and Byzantine civilizations, which had kept alive the Greek inheritance. By translating Greek works into Arabic and commenting on them, Muslim scholars performed the great historical task of preserving the philosophical and scientific heritage of ancient Greece. This Greek learning, supplemented by original contributions of Muslim scholars and scientists, was eventually passed on to Christian Europe.

The Arab empire, stretching from Spain to India, was unified by a common language (Arabic), a common faith, and a common culture. By the eleventh century, however, the Arabs began losing their dominance in the Islamic world. The Seljuk Turks, who had taken Asia Minor from the Byzantines, also conquered the Arabic lands of Syria, Palestine, and much of Persia. Although the Abbasid caliphs remained the religious and cultural leaders of Islam, political power was exercised by Seljuk sultans. In the eleventh and twelfth centuries, the Muslims lost Sicily and most of Spain to Christian knights, and European Crusaders carved out kingdoms in the Near East.

In the thirteenth century, Mongols led by Genghis Khan devastated Muslim lands; in the late fourteenth century, this time led by Tamerlane, they again plundered and massacred their way through Arab territory. After Tamerlane's death in 1404, his empire disintegrated, and its collapse left the way open for the Ottoman Turks.

The Ottoman Empire reached its height in the sixteenth century with the conquest of Egypt, North Africa, Syria, and the Arabian coast. The Ottomans developed an effective system of administration, but they could not restore the cultural brilliance, the thriving trade, or the prosperity that the Muslim world had known under the Abbasid caliphs of Baghdad.

Latin Christendom in the Early Middle Ages

The centuries of cultural greatness of both the Islamic and the Byzantine civilizations enriched the Western world. However, neither Islam nor Byzantium made the breakthroughs in science, technology, philosophy, the arts, economics, and political thought that gave rise to the modern world. That process was the singular achievement of Europe. During the Early Middle Ages (500–1050), Latin Christendom was culturally far behind the two Eastern civilizations, but by the twelfth century it had caught up. In succeeding centuries, it produced the movements that ushered in the modern age: the Renaissance, the Reformation, the Scientific Revolution, the Age of Enlightenment, the French Revolution, and the Industrial Revolution.

Political, Economic, and Intellectual Transformation

From the sixth to the eighth century, Europeans struggled to overcome the disorder created by the breakup of the Roman Empire and the deterioration of Greco-Roman civilization. In the process, a new civilization, with its own distinctive style, took root. It grew out of the intermingling of Greco-Roman civilization, the Christian outlook, and Germanic traditions. But centuries would pass before it would come to fruition.

In the fifth century, German invaders founded kingdoms in North Africa, Italy, Spain, Gaul, and Britain — lands formerly belonging to Rome. Even before the invasions, the Germans had acquired some knowledge of Roman culture and were attracted to it. Therefore, the new Germanic rulers did not seek to destroy Roman civilization, they sought to share in its advantages. For example, Theodoric the Great (476–526), the Ostrogoth ruler of Italy, retained the Roman Senate, government officials, civil service, and schools, and rich aristocratic Roman families continued to hold high government offices. The Burgundians in Gaul and the Visigoths in Spain maintained Roman law for their conquered subjects. All the Germanic kingdoms tried to keep Roman systems of taxation; furthermore, Latin remained the official language of administration.

But the Germanic kingdoms, often torn by warfare, internal rebellion, and assassination, provided a poor political base on which to revive a decadent and dying classical civilization. Most of the kingdoms survived for only a short time and had no enduring impact. An exception to this trend occurred in Gaul and south-central Germany, where the most successful of the Germanic kingdoms was established by the Franks — the founders of the new Europe.

The Roman world was probably too far gone to be rescued, but even if it had not been, the Germans were culturally unprepared to play the role of rescuer. By the end of the seventh century, the old Roman lands in the west showed a marked decline in central government, town life, commerce, and learning. While vigorous and brave, the German invaders were essentially a rural and warrior people, tribal in organization and outlook. Their native culture, which was without cities or written literature, was primitive compared with the literary, philosophical, scientific, and artistic achievements of the Greco-Roman world. The Germans were not equipped to reform the decaying Roman system of administration and taxation or to cope with the economic problems that had burdened the Empire. Nor could they maintain roads and irrigation systems, preserve skills in the arts of stoneworking and glassmaking, or breathe new life into the dying humanist culture.

The distinguishing feature of classical civilization, its vital urban institutions, had deteriorated in the Late Roman Empire. Under the kingdoms created by Germanic chieftains, the shift from an urban to a rural economy accelerated. Although towns did not vanish altogether, they continued to lose control over the surrounding countryside and to decline in wealth and importance. They were the headquarters of bishops, rather than centers of commerce and intellectual life. Italy remained an exception to this general trend. There, Roman urban institutions persisted, even during the crudest period of the Early Middle Ages. Italian cities kept some metal currency in circulation and traded with one another and with Byzantium.

In retreat since the Late Roman Empire, Greco-Roman humanism continued its decline in the centuries immediately following Rome's demise. The old Roman upper classes abandoned their heritage and absorbed the ways of their Germanic conquerors, the Roman schools closed, and Roman law faded into disuse. Aside from clerics, few people could read and write Latin, and even learned clerics were rare. Knowledge of the Greek language in Western Europe was almost totally lost, and the Latin rhetorical style deteriorated. Many literary works of classical antiquity were either lost or neglected. European culture was much poorer than the high civilizations of Byzantium, Islam, and ancient Rome.

During this period of cultural poverty, the few persons who were learned generally did not engage in original thought, but rather salvaged and transmitted remnants of classical civilization. In a rudimentary way, they were struggling to create a Christian culture that combined the intellectual tradition of Greece and Rome with the religious teachings of the Christian church.

An important figure in the intellectual life of this transitional period was Boethius (480–c. 525), a descendant of a noble Italian family. Aspiring to rescue the intellectual heritage of antiquity, Boethius translated into Latin some of Aristotle's treatises on logic and wrote commentaries on Aristotle, Cicero, and Porphyry (a Neo-Platonist philosopher). Until the twelfth century, virtually all that Latin Christendom knew of Aristotle came from Boethius's translations and commentaries. Similarly, his work in mathematics, which contains fragments from Euclid, was the main source for the study of that discipline in the Early Middle Ages. In his theological writings, Boethius tried to demonstrate that reason did not conflict with orthodoxy — an early attempt to attain a rational comprehension of belief, or, as he expressed it, to join faith to reason. Boethius's effort to examine Christian doctrines rationally, a salient feature of medieval philosophy, was to grow to maturity in the twelfth and thirteenth centuries.

Cassiodorus (c. 490–575), another Italian, collected Greek and Latin manuscripts and started the monastic practice of copying classical texts. Without this tradition, many key Christian and pagan works would undoubtedly have perished. In Spain, another "preserver" of ancient works, Isidore of Seville (c. 576–636), compiled an encyclopedia, *Etymologiae,* covering a diversity of topics, from arithmetic and furniture to God. Isidore derived his information from many secular and religious sources. Quite understandably, his work contained many errors, particularly in its references to nature. For centuries, though, the *Etymologiae* served as a standard reference work and was found in every monastic library of note.

The translations and compilations made by Boethius, Cassiodorus, and Isidore, the books collected and copied by monks and nuns, and the schools established in monasteries (particularly those in Ireland, England, and Italy) kept intellectual life from dying out completely in the Early Middle Ages.

The Church: Shaper of Medieval Civilization

Christianity was the integrating principle and the church was the dominant institution of the Middle Ages. During the Late Roman Empire, as the Roman state and its institutions decayed, the church gained in power and importance. Its organization grew stronger, and its membership increased. Unlike the Roman state, the church was a healthy and vital organism. The elite of the Roman Empire had severed its commitment to the values of classical civilization, whereas the church leaders were intensely devoted to their faith.

When the Empire collapsed, the church retained the Roman administrative system and preserved elements of Greco-Roman civilization. A unifying and civilizing agent, the church provided people with an intelligible and purposeful conception of life and death. In a dying world, the church was the only

Painting of Saint Matthew from the Gospel Book of Charlemagne, c. 800–810. Handwritten and very costly, sacred books were often lavishly illustrated with minature paintings. In this painting, Saint Matthew, wearing a Roman toga, is depicted with his pen poised, writing his gospel. Because of the painting's clear Hellenistic style, scholars believe its artist was trained in an Italian or Byzantine school. (*Kunsthistorisches Museum, Vienna*)

institution capable of reconstructing civilized life. Thus, the Christian outlook, rather than the traditions of the German tribes, formed the foundation of medieval civilization. During the course of the Middle Ages, people came to see themselves as participants in a great drama of salvation. There was only one truth: God's revelation to humanity. There was only one avenue to heaven, and it passed through the church. Membership in a universal church replaced citizenship in a universal empire. Across Europe, from Italy to Ireland, a new society centered on Christianity was taking shape.

Monks helped build the foundation of medieval civilization. During the seventh century, intellectual life on the Continent continued its steady decline. In the monasteries of Ireland and England, however, a tradition of learning persisted. Early in the fifth century, Saint Patrick began the conversion of the Irish to Christianity. In Ireland, Latin became firmly entrenched as the language of both the church and scholars at a time when it was in danger of disappearing in many parts of the Continent. Irish monks preserved and cultivated Latin and even preserved some knowledge of Greek, and during their missionary activities, they revived the use of Latin on the Continent. In England, the Anglo-Saxons, both men and women, who converted to Christianity mainly in the seventh century, also established monasteries that kept learning alive. In the sixth and seventh centuries, Irish and Anglo-Saxon monks became the chief agents for converting people in northern Europe. Thus, monks and nuns made possible a unitary European civilization, based on a Christian foundation. By copying and preserving ancient texts, they also kept alive elements of ancient civilization.

During the Early Middle Ages, when cities were in decay, monasteries, whose libraries contained theological works and ancient Latin classics, were the principal cultural centers; they would remain so until the rebirth of towns in the High Middle Ages. Monasteries also offered succor to the sick and the destitute and served as places of refuge for travelers. To the medieval mind, the monks' and nuns' selfless devotion to God, adoption of apostolic poverty, and dedication to prayer and contemplation represented the highest expression of the Christian way of life; it was the finest and most certain path to salvation.

The Early Middle Ages were a formative period for the papacy, as well as for society in general. A decisive figure in the strengthening of the papacy was Gregory I, known as the Great (590–604). One of the ablest of medieval popes, Gregory used Roman methods of administration to organize papal property in Italy, Sicily, Sardinia, Gaul, and other regions effectively. He strengthened his authority over bishops and monks, dispatched missionaries to England to win over the Anglo-Saxons, and set his sights on an alliance with the Franks. Finally materializing 150 years later, this alliance helped shape medieval history.

The Kingdom of the Franks

From their homeland in the Rhine River valley, the Frankish tribes had expanded into Roman territory during the fourth and fifth centuries. The ruler Clovis united the various Frankish tribes and conquered most of Gaul. In 496, he converted to Roman Christianity. Clovis's conversion to Catholicism was an event of great significance. A number of other German kings had adopted the Arian form of Christianity, which the church had declared heretical. By embracing Roman Christianity, the Franks became a potential ally of the papacy.

Clovis's successors could not maintain control over their lands, and power passed to the mayor of the palace, the king's chief officer. Serving as mayor of the palace from 717 to 741, Charles Martel subjected all Frankish lands to his rule. In addition, at the battle of Tours in 732, he defeated the Muslims. Although the Muslims continued to occupy the Iberian Peninsula, they would advance no farther north into Europe.

Charles Martel was succeeded by his son Pepin the Short, who in 751 deposed the king. With the approval of the papacy and his nobles, Pepin was crowned king by Boniface, a prominent bishop. Two years later, Pope Stephen II anointed Pepin again as king of the Franks and appealed to him to protect the papacy from the Lombards, the last German tribe to invade formerly Roman territory. Pepin crossed into Italy, defeated the Lombards, and turned over captured lands to the papacy. This famous Donation of Pepin made the pope ruler of the territory between Rome and Ravenna, which became known as the Papal States.

The Era of Charlemagne

The alliance between the Franks and the papacy was continued by Pepin's successor, Charlemagne (Charles the Great), who ruled from 768 to 814.

Map 6.1   The Carolingian World

Charlemagne continued the Carolingian policy of expanding the Frankish kingdom. He destroyed the Lombard kingdom and declared himself king of the Lombards. He added Bavaria to his kingdom, and after long, terrible wars, he forced the Saxons to submit to his rule and convert to Christianity. He also conquered a region in northern Spain, the Spanish March, which served as a buffer between the Christian Franks and the Muslims in Spain.

Immense difficulties arose in governing the expanded territories. Size seemed an insuperable obstacle to effective government, particularly since Charlemagne's administrative structure, lacking in trained personnel, was primitive by Islamic, Byzantine, or Roman standards. The empire was divided into about 250 counties, administered by counts — nobles who were personally loyal to the ruler and who implemented the king's decisions.

On Christmas Day in Rome in the year 800, Pope Leo III crowned Charlemagne emperor of the Romans. The title signified that the tradition of a world empire still survived, despite the demise of the Western Roman Empire three hundred years earlier. But because the pope crowned Charlemagne, the emperor now had a spiritual responsibility to spread and defend the faith. Thus, Roman universalism was fused with Christian universalism.

The Frankish empire, of course, was only a dim shadow of the Roman Empire. The Franks had no Roman law or Roman legions; there were no cities that were centers of economic and cultural activity; and officials were not trained civil servants with a world outlook, but uneducated war chieftains with a tribal viewpoint. Yet Charlemagne's empire did embody the concept of a universal Christian empire — an ideal that would endure throughout the Middle Ages.

The crowning of a German ruler as emperor of the Romans by the head of the church represented the merging of German, Christian, and Roman traditions, which is the essential characteristic of medieval civilization. This blending of traditions was also evident on a cultural plane, for Charlemagne, a German warrior-king, showed respect for classical learning and Christianity, both non-Germanic traditions.

Charlemagne believed that it was his religious duty to raise the educational level of the clergy so that they understood and could properly teach the faith. He also fostered education to train administrators who would be capable of overseeing his empire and royal estates; such men had to be literate. To achieve his purpose, Charlemagne gathered some of the finest scholars in Europe. Alcuin of York, England (735–804), was given charge of the palace school, attended by Charlemagne and his family, high lords, and youths training to serve the emperor. Throughout Gaul, Alcuin expanded schools and libraries, promoted the copying of ancient manuscripts, and imposed basic literacy standards on the clergy.

The focus of the Carolingian Renaissance — the cultural revival produced by Charlemagne's teachers and scholars — was predominantly Christian: an effort to train clergymen and improve their understanding of the Bible and the writings of the church fathers. This process raised the level of literacy and improved the Latin style. Most important, monastic copyists continued to preserve ancient texts, which otherwise might never have survived. The oldest surviving manuscripts of many ancient works are Carolingian copies.

Compared with the Greco-Roman past, with the cultural explosion of the twelfth and thirteenth centuries, or with the great Italian Renaissance of the fifteenth century, the Carolingian Renaissance seems slight indeed. But we must bear in mind the cultural poverty that prevailed before the era of Charlemagne. The Carolingian Renaissance reversed the process of cultural decay that characterized much of the Early Middle Ages. Learning would never again fall to the low level it had reached in the centuries following the decline of Rome.

During the era of Charlemagne, a distinct European civilization emerged. It blended the Roman heritage of a world empire, the intellectual achievement of the Greco-Roman mind, Christian otherworldliness, and the customs of the Germanic peoples. This nascent Western European civilization differed from Byzantine and Islamic civilizations, and Europeans were growing conscious of the difference. But the new medieval civilization was still centuries away from its high point, which would be reached in the twelfth and thirteenth centuries.

Charlemagne's empire also engendered the ideal of a unified Latin Christendom: a single Christian community under one government. Over the centuries, the pursuit of this ideal of a Christian world-state, Christendom, would inspire many people, both clergy and laity.

The Breakup of Charlemagne's Empire

After Charlemagne's death in 814, his son, Louis the Pious, inherited the throne. Louis aimed to preserve the empire, but the task was virtually impossible. The empire's strength rested more on Charlemagne's personal qualities than on any firm economic or political foundation. Moreover, the empire was simply too large and consisted of too many diverse peoples to be governed effectively. Besides Frankish nobles, who sought to increase their own power at the emperor's expense, Louis had to deal with his own rebellious sons. After Louis died in 840, the empire was divided among the three surviving sons.

The Treaty of Verdun in 843 gave Louis the German the eastern part of the empire, which marked the beginning of Germany; to Charles the Bald went the western part, which was the start of France; and Lothair received the Middle Kingdom, which extended from Rome to the North Sea. This Middle Kingdom would be an area of conflict between France and Germany right into the twentieth century. As central authority waned, large landowners increasingly exercised authority in their own regions. Simultaneous invasions from all directions furthered this movement toward localism and decentralization.

In the ninth and tenth centuries, Latin Christendom was attacked on all sides. From bases in North Africa, Spain, and southern Gaul, Muslims ravaged regions of southern Europe, even as far as the suburbs of Rome. The Magyars, originally from Western Asia, had established themselves on the plains of the Danube; their horsemen launched lightning raids into northern Italy, Western Germany, and parts of France. Defeated in Germany in 933 and again in 955, the Magyars withdrew to what is now Hungary; they ceased their raids and adopted Christianity.

Still another group of invaders, the Northmen, or Vikings, sailed south from Scandinavia in their long, wooden ships to raid the coasts and river valleys of Western Europe. Villages were devastated, ports were destroyed, and the population was decimated. Trade came to a standstill, coins no longer circulated, and farms turned into wastelands. Already gravely weakened, the European economy collapsed. The political authority of kings disappeared, and cultural life and learning withered.

These terrible attacks heightened political insecurity and accelerated anew the process of decentralization that had begun with the decline of Rome. During these chaotic times, counts came to regard as their own the land that they administered and defended for their king. Similarly, the inhabitants of a district looked on the count or local lord as their ruler, for his men and fortresses protected them. In their regions, nobles exercised public power formerly held by kings. Europe had entered an age of feudalism, in which the essential unit of government was not a kingdom but a county or castellany, and political power was the private possession of local lords.

Feudal Society

Arising during a period of collapsing central authority, invasion, scanty public revenues, and declining commerce and town life, feudalism attempted to provide some order and security. Feudalism was not a planned system derived logically from general principles, but rather an improvised response to the challenge posed by ineffectual central authority. Feudal practices were not uniform; they differed from locality to locality, and in some regions they barely took root. Although it was only a stopgap means of governing, feudalism did bring some order, justice, and law during an era of breakdown, localism, and transition. It remained the predominant political arrangement until kings reasserted their authority in the High and Late Middle Ages.

Vassalage

Feudal relationships enabled lords to increase their military strength. The need for military support was the principal reason for the practice of vassalage, in which a knight, in a solemn ceremony, pledged loyalty to a lord. This feature of feudalism derived from an ancient German ceremony, during which warriors swore personal allegiance to the head of the war-band. Among other things, the vassal gave military service to his lord and received in return a *fief,* which was usually land. This fief was inhabited by peasants, and the crops that they raised provided the vassal with his means of support.

Besides rendering military assistance and supplying knights, the vassal owed several other obligations to his lord in return for the fief and the lord's protection. These duties included sitting in the lord's court and judging cases, such as the breach of feudal agreements between the lord and his other vassals; providing lodgings when the lord traveled through the vassal's territory; offering a gift when the lord's son was knighted or when his eldest daughter married; and raising a ransom should the lord be captured by an enemy.

Generally, both lord and vassal felt honor-bound to abide by the oath of loyalty. It became an accepted custom for a vassal to renounce his loyalty to his lord if the latter failed to protect the vassal from enemies, mistreated him, or increased his obligations as fixed by the feudal contract. On the other hand, if a vassal did not live up to his obligations, the lord would summon him to his court, where he would be tried for treachery. If found guilty, the vassal could lose his fief and perhaps his life. At times, disputes between vassals and lords erupted into warfare. Because a vassal often held land from more than one lord and sometimes was himself a lord to vassals, situations frequently became awkward, complex, and confusing. On occasion, a vassal had to decide to which lord he owed *liege homage* (prime loyalty).

As feudalism evolved, the king came to be regarded as the chief lord, who had granted fiefs to the great lords, who in turn had divided them into smaller units and regranted them to vassals. Thus, all members of the ruling class, from the lowliest knights to the king, occupied a place in the feudal hierarchy. In theory, the king was the highest political authority and the source of land tenure, but in actual fact he was often less powerful than other nobles of the realm. Feudalism declined when kings converted their theoretical powers into actual powers. The decline of feudalism was a gradual process; conflict between the crown and the aristocracy persisted, with varying degrees of intensity, for several centuries, but the future belonged to the centralized state being shaped by kings, not to feudal fragmentation.

Feudal Warriors

Feudal lords viewed manual labor and commerce as degrading for men of their rank. They considered only one vocation worthy: that of warrior. Through combat, the lord demonstrated his valor, earned his reputation, measured his individual worth, derived excitement, added to his wealth, and defended his rights. Warfare gave meaning to his life. During the twelfth century, to relieve the boredom of peacetime, nobles staged gala tournaments in which knights, fighting singly or in teams, engaged each other in battle to prove their skill and courage and to win honor. The feudal glorification of combat became deeply ingrained in Western society and endured into the twentieth century. Over the centuries, a code of behavior, called *chivalry*, evolved for the feudal nobility. A true knight was expected to fight bravely, demonstrate loyalty to his lord, and treat other knights with respect and courtesy.

In time, the church interjected a religious element into the warrior culture of the feudal knight. It sought to use the fighting spirit of the feudal class for Christian ends: knights could assist the clergy in enforcing God's will. Thus, a Christian component was added to the Germanic tradition of loyalty and courage. As a Christian gentleman, a knight was expected to honor the laws of the church and to wield his sword in the service of God.

Regarding the private warfare of lords as lawless violence that menaced social life, the church, in the eleventh century, imposed strictures called the Peace of God and the Truce of God. These restrictions limited feudal warfare to certain days of the week and certain times of the year. Although only partially effective, the Peace of God did offer Christian society some respite from plundering and incessant warfare.

Noblewomen

Feudal society was very much a man's world. In theory, women were deemed to be physically, morally, and intellectually inferior to men. Although the church taught that both men and women were precious to God and that mar-

Noblewomen. At times, a medieval lady would join her husband's hunting party. *(Universitat Bibliothek, Heidelberg, cod. Pal. Germ.048 Fol, 64r/AKG London)*

riage was a sacred rite, clergymen viewed women as agents of the Devil — evil temptresses who, like the biblical Eve, lured men into sin. Women were subjected to male authority. Fathers arranged the marriages of their daughters. Girls from aristocratic families were generally married at age sixteen or younger to men often twice their age; frequently, aristocratic girls who did not marry had to enter a convent. The wife of a lord was at the mercy of her husband; if she annoyed him, she might expect a beating. But as the lady of the castle, she performed important duties. She assigned tasks to the servants; made medicines; preserved food; taught young girls how to sew, spin, and weave; and, despite her subordinate position, took charge of the castle when her husband was away.

The nunneries provided an outlet for the talents of unmarried noblewomen. Abbesses demonstrated organizational skills in supervising the convent's affairs. Some nuns acquired an education and, like their male counterparts, copied manuscripts and thus preserved knowledge and ideas of the past. The nun Hroswitha (c. 935–c. 1001) of Gandersheim, in Saxony, Germany, produced poetry, history, and plays. Inspired by the Roman poet Terence, she wrote six dramas — the first since Roman times — along with a history of German rulers and one of her own convent.

Agrarian Society

Feudalism was built on an economic foundation known as *manorialism*. Although pockets of free peasantry remained, a village community (manor) consisting of serfs bound to the land became the essential agricultural arrangement for much of the Middle Ages. The manorial village was the means of organizing an agricultural society with limited markets and money. Neither the lords who warred nor the clergy who prayed performed economically productive work. Their ways of life were made possible by the toil of serfs.

The origins of manorialism can be traced in part to the Late Roman Empire, when peasants depended on the owners of large estates for protection and security. This practice developed further during the Early Middle Ages, especially during the invasions of Northmen, Magyars, and Muslims in the ninth and tenth centuries. Peasants continued to sacrifice their freedom in exchange for protection; in some cases, they were too weak to resist the encroachments of local magnates. Like feudalism, manorialism was not an orderly system; it consisted of improvised relationships and practices that varied from region to region.

A lord controlled at least one manorial village; great lords might possess hundreds. A small manor had a dozen families; a large one had as many as fifty or sixty. The manorial village was never completely self-sufficient because salt, millstones, and metalware were generally obtained from outside sources. It did, however, constitute a balanced economic setting. Peasants grew grain and raised cattle, sheep, goats, and hogs; blacksmiths, carpenters, and stonemasons did the building and repairing; the village priest cared for the souls of the inhabitants; and the lord defended the manor and administered the customary law. The serf and his family lived in a dismal, one-room cottage that they shared with chickens and pigs. In the center burned a small fire, the smoke escaping through a hole in the roof. In cold weather when the fire was strong, the room was filled with smoke. When it rained, water came through the thatched roof and turned the earth floor into mud. The odor from animal excrement was ever present.

When a manor was attacked by another lord, the peasants found protection inside the walls of their lord's house. By the twelfth century, in many places, this building had become a well-fortified stone castle. Peasants generally lived, worked, and died on the lord's estate and were buried in the village churchyard. Few had any contact with the world beyond the village of their birth.

In return for protection and the right to cultivate fields and to pass these holdings on to their children, the serfs owed obligations to their lord, and their personal freedom was restricted in a variety of ways. Bound to the land, they could not leave the manor without the lord's consent. Before a serf could marry, he had to obtain the lord's permission and pay a fee. The lord could select a wife for his serf and force him to marry her. Sometimes, a serf, objecting to the lord's choice, preferred to pay a fine. These rules also applied to the serf's children, who inherited their parents' obligations. In addition to working their allotted land, the serfs had to tend the fields reserved for the lord.

Other services exacted by the lord included digging ditches, gathering fire-wood, building fences, repairing roads and bridges, and sewing clothes. Probably somewhat more than half of a serf's workweek was devoted to fulfilling these labor obligations. Serfs also paid a variety of dues to the lord, including payments for using the lord's mill, bake-oven, and winepress.

Serfs did derive some benefits from manorial relationships. They received protection during a chaotic era, and they possessed customary rights, which the lord often respected, to cottages and farmlands. If a lord demanded more services or dues than was customary, or if he interfered with their right to cottages or strips of farmland, the peasants might demonstrate their discontent by refusing to labor for the lord. Until the fourteenth century, however, open rebellion was rare because lords possessed considerable military and legal power. The manorial system promoted attitudes of dependency and servility among the serfs; their hopes for a better life were directed toward heaven.

Economic Expansion During the High Middle Ages

Manorialism and feudalism presupposed a hierarchical, organic, and stable social order: clergy who prayed, lords who fought, and peasants who toiled. People believed that society functioned smoothly when all individuals accepted their status and performed their proper role. Consequently, a person's rights, duties, and relationship to law depended on his or her ranking in the social order. To change position was to upset the organic unity of society. And no one, serfs included, should be deprived of the traditional rights associated with his or her rank. This arrangement was justified by the clergy, who maintained that "God himself has willed that among men, some must be lords and some serfs."[2]

During the High Middle Ages (1050–1300), however, the revival of urban economy and the reemergence of central authority undermined feudal and manorial relationships. By the end of the eleventh century, Europe showed many signs of recovery. The invasions of Magyars and Vikings had ended, and powerful lords and kings imposed greater order in their territories. A period of economic vitality, the High Middle Ages witnessed an agricultural revolution, a commercial revolution, the rebirth of towns, and the rise of an enterprising and dynamic middle class.

An Agricultural Revolution

Important advances were made in agriculture during the Middle Ages. Many of these innovations occurred in the Early Middle Ages but were only gradually adopted and were not used everywhere. In time, however, they markedly increased production. By the end of the thirteenth century, medieval agriculture had reached a technical level far superior to that of the ancient world.

One innovation was a heavy plow that cut deeply into the soil. This new plow enabled farmers to work more quickly and effectively. As a result, they could cultivate more land, including the heavy, moist soils of northern Europe, which had offered too much resistance to the light plow. Another important advance in agricultural technology was the invention of the collar harness. The old yoke harness worked well with oxen, but it tended to choke horses — and horses, because they move faster and have greater stamina than oxen, are more valuable for agricultural work. The widening use of the water mill by the tenth century and the introduction of windmills in the twelfth century saved labor in grinding grain; these inventions replaced ancient hand-worked mills.

The gradual emergence of the three-field system of managing agricultural land, particularly in northern Europe, increased production. In the old, widely used two-field system, half the land was planted in autumn with winter wheat, while the other half was left fallow to restore its fertility. In the new three-field system, one third of the land was planted in autumn with winter wheat, a second third was planted the following spring with oats and vegetables, and the last third remained fallow. The advantages of the three-field system were that two-thirds of the land was farmed and only one-third left unused and that the diversification of crops made more vegetable protein available.

Higher agricultural production reduced the number of deaths from starvation and dietary disease and thus contributed to a population increase. Soon the farmlands of a manorial village could not support its growing population. Consequently, peasants had to look beyond their immediate surroundings and colonize trackless wastelands. Lords vigorously promoted this conversion of uncultivated soil into agricultural land because it increased their incomes. Monastic communities also actively engaged in this enterprise. Almost everywhere, peasants were draining swamps, clearing forests, and establishing new villages. Their endeavors during the eleventh and twelfth centuries brought vast areas of Europe under cultivation for the first time. New agricultural land was also acquired through expansion, the most notable example being the organized settlement of lands to the east by German colonists.

The colonizing and cultivation of virgin lands contributed to the decline of serfdom. Lords owned vast tracts of forests and swamps that would substantially increase their incomes if cleared, drained, and farmed. But serfs were often unwilling to move from their customary homes and fields to do the hard labor needed to cultivate these new lands. To lure serfs away from their villages, lords promised them freedom from most or all personal services. In many cases, the settlers fulfilled their obligations to the lord by paying rent rather than by performing services or providing foodstuffs, thus making the transition from serfs to freemen. In time, they came to regard the land as their own.

The improvement in agricultural technology and the colonization of new lands altered the conditions of life in Europe. Surplus food and the increase in population freed people to work at nonfarming occupations, making possible the expansion of trade and the revival of town life.

The Revival of Trade

Expanding agricultural production, the end of Viking attacks, greater political stability, and an increasing population brought about a revival of commerce. During the Early Middle Ages, Italians and Jews kept alive a small amount of long-distance trade between Catholic Europe and the Byzantine and Islamic worlds. In the eleventh century, sea forces of Italian trading cities cleared the Mediterranean of Muslim fleets that preyed on Italian shipping. As in Roman times, goods could circulate once again from one end of the sea to the other. In the twelfth and thirteenth centuries, local, regional, and long-distance trade gained such momentum that some historians describe the period as a commercial revolution that surpassed the commercial activity of the Roman Empire during the Pax Romana.

Crucial to the growth of trade were international fairs, where merchants and craftspeople set up stalls and booths to display their wares. Because of ever-present robbers, lords provided protection for merchants carrying their wares to and from fairs. Each fair lasted about three to six weeks; then the merchants would move on to another site. The Champagne region in northeastern France was the great center for fairs.

The principal arteries of trade flowed between the Eastern Mediterranean and the Italian cities; between Scandinavia and the Atlantic coast; between northern France, Flanders, and England; and from the Baltic Sea in the north to the Black Sea and Constantinople via Russian rivers.

Increased economic activity led to advances in business techniques. Since individual merchants often lacked sufficient capital for large-scale enterprises, groups of merchants formed partnerships. By enabling merchants to pool their capital, reduce their risks, and expand their knowledge of profit-making opportunities, these arrangements furthered commerce. Underwriters insured cargoes; the development of banking and credit instruments made it unnecessary for merchants to carry large amounts of cash. The international fairs not only were centers of international trade, but also served as capital markets for international credit transactions. The arrangements made by fair-going merchants to settle their debts were the origin of the bill of exchange, which allowed one currency to be converted into another. The invention of double-entry bookkeeping gave merchants an overview of their financial situation: the value of their goods and their ready cash. Without such knowledge, no large-scale commercial activity could be conducted on a continuous basis. Another improvement in business techniques was the formation of commercial law, which defined the rules of conduct for debts and contracts.

The Rise of Towns

In the eleventh century, towns emerged anew throughout Europe, and in the twelfth, they became active centers of commercial and intellectual life. Towns were a new and revolutionary force — socially, economically, and culturally. A new class of merchants and craftspeople came into being. This new class —

the middle class — was made up of those who, unlike the lords and serfs, were not affiliated with the land. The townsman was a new man, with a different value system from that of the lord, the serf, and the clergyman.

One reason for town growth was the increased food supply stemming from advances in agricultural technology. Surplus farm production meant that the countryside could support an urban population of artisans and professionals. Another reason for the rise of urban centers was the expansion of trade. Towns emerged in locations that were natural for trade: seacoasts, river-banks, crossroads, and market sites; they also sprang up outside fortified castles and monasteries and on surviving Roman sites. The colonies of merchants who gathered at these places were joined by peasants skilled in crafts or willing to work as laborers. Most towns had a small population. The largest ones — Florence, Ghent, and Paris — had between fifty thousand and a hundred thousand inhabitants. Covering only small areas, these walled towns were crowded with people.

Merchants and artisans organized guilds to protect their members from outside competition. The merchant guild in a town prevented outsiders from doing much business. A craftsman new to a town had to be admitted to the guild of his trade before he could open a shop. Competition between members of the same guild was discouraged. To prevent one guild member from making significantly more money than another, a guild required its members to work the same number of hours, pay employees the same wages, produce goods of equal quality, and charge customers a just price. These rules were strictly enforced.

Women took an active part in the economic life of towns, working with men, usually their husbands, in the various crafts — as cobblers, tailors, hatters, bakers, goldsmiths, and so forth. Women brewed beer, made and sold charcoal, sold vegetables, fish, and poultry, and ran inns. In many towns, the wives and widows of master craftsmen were admitted to guilds. These guildswomen had many of the privileges of a master, including the right to train apprentices.

Because many towns were situated on land belonging to lords or on the sites of old Roman towns ruled by bishops, these communities at first came under feudal authority. In some instances, lords encouraged the founding of towns, for urban industry and commerce brought wealth to the region. However, tensions soon developed between merchants, who sought freedom from feudal restrictions, since they interfered with the pursuit of financial gain, and lords and bishops, who wanted to preserve their authority over the towns. Townspeople, or burghers, refused to be treated as serfs bound to a lord and liable for personal services and customary dues. The burghers wanted to travel, trade, marry, and dispose of their property as they pleased; they wanted to make their own laws and levy their own taxes. Sometimes by fighting, but more often by payments of money, the townspeople obtained charters from the lords giving them the right to set up their own councils. These assemblies passed laws, collected taxes, and formed courts that enforced the laws. Towns became more or less self-governing city-states, the first since Greco-Roman days.

In a number of ways, towns loosened the hold of lords on serfs. Seeking freedom and fortune, serfs fled to the new towns, where, according to custom, lords could no longer reclaim them after a year and a day. Enterprising serfs earned money by selling food to the townspeople. When they acquired a sufficient sum, they bought their freedom from lords, who needed cash to pay for goods bought from merchants. Lords increasingly began to accept fixed cash payments from serfs in place of labor services or foodstuffs. As serfs met their obligations to lords with money, they gradually became rent-paying tenants and, in time, were no longer bound to the lord's land. The manorial system of personal relations and mutual obligations was disintegrating.

The activities of townspeople made them a new breed; they engaged in business and had money and freedom. Their world was the market rather than the church, the castle, or the manor. Townspeople were freeing themselves from the prejudices both of feudal aristocrats, who considered trade and manual work degrading, and of the clergy, who cursed the pursuit of riches as an obstacle to salvation. The townspeople were critical, dynamic, and progressive — a force for change. Medieval towns nurtured the origins of the *bourgeoisie* (literally, "citizens of the burg," the walled town), the urban middle class, which would play a crucial role in modern European history.

The Rise of States

The revival of trade and the growth of towns were signs of the vitality of Latin Christendom. Another sign of strength was the greater order and security provided by the emergence of states. Aided by educated and trained officials who enforced royal law, tried people in royal courts, and collected royal taxes, kings expanded their territory and slowly fashioned strong central governments. These developments laid the foundations of European states. Not all areas followed the same pattern. Whereas England and France achieved a large measure of unity during the Middle Ages, Germany and Italy remained divided into numerous independent territories.

England

In 1066, the Normans — those Northmen who had first raided and then settled in France — conquered Anglo-Saxon England. Determined to establish effective control over his new kingdom, William the Conqueror (1027–1087), duke of Normandy, kept a sixth of conquered England for himself. In accordance with feudal practice, he distributed the rest among his Norman nobles, who swore an oath of loyalty to William and provided him with military assistance. But William made certain that no feudal baron had enough land or soldiers to threaten his power. Because he had conquered England in one stroke, his successors did not have to travel the long, painful road to national unity that French monarchs had to take.

To strengthen royal control, William retained some Anglo-Saxon administrative practices. The land remained divided into *shires* (counties) administered by *sheriffs* (royal agents). This structure gave the king control over local government. To determine how much money he could demand, William ordered a vast census to be taken of people and property in every village. These data were compiled in the *Domesday Book,* which listed the number of tenants, cattle, sheep, and pigs and the quantities of farm equipment throughout the realm. Thus, William knew his kingdom's assets better than any other monarch of his day.

A crucial development in shaping national unity was the emergence of common law. During the reigns of Henry I (1100–1135) and Henry II (1154–1189), royal judges traveled to different parts of the kingdom. Throughout England, important cases began to be tried in the king's court rather than in local courts, thereby increasing royal power. The decisions of royal judges were recorded and used as guides for future cases. In this way, a law common to the whole land gradually came to prevail over the customary law of a specific locality. Because common law applied to all England, it served as a force for unity. It also provided a fairer system of justice. Common law remains the foundation of the English legal system and the legal systems of lands settled by English people, including the United States.

Henry II made trial by jury a regular procedure for many cases heard in the king's court, thus laying the foundations of the modern judicial system. Twelve men familiar with the facts of the case appeared before the king's justices and were asked under oath if the plaintiff's statement was true. The justices based their decisions on the answers. Henry II also ordered representatives of a given locality to report under oath to visiting royal judges any local persons who were suspected of murder or robbery. This indictment jury was the ancestor of the modern grand jury system.

King John (1199–1216) inadvertently precipitated a situation that led to another step in the political development of England. Fighting a costly and losing war with the king of France, John coerced his vassals into giving him more and more revenue; he had also punished some vassals without a proper trial. In 1215, the angry barons rebelled and compelled John to fix his seal to a document called the *Magna Carta,* or Great Charter. The Magna Carta is celebrated as the root of the uniquely English respect for basic rights and liberties. Although essentially a feudal document directed against a king who had violated the rights of feudal barons, the Magna Carta stated certain principles that could be interpreted more widely.

Over the centuries, these principles were expanded to protect the liberties of the English against governmental oppression. The Magna Carta stated that no unusual feudal dues "shall be imposed in our kingdom except by the common consent of our kingdom." In time, this right came to mean that the king could not levy taxes without the consent of Parliament, the governmental body that represents the English people. The Magna Carta also provided that "no freeman shall be taken or imprisoned . . . save by the lawful judgment of his peers or by the law of the land." The barons who drew up the document had in-

The Battle of Hastings A.D. **1066: Scene from the Bayeux Tapestry, France, Eleventh Century.**   This battle sealed the conquest of England by William, Duke of Normandy. The French-speaking Normans now governed the native Anglo-Saxons; eventually both Normans and Anglo-Saxons fused into a single people, the English. The Bayeux Tapestry depicts seventy scenes of the conquest and is significant as both a work of art and a historical source. (*Tapisserie de la Reine Mathilde, Ville de Bayeux, France*)

tended it to mean that they must be tried by fellow barons. As time passed, these words were regarded as a guarantee of trial by jury for all men, a prohibition against arbitrary arrest, and a command to dispense justice fully, freely, and equally. Implied in the Magna Carta is the idea that the king cannot rule as he pleases but must govern according to the law — that not even the king can violate the law of the nation. Centuries afterward, when Englishmen sought to limit the king's power, they would interpret the Magna Carta in this way.

Anglo-Saxon England had retained the Germanic tradition that the king should consider the advice of the leading men in the land. Later, William the Conqueror continued this practice by seeking the opinions of leading nobles and bishops. In the thirteenth century, it became accepted custom that the king should not decide major issues without consulting these advisers, who assembled in the Great Council. Lesser nobility and townspeople also began to be summoned to meet with the king. These two groups were eventually called the House of Lords (bishops and nobles) and the House of Commons (knights and burghers). Thus, the English Parliament evolved; by the mid-fourteenth century, it had become a permanent institution of government. Frequently in need of money but unable to levy new taxes without the approval of Parliament, the king had to turn to that body for help. Over the centuries, Parliament would use this control over money matters to increase its power. The tradition grew that the power to govern rested not with the king alone, but with the king and Parliament together.

During the Middle Ages, England became a centralized and unified state. The king, however, did not have unlimited power; he was not above the law.

The rights of the people were protected by certain principles implicit in the common law and the Magna Carta and by the emergence of Parliament.

France

In the 150 years after Charlemagne's death, the western part of his empire, which was destined to become France, faced terrible ordeals. Charlemagne's heirs fought one another for the crown; the Vikings raided everywhere their ships would carry them; Muslims from Spain plundered the southern coast; and strong lords usurped power for themselves. With the Carolingian family unable to maintain the throne, the great lords bestowed the title of king on one of their own. In 987, they chose Hugh Capet (987–996), the count of Paris. Because many great lords held territories far larger than those of Hugh, the French king did not seem a threat to noble power. But Hugh strengthened the French monarchy by having the lords also elect his son as his coruler. This practice continued until it became understood that the crown would remain with the Capetian family.

With the accession of Louis VI (1108–1137), a two-hundred-year period of steadily increasing royal power began. Louis started this trend by successfully subduing the barons in his own duchy. A decisive figure in the expansion of royal power was Philip Augustus (1180–1223). Philip struck successfully at King John of England (of Magna Carta fame), who held more territory as feudal lord in France than Philip did. When William, duke of Normandy, in Western France, conquered England in 1066, he became ruler of England and Normandy; William's great-grandson Henry II acquired much of southern France through his marriage to Eleanor of Aquitaine (c. 1122–1204) in 1152. Thus, as a result of the Norman Conquest and intermarriage, the destinies of France and England were closely intertwined until the end of the Middle Ages. By stripping King John of most of his French territory (Normandy, Anjou, and much of Aquitaine), Philip trebled the size of his kingdom and became stronger than any French lord.

In the thirteenth century, the power of the French monarch continued to grow. Departing from feudal precedent, Louis IX (1226–1270) issued ordinances for the entire realm without seeking the consent of his vassals. Kings added to their lands through warfare and marriage. They also devised new ways of raising money, including taxing the clergy. A particularly effective way of increasing the monarch's power was by extending royal justice; many cases previously tried in lords' courts were transferred to the king's court.

At the beginning of the fourteenth century, Philip IV (the Fair) engaged in a struggle with the papacy. Seeking to demonstrate that he had the support of his subjects, Philip convened a national assembly — the Estates General — representing the clergy, the nobility, and the townspeople. This assembly would be called again to vote funds for the crown. But unlike the English Parliament, the Estates General never became an important body in French political life, and it never succeeded in controlling the monarch. Whereas the basis for limited monarchy had been established in England, no comparable checks on the king's power developed in France. By the end of the Middle Ages, French kings had succeeded in creating a unified state. But regional and local loyalties remained strong and persisted for centuries.

Germany

After the destruction of Charlemagne's empire, its German territories were broken into large duchies. Following an ancient German practice, the ruling dukes elected one of their own as king. The German king, however, had little authority outside his own duchy. Some German kings tried not to antagonize the dukes, but Otto the Great (936–973) was determined to control them. He entered into an alliance with German bishops and archbishops, who could provide him with fighting men and trained administrators — a policy continued by his successors. In 962, emulating the coronation of Charlemagne, the pope crowned Otto "Emperor of the Romans." (Later the title would be changed to Holy Roman emperor.)

Otto and his successors wanted to dominate Italy and the pope — an ambition that embroiled the Holy Roman emperor in a life-and-death struggle with the papacy. The papacy allied itself with the German dukes and the Italian cities, enemies of the emperor. The intervention in papal and Italian politics was the principal reason why German territories did not achieve unity in the Middle Ages.

The Growth of Papal Power

In the High Middle Ages, a growing spiritual vitality accompanied the economic recovery and increased political stability. It was marked by several developments. Within the church, reform movements were attacking clerical abuses, and the papacy was gaining power. A holy war against the Muslims was drawing the Christian community closer together. Furthermore, the church tried with great determination to make society follow divine standards — that is, it tried to shape all institutions and cultural expressions according to a comprehensive Christian outlook.

As the sole interpreters of God's revelation and the sole ministers of his sacraments — sacred rites — the clergy imposed and supervised the moral standards of Christendom. Divine grace was channeled through the sacraments, which could be administered only by the clergy, the indispensable intermediary between the individual and God. On those who resisted its authority, the church could impose the penalty of excommunication (expulsion from the church and denial of the sacraments, without which there could be no salvation).

Gregorian Reform

By the tenth century, the church was Western Europe's leading landholder, owning perhaps a third of the land in Italy and vast properties in other lands.

0   200   400 Km.

0   200   400 Mi.

Baltic Sea

North Sea

ATLANTIC OCEAN

DENMARK

ENGLAND

FRISIA

POMERANIA

POLAND

SAXONY

LUSATIA

THURINGIA

MORAVIA

BOHEMIA

LOWER LORRAINE

UPPER LORRAINE

FRANCONIA

Worms

BAVARIA

AUSTRIA

SWABIA

HUNGARY

BURGUNDY-ARLES

Lyons

FRANCE

Clermont

Avignon

PROVENCE

LOMBARDY

TUSCANY

REPUBLIC OF VENICE

Venice

Zara

Adriatic Sea

PAPAL STATES

Assisi

Rome

Naples

KINGDOM OF SICILY

APULIA

Sicily

BULGARIA

Constantinople

Mediterranean Sea

PORTUGAL

LEON

CASTILE

ARAGON

CATALONIA

VALENCIA

However, the papacy was in no position to exercise commanding leadership over Latin Christendom. The office of pope had fallen under the domination of aristocratic families; they conspired and on occasion murdered in order to place one of their own on the wealthy and powerful throne of Saint Peter. As the papacy became a prize for Rome's leading families, it was not at all unusual for popes themselves to be involved in conspiracies and assassinations. Also weakening the authority of the papacy were local lords, who dominated churches and monasteries by appointing bishops and abbots and by collecting the income from church taxes. These bishops and abbots appointed by lords for political reasons lacked the spiritual devotion to maintain high standards of discipline among the priests and monks.

What raised the power of the papacy to unprecedented heights was the emergence of a reform movement, particularly in French and German monasteries. High-minded monks called for a reawakening of spiritual fervor and the elimination of moral laxity among the clergy. They particularly denounced the concern for worldly goods, the taking of mistresses, and the diminishing commitment to the Benedictine rule. Of the many monasteries that took part in this reform movement, the Benedictine monks of Cluny, in Burgundy, France, were the most influential.

In the middle of the eleventh century, popes came under the influence of the monastic reformers. In 1059, a special synod, convened by the reform-minded Pope Nicholas II, moved to end the interference of Roman nobles and German Holy Roman emperors in choosing the pope. Henceforth, a select group of clergymen in Rome, called *cardinals,* would be responsible for picking a new pontiff.

The reform movement found its most zealous exponent in the person of Hildebrand, who became Pope Gregory VII in 1073. For Gregory, human society was part of a divinely ordered universe, governed by God's universal law. As the supreme spiritual leader of Christendom, the pope was charged with the mission of establishing a Christian society on earth. As successor to Saint Peter, the pope had the final word on matters of faith and doctrine. All bishops came under his authority; so did kings, whose powers should be used for Christian ends. The pope was responsible for instructing rulers in the proper use of their God-given powers, and kings had a solemn duty to obey these instructions. If the king failed in his Christian duty, the pope could deny him his right to rule. Responsible for implementing God's law, the pope could never take a subordinate position to kings.

Like no other pope before him, Gregory VII made a determined effort to assert the preeminence of the papacy over both the church hierarchy and secular rulers. This determination led to a bitter struggle between the papacy and the German monarch and future Holy Roman emperor Henry IV. The dispute was a dramatic confrontation between two competing versions of the relationship between secular and spiritual authority.

◄ **Map 6.2**   The Holy Roman Empire, c. 1200

Through his reforms, Gregory VII intended to improve the moral quality of the clergy and to liberate the church from all control by secular authorities. He forbade priests who had wives or concubines to celebrate Mass, deposed clergy who had bought their offices, excommunicated bishops and abbots who had received their estates from a lay lord, and expelled from the church lay lords who invested bishops with their office. The appointment of bishops, Pope Gregory insisted, should be controlled by the church.

This last point touched off the conflict, called the Investiture Controversy, between Henry and Pope Gregory. Bishops served a dual function. On the one hand, they belonged to the spiritual community of the church; on the other, as members of the nobility and holders of estates, they were also integrated into the feudal order. Traditionally, emperors had both granted bishops their feudal authority and invested them with their spiritual authority. In maintaining that no lay rulers could confer ecclesiastical offices on their appointees, Pope Gregory threatened Henry's authority.

Seeking allies in the conflict with feudal nobility in earlier times, German kings had made vassals of the upper clergy. In return for a fief, bishops had agreed to provide troops for a monarch in his struggle against the lords. But if kings had no control over the appointment of bishops — in accordance with Pope Gregory's view — they would lose the allegiance, military support, and financial assistance of their most important allies. To German monarchs, bishops were officers of the state who served the throne. Moreover, if they agreed to Gregory's demands, German kings would lose their freedom of action and be dominated by the Roman pontiff. Henry IV regarded Gregory VII as a fanatic who trampled on custom, meddled in German state affairs, and challenged legitimate rulers established by God, thereby threatening to subordinate kingship to the papacy.

With the approval of the German bishops, Henry called for Pope Gregory to descend from the throne of Saint Peter. Gregory in turn excommunicated Henry and deposed him as king. German lands were soon embroiled in a civil war, as German lords used the quarrel to strike at Henry's power. Finally, Henry's troops crossed the Alps, successfully attacked Rome, and installed a new pope, who crowned Henry emperor of the Romans. Gregory died in exile in 1085.

In 1122, the papacy and Emperor Henry V reached a compromise. Bishops were to be elected exclusively by the church and invested with the staff and the ring — symbols of spiritual power — by the archbishop, not the king. This change signified that the bishop owed his role as spiritual leader to the church only. But the king would grant the bishop the scepter, to indicate that the bishop was also the recipient of a fief and the king's vassal, owing feudal obligations to the crown. This compromise, called the Concordat of Worms, recognized the dual function of the bishop as a spiritual leader in the church and a feudal landowner. Similar settlements had been reached with the kings of France and England several years earlier.

The conflict between the papacy and the German rulers continued after the Concordat of Worms — a contest for supremacy between the heir of Saint

Peter and the heir of Charlemagne. German monarchs wanted to control the papacy and the prosperous northern Italian cities. When Frederick I (1152–1190), known as Frederick Barbarossa (Red Beard), tried to assert authority over these cities, they resisted. In 1176, the armies of an alliance of Italian cities, supported by the pope, trounced Frederick's forces at the battle of Legnano. The Italian infantry showed that it could defeat knights on horseback, and Frederick was compelled to recognize the independence of the Italian cities. His numerous expeditions to Italy weakened his authority. German princes strengthened themselves at the expense of the monarchy, thereby continuing to preclude German unity.

The Crusades

Like the movement for spiritual renewal associated with the Cluniac reformers, the Crusades — wars to regain the Holy Land from the Muslims — were an outpouring of Christian zeal and an attempt by the papacy to assert its preeminence. Along with the renewal of commerce and the growth of towns, the Crusades signaled the increased vitality and self-confidence of Western Europe. The victims of earlier Muslim attacks, Latin Christians now took the offensive.

The Crusades were also part of a general movement of expansion that took place in Europe during the High Middle Ages. By the middle of the eleventh century, Genoese and Pisans had driven the Muslims from Sardinia. By 1091, Normans from France had taken Sicily from the Muslims and southern Italy from Byzantium. With the support of the papacy, Christian knights engaged in the long struggle to drive the Muslims from Spain; by 1248, after more than two centuries of conflict, only the small southern kingdom of Granada remained in Muslim hands. Germans conquered and colonized lands south of the Baltic coast inhabited by non-Christian Slavs, Balts, and Prussians. German settlers brought with them Christianity and German language and culture. They cleared vast tracts of virgin land for farming and established towns, bishoprics, and monasteries in a region where urban life had been virtually unknown.

Seeking to regain lands taken from Byzantium by the Seljuk Turks, the Byzantine emperor Alexius appealed to the West for mercenaries. Pope Urban II, at the Council of Clermont (in France) in 1095, exaggerated the danger confronting Eastern Christianity. He called for a holy crusade against the heathen Turks, whom he accused of defiling and destroying Christian churches. A Christian army, mobilized by the papacy to defend the faith and to regain the Holy Land from nonbelievers, accorded with the papal concept of a just war; it would channel the endemic violence of Europe's warrior class in a Christian direction.

What motivated the knights and others who responded to Urban's appeal? No doubt the Crusaders regarded themselves as armed pilgrims dedicated to rescuing holy places from the hated Muslims. Moreover, Urban declared that participation in a crusade was itself an act of penance, an acceptable way

Depiction of the Siege of Tyre in 1124.   The fall of the city gave Christians control of the Syrian coast. (*Biliothèque Nationale, Paris*)

of demonstrating sorrow for sin. To the warrior nobility, a crusade was a great adventure, promising land, glory, and plunder, but it was also an opportunity to remit sins by engaging in a holy war. The enthusiasm with which knights became Christian warriors revealed the extent to which Christian principles had permeated the warrior mentality of the nobles.

Stirred by popular preachers, the common people also became gripped by the crusading spirit. The most remarkable of the evangelists was Peter the Hermit. Swayed by this old man's eloquence, thousands of poor people abandoned their villages and joined Peter's march to Jerusalem. After reaching Constantinople, Peter's recruits crossed into Turkish territory, where they were massacred.

An army of Christian knights also departed from Constantinople. In June 1099, three years after leaving Europe, this army stood outside the walls of Jerusalem. Using siege weapons, it broke into the city and slaughtered the Muslim and Jewish inhabitants. Besides capturing Jerusalem, the Crusaders carved out four principalities in the Near East.

Never resigned to the establishment of Christian states in their midst, Muslim leaders called for a jihad, or holy war. In 1144, one of the Crusader states, the County of Edessa, fell to the resurgent forces of Islam. Alarmed by the loss of Edessa, Pope Eugenius II called for the Second Crusade, which was a complete failure.

After 1174, Saladin, a brilliant commander, became the most powerful leader in the Muslim Near East. In 1187, he invaded Palestine, annihilating a Christian army near Nazareth and recapturing Jerusalem. This led to the Third Crusade, in which some of Europe's most prominent rulers took part — Richard I, the Lion-Hearted, of England, Philip Augustus of France, and Frederick Barbarossa of Germany. The Crusaders captured Acre and Jaffa, but Jerusalem remained in Muslim hands.

Pope Innocent III, who called the Fourth Crusade (1202–1204), was enraged by the actions of the Crusaders. They had first attacked the Christian port of Zara, controlled by the king of Hungary, and then looted and defiled churches and massacred Byzantines in Constantinople. This shameful behavior, along with the belief that the papacy was exploiting the crusading ideal to extend its own power, weakened both the crusading zeal of Christendom and the moral authority of the papacy. Other Crusades followed, but the position of the Christian states in the Near East continued to deteriorate. In 1291, almost two centuries after Pope Urban's appeal, the last Christian strongholds in the Near East fell.

The Crusades increased the wealth of the Italian cities that furnished transportation for the Crusaders and benefited from the increased trade with the East. They may have contributed to the decline of feudalism and the strengthening of monarchy because many lords were killed in battle or squandered their wealth financing expeditions to the Holy Land. Over the centuries, some have praised the Crusades for inspiring idealism and heroism. Others, however, have castigated the movement for corrupting the Christian spirit and unleashing religious intolerance and fanaticism — including the massacre of Jews in the Rhineland and of Muslims and Jews in Jerusalem — that would lead to strife in future centuries.

Dissenters and Reformers

Freedom of religion is a modern concept; it was totally alien to the medieval outlook. Regarding itself as the possessor and guardian of divine truth, the church felt a profound obligation to purge Christendom of heresy — beliefs that challenged Christian orthodoxy. To the church, heretics had committed treason against God and were carriers of a deadly infection. Heresy was the work of Satan; lured by false ideas, people might abandon the true faith and deny themselves salvation. In the eyes of the church, heretics not only obstructed individual salvation but also undermined the foundations of society.

To compel obedience, the church used its power of excommunication. An excommunicated person could not receive the sacraments or attend church services — fearful punishments in an age of faith. In dealing with a recalcitrant ruler, the church could declare an interdict on his territory, which in effect denied the ruler's subjects the sacraments (although exceptions could be made). The church hoped that the pressure exerted by an aroused populace would compel the offending ruler to mend his ways.

The church also conducted heresy trials. Before the thirteenth century, local bishops were responsible for finding heretics and putting them on trial. In 1233, the papacy established the Inquisition, a court specially designed to fight heresy. The accused were presumed guilty until proven innocent; they were not told the names of their accusers, nor could they have legal defense. To wrest a confession from the accused, torture (which had been sanctioned by Roman law) was permitted. Those who persisted in their beliefs might be turned over to the civil authorities to be burned at the stake.

The Waldensians   Dissent in the Middle Ages was often reformist in character. Inspired by the Gospels, reformers criticized the church for its wealth and involvement in worldly affairs. They called for a return to the simpler, purer life of Jesus and the Apostles.

In their zeal to emulate the moral purity and material poverty of the first followers of Jesus, these reform-minded dissenters attacked ecclesiastical authority. The Waldensians, followers of Peter Waldo, a rich merchant of Lyons, were a case in point. In the 1170s, Peter distributed his property to the poor and attracted both male and female supporters. Like their leader, the Waldensians committed themselves to poverty and to preaching the Gospel in the vernacular, or native tongue, rather than in the church's Latin, which many Christians did not understand.

The Waldensians considered themselves true Christians, faithful to the spirit of the apostolic church. Repelled by Waldensian attacks against the immorality of the clergy and by the fact that these laypeople were preaching the Gospel without the permission of ecclesiastical authorities, the church condemned the movement as heretical. Despite persecution, however, the Waldensians continued to survive as a group in northern Italy.

The Cathari   Catharism was the most radical heresy to confront the medieval church. This belief represented a curious mixture of Eastern religious movements that had competed with Christianity in the days of the Roman Empire. Cathari tenets differed considerably from those of the church. The Cathari believed in an eternal conflict between the forces of the god of good and those of the god of evil. Because the evil god, whom they identified with the God of the Old Testament, had created the world, this earthly home was evil. The soul, spiritual in nature, was good, but it was trapped in wicked flesh.

The Cathari taught that, since the flesh is evil, Christ would not have taken a human form; hence, he could not have suffered on the cross or have been resurrected. Nor could God have issued forth from the evil flesh of the Virgin. According to Catharism, Jesus was not God but an angel. In order to enslave people, the evil god created the church, which demonstrated its wickedness by pursuing power and wealth. Repudiating the church, the Cathari organized their own ecclesiastical hierarchy.

The center for the Catharist heresy was southern France, where a strong tradition of protest against the moral laxity and materialism of the clergy existed. When the Cathari did not submit to peaceful persuasion, Innocent III called on kings and lords to exterminate Catharism with the sword. Lasting from 1208 to 1229, the war against the Cathari was marked by brutality and fanaticism. Under Innocent's successor, Dominican and Franciscan inquisitors completed the task of exterminating them.

The Franciscans and the Dominicans   Driven by a zeal for reform, devout laypeople condemned the clergy for moral abuses. Sometimes their piety and resentment exploded into heresy; at other times it was channeled into movements that served the church. Such was the case with the two great orders of friars, the Franciscans and the Dominicans.

Like Peter Waldo, Saint Francis of Assisi (c. 1181–1226) came from a wealthy merchant family. After undergoing an intense religious experience, Francis abandoned his possessions and devoted his life to imitating Christ. Dressed as a beggar, he wandered into villages and towns, preaching, healing, and befriending the poor, the helpless, the sick, and even lepers, whom everyone feared to approach. The saintly Francis soon attracted disciples, called Little Brothers, who followed in their leader's footsteps.

As the Franciscans grew in popularity, the papacy exercised greater control over their activities. In time, the order was transformed from a spontaneous movement of inspired laymen into an organized agent of papal policy. The Franciscans served the church as teachers and missionaries in Eastern Europe, North Africa, the Near East, and China. The papacy set aside Francis's prohibition against the Brothers owning churches, houses, and lands corporately. His desire to keep the movement a lay order was abandoned when the papacy granted the Brothers the right to hear confession. Francis's opposition to formal learning as irrelevant to preaching Gospel love was rejected when the movement began to urge university education for its members. Those who protested against these changes as a repudiation of Francis's spirit were persecuted, and a few were even burned at the stake as heretics.

The Dominican order was founded by Saint Dominic (c. 1170–1221), a Spanish nobleman who had preached against the Cathari in southern France. Believing that those who were well versed in Christian teaching could best combat heresy, Dominic, unlike Francis, insisted that his followers engage in study. Eventually, the Dominicans became some of the leading theologians in the universities. Like the Franciscans, they went out into the world to preach the Gospel and to proselytize. Dominican friars became the chief operators of the Inquisition. For their zeal in fighting heresy, they were known as the hounds of the Lord.

Innocent III: The Apex of Papal Power

During the pontificate of Innocent III (1198–1216), papal theocracy reached its zenith. More than any earlier pope, Innocent made the papacy the center of European political life; in the tradition of Gregory VII, he forcefully asserted the theory of papal monarchy. As head of the church, Vicar of Christ, and successor of Saint Peter, Innocent claimed the authority to intervene in the internal affairs of secular rulers when they threatened the good order of Christendom. According to Innocent, the pope, "lower than God but higher than man . . . judges all and is judged by no one."3

Innocent applied these principles of papal supremacy in his dealings with the princes of Europe. When King Philip Augustus of France repudiated Ingeborg of Denmark the day after their wedding and later divorced her to marry someone else, Innocent placed an interdict on France to compel Philip to take Ingeborg back. For two decades, Innocent III championed Ingeborg's cause, until she finally became the French queen. When King John of England rejected the papal candidate for archbishop of Canterbury, Stephen Langton, Innocent first laid an interdict on the country. Then he excommunicated John, who expressed his defiance by confiscating church property and by forcing many bishops into exile. However, when Innocent urged Philip Augustus of France to invade England, John backed down.

Innocent called the Fourth Crusade against the Muslims and a crusade against the heretical Cathari. The culminating expression of Innocent's supremacy was the Fourth Lateran Council, convened in 1215. Comprising some twelve hundred clergy and representatives of secular rulers, the council issued several far-reaching decrees. It maintained that the Eastern Orthodox church was subordinate to the Roman Catholic church. It prohibited the state from taxing the clergy and declared laws detrimental to the church null and void. It also made bishops responsible for ferreting out heretics in their dioceses and ordered secular authorities to punish convicted heretics. Furthermore, the council insisted on high standards of behavior for the clergy and required each Catholic to confess his or her sins to a priest at least once a year and to perform the prescribed penance. Through this directive, the church tightened its control over the conscience of Europe. The council also decreed that in the sacrament of the Eucharist, the body and blood of Christ are actually present in the bread and wine used in the sacrament. This meant that the priest at the altar was God's agent in the performance of a wondrous miracle.

Christians and Jews

In their relations with heretics, pagans, and Muslims, medieval Christians demonstrated a narrow and hostile attitude that ran counter to the Gospel message that all human beings were children of God and that Christ had suffered for all humanity. Muslims were seen, in the words of Pope Urban II, as a "vile breed," "infidels," and "enemies of God."

Medieval Christians also showed hatred for Jews — a visibly alien group in a society dominated by the Christian world-view. In 1096, bands of Crusaders massacred Jews in French and German towns. In 1290, Jews were expelled from England, and in 1306, from France. Between 1290 and 1293, expulsions, massacres, and forced conversions led to the virtual disappearance of a centuries-old Jewish community life in southern Italy. In Germany, savage riots periodically led to the torture and murder of Jews. In 1348–49, when the Black Death (see page 196) raged across Europe, thousands of Jews were burned alive in Basel, Freiburg, Strasbourg, Mainz, and other towns.

Several factors contributed to anti-Jewish feelings during the Middle Ages. To medieval Christians, the refusal of the Jews to embrace Christianity was an act of wickedness, particularly since the church taught that the coming of Christ had been prophesied by the Old Testament. Related to this prejudice was the portrayal of the Crucifixion in the Gospels. In the minds of medieval Christians, the crime of deicide — the killing of God — eternally tainted the Jews as a people. The flames of hatred were fanned by the absurd allegation that Jews, made bloodthirsty by the spilling of Christ's blood, tortured and murdered Christians, particularly children, to obtain blood for ritual purposes. This blood libel was widely believed and incited numerous riots that led to the murder, torture, and expulsion of countless Jews, despite the fact that popes condemned the charge as groundless.

The role of Jews as moneylenders also provoked animosity toward them. Increasingly excluded from international trade and most professions, barred from the guilds, and in some areas barred from landholding as well, Jews found that virtually the only means of livelihood open to them was moneylending. This activity, which was in theory forbidden to Christians, aroused the hatred of the individual peasants, clergy, lords, and kings who did the borrowing.

The policy of the church toward the Jews was that they should not be harmed, but that they should live in humiliation, a fitting punishment for their act of deicide and continued refusal to embrace Christianity. Thus, the Fourth Lateran Council barred Jews from public office, required them to wear a distinguishing badge on their clothing, a symbol of their degradation, and ordered them to remain off the streets during Christian festivals. Christian art, literature, and religious instruction depicted the Jews in a derogatory manner, often identifying them with the Devil, who was very real and very terrifying to medieval Christians. Such people deserved no mercy, reasoned medieval Christians. Indeed, nothing was too bad for them. Deeply etched into the minds and hearts of Christians, the distorted image of the Jew as a contemptible creature persisted in the European mentality into the twentieth century.

Despite their precarious position, medieval Jews maintained their faith, expanded their tradition of biblical and legal scholarship, and developed a flourishing Hebrew literature. The work of Jewish translators, doctors, and philosophers contributed substantially to the flowering of medieval culture in the High Middle Ages.

The foremost Jewish scholar of the Middle Ages was Moses ben Maimon (1135–1204), also called by the Greek name Maimonides. He was born in Córdoba, Spain, then under Muslim rule. After his family emigrated from Spain, Maimonides went to Egypt, where he became physician to the sultan.

During his lifetime, Maimonides achieved fame as a philosopher, theologian, mathematician, and physician. He was recognized as the leading Jewish sage of his day, and his writings were respected by Christian and Muslim thinkers as well. Like Christian and Muslim philosophers, Maimonides sought to harmonize faith with reason, to reconcile the Hebrew Scriptures and the Talmud (Jewish biblical commentary) with Greek philosophy. In his writings on ethical themes, Maimonides demonstrated piety, wisdom, and humanity.

Notes

1. The Koran, trans. N. J. Dawood (Baltimore: Penguin Books, 1961), pp. 108–109.
2. Quoted in V. H. H. Green, *Medieval Civilization in Western Europe* (New York: St. Martin's Press, 1971), p. 35.
3. Excerpted in Brian Tierney, ed., *The Crisis of Church and State, 1050–1300* (Englewood Cliffs, N.J.: Prentice-Hall, 1964), p. 132.

Suggested Reading

Bark, W. C., *Origins of the Medieval World* (1960). The Early Middle Ages as a fresh beginning.

Cantor, Norman F., ed., *The Medieval Reader* (1994). Well-chosen first-hand accounts.

Chazan, Robert, *Medieval Stereotypes and Modern Antisemitism* (1997). The deterioration of the image of the Jew in the High Middle Ages.

Cohen, Jeremy, *The Friars and the Jews* (1982). The evolution of medieval anti-Judaism among the Dominicans and Franciscans.

Cohen, Mark, *Under Crescent and Crow* (1994). A comparison of the legal, economic, and social situations of Jews in medieval Islam and Christendom.

Dawson, Christopher, *The Making of Europe* (1957). Stresses the role of Christianity in shaping European civilization.

Gies, Frances, and Joseph Gies, *Women in the Middle Ages* (1978). The narrative weaves in valuable quotations from medieval sources.

———, *Life in a Medieval Castle* (1974). The castle as the center of medieval life; passages from journals, songs, and account books permit medieval people to speak for themselves.

Gimpel, Jean, *The Medieval Machine* (1977). The Technological advances in the Middle Ages.

Focillon, Henri, *The Year 1000* (1971). Conditions of life toward the end of the Early Middle Ages.

Herrin, Judith, *The Formation of Christendom* (1987). The transition from antiquity to the Middle Ages.

Holmes, George, ed., *The Oxford History of Medieval Europe* (1988). Essays by several scholars; good opening essay on transformation of the Roman world.

Kritzeck, James, ed., *Anthology of Islamic Literature*. A rich sampling (1964).

Laistner, M. L. W., *Thought and Letters in Western Europe A.D. 500 to 900* (1957). A comprehensive survey of European thought in the Early Middle Ages.

Lewis, A. R., *Emerging Medieval Europe* (1967). Good discussions of economic and social changes.

Lewis, Bernard, *The Arabs in History* (1966). A valuable survey.

Lopez, R. S., *The Commercial Revolution of the Middle Ages, 950–1350* (1976). How an undeveloped society succeeded in developing itself.

Lucas, Angela M., *Women in the Middle Ages* (1983). Women and religion, marriage, and letters.

Mayer, H. E., *The Crusades* (1972). A short, scholarly treatment.

Mundy, J. H., *Europe in the High Middle Ages, 1150–1309* (1973). All phases of society in the High Middle Ages.

Nasr, Seyyed Hossein, *Science and Civilization in Islam* (1968). An analysis of Islamic science with many illuminating extracts from medieval works.

Perry, Marvin, and Frederick M. Schweitzer, eds. *Jewish-Christian Encounters over the Centuries* (1994). Excellent essay by Schweitzer on the medieval view of Jews and Judaism.

Pounds, N. J. G., *An Economic History of Medieval Europe* (1974). A lucid survey.

Rorig, Fritz, *The Medieval Town* (1971). A study of medieval urban life.

Shahar, Shulamith, *The Fourth Estate* (1983). Women in the Middle Ages.

Trachtenberg, Joshua, *The Devil and the Jews* (1961). The medieval conception of the Jew and its relationship to modern anti-Semitism.

Tierney, Brian, ed., *The Crisis of Church and State, 1050–1300* (1964). Contains many documents illustrating this crucial medieval development.

White, Lynn, Jr., *Medieval Technology and Social Change* (1964). A study of medieval advances in technology.

Zacour, Norman, *An Introduction to Medieval Institutions* (1969). Comprehensive essays on all phases of medieval society.

Review Questions

1. What was the long-term influence of Byzantium on world history?
2. Characterize and discuss the significance of the Muslim intellectual achievement.
3. The civilization of Latin Christendom was a blending of Christian, Greco-Roman, and Germanic traditions. Explain this statement.
4. What was the significance of monks and nuns to medieval civilization?
5. What crucial developments occurred during the reign of Charlemagne? Why were they important?
6. What conditions led to the rise of feudalism? How did feudal law differ from Roman law?
7. What advances in agriculture occurred during the Middle Ages, and what effect did they have?
8. What factors contributed to the rise of towns? What was the significance of the medieval town?
9. Identify the following and explain their importance: William the Conqueror, common law, Magna Carta, and Parliament.
10. Why did Germany fail to achieve unity during the Middle Ages?
11. What prompted Urban II to call a crusade against the Turks? What caused lords and commoners to go on a crusade? What was the final importance and outcome of the Crusades?
12. Why did the church regard Waldensians and Cathari as heretics?
13. What factors contributed to the rise of anti-Semitism during the Middle Ages? How does anti-Semitism demonstrate the power of mythical thinking?
14. The High Middle Ages showed many signs of recovery and vitality. Discuss this statement.

❖ CHAPTER 7

The Flowering and Dissolution of Medieval Civilization

*E*urope in the High Middle Ages showed considerable vitality. The population increased, long-distance trade revived, new towns emerged, states started to take shape, and papal power grew. The culminating expression of this recovery and resurgence was the cultural flowering in philosophy, the visual arts, and literature. Creative intellects achieved on a cultural level what the papacy accomplished on an institutional level: the integration of life around a Christian viewpoint. The High Middle Ages saw the restoration of some of the learning of the ancient world, the rise of universities, the emergence of an original form of architecture (the Gothic), and the erection of an imposing system of thought, called *scholasticism*. Medieval theologian-philosophers fashioned Christian teachings into an all-embracing philosophy that represented the spiritual essence, the distinctive style of medieval civilization. They perfected what Christian thinkers in the Roman Empire had initiated and what the learned men of the Early Middle Ages had been groping for: a synthesis of Greek philosophy and Christian revelation. ❖

Revival of Learning

In the late eleventh century, Latin Christendom began to experience a cultural revival; all areas of life showed vitality and creativeness. In the twelfth and thirteenth centuries, a rich civilization with a distinctive style united the educated elite in the lands from Britain to Sicily. Gothic cathedrals, an enduring testament to the creativity of the religious impulse, were erected throughout Europe. Universities sprang up in many cities. Roman authors were again read and their style imitated. The quality of written Latin — the language of the church, learning, and education — improved, and secular and religious poetry, both in Latin and in the vernacular, abounded. Roman law emerged anew in Italy, spread to northern Europe, and regained its importance (lost since Roman times) as worthy of study and scholarship. Some key works of ancient Greece were translated into Latin and studied in universities. Employing the rational tradition of Greece, men of genius harmonized Christian doctrines and Greek philosophy.

Chronology 7.1 ❖ The High and Late Middle Ages

c. 1100	Revival of the study of Roman law at Bologna
1163	Start of the construction of the Cathedral of Notre Dame
1267–1273	Saint Thomas Aquinas writes *Summa Theologica*
1309–1377	Babylonian Captivity; the popes, all French, reside at Avignon and are influenced by the French monarchy
c. 1321	Dante completes *Divine Comedy*
1337–1453	Hundred Years' War between England and France
1347–1351	Black Death reaches Italian ports and ravages Europe
1377	Pope Gregory XI returns the papacy to Rome
1378–1417	Great Schism; Christendom has two and then three popes
1415	The battle of Agincourt: Henry V of England defeats the French; Jan Hus, a Bohemian religious reformer, is burned at the stake
1453	The English are driven from France, except Calais; the end of the Hundred Years' War
1460	Pope Pius II condemns the Conciliar Movement as heretical

---

Several conditions contributed to this cultural explosion, known as the Twelfth-Century Awakening. As attacks of Vikings, Muslims, and Magyars ended and kings and great lords imposed more order and stability, people found greater opportunities for travel and communication. The revival of trade and the growth of towns created a need for literacy and provided the wealth required to support learning. Increasing contact with Islamic and Byzantine cultures in Spain, Sicily, and Italy led to the translation into Latin of ancient Greek works preserved by these Eastern civilizations. By preserving Greek philosophy and science — and by making creative commentaries on these classical works — Islamic civilization acted as a bridge between antiquity and the cultural revival of the High Middle Ages. The Twelfth-Century Awakening was also prompted by the legacy of the Carolingian Renaissance, whose cultural lights had dimmed but never wholly vanished in the period of disorder after the dissolution of Charlemagne's empire.

In the Early Middle Ages, the principal educational centers were the monastic schools. During the twelfth century, cathedral schools in towns gained importance. Their teachers, paid a stipend by a local church, taught grammar, rhetoric, and logic. However, the chief expression of expanding intellectual life was the university, a distinct creation of the Middle Ages. The first universities were not planned but grew spontaneously. They developed as students, eager for knowledge, gathered around prominent teachers. The renewed importance of Roman law for business and politics, for example, drew students to Bologna to study with acknowledged masters.

University students attended lectures, prepared for examinations, and earned degrees. They studied grammar, rhetoric, logic, arithmetic, geometry, astronomy, medicine, music, and, when ready, church law and theology, which was considered the queen of the sciences. The curriculum relied heavily on Latin translations of ancient texts, chiefly the works of Aristotle. Students in mathematics and astronomy read Latin translations of Euclid and Ptolemy, while those in medicine studied the works of two great medical men of the ancient world, Hippocrates and Galen.

Universities performed a crucial function in the Middle Ages. Students learned the habit of reasoned argument. Universities trained professional secretaries and lawyers, who administered the affairs of church, state, and the growing cities. These institutions of learning also produced theologians and philosophers, who shaped the climate of public opinion. Since the curriculum and the texts studied were essentially the same in all lands, the learning disseminated by universities tightened the cultural bonds that united Christian Europe. Medieval universities established in the West a tradition of learning that has never died. There is direct continuity between the universities of our own day and medieval centers of learning.

The Medieval World-View

A distinctive world-view, based essentially on Christianity, evolved during the Middle Ages. This outlook differed from both the Greco-Roman and the modern scientific and secular views of the world. In the Christian view, not the individual but the Creator determined what constituted the good life. Thus, reason that was not illuminated by revelation was either wrong or inadequate, for God had revealed the proper rules for the regulation of individual and social life. Ultimately, the good life was not of this world but came from a union with God in a higher world. This Christian belief, as formulated by the church, made life and death purposeful and intelligible; it dominated the thought of the Middle Ages.

The Universe: Higher and Lower Worlds

Medieval thinkers sharply differentiated between spirit and matter, between a realm of grace and an earthly realm, between a higher world of perfection and a lower world of imperfection. Moral values derived from the higher world, which was also the final destination for the faithful. Two sets of laws operated in the medieval universe, one for the heavens and one for the earth. The cosmos was a giant ladder, with God at the summit; earth, composed of base matter, stood at the bottom, just above hell.

Theology Lecture.   At the University of Paris, students listen attentively to a theology lecture. (*Bibliotèque Municipale de Troyes*)

From Aristotle and Ptolemy, medieval thinkers inherited the theory of an earth-centered universe — the *geocentric theory* — which they imbued with Christian meaning. The geocentric theory held that revolving around the motionless earth at uniform speeds were seven transparent spheres, in which were embedded the seven "planets" — the moon, Mercury, Venus, the sun, Mars, Jupiter, and Saturn. A sphere of fixed stars — that is, the stars stayed in a constant relationship to one another — enclosed this planetary system. Above the firmament of the stars were the three heavenly spheres. The outermost, the Empyrean Heaven, was the abode of God and the Elect. Through the sphere below — the Prime Mover — God transmitted motion to the planetary spheres. Beneath this was the lowest sphere, the invisible Crystalline Heaven.

An earth-centered universe accorded with the Christian idea that God had created the universe for men and women and that salvation was the primary aim of life. Because God had created people in his image, they deserved this central position in the universe. Although they might be living at the bottom rung of the cosmic ladder, only they, of all living things, had the capacity to ascend to heaven, the realm of perfection.

Also acceptable to the Christian mentality was the sharp distinction drawn by Aristotle between the world above the moon and the one below it. Aristotle held that terrestrial bodies were made of four elements: earth, water, air, and fire. Celestial bodies, which occupied the region above the moon, were composed of a fifth element, ether — too clear, too pure, and too perfect to be found on earth. The planets and stars existed in a world apart; they were made of the divine ether and followed celestial laws, which did not apply to earthly objects. Whereas earthly bodies underwent change — ice converting to water, a burning log converting to ashes — heavenly objects were incorruptible, immune to all change. Unlike earthly objects, they were indestructible.

Heavenly bodies also followed different laws of motion from earthly objects. Aristotle said that it was natural for celestial bodies to move eternally in uniform circles, such motion being considered a sign of perfection. According to Aristotle, it was also natural for heavy bodies (stone) to fall downward and for light objects (fire, smoke) to move upward toward the celestial world; the falling stone and the rising smoke were finding their natural place in the universe.

The Individual: Sinful but Redeemable

At the center of medieval belief was the idea of a perfect God and a wretched and sinful human being. God, who had conceived and created the universe, had given Adam and Eve freedom to choose; rebellious and presumptuous, they had used their freedom to disobey God. In doing so, they made evil an intrinsic part of the human personality. But God, who had not stopped loving human beings, showed them the way out of sin. God became man and died so that human beings might be saved. Men and women were weak, egocentric, and sinful. With God's grace, they could overcome their sinful nature and gain salvation; without grace, they were utterly helpless.

The medieval individual's understanding of self stemmed from a comprehension of the universe as a hierarchy instituted by and culminating in God. On earth, the basest objects were lifeless stones, devoid of souls. Higher than stones were plants, endowed with a primitive type of soul that allowed reproduction and growth. Still higher were animals, which had the capacity for motion and sensation. The highest of the animals were human beings; unlike other animals, they could grasp some part of universal truth. Far superior to them were the angels, who apprehended God's truth without difficulty. At the summit of this graduated universe (the Great Chain of Being) was God, who was pure Being, without limitation, and the source of all existence. God's revelation reached down to humanity through the hierarchical order. From God, revelation passed to the angels, who were also arranged hierarchically. From the angels, the truth reached men and women; it was grasped first by prophets and apostles and then by the multitudes. Thus, all things in the universe, from God to angels to men and women to the lowest earthly objects, occupied a place peculiar to their nature and were linked by God in a great, unbroken chain.

Medieval individuals derived a sense of security from this hierarchical universe, in which the human position was clearly defined. True, they were sinners who dwelt on a corruptible earth at the bottom of the cosmic hierarchy. But they could ascend to the higher world of perfection above the moon. As children of God, they enjoyed the unique distinction that each human soul was precious and commanded respect.

Medieval thinkers also arranged knowledge in a hierarchical order: knowledge of spiritual things surpassed all worldly knowledge, all human sciences.

To know what God wanted of the individual was the summit of self-knowledge and permitted entry into heaven. Thus, God was both the source and the end of knowledge. The human capacity to think and to act freely reflected the image of God within each individual; it ennobled men and women and offered them the promise of associating with God in heaven. Human nobility might derive from intelligence and free will, but if individuals used these attributes to disobey God, they brought misery on themselves.

Philosophy, Science, and Law

Medieval philosophy, or scholasticism, applied reason to revelation. It explained and clarified Christian teachings by means of concepts and principles of logic derived from Greek philosophy. Scholastics tried to show that the teachings of faith, although not derived from reason, were not contrary to reason. They tried to prove through reason what they already held to be true through faith. For example, the existence of God and the immortality of the soul, which every Christian accepted as articles of faith, could also, they thought, be demonstrated by reason. In struggling to harmonize faith with reason, medieval thinkers constructed an extraordinary synthesis of Christian revelation and Greek rationalism.

The scholastic masters used reason not to challenge but to serve faith: to elucidate, clarify, and buttress it. They did not break with the central concern of Christianity: earning God's grace and achieving salvation. Although this goal could be realized solely by faith, scholastic thinkers insisted that a science of nature did not obstruct the pursuit of grace and that philosophy could assist the devout in contemplating God. They did not reject those Christian beliefs that were beyond the grasp of human reason and therefore could not be deduced by rational argument. Instead, they held that such truths rested entirely on revelation and were to be accepted on faith. To medieval thinkers, reason did not have an independent existence but ultimately had to acknowledge a suprarational, superhuman standard of truth. They wanted rational thought to be directed by faith for Christian ends and guided by scriptural and ecclesiastical authority. Ultimately, faith had the final word.

Not all Christian thinkers welcomed the use of reason. Regarding Greek philosophy as an enemy of faith (would not reason lead people to question belief in miracles?), a fabricator of heresies (would not reason encourage disbelief in essential church teachings?), and an obstacle to achieving communion of the soul with God (would not a deviation from church teachings, under the influence of pagan philosophy, deprive people of salvation?), conservative theologians opposed the application of reason to Christian revelation. In a sense, the conservatives were right. By giving renewed vitality to Greek thought, medieval philosophy nurtured a powerful force that would eventually shatter the medieval concepts of nature and society and weaken

Christianity. Modern Western thought was created by thinkers who refused to subordinate reason to Christian authority. Reason proved a double-edged sword: it both ennobled and undermined the medieval world-view.

Saint Anselm and Abelard

An early scholastic, Saint Anselm (1033–1109) was abbot of the Benedictine monastery of Le Bec in Normandy. He used rational argument to serve the interests of faith. Like Augustine before him and other thinkers who followed him, Anselm said that faith was a precondition for understanding. Without belief there could be no proper knowledge. He developed a philosophical proof for the existence of God. Anselm argued as follows: we can conceive of no being greater than God. But if God were to exist only in thought and not in actuality, his greatness would be limited; he would be less than perfect. Hence, he exists.

Anselm's motive and method reveal something about the essence of medieval philosophy. He does not begin as a modern might: "If it can be proven that God exists, I will adopt the creed of Christianity; if not, I will either deny God's existence (atheism) or reserve judgment (agnosticism)." Rather, Anselm accepts God's existence as an established fact because he believes what Holy Scripture says and what the church teaches. He then proceeds to employ logical argument to demonstrate that God can be known not only through faith, but also through reason. He would never use reason to subvert what he knows to be true by faith. This attitude would generally characterize later medieval thinkers, who also applied reason to faith.

As a young teacher of theology at the Cathedral School of Notre Dame, Peter Abelard (1079–1142) acquired a reputation for brilliance and combativeness. His tragic affair with Héloise, whom he tutored and seduced, has become one of the great romances in Western literature. Abelard's most determined opponent, Bernard of Clairvaux, accused him of using the method of dialectical argument to attack faith. To Bernard, a monk and mystic, subjecting revealed truth to critical analysis was fraught with danger. Hearkening to Bernard's powerful voice, the church condemned Abelard and confined him to a monastery for the rest of his days.

Abelard believed that it was important to apply reason to faith and that careful and constant questioning led to wisdom. In *Sic et Non* (Yes and No), he took 150 theological issues and, by presenting passages from the Bible and the church fathers, showed that there were conflicting opinions. He suggested that the divergent opinions of authorities could be reconciled through proper use of dialectics. But like Anselm before him, Abelard did not intend to refute traditional church doctrines. Reason would buttress, not weaken, the authority of faith. He wrote after his condemnation in 1141: "I will never be a philosopher, if this is to speak against St. Paul; I would not be an Aristotle if this were to separate me from Christ. . . . I have set my building on the cornerstone on which Christ has built his Church. . . . I rest upon the rock that cannot be moved."[1]

Saint Thomas Aquinas: The Synthesis of Faith and Reason

The introduction into Latin Christendom of the major works of Aristotle created a dilemma for religious authorities. Aristotle's comprehensive philosophy of nature and man, a product of human reason alone, conflicted in many instances with essential Christian doctrine. Whereas Christianity taught that God created the universe at a specific point in time, Aristotle held that the universe was eternal. Nor did Aristotle believe in the personal immortality of the soul, another cardinal principle of Christianity.

Some church officials feared that the dissemination of Aristotle's ideas and the use of Aristotelian logic would endanger faith. At various times in the first half of the thirteenth century, they forbade teaching the scientific works of Aristotle at the University of Paris. But because the ban did not apply throughout Christendom and was not consistently enforced in Paris, Aristotle's philosophy continued to be studied. Rejecting the position of conservatives, who insisted that philosophy would contaminate faith, Saint Thomas Aquinas (c. 1225–1274) upheld the value of human reason and natural knowledge. He set about reconciling Aristotelianism with Christianity. Aquinas taught at Paris and in Italy. His greatest work, *Summa Theologica*, is a systematic exposition of Christian thought.

Can the teachings of faith conflict with the evidence of reason? For Aquinas, the answer was emphatically no. Since both faith and reason came from God, they were not in competition with each other but, properly understood, supported each other and formed an organic unity. Consequently, reason should not be feared, for it was another avenue to God. Because there was an inherent agreement between true faith and correct reason — they both ultimately stemmed from God — contradictions between them were only a misleading appearance. Although philosophy had not yet been able to resolve the dilemma, for God no such contradictions existed. In heaven, human beings would attain complete knowledge, as well as complete happiness. While on earth, however, they must allow faith to guide reason; they must not permit reason to oppose or undermine faith.

Thus, in exalting God, Aquinas also paid homage to human intelligence, proclaimed the value of rational activity, and asserted the importance of physical reality discovered through human senses. Consequently, he prized the natural philosophy of Aristotle. Correctly used, Aristotelian thought would assist faith. Aquinas's great effort was to synthesize Aristotelianism with the divine revelation of Christianity. That the two could be harmonized he had no doubt. He made use of Aristotelian categories in his five proofs of God's existence. In his first proof, for example, Aquinas argued that a thing cannot move itself. Whatever is moved must be moved by something else, and that by something else again. "Therefore, it is necessary to arrive at a first mover, moved by no other; and this everyone understands to be God."[2]

Aquinas upheld the value of reason. To love the intellect was to honor God and not to diminish the truth of faith. He had confidence in the power of the rational mind to comprehend most of the truths of revelation, and he insisted that in nontheological questions about specific things in nature — those questions not affecting salvation — people should trust only reason and experience. Thus, Aquinas gave new importance to the empirical world and to scientific speculation and human knowledge.

The traditional medieval view, based largely on Saint Augustine, drew a sharp distinction between the higher world of grace and the lower world of nature, between the world of spirit and the world of sense experience. Knowledge derived from the natural world was often seen as an obstacle to true knowledge. Aquinas altered this tradition by affirming the importance of knowledge of the social order and the physical world. He gave human reason and worldly knowledge a new dignity. Thus, the City of Man was not merely a sinful place from which people tried to escape in order to enter God's city; it was worthy of investigation and understanding. But Aquinas remained a medieval thinker, for he always maintained that secular knowledge should be supervised and corrected by revealed truth, and he never questioned the truth of the medieval Christian view of the world and the individual.

Science

During the Early Middle Ages, few scientific works from the ancient world were available to Western Europeans. Scientific thought was at its lowest ebb since its origination more than a thousand years earlier in Greece. In contrast, both the Islamic and Byzantine civilizations preserved and, in some instances, added to the legacy of Greek science. In the High Middle Ages, however, many ancient texts were translated from Greek and Arabic into Latin and entered Latin Christendom for the first time. Spain, where Christian and Muslim civilizations met, was one of the two principal centers of translation. The other was Sicily, which had been controlled by Byzantium up to the last part of the ninth century and then by Islam until Christian Normans completed the conquest of the island by 1091.

In the thirteenth and fourteenth centuries, a genuine scientific movement did occur. Impressed with the naturalistic and empirical approach of Aristotle, some medieval schoolmen spent time examining physical nature. Among them was the Dominican Albert the Great (Albertus Magnus, c. 1206–1280). Born in Germany, he studied at Padua and taught at the University of Paris, where Thomas Aquinas was his student. To Albert, philosophy meant more than employing Greek reason to contemplate divine wisdom; it also meant making sense of nature. Albert devoted himself to editing and commenting on the vast body of Aristotle's works.

While retaining the Christian emphasis on God, revelation, the supernatural, and the afterlife, Albert (unlike many earlier Christian thinkers) considered nature a valid field for investigation. In his writings on geology, chemistry, botany, and zoology, Albert, like Aristotle, displayed a respect for the concrete details of nature, utilizing them as empirical evidence. Albert approved of inquiry into the material world, stressed the value of knowledge derived from experience with nature, sought rational explanations for natural occurrences, and held that theological debates should not stop scientific investigations.

Other scholars in the scientific movement included Robert Grosseteste (c. 1175–1253), the chancellor of Oxford University. He declared that the roundness of the earth could be demonstrated by reason. In addition, he insisted that mathematics was necessary in order to understand the physical world, and he carried out experiments on the refraction of light. Another Englishman, the monk and philosopher Roger Bacon (c. 1214–1294), foreshadowed the modern attitude of using science to gain mastery over nature. Bacon valued the study of mathematics and read Arabic works on the reflection and refraction of light. Among his achievements were experiments in optics and the observation that light travels much faster than sound. His description of the anatomy of the vertebrate eye and optic nerves was the finest of that era, and he recommended dissecting the eyes of pigs and cows to obtain greater knowledge of the subject.

Medieval scholars did not make the breakthrough to modern science. They retained the belief that the earth was at the center of the universe and that different sets of laws operated on earth and in the heavens. They did not invent analytic geometry or calculus or arrive at the concept of inertia — all crucial for modern science. Moreover, medieval science was never wholly removed from a theological setting. Modern science self-consciously seeks the advancement of specifically scientific knowledge, but in the Middle Ages, many questions involving nature were raised merely to clarify a religious problem.

Medieval scholars and philosophers did, however, advance knowledge about optics, the tides, and mechanics. They saw the importance of mathematics for interpreting nature, and they performed some experiments. By translating and commenting on ancient Greek and Arabic works, medieval scholars provided future ages with ideas to reflect on and to surpass, a necessary precondition for the emergence of modern science. Medieval thinkers also developed an anti-Aristotelian physics, which some historians of science believe influenced Galileo, the creator of modern mechanics, more than two centuries later.

Recovery of Roman Law

During the Early Middle Ages, Western European law essentially consisted of Germanic customs, some of which had been put into writing. Some elements of Roman law endured as custom and practice, but the formal study of Roman law had disappeared. The late eleventh and twelfth centuries saw the revival of Roman law, particularly in Bologna, Italy. Irnerius lectured on the *Corpus Juris Civilis*, codified by Byzantine jurists in the sixth century, and made Bologna the leading center for the study of Roman law. Irnerius and his students employed the methods of organization and logical analysis that scholastic theologians used in studying philosophical texts.

Unlike traditional Germanic law, which was essentially tribal and parochial, Roman law assumed the existence of universal principles, which could be grasped by the human intellect and expressed in the law of the state.

Roman jurists had systematically and rationally structured the legal experience of the Roman people. The example of Roman law stimulated medieval jurists to organize their own legal tradition. Intellectuals increasingly came to insist on both a rational analysis of evidence and judicial decisions based on rational procedures. Law codes compiled in parts of France and Germany and in the kingdom of Castile were influenced by the recovery of Roman law.

Literature

Medieval literature was written both in Latin and in the vernacular. Much of medieval Latin literature consisted of religious hymns and dramas depicting the life of Christ and saints. In their native tongues, medieval writers created different forms of poetry: *chansons de geste,* the *roman,* and *troubadour* songs, which emerged during the High Middle Ages.

The French *chansons de geste* — epic poems of heroic deeds that had first been told orally — were written in the vernacular of northern France. These poems dealt with Charlemagne's battles against the Muslims, with rebellious nobles, and with feudal warfare. The finest of these epic poems, *The Song of Roland,* expressed the vassal's loyalty to his lord and the Christian's devotion to his faith. Roland, Charlemagne's nephew, was killed in a battle with the Muslims. The *Nibelungenlied,* the best expression of the heroic epic in Germany, is often called "the *Iliad* of the Germans." Like its French counterpart, it dealt with heroic feats.

The roman — a blending of old legends, chivalric ideals, and Christian concepts — combined love with adventure, war, and the miraculous. Among the romans were the tales of King Arthur and his Round Table. Circulating by word of mouth for centuries, these tales spread from the British Isles to France and Germany. In the twelfth century, they were put into French verse.

Another form of medieval poetry, which flourished particularly in Provence, in southern France, dealt with the romantic glorification of women. Sung by troubadours, many of them nobles, the courtly love poetry expressed a changing attitude toward women. Although medieval men generally regarded women as inferior and subordinate, courtly love poetry ascribed to noble ladies superior qualities of virtue. To the nobleman, the lady became a goddess worthy of all devotion, loyalty, and worship. He would honor her and serve her as he did his lord; for her love he would undergo any sacrifice.

Noblewomen actively influenced the rituals and literature of courtly love. They often invited poets to their courts and wrote poetry themselves. They demanded that knights treat them with gentleness and consideration and that knights dress neatly, bathe often, play instruments, and compose (or at least recite) poetry. To prove worthy of his lady's love, a knight had to demonstrate patience, charm, bravery, and loyalty. By devoting himself to a lady, it was believed, a knight would ennoble his character.

Courtly love did not involve a husband-wife relationship, but rather a noble's admiration of and yearning for another woman of his class. Among nobles, marriages were arranged for political and economic reasons. The ritu-

Art as History:
The Ancient World
Through the Middle Ages

Historians rely on many different sources to arrive at a knowledge of the past. These sources include not only the written documents and literature of a people, but also their artistic creations—their architecture, sculpture, and painting. As you look at these works of art, what insights do they suggest about the historical times in which they were produced?

The Parthenon, Athens, 447–432 B.C.   This Greek classical temple crowns the Acropolis above Athens. Dedicated to Athena, patron goddess of the city and of wisdom and the arts, the marble Parthenon once contained a huge ivory and gold statue of her. The temple ruins reveal the perfect proportions and placement of the Parthenon, but they do not show that its facade was painted, as were the life-size sculptures that filled the triangular spaces above the rows of columns. What do the structure and style of the Parthenon suggest about Greek civilization? (*Scala/Art Resource, NY*)

Black-figured Amphora: Achilles and Ajax Playing a Board Game, 540–530 B.C. Greeks not only built beautiful temples and skillfully sculpted ideal figures possessing grace; they also imparted beauty to everyday utensils, such as this amphora, a "vase" used to hold wine or oil. Here, figures from Homer's *Iliad* are shown enjoying a respite from the siege of Troy. What does this vessel and its ornamentation reveal about the Hellenic Greeks? (*Scala/Art Resource, NY*)

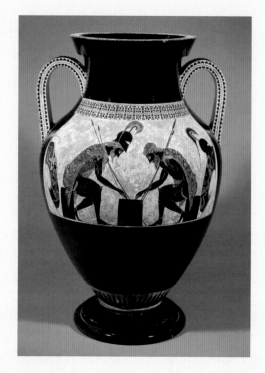

Hellenistic Sculpture: *The Laocoön*, Second Century B.C. This Hellenistic sculpture, attributed to three artists, depicts the suffering, anguish, and death of the mythological Laocoön and his sons as divine retribution for his having broken an oath. It presents an interesting contrast to earlier Hellenic art, which was characteristically harmonious and serene. What statement does the shape and arrangement of the figures in the group seem to be making about human destiny? How does it differ from the usual approach of Hellenic art in protraying the human figure? (*Museo Pio Clementino, Vatican Museums, Vatican State/Scala/Art Resource*)

Detail of Pompeian Wall Fresco: Lady Playing the Cithara. Upon the removal of lava and ash from Pompeii, a first-century Roman city appeared, providing historians with data on the daily life of almost twenty centuries ago. What does this fresco scene disclose about the state of Roman culture and the lives of Roman matrons?
(*Copyright © 1996 by The Metropolitan Museum of Art, Rogers Fund, 1903*)

Apse Mosaic: Justinian and Attendants, Church of San Vitale, Ravenna. Emperor Justinian, who ruled Byzantium from 527 to 565, appears in this mosaic as a symbol of Christ rather than as an ordinary ruler on earth. The golden halo and the presence of exactly twelve attendants, reminiscent of the Twelve Apostles, confirm this impression. The way in which an artist depicts the human figure reveals a lot about past cultures. What can we learn about Byzantium by comparing the portrayal of Justinian with that of the Roman matron playing the cithara on the previous page? (*Scala/Art Resource, NY*)

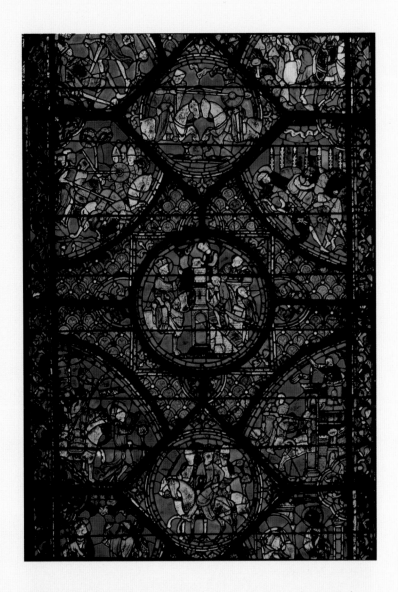

Stained Glass from Chartres Cathedral: Charlemagne Giving Orders for Building the Church of Saint James. Dating from the early thirteenth century, Chartres is one of the outstanding Gothic cathedrals. Its stained-glass windows shed light in jeweled colors on the interior of the sanctuary, uplifting the spirit and raising the eyes of the worshiper. However, these windows also instruct: they tell stories about heroes, such as Emperor Charlemagne, and about saints and the Trinity. What might a medieval churchgoer have learned from this window? (*Copyright Sonia Halliday and Laura Lushington*)

April from *Les très riches heures* of Jean, Duke of Berry. This page from a beautifully illustrated volume of prayers, which was made during 1413–1416, is one of the paintings of months appearing in this nobleman's book. What does this scene reveal about the lifestyle of nobles, both men and women? (*Giraudon/Art Resource, NY*)

Domenico Veneziano (c. 1410–1461): *Madonna and Child with Saints,* c. 1445.
This Florentine master painted the altar panel (6′ 7½″ × 6′ 11⅞″) in a new style,
called *sacra conversazione* (sacred conversation). The enthroned Madonna and child
are framed by architectural elements and flanked by the formal, solemn figures of
saints, who seem to converse with her or between themselves, or even with the onlooker. Saint John, to the left of the child and the Madonna, gazes out of the painting
as he points to them, in effect directing the onlooker's eyes. In his color scheme,
Domenico uses sunlight and spots of bright primary colors, along with pastels, to present a glowing scene. What elements in the painting indicate that it is an Early Renaissance work? (*Alinari/Art Resource, NY*)

Hubert or Jan van Eyck: *The Last Judgment,* **c. 1420–1425.** The major concern of medieval people was the salvation of their souls. At the Last Judgment, the good would be drawn to heaven while the damned would be sealed in hell. In *The Last Judgment,* the Flemish artist van Eyck depicts this final division in graphic detail. How does the relationship between man and the divine portrayed by van Eyck differ from the classical humanism of ancient Greek art? *(Copyright © 1996 by The Metropolitan Museum of Art, Fletcher Fund, 1933)*

Virgil and Dante Watch Lucifer: A Miniature Painting in an Early Manuscript of *The Divine Comedy*.   Dante reserved the lowest depth of Hell for those guilty of treason. Lucifer, the angel who betrayed God, is depicted as a monster with three mouths. With these he perpetually chews the bodies of the arch-traitors Judas Iscariot, Brutus, and Cassius. *The Divine Comedy* exemplifies the medieval mind's overriding concern with God and the afterlife. (*Trivulzian Library, Milan*)

als of courtly love, it has been suggested, provided an outlet for erotic feelings condemned by the church. They also expanded the skills and refined the tastes of the noble. The rough warrior acquired wit, manners, charm, and skill with words. He was becoming a courtier and a gentleman.

The greatest literary figure of the Middle Ages was Dante Alighieri (1265–1321) of Florence. Dante appreciated the Roman classics and wrote not just in Latin, the traditional language of intellectual life, but in Italian, his native tongue. In this respect, he anticipated the Renaissance (see Chapter 8). In the tradition of the troubadours, Dante wrote poems to his beloved Beatrice.

In *The Divine Comedy,* Dante synthesized the various elements of the medieval outlook and summed up, with immense feeling, the medieval understanding of the purpose of life. Written while Dante was in exile, *The Divine Comedy* describes the poet's journey through hell, purgatory, and paradise.

The Romanesque Nave of the Cathedral of St. Sernin, Toulouse. The nave is covered by a stone barrel vault, replacing earlier wooden roofs, which were susceptible to fire. The columns, thick walls, and small windows were required structurally to bear the great weight of the roof vaulting. Little light penetrated the interior. (*Caisse Nationale des Monuments Historiques, Paris*)

Dante arranges hell into nine concentric circles; in each region, sinners are punished in proportion to their earthly sins. The poet experiences all of hell's torments — burning sand, violent storms, darkness, and fearful monsters that whip, claw, bite, and tear sinners apart. The ninth circle, the lowest, is reserved for Lucifer and traitors. Lucifer has three faces, each a different color, and two batlike wings. In each mouth he gnaws on one of the greatest traitors in history: Judas Iscariot, who betrayed Jesus, and Brutus and Cassius, who assassinated Caesar. Those condemned to hell are told: "All hope abandon, ye who enter in." In purgatory, Dante meets sinners who, although they undergo punishment, will eventually enter paradise. In paradise, an abode of light, music, and gentleness, the poet, guided by Beatrice, meets the great saints and the Virgin Mary. For an instant, he glimpses the Vision of God. In this mystical experience, the aim of life is realized.

Written in the vernacular, *The Canterbury Tales* of Geoffrey Chaucer (c. 1340–1400) is a masterpiece of English literature. Chaucer chose as his theme twenty-nine pilgrims en route from London to the religious shrine at Canterbury. In describing the pilgrims, Chaucer displayed humor, charm, an understanding of human nature, and a superb grasp of the attitudes of the English. Few writers have pictured their times better.

Architecture

Two styles of architecture evolved during the Middle Ages: Romanesque and Gothic. The Romanesque style dominated the eleventh century and the greater part of the twelfth. In imitation of ancient Roman structures, Romanesque buildings had massive walls that supported stone barrel and groin vaults with rounded arches. The thick walls were needed to hold up the great weight of the roofs. The walls left few spaces for windows, and so little light entered the interior. However, the development of the pointed arch permitted supports that lessened the bearing pressure of the roof on the walls. This new style, called Gothic, allowed buildings to have lofty, vaulted ceilings and huge windows. The Romanesque building produced an impression of massive solidity; Gothic buildings created an illusion of soaring energy.

The Gothic cathedral gave visual expression to the medieval conception of a hierarchical universe. As historian Joan Gadol puts it, "Inside and out, the Gothic cathedral is one great movement upward through a mounting series of grades, one ascent through horizontal levels marked by arches, galleries, niches, and towers . . . the material ascends to the spiritual, the natural is assumed into the supernatural—all in a graduated rise."[3] This illusion is created by the tall and narrow proportions of the interior spaces, the springing pointed arches, and the marching patterns of closely spaced columns and colonnettes.

The magnificently designed stained-glass windows and complex sculptural decoration of Gothic cathedrals depicted scenes from the Bible and the lives of saints—as well as scenes from daily life—for the worshipers, many of whom were illiterate. The reduction of wall space, which allowed these massive glass illustrations, was made possible by the flying buttresses on the buildings' exteriors. These great arcs of masonry carry the weight and thrust of the stone vaults out to the exterior walls.

The Gothic style was to remain vigorous until the fifteenth century, spreading from France to England, Germany, Spain, and beyond. Revived from time to time thereafter, it has proved to be one of the most enduring styles in Western art and architecture.

The Fourteenth Century: An Age of Adversity

By the fourteenth century, Latin Christendom had experienced more than 250 years of growth. On the economic level, agricultural production had expanded, commerce and town life had revived, and the population had increased. On the political level, kings had become more powerful, bringing greater order and security to large areas. On the religious level, the papacy had demonstrated its strength as the spiritual leader of Christendom, and the clergy had been reformed. On the cultural level, a unified world-view, blending faith and reason, had been forged.

The Gothic Nave and Choir of Notre Dame Cathedral, Paris, Twelfth Century. The Gothic nave is wider than a Romanesque nave because pointed arches can bridge a wider space and carry a roof with less heavy vaulting. The walls are raised higher, are thinner, and are punctured with larger open spaces for windows than was possible in Romanesque buildings. The weight of the roof and walls is born by "flying buttresses," stone arched supports external to the walls. (*Jean Roubier*)

During the Late Middle Ages (roughly the fourteenth century), however, Latin Christendom was afflicted with severe problems. The earlier increases in agricultural production did not continue. Limited use of fertilizers and limited knowledge of conservation exhausted the topsoil. From 1301 to 1314, there was a general shortage of food, and from 1315 to 1317, famine struck Europe. Throughout the century, starvation and malnutrition were widespread.

Adding to the economic crisis was the Black Death, or bubonic plague. This disease was carried by fleas on black rats and probably first struck Mongolia in 1331–32. From there, it crossed into Russia. Carried back from Black Sea ports, the plague reached Sicily in 1347. Spreading swiftly throughout much of Europe, it attacked an already declining and undernourished population. The first onslaught lasted until 1351, and other serious outbreaks occurred in later decades. The crowded cities and towns had the highest mortalities. Perhaps twenty million people — about one-quarter to one-third of the European population — perished in the worst natural disaster in recorded history.

Panic-stricken people drifted into debauchery, lawlessness, and frenzied forms of religious life. Organized bands of flagellants marched from region to region, beating themselves and each other with sticks and whips in a desperate effort to appease God, who, they believed, had cursed them with the plague. Art concentrated on morbid scenes of decaying flesh, open graves laden with worm-eaten corpses, dances of death, and the torments of hell. Sometimes, this hysteria was directed against Jews, who were accused of causing the plague by poisoning wells. Terrible massacres of Jews, often by mass burnings, occurred despite the pleas of the papacy.

The millions of deaths caused production of food and goods to plummet and some prices to soar. Economic and social tensions, some of them antedating the Black Death, escalated into rebellions. Each rebellion had its own specific causes, but a general pattern characterized the uprisings in the countryside. When kings and lords, breaking with customary social relationships, imposed new and onerous regulations, the peasants rose in defense of their traditional rights.

In 1323, the lords' attempt to reimpose old manorial obligations infuriated the free peasants of Flanders, whose condition had improved in earlier decades. The Peasants' Revolt lasted five bloody years. In 1358, French peasants took up arms in protest against the plundering of the countryside by soldiers. Perhaps twenty thousand peasants died in the uprising known as the *Jacquerie*. In 1381, English peasants revolted, angered over legislation that tied them to the land and imposed new taxes. Like the revolts in Flanders and France, the uprising in England failed. To the landed aristocracy, the peasants were sinners attacking a social system ordained by God. Possessing superior might, the nobility suppressed the peasants, sometimes with savage cruelty.

Social unrest also afflicted towns. The wage earners of Florence (1378), the weavers of Ghent (1382), and the poor of Paris (1382) rose up against the ruling oligarchies. These revolts were generally initiated not by the poorest and most downtrodden, but by those who had made some gains and were eager for more. The rebellions of the urban poor were crushed just like the peasant uprisings.

Compounding the adversity was the series of conflicts known as the Hundred Years' War (1337–1453). Because English kings ruled parts of France, conflicts between the two monarchies were common. In the opening phase of the war, the English inflicted terrible defeats on French knights at the battles of Crécy (1346) and Poitiers (1356). Using longbows, which allowed them to shoot arrows rapidly, English archers cut down wave after wave of charging French cavalry. The war continued on and off throughout the fourteenth century. During periods of truce, gangs of unemployed soldiers roamed the French countryside killing and stealing, actions that precipitated the Jacquerie.

After the battle of Agincourt (1415), won by the English under Henry V, the English controlled most of northern France. It appeared that England would shortly conquer France and join the two lands under one crown. At this crucial moment in French history, a young and illiterate peasant girl, Joan of Arc (1412–1431), helped rescue France. Believing that God commanded her to drive the English out of France, Joan rallied the demoralized French troops, leading them in battle. In 1429, she liberated the besieged city of

The Jacquerie.   Enraged French peasants attack the castle of a lord. (*Bibliothèque Nationale, Paris*)

Orléans. Imprisoned by the English, Joan was condemned as a heretic and a witch in 1431 by a handpicked church court. She was burned at the stake. Inspired by Joan's death, the French drove the English from all French territory except the port of Calais.

During the Hundred Years' War, French kings introduced new taxes, which added substantially to their incomes. These monies furnished them with the means to organize a professional army of well-paid and loyal troops. By evoking a sense of pride and oneness in the French people, the war also contributed to a growing, but still incomplete, national unity. The English, too, emerged from the war with a greater sense of solidarity, and Parliament, because it had to finance the war, gained in stature. However, the war had horrendous consequences for the French peasants. Thousands of farmers were killed, and valuable farmland was destroyed by English armies and marauding bands of mercenaries. In a portentous development, the later stages of the Hundred Years' War saw the use of gunpowder and heavy artillery.

The Decline of the Papacy

The principal sign of the decline of medieval civilization in the Late Middle Ages was the waning authority and prestige of the papacy. In the High Middle Ages, the papacy had been the dominant institution in Christendom, but in the Late Middle Ages, its power disintegrated. The medieval ideal of a unified Christian commonwealth guided by the papacy was shattered. Papal authority declined in the face of the growing power of kings, who championed the parochial interests of states. As the pope became more embroiled in European politics, papal prestige and the pope's capacity to command diminished. Many pious Christians felt that the pope was behaving more like a secular ruler than like an Apostle of Christ. Political theorists and church reformers further undermined papal authority.

Conflict with France

Philip IV of France (1285–1314) taxed the church in his land to raise revenue for war. In doing so, he disregarded the church prohibition against the taxing of its property without papal permission. In 1296, in the bull *Clericis Laicos,* Pope Boniface VIII (1294–1303) decreed that kings and lords who imposed taxes on the clergy and the clergy who paid them would be excommunicated. Far from bowing to the pope's threat, Philip acted forcefully to assert his authority over the church in his kingdom. Boniface backed down from his position, declaring that the French king could tax the clergy in times of national emergency. Thus, the matter was resolved to the advantage of the state.

A second dispute had more disastrous consequences for Boniface. Philip tried and imprisoned a French bishop despite Boniface's warning that this was an illegal act and a violation of church law and tradition, which held that the church, not the state, must judge the clergy. Philip summoned the first meeting of the Estates General to gain the backing of the nation. Shortly afterward, Boniface threatened to excommunicate Philip. The outraged monarch raided the papal summer palace at Anagni in September 1303 and captured the pope. Although Boniface was released, this shocking event proved too much for him, and a month later he died.

Boniface's two successors, Benedict XI (1303–1304) and Clement V (1305–1314), tried to conciliate Philip. In particular, Clement decided to remain at Avignon, a town on the southeastern French frontier, where he had set up a temporary residence.

From 1309 to 1377, a period known as the Babylonian Captivity, the popes were all French and resided in Avignon, not Rome. During this time, the papacy, removed from Rome and deprived of revenues from the Papal States in Italy, was often forced to pursue policies favorable to France. The growing antipapalism among the laity further damaged the papal image. Laypeople were repelled by the luxurious style of living at Avignon and by the appointment of high churchmen to lands where they did not know the language and showed little concern for the local population. Criticism of the papacy increased. The conflict between Boniface and Philip provoked a battle of words between proponents of papal supremacy and defenders of royal rights.

The most important critique of clerical intrusion into worldly affairs was *The Defender of the Peace* (1324) by Marsiglio of Padua (c. 1290–c. 1343). Marsiglio held that the state ran according to its principles, which had nothing to do with religious commands originating in a higher realm. Religion dealt with a supranatural world and with principles of faith that could not be proved by reason, wrote Marsiglio. Politics, on the other hand, dealt with the natural world and the affairs of the human community. Political thinkers should not try to make the earthly realm conform to articles of faith. For Marsiglio, the state was self-sufficient; it needed no instruction from a higher authority. Thus, Marsiglio denied the essential premises of medieval papal political theory: that the pope, as God's vicar, was empowered to guide kings; that the state, as part of a divinely ordered world, must conform to and fulfill supranatural ends; and that the clergy were above the laws of the state. Marsiglio viewed the church as a spiritual institution with no temporal power.

The Great Schism and the Conciliar Movement

Pope Gregory XI returned the papacy to Rome in 1377, ending the Babylonian Captivity. But the papacy was to endure an even greater humiliation: the Great Schism. Elected pope in 1378, Urban VI abused and imprisoned a number of cardinals. Fleeing from Rome, the cardinals declared that the election of Urban had been invalid and elected Clement VII as the new pope. Refusing to step down, Urban excommunicated Clement, who responded in kind. To the utter confusion and anguish of Christians throughout Europe, there were now two popes: urban ruling from Rome and Clement from Avignon.

Prominent churchmen urged the convening of a general council — the Council of Pisa — to end the disgraceful schism, which obstructed the papacy from performing its sacred duties. Held in 1409 and attended by hundreds of churchmen, the Council of Pisa deposed both Urban and Clement and elected a new pope. Neither deposed pope recognized the council's decision, so Christendom then had three popes. A new council was called at Constance in 1414. In the struggle that ensued, each of the three popes either abdicated or was deposed in favor of an appointment by the council. In 1417, the Great Schism ended.

During the first half of the fifteenth century, church councils met at Pisa (1409), Constance (1414–1418), and Basel (1431–1449) in order to end the schism, combat heresy, and reform the church. The Conciliar Movement attempted to transform the papal monarchy into a constitutional system, in which the pope's power would be regulated by a general council. Supporters of the movement held that the papacy could not reform the church as effectively as a general council representing the clergy. But the Conciliar Movement ended in failure. As the Holy Roman emperor and then the French monarch withdrew support from the councils, the papacy regained its authority over the higher clergy. In 1460, Pope Pius II condemned the Conciliar Movement as heretical.

Deeply embroiled in European power politics, the papacy often neglected its spiritual and moral responsibilities. Many devout Christians longed for a religious renewal, a return to simple piety. The papacy barely heard this cry for reform. Its failure to provide creative leadership for reform made possible the Protestant Reformation of the sixteenth century. By splitting Christendom into Catholic and Protestant, the Reformation destroyed forever the vision of a Christian world commonwealth guided by Christ's vicar, the pope.

Fourteenth-Century Heresies

Another threat to papal power and to the medieval ideal of a universal Christian community guided by the church came from radical reformers, who questioned the function and authority of the entire church hierarchy. These heretics in the Late Middle Ages were forerunners of the Protestant Reformation.

The two principal dissenters were the Englishman John Wycliffe (c. 1320–1384) and the Bohemian (Czech) Jan Hus (c. 1369–1415). By stressing a personal relationship between the individual and God and by claiming that the Bible itself, rather than church teachings, was the ultimate Christian authority, Wycliffe challenged the fundamental position of the medieval church: that the avenue to salvation passed through the church alone. He denounced the wealth of the higher clergy and sought a return to the spiritual purity and material poverty of the early church.

To Wycliffe, the wealthy, elaborately organized hierarchy of the church was unnecessary and wrong. The splendidly dressed and propertied bishops had no resemblance to the simple people who first followed Christ. Indeed, these worldly bishops, headed by a princely and tyrannical pope, were really anti-Christians, the "fiends of Hell." Wycliffe wanted the state to confiscate church property and the clergy to embrace poverty. By denying that priests changed the bread and wine of communion into the substance of the body and blood of Christ, Wycliffe rejected the sacramental power of the clergy. The church, in response, deprived the Lollards — an order of poor priests that spread Wycliffe's teachings — of their priestly functions. In the early fifteenth century, some of Wycliffe's followers were burned at the stake.

Wycliffe's ideas were enthusiastically received by Czech reformers in Bohemia led by Jan Hus. Like Wycliffe, Hus advocated vernacular translations of the Bible, which would be accessible to common people, and upbraided the upper clergy for their luxury and immorality.

Although both movements were declared heretical and Hus was burned at the stake, the church could not crush the dissenters' followers or eradicate their teachings. To some extent, the doctrines of the Reformation would parallel the teachings of Wycliffe and Hus.

Breakup of the Thomistic Synthesis

In the Late Middle Ages, the papacy lost power as kings, political theorists, and religious dissenters challenged papal claims to supreme leadership. The great theological synthesis constructed by the scholastic theologians of the twelfth and thirteenth centuries was also breaking down. The process of fragmentation seen in the history of the church took place in philosophy as well.

Saint Thomas Aquinas's system was the culmination of the scholastic attempt to show the basic agreement of philosophy and religion. In the fourteenth century, a number of thinkers cast doubt on the possibility of synthesizing Aristotelianism and Christianity, that is, reason and faith. Denying that reason could demonstrate the truth of Christian doctrines with certainty, philosophers tried to separate reason from faith. Whereas Aquinas had said that reason proved or clarified much of revelation, fourteenth-century thinkers asserted that the basic propositions of Christianity were not open to rational proof. Whereas Aquinas had held that faith supplemented and perfected reason, some philosophers were now proclaiming that reason often contradicted faith.

To be sure, this new outlook did not urge abandoning faith in favor of reason. Faith had to prevail in any conflict with reason because faith rested on God, the highest authority in the universe. But the relationship between reason and revelation was altered. Articles of faith, it was now held, had nothing to do with reason; they were to be believed, not proved. Reason was not an aid to theology but a separate sphere of activity. This new attitude snapped the link between reason and faith that Aquinas had so skillfully forged. The scholastic synthesis was disintegrating.

The chief proponent of this new outlook was William of Ockham (c. 1285–1349). In contrast to Aquinas, Ockham insisted that natural reason could not prove God's existence, the soul's immortality, or any other essential Christian doctrine. Reason could say only that God probably exists and that he probably endowed human beings with an immortal soul; it could not prove these propositions with certainty. The tenets of faith were beyond the reach of reason, said Ockham; there was no rational foundation to Christianity. For Ockham, reason and faith did not necessarily complement each other as they did for Aquinas; it was neither possible nor helpful to join reason to faith. He did not, however, seek to undermine faith — only to disengage it from reason.

In the process of proclaiming the authority of faith, Ockham also furthered the use of reason to comprehend nature. Ockham's approach, separating natural knowledge from religious dogma, made it easier to explore the natural world empirically, without fitting it into a religious framework. Ockham thus is a forerunner of the modern mentality, which is characterized by the separation of reason from religion and by an interest in the empirical investigation of nature.

The Middle Ages and the Modern World: Continuity and Discontinuity

Medieval civilization began to decline in the fourteenth century, but no dark age comparable to the three centuries following Rome's fall descended on Europe; its economic and political institutions and technological skills had grown too strong. Instead, the waning of the Middle Ages opened up possibilities for another stage in Western civilization: the modern age.

The modern world is linked to the Middle Ages in innumerable ways. European cities, the middle class, the state system, English common law, universities — all had their origins in the Middle Ages. During medieval times, important advances were made in business practices, including partnerships, systematic bookkeeping, and the bill of exchange. By translating and commenting on the writings of Greek and Arabic thinkers, medieval scholars preserved a priceless intellectual heritage, without which the modern mind could never have evolved. In addition, numerous strands connect the thought of the scholastics and that of early modern philosophers.

Feudal traditions lasted long after the Middle Ages. Up until the French Revolution, for instance, French aristocrats enjoyed special privileges and exercised power over local government. In England, the aristocracy controlled local government until the Industrial Revolution transformed English society in the nineteenth century. Retaining the medieval ideal of the noble warrior, aristocrats continued to dominate the officer corps of European armies through the nineteenth century and even into the twentieth. Aristocratic notions of duty, honor, loyalty, and courtly love have endured into the twentieth century.

During the Middle Ages, Europeans began to take the lead over the Muslims, the Byzantines, the Chinese, and all the other peoples in the use of technology. Medieval technology and inventiveness stemmed in part from Christianity, which taught that God had created the world specifically for human beings to subdue and exploit. Consequently, medieval people tried to employ animal power and laborsaving machinery to relieve human drudgery. Moreover, Christianity taught that God was above nature, not within it, so the Christian had no spiritual obstacle to exploiting nature — unlike, for instance, the Hindu. In contrast to classical humanism, the Christian outlook did not consider manual work degrading; even monks combined it with study.

The Christian stress on the sacred worth of the individual and on the higher law of God has never ceased to influence Western civilization. Even though in modern times the various Christian churches have not often taken the lead in political and social reform, the ideals identified with the Judeo-Christian tradition have become part of the Western heritage. As such, they have inspired social reformers who may no longer identify with their ancestral religion.

Believing that God's law was superior to state or national decrees, medieval philosophers provided a theoretical basis for opposing tyrannical kings who violated Christian principles. The idea that both the ruler and the ruled are bound by a higher law would, in a secularized form, become a principal element of modern liberal thought.

Feudalism also contributed to the history of liberty. According to feudal theory, the king, as a member of the feudal community, was duty-bound to honor agreements made with his vassals. Lords possessed personal rights, which the king was obliged to respect. Resentful of a king who ran roughshod over customary feudal rights, lords also negotiated contracts with the crown, such as the famous Magna Carta, to define and guard their customary liberties.

Wisdom Urges Medieval Scholars Forward.   During the Middle Ages, Europeans made considerable advances in technology. The astrolabe, quadrant, sundials, and mechanical clocks shown here illustrate medieval technical skills. (*Bibliothèque Royale Albert I, Brussels*)

To protect themselves from the arbitrary behavior of a king, feudal lords initiated what came to be called *government by consent* and the *rule of law*.

During the Middle Ages, then, there gradually emerged the idea that law was not imposed on inferiors by an absolute monarch but required the collaboration of the king and his subjects; that the king, too, was bound by the law; and that lords had the right to resist a monarch who violated agreements. A related phenomenon was the rise of representative institutions, with which the king was expected to consult on the realm's affairs. The most notable such institution was the British Parliament; although subordinate to the king, it became a permanent part of the state. Later, in the seventeenth century, Parliament would successfully challenge royal authority. Thus, continuity exists between the feudal tradition of a king bound by law and the modern practice of limiting the authority of the head of state.

Although the elements of continuity are clear, the characteristic outlook of the Middle Ages is as different from that of the modern age as it was from the outlook of the ancient world. Religion was the integrating feature of the Middle Ages, whereas science and secularism — a preoccupation with worldly life — determine the modern outlook. The period from the Italian Renaissance of the fifteenth century through the eighteenth-century Age of Enlightenment constituted a gradual breaking away from the medieval world-view: a rejection of the medieval conception of nature, the individual, and the purpose of life. The transition from medieval to modern was neither sudden nor complete, for there are no sharp demarcation lines separating historical periods. While many distinctively medieval ways endured into the sixteenth, seventeenth, and even eighteenth centuries, these centuries saw as well the rise of new intellectual, political, and economic forms that marked the emergence of modernity.

Medieval thought began with the existence of God and the truth of his revelation as interpreted by the church, which set the standards and defined the purposes for human endeavor. The medieval mind rejected the fundamental principle of Greek philosophy: the autonomy of reason. Without the guidance of revealed truth, reason was seen as feeble.

Scholastics engaged in genuine philosophical speculation, but they did not allow philosophy to challenge the basic premises of their faith. Unlike either ancient or modern thinkers, medieval schoolmen ultimately believed that reason alone could not provide a unified view of nature or society. A rational soul had to be guided by a divine light. For all medieval philosophers, the natural order depended on a supernatural order for its origin and purpose. To understand the natural world properly, it was necessary to know its relationship to the higher world. The discoveries of reason had to accord with Scripture as interpreted by the church.

In the modern view, both nature and the human intellect are self-sufficient. Nature is a mathematical system that operates without miracles or any other form of divine intervention. To comprehend nature and society, the mind needs no divine assistance; it accepts no authority above reason. The modern mentality finds it unacceptable to reject the conclusions of science on the basis of clerical authority and revelation or to ground politics, law, or economics on religious dogma. It refuses to settle public issues by appeals to religious belief.

The medieval philosopher understood both nature and society to be hierarchical. God was the source of moral values, and the church was responsible for teaching and upholding these ethical norms. Kings acquired their right to rule from God. The entire social structure constituted a hierarchy: the clergy guided society according to Christian standards; lords defended Christian society from its enemies; and serfs, lowest in the social order, toiled for the good of all. In the hierarchy of knowledge, a lower form of knowledge derived from the senses, and the highest type of knowledge, theology, dealt with God's revelation. To the medieval mind, this hierarchical ordering of nature, society, and knowledge had divine sanction.

Rejecting the medieval division of the universe into higher and lower realms and superior and inferior substances, the modern view postulates the uniformity of nature and of nature's laws: the cosmos knows no privilege of rank; heavenly bodies follow the same laws of nature as earthly objects. Space is geometric and homogeneous, not hierarchical, heterogeneous, and qualitative. The universe is no longer conceived of as finite and closed, but seen as infinite, and the operations of nature are explained mathematically. The modern thinker studies mathematical law and chemical composition, not grades of perfection. Spiritual meaning is not sought in an examination of the material world. Roger Bacon, for example, described seven coverings of the eye and then concluded that God had fashioned the eye in this manner in order to express the seven gifts of the Spirit. This way of thinking is alien to the modern outlook. So, too, is the medieval belief that natural disasters, such as plagues and famines, are God's punishments for people's sins.

The outlook of the modern West also broke with the rigid division of medieval society into three orders: clergy, nobles, and commoners. The intellectual justification for this arrangement, as expressed by the English prelate John of Salisbury (c. 1115–1180), has been rejected by modern westerners: "For inferiors owe it to their superiors to provide them with service, just as the superiors in their turn owe it to their inferiors to provide them with all things needful for their protection and succor."[4] Opposing the feudal principle that an individual's obligations and rights are a function of his or her rank in society, the modern view stresses equality of opportunity and equal treatment under the law. It rejects the idea that society should be guided by clergy, who are deemed to possess a special wisdom; by nobles, who are entitled to special privileges; and by monarchs, who are thought to receive their power from God.

The modern West has also rejected the personal and customary character of feudal law. As the modern state developed, law assumed an impersonal and objective character. For example, if a lord demanded more than the customary forty days of military service, a vassal might refuse to comply because he would see the lord's request as an unpardonable violation of custom and agreement, as well as an infringement on his liberties. In the modern state, with a constitution and a representative assembly, if a new law increasing the length of military service is passed, it merely replaces the old law. People do not refuse to obey it because the government has broken faith or violated custom.

In the modern world, the individual's relationship to the universe has been radically transformed. Medieval people lived in a geocentric universe that was finite in space and time. The universe was small, enclosed by a sphere of stars, beyond which were the heavens. The universe, it was believed, was some four thousand years old, and, in the not-too-distant future, Christ would return and human history would end. People in the Middle Ages knew why they were on earth and what was expected of them; they never doubted that heaven would be their reward for living a Christian life. Preparation for heaven was the ultimate aim of life. J. H. Randall, Jr., a historian of ideas, eloquently sums up the medieval view of a purposeful universe, in which the human being's position was clearly defined:

> *The world was governed throughout by the omnipotent will and omniscient mind of God, whose sole interests were centered in man, his*

trial, his fall, his suffering and his glory. Worm of the dust as he was, man was yet the central object in the whole universe. . . . And when his destiny was completed, the heavens would be rolled up as a scroll and he would dwell with the Lord forever. Only those who rejected God's freely offered grace and with hardened hearts refused repentance would be cut off from this eternal life.[5]

This comforting medieval vision is alien to the modern outlook. Today, in a universe some twelve billion years old, in which the earth is a tiny speck floating in an endless cosmic ocean, where life evolved over tens of millions of years, many westerners no longer believe that human beings are special children of God; that heaven is their ultimate goal; that under their feet is hell, where grotesque demons torment sinners; and that God is an active agent in human history. To many intellectuals, the universe seems unresponsive to people's religious supplications, and life's purpose is sought within the limits of earthly existence. Science and secularism have driven Christianity and faith from their central position to the periphery of human concerns.

The modern outlook developed gradually in the period from the Renaissance to the eighteenth-century Age of Enlightenment. Mathematics rendered the universe comprehensible. Economic and political thought broke free of the religious frame of reference. Science became the great hope of the future. The thinkers of the Enlightenment wanted to liberate humanity from superstition, ignorance, and traditions that could not pass the test of reason. They saw themselves as emancipating culture from theological dogma and clerical authority. Rejecting the Christian idea of a person's inherent sinfulness, they held that the individual was basically good and that evil resulted from faulty institutions, poor education, and bad leadership. Thus, the concept of a rational and free society in which individuals could realize their potential slowly emerged.

Notes

1. Quoted in David Knowles, *The Evolution of Medieval Thought* (New York: Vintage Books, 1964), p. 123.
2. Thomas Aquinas, *Summa Theologica,* Pt. 1, question 2, art. 3. Excerpted in Anton C. Pegis, ed., *Introduction to Saint Thomas Aquinas* (New York: Modern Library, 1948), p. 25.
3. Joan Gadol, *Leon Battista Alberti,*

Universal Man of the Early Renaissance (Chicago: University of Chicago Press, 1969), pp. 149–150.
4. John of Salisbury, *Policraticus,* trans. John Dickinson (New York: Russell & Russell, 1963), pp. 243–244.
5. J. H. Randall, Jr., *The Making of the Modern Mind* (Boston: Houghton Mifflin, 1940), p. 34.

Suggested Reading

Baldwin, John W., *The Scholastic Culture of the Middle Ages* (1971). A useful introductory survey.

Bonner, Anthony, ed., *Songs of the Troubadours* (1972). Collection of troubadour poetry.

Brooke, Christopher, *The Twelfth-Century Renaissance* (1969). Surveys schools, learning, theology, literature, and leading figures.

Copleston, F. C., *A History of Medieval Philosophy* (1974). A lucid, comprehensive survey of medieval philosophy.

Flanagan, Sabina, *Hildegard of Bingen* (1989). A biography of a remarkable medieval woman who distinguished herself as a mystic, poet, and naturalist.

Gilson, Etienne, *Reason and Revelation in the Middle Ages* (1966). A superb brief exposition of the medieval philosophical tradition.

Gimpel, Jean, *The Cathedral Builders* (1984). The financial, political, and spiritual forces behind the building of cathedrals.

Haskins, C. H., *The Renaissance of the Twelfth Century* (1957). Reprint of a still useful work.

Hay, Denys, *Europe in the Fourteenth and Fifteenth Centuries* (1966). A good survey of the Late Middle Ages.

Lerner, Robert E., *The Age of Adversity* (1968). A short, readable survey of the fourteenth century.

Ozment, Steven E., *The Age of Reform, 1250–1550* (1980). An intellectual and religious history of late medieval and Reformation Europe.

Pieper, Josef, *Scholasticism* (1964). Written with intelligence and grace.

Piltz, Anders, *The World of Medieval Learning* (1981). A clearly written, informative survey of medieval education and learning.

Wagner, David L., ed., *The Seven Liberal Arts in the Middle Ages* (1983). Essays on the place of the liberal arts in medieval culture.

Wieruszowski, Helene, *The Medieval University* (1966). A good survey, followed by documents.

Review Questions

1. What factors contributed to the revival of learning in the late eleventh and twelfth centuries?
2. Describe the essential features of the medieval view of the universe. How does it differ from the modern view?
3. The medieval individual's understanding of self was related to a comprehension of the universe as a hierarchy culminating in God. Explain this statement.
4. What were scholastic philosophers trying to accomplish?
5. What was the significance of Aquinas's thought?
6. Describe what each of the following tells about the attitudes and interests of medieval people: troubadour poetry, *The Canterbury Tales, The Divine Comedy,* and Gothic cathedrals.
7. What economic problems made the fourteenth century an age of adversity?
8. How was the church's authority weakened in the Late Middle Ages?
9. What is the legacy of the Middle Ages to the modern world?
10. How does the characteristic outlook of the Middle Ages differ from that of the modern age?

❖ PART THREE

The Rise of Modernity: From the Renaissance to the Enlightenment

1350–1789

Departure from Lisbon for Brazil, the East Indies, and America, by Theodore de Bry, 1562. (*Giraudon/Art Resource, NY*)

POLITICS AND SOCIETY	THOUGHT AND CULTURE
1300 Hundreds Years' War (1337–1453)	Italian Renaissance begins (c. 1350)
1400 War of Roses in England (1455–1485) Rule of Ferdinand and Isabella in Spain (1469–1516) Charles VIII of France (1483–1498) Henry VII, beginning of Tudor dynasty in England (1485–1509) Columbus reaches America (1492)	Early Renaissance artists: Brunelleschi, Masaccio, van Eyck Printing with movable type (c. 1450) Humanists: Valla, Pico della Mirandola Late Renaissance artists: Botticelli, Leonardo da Vinci, Michelangelo, Raphael, Bellini, Giorgione, Titian Renaissance spreads to northern Europe (late fifteenth and early sixteenth cent.)
1500 Henry VIII of England (1509–1547) Francis I of France (1515–1547) Charles V, Holy Roman Emperor (1519–1556) Henry VIII of England breaks with Rome (1529–1536) Council of Trent (1545–1563) Peace of Augsburg in Germany (1555) Philip II of Spain (1556–1598) Elizabeth I of England (1558–1603) Religious wars in France (1562–1598) Revolt of the Netherlands from Spain (1566–1609) Defeat of Spanish Armada (1588)	Humanists: Castiglione, Erasmus, Montaigne, Rabelais, More, Cervantes, Shakespeare Machiavelli, *The Prince* (1513) Luther writes his Ninety-Five Theses (1517) Copernicus, *On the Revolution of the Heavenly Spheres* (1543)
1600 Thirty Years' War (1618–1648) English Revolution (1640–1660, 1688–1689) Louis XIV of France (1643–1715) Peter the Great of Russia (1682–1725)	Scientists: Kepler, Galileo, Newton Philosophers: Bacon, Descartes, Hobbes, Locke
1700 War of Spanish Succession (1702–1714) War of Austrian Succession (1740–1748) Frederick the Great of Prussia (1740–1786) Maria Theresa of Austria (1740–1780) Seven Years' War (1756–1763) American Declaration of Independence (1776) American Revolution (1776–1783) Beginning of French Revolution (1789)	Enlightenment thinkers: Voltaire, Montesquieu, Rousseau, Diderot, Hume, Adam Smith, Thomas Jefferson, Kant

❖ CHAPTER 8

Transition to the Modern Age: Renaissance and Reformation

*F*rom the Italian Renaissance of the fifteenth century through the Age of Enlightenment of the eighteenth century, the outlook and institutions of the Middle Ages disintegrated and distinctly modern forms emerged. The radical change in European civilization affected every level of society. On the economic level, commerce and industry expanded greatly, and capitalism largely replaced medieval forms of economic organization. On the political level, central government grew stronger at the expense of feudalism. On the religious level, the rise of Protestantism fragmented the unity of Christendom. On the social level, middle-class townspeople, increasing in number and wealth, began to play a more important role in economic and cultural life. On the cultural level, the clergy lost its monopoly over learning, and the otherworldly orientation of the Middle Ages gave way to a secular outlook in literature and the arts. Theology, the queen of knowledge in the Middle Ages, surrendered its crown to science, and reason, which had been subordinate to revelation, asserted its independence.

Many of these tendencies manifested themselves dramatically during the Renaissance (1350–1600). The word *renaissance* means "rebirth," and it is used to refer to the attempt by artists and thinkers to recover and apply the ancient learning and standards of Greece and Rome. During the Renaissance, individuals showed an increasing concern for worldly life and self-consciously aspired to shape their destinies, an attitude that is the key to modernity.

To be sure, the Renaissance was not a complete and sudden break with the Middle Ages. Many medieval ways and attitudes persisted. Nevertheless, the view that the Renaissance represents the birth of modernity has much to recommend it. Renaissance writers and artists themselves were aware of their age's novelty. They looked back on the medieval centuries as a "Dark Age" that followed the grandeur of ancient Greece and Rome, and they believed that they were experiencing a rebirth of cultural greatness. Renaissance artists and writers were fascinated by the cultural forms of Greece and Rome; they sought to imitate classical style and to capture the secular spirit of antiquity. In the process, they broke with medieval artistic and literary forms. They valued the full development of human talent and expressed a new excitement about the possibilities of life in this world. This outlook represents a break with the Middle Ages and the emergence of modernity.

The Renaissance, then, was an age of transition. It saw the rejection of certain elements of the medieval outlook, the revival of classical cultural forms, and the emergence of distinctly modern attitudes. This rebirth began in Italy during the fourteenth century and gradually spread north and west to Germany, France, England, and Spain during the late fifteenth and sixteenth centuries.

The Renaissance was one avenue to modernity; another was the Reformation. By dividing Europe into Catholic and Protestant, the Reformation ended medieval religious unity. It also accentuated the importance of the individual person, a distinctive feature of the modern outlook. It stressed individual conscience rather than clerical authority, insisted on a personal relationship between each man or woman and God, and called attention to the individual's inner religious capacities. ❖

Italy: Birthplace of the Renaissance

The city-states of northern Italy that spawned the Renaissance were developed urban centers, where people had the wealth, freedom, and inclination to cultivate the arts and to enjoy the fruits of worldly life. In Italy, moreover, reminders of ancient Rome's grandeur were visible everywhere: Roman roads, monuments, and manuscripts intensified the Italians' links to their Roman past. Northern Italian city-states had developed into flourishing commercial and banking centers and had monopolized trade in the Mediterranean during the twelfth and thirteenth centuries. The predominance of business and commerce within these city-states meant that the feudal nobility, which held the land beyond the city walls, played a much less important part in government than it did elsewhere in Europe. By the end of the twelfth century, these city-states had adopted a fairly uniform pattern of republican self-government, built around the office of a chief magistrate.

This republicanism proved precarious, however. During the fourteenth and early fifteenth centuries, republican institutions in one city after another toppled, giving way to rule by despots. The city-states had come to rely on mercenary troops, whose leaders, the notorious *condottieri* — unschooled in and owing no loyalty to the republican tradition — simply seized power during emergencies.

Florence, the leading city of the Renaissance, held out against the trend toward despotism for a long time. But by the mid-fifteenth century, even Florentine republicanism was giving way before the intrigues of a rich banking family, the Medici. They had installed themselves in power in the 1430s with

Chronology 8.1 ❖ The Renaissance and the Reformation

1304–1374	Petrarch, "father of humanism"
c. 1445	Johann Gutenberg invents movable metal type
1513	Machiavelli writes *The Prince*
1517	Martin Luther writes his Ninety-five Theses and the Reformation begins
1520	Pope Leo X excommunicates Luther
1524–1526	German peasants revolt
1529	English Parliament accepts Henry VIII's Reformation
1534	Henry VIII is declared head of the Church of England; King Francis I of France declares Protestants to be heretics; Ignatius Loyola founds the Society of Jesus; Anabaptists, radical reformers, capture Münster in Westphalia
1535	Sir Thomas More, English humanist and author of *Utopia*, is executed for treason
1536–1564	Calvin leads the Reformation in Geneva
1545–1563	Council of Trent
1555	Peace of Augsburg

the return of Cosimo de' Medici from exile. Cosimo's grandson, Lorenzo the Magnificent, completed the destruction of the republican constitution in 1480, when he managed to set up a government staffed by his supporters.

New ways of life developed within the Italian city-states. Prosperous business people played a leading role in the political and cultural life of the city. With the expansion of commerce and industry, the feudal values of birth, military prowess, and a fixed hierarchy of lords and vassals decayed in favor of ambition and individual achievement, whether at court, in the counting house, or inside the artist's studio.

Art served as a focus of civic pride and patriotism. Members of the urban upper class became patrons of the arts, providing funds to support promising artists and writers. Just as they contended on the battlefield, rulers competed for art and artists to bolster their prestige. The popes, too, heaped wealth on artists to enhance their own flagging prestige. They became the most lavish patrons of all, as the works of Michelangelo and Raphael testify.

Some women of wealthy and noble Italian families were educated in classical languages and literature and served as patrons of the arts. Thus, Isabella d'Este,

Ludovico Gonzaga, His Family and Court: A Fresco Painted by Andrea Mantegna, A.D. 1465–1474.   The Gonzaga family came to power as princes of Mantua, selling their services as condottieri to the Venetians, Milanese, or others as their interests dictated. Ludovico (1414–1478) presided over the city at a time of great prosperity. He commissioned the famous painter Andrea Mantegna to decorate his palace and the architect Leon Battista Alberti to build several churches. His patronage of humanistic scholars, poets, and philosophers added to the prestige of the city and its princely ruler. (*Alinari/Art Resource, NY*)

wife of the ruler of a small state in northern Italy, knew Latin and Greek, collected books, and displayed works of artists that she had commissioned.

The result of this new patronage by popes and patricians was an explosion of artistic creativity. The amount, and especially the nature, of this patronage also helped shape both art and the artist. Portraiture became a separate genre for the first time since antiquity and was developed much further than ever before. Patrician rivalry and insecurity of status, fed by the Renaissance ethic of individual achievement and reward, produced a scramble for honor and reputation. This pursuit fostered the desire to be memorialized in a painting, if not in a sculpture. Distinguished portrait painters and sculptors were in great demand.

The great artists emerged as famous men by virtue of their exercise of brush and chisel. In the Middle Ages, artists had been regarded as craftsmen who did lowly (manual) labor and who, as a result, were to be accorded little, if any, status. Indeed, for the most part they remained anonymous. But the unparalleled Renaissance demand for art brought artists public recognition.

The Renaissance Outlook

Increasingly, a secular outlook came to dominate Renaissance society. Intrigued by the active life of the city and eager to enjoy the worldly pleasures that their money could obtain, wealthy merchants and bankers moved away from the medieval preoccupation with salvation. To be sure, they were neither nonbelievers nor atheists, but more and more, religion had to compete with worldly concerns. Consequently, members of the urban upper class paid religion less heed, or at least did not allow it to interfere with their quest for the full life. The challenge and pleasure of living well in this world seemed more exciting than the promise of heaven. This outlook found concrete expression in Renaissance art and literature.

Individualism was another hallmark of the Renaissance. In contrast to medieval thinkers, who emphasized the Christian belief in human weakness, sinfulness, and dependency, Renaissance figures revived the classical confidence in human capacities and extolled the infinite possibilities of individual life. The urban elite sought to assert their own personalities, demonstrate their unique talents, and gain recognition for their accomplishments. Traditional feudal values of birth and place in a fixed hierarchy were superseded by the desire for individual achievement. Individual worth was interpreted far more broadly than it had been by feudal lords, who had equated worth with military prowess. Renaissance Italy produced a distinctive human type, the "universal man": a many-sided person, who not only showed mastery of the ancient classics, an appreciation of and even talent for the visual arts, and a concern for the day-to-day affairs of his city, but also aspired to mold his life into a work of art. Disdaining Christian humility, Renaissance individuals took pride in their talents and worldly accomplishments — "I can work miracles," said the great Leonardo da Vinci. Renaissance artists portrayed the individual character of human beings, captured the rich diversity of human personality, produced the first portraits since Roman times, and affixed their signatures to their works. Renaissance writers probed their own feelings and manifested a self-awareness that characterizes the modern outlook.

In later centuries, as the secular outlook gathered strength, it focused even more intently on the individual. It led to the conviction that the individual should be freed from domination by otherworldly concerns, theological dogma, and ecclesiastical authority and should concentrate on the full development of human talents and on improving the quality of earthly existence.

During the Renaissance, the secular spirit and the concern with the individual found expression in the intellectual movement called humanism and in a political theory that separated politics from Christian principles.

Humanism

Humanism, the most characteristic intellectual movement of the Renaissance, was an educational and cultural program based on the study of ancient Greek and Roman literature. The humanist attitude toward antiquity differed from that of medieval scholars, who had taken pains to fit classical learning into a Christian world-view. Renaissance humanists did not subordinate the classics to the requirements of Christian doctrines. Rather, they valued ancient literature for its own sake — for its clear and graceful style and for its insights into human nature. From the ancient classics, humanists expected to learn much that could not be provided by medieval writings: for instance, how to live well in this world and how to perform one's civic duties. For the humanists, the classics were a guide to the good life, the active life. To achieve self-cultivation, to write well, to speak well, and to live well, it was necessary to know the classics. In contrast to scholastic philosophers, who used Greek philosophy to prove the truth of Christian doctrines, Italian humanists used classical learning to nourish their new interest in a worldly life. Whereas medieval scholars were familiar with only some ancient Latin writers, Renaissance humanists restored to circulation every Roman work that could be found. Similarly, knowledge of Greek was very rare in Latin Christendom during the Middle Ages, but Renaissance humanists increasingly cultivated the study of Greek in order to read Homer, Demosthenes, Plato, and other ancients in the original.

Although predominantly a secular movement, Italian humanism was not un-Christian. True, humanists often treated moral problems in a purely secular manner. Yet in dealing with religious and theological issues, they did not challenge Christian belief or question the validity of the Bible. They did, however, attack scholastic philosophy for its hairsplitting arguments and preoccupation with trivial matters. They stressed instead a purer form of Christianity, based on the direct study of the Bible and the writings of the church fathers.

One of the early humanists, sometimes called the father of humanism, was Petrarch (1304–1374). Petrarch and his followers carried the recovery of the classics further through their systematic attempt to discover the classical roots of medieval Italian rhetoric. Petrarch's own efforts to learn Greek were largely unsuccessful, but he advanced humanist learning by encouraging his students to master the ancient tongue. Petrarch was particularly drawn to Cicero, the ancient Roman orator. Following Cicero's example, he maintained that education should consist not only of learning and knowing things, but also of learning how to communicate one's knowledge and how to use it for the public good. Therefore, the emphasis in education should be on rhetoric and moral philosophy — wisdom combined with eloquence. This was the key to virtue in the ruler, the citizen, and the republic. Petrarch helped to make Ciceronian values dominant among the humanists. His followers set up schools to inculcate the new Ciceronian educational ideal.

Implicit in the humanist educational ideal was a radical transformation of the Christian idea of human beings. According to the medieval (Augustinian) view, men and women, because of their sinful nature, were incapable of attaining excellence through their own efforts. They were completely subject to divine will. In contrast, the humanists, recalling the classical Greek concept of human beings, made the achievement of excellence through individual striving the end not only of education, but of life itself. Moreover, because individuals were capable of this goal, it was their duty to pursue it as the end of life. The pursuit was not effortless; indeed, it took extraordinary energy and skill.

People, then, were deemed capable of excellence in every sphere and duty-bound to make the effort. This emphasis on human creative powers was one of the most characteristic and influential doctrines of the Renaissance. A classic expression of it is found in the *Oration on the Dignity of Man* (1486) by Giovanni Pico della Mirandola (1463–1494). Man, said Pico, has the freedom to shape his own life. Pico has God say to man: "We have made you a creature" such that "you may, as the free and proud shaper of your own being, fashion yourself in the form you may prefer."[1]

An attack on the medieval scholastics was also implicit in the humanist educational ideal. Humanists accused scholastics of corrupting the Latin style of ancient Rome and of dealing with useless questions. This humanist emphasis on the uses of knowledge offered a stimulus to science and art.

So hostile were the humanists to things scholastic and medieval that they reversed the prevailing view of history. According to the Christian view, history was a simple unfolding of God's will and providence. The humanists, however, stressed the importance of human actions and human will in history — the importance of people as active participants in the shaping of events. They characterized the epoch preceding their own as a period of decline from classical heights — a dark age — and saw their own time as a period of rebirth, representing the recovery of classical wisdom and ideals. Thus, the humanists invented the notion of the Middle Ages as the period separating the ancient world from their own. To the humanists, then, we owe the current periodization of history into ancient, medieval, and modern. The humanists' view also contained an element of today's idea of progress: they dared to think that they, "the moderns," might even surpass the ancient glories of Greece and Rome.

The humanist emphasis on historical scholarship yielded a method of critical inquiry that could help to undermine traditional loyalties and institutions. The work of Lorenzo Valla (c. 1407–1457) provides the clearest example of this trend. Educated as a classicist, Valla trained the guns of critical scholarship on the papacy in his most famous work, *Declamation Concerning the False Decretals of Constantine*. The papal claim to temporal authority rested on a document that purported to verify the so-called Donation of Constantine, through which the Emperor Constantine, when he moved the capital of the Roman Empire to Constantinople in the fourth century, had given the pope dominion over the entire Western Empire. But Valla proved that the document was based on an eighth-century forgery because the language at certain points was unknown in Constantine's time and did not come into use until much later.

Also embedded in the humanist reevaluation of individual potential was a new appreciation of the moral significance of work. For the humanist, the honor, fame, and even glory bestowed by one's city or patron for meritorious deeds was the ultimate reward for effort. The humanist pursuit of praise and reputation became something of a Renaissance cult.

A Revolution in Political Thought

By turning away from the religious orientation of the Middle Ages and discussing the human condition in secular terms, Renaissance humanists opened up new possibilities for thinking about political and moral problems. Niccolò Machiavelli (1469–1527), a keen observer of Italian politics, saw the Italian city-states, ruled by men whose authority rested solely on their cunning and effective use of force, as a new phenomenon. He recognized that traditional political theory, concerned with ideal Christian ends, could not adequately explain it. Italian princes made no effort to justify their policies on religious grounds; war was endemic, and powerful cities took over weaker ones; diplomacy was riddled with intrigue, betrayal, and bribery. In such a tooth-and-claw world — where political survival depended on alertness, cleverness, and strength — medieval theorists, who expected the earthly realm to accord with standards revealed by God, seemed utterly irrelevant. Machiavelli simply wanted rulers to understand how to prepare and expand the state's power. In his book *The Prince*, he expounded a new political theory — one that had no place for Christian morality but coincided with the emerging modern secular state. He himself was aware that his study of statecraft in the cold light of reason, free of religious and moral illusions, represented a new departure.

For Machiavelli, survival was the state's overriding aim; it transcended any concern with moral or religious values and the interests of individual subjects. Removing questions of good and evil from the political realm, Machiavelli maintained that the prince may use any means to save the state when its survival is at stake. Successful princes, he contended, have always been indifferent to moral and religious considerations — a lesson of history that rulers ignore at their peril. Thus, if the situation warrants it, the prince can violate agreements with other rulers, go back on his word with his subjects, and resort to cruelty and terror.

Machiavelli broke with the distinguishing feature of medieval thought: the division of the universe into the higher world of the heavens and a lower earthly realm. To this extent, he did for politics what Galileo accomplished a century later for physics. Medieval thinkers believed that rulers derived their power from God and had a religious obligation to govern in accordance with God's commands. Rejecting completely this otherworldly, theocentric orientation, Machiavelli ascribed no divine origin or purpose to the state. He saw it as a natural entity; politics had nothing to do with God's intent or with moral precepts originating in a higher world. Machiavelli's significance as a political thinker rests on the fact that he removed political thought from a religious frame of reference and viewed the state and political behavior in the detached and dispassionate manner of a scientist. In secularizing and rationalizing political philosophy, he initiated a trend of thought that we recognize as distinctly modern.

Renaissance Art

The essential meaning of the Renaissance is conveyed through its art, particularly architecture, sculpture, and painting. Renaissance examples of all three art forms reflect a style that stressed proportion, balance, and harmony. These artistic values were achieved through a new, revolutionary conceptualization of space and spatial relations. To a considerable extent, Renaissance art also reflects the values of Renaissance humanism: a return to classical models in architecture, to the rendering of the nude figure, and to a heroic vision of human beings.

Medieval art served a religious function and sought to represent spiritual aspiration; the world was a veil merely hinting at the other perfect and eternal world. Renaissance art did not stop expressing spiritual aspiration, but its setting and character differ altogether. No longer a shroud, this world becomes the place where people live, act, and worship. The reference is less to the other world and more to this world, and people are treated as creatures who find their spiritual destiny as they fulfill their human one. At its most distinctive, Renaissance art represents a conscious revolt against the art of the Middle Ages. This revolt produced revolutionary discoveries that served as the foundation of Western art up to this century.

In art, as in philosophy, the Florentines played a leading role in this esthetic transformation. They, more than anyone else, were responsible for the way artists saw and drew for centuries and for the way most Western people still see or want to see. The first major contributor to Renaissance painting was the Florentine painter Giotto (c. 1276–1337). Borrowing from Byzantine painting, he created figures delineated by alterations in light and shade. He also developed several techniques of perspective, representing three-dimensional figures and objects on two-dimensional surfaces so that they appear to stand in space. Giotto's figures look remarkably alive. They are drawn and arranged in space to tell a story, and their expressions and the illusion of movement they convey heighten the dramatic effect. Giotto's best works were *frescoes,* wall paintings painted while the plaster was still wet, or *fresh.* Lionized in his own day, Giotto had no immediate successors, and his ideas were not taken up and developed further for almost a century.

By the early fifteenth century, the revival of classical learning had begun in earnest. In Florence, it had its artistic counterpart among a circle of architects, painters, and sculptors who sought to revive classical art. The leader of this group was an architect, Filippo Brunelleschi (1377–1446). He designed churches reflecting classical models. To him we also owe a scientific discovery of the first importance in the history of art: the rules of perspective. Giotto had revived the ancient technique of foreshortening; Brunelleschi completed the discovery by rendering perspective in mathematical terms. Brunelleschi's devotion to ancient models and his new tool of mathematical perspective set the stage for the further development of Renaissance painting. Brunelleschi's young Florentine friend Masaccio (1401–1428) took up the challenge. Faithful to the new rules of perspective, Masaccio was also concerned with painting statuesque figures and endowing his paintings with a grandeur and

The Birth of Venus by Sandro Botticelli (1444–1510).   A member of the Florentine circle of Neo-Platonists, Botticelli celebrated classical myths, such as the rising of Venus, goddess of love, who was born in the sea. The use of classical deities and myths in Western art and literature took on new force during the Renaissance. (*Alinari/Art Resource, NY*)

simplicity whose inspiration was classical. Perspective came with all the force of religious revelation.

In his work *On Painting,* Leon Battista Alberti (1404–1472), a humanist, scholar, and art theoretician, brought the Renaissance trend toward perspectival art to a summation by advancing the first mathematical theory of artistic perspective. By defining visual space and the relationship between the object and the observer in mathematical terms, Renaissance art and artistic theory helped to pave the way for the development of the modern scientific approach to nature, which later found expression in the astronomy of Copernicus and the physics of Galileo.

Renaissance artists were dedicated to representing things as they are, or at least as they are seen to be. Part of the inspiration for this was also classical. The ancient ideal of beauty was the beautiful nude. Renaissance admiration for ancient art meant that for the first time since the fall of Rome, artists studied anatomy; they learned to draw the human form by having models pose for them, a practice fundamental to artistic training to this day. Another member of Brunelleschi's circle, the Florentine sculptor Donatello (1386–1466), also showed renewed interest in the human form.

The great Renaissance artists included Leonardo da Vinci (1452–1519), Michelangelo Buonarroti (1475–1564), and Raphael Santi (1483–1520). All of them were closely associated with Florence. Leonardo was a scientist and engineer as well as a great artist. He was an expert at fortifications and gunnery, an inventor, an anatomist, and a naturalist. Bringing careful observation of nature to his paintings, he combined it with powerful psychological insight to produce works of unsurpassed genius, though few in number. Among his most important paintings are *The Last Supper* and *La Gioconda,* or the Mona Lisa. The Mona Lisa is an example of an artistic invention of Leonardo's — what the Italians call *sfumato.* Leonardo left the outlines of the face a little vague and shadowy; this freed it of any wooden quality, which more exact drawing would impart, and thus made it more lifelike and mysterious.

Michelangelo's creation of artistic harmony derived from a mastery of anatomy and drawing. His model in painting came from sculpture: his paintings are sculpted drawings. He was, of course, a sculptor of the highest genius whose approach to his art was poetic and visionary. Instead of trying to impose form on marble, he thought of sculpting as releasing the form from the rock. Among his greatest sculptures are *David, Moses,* and *The Dying Slave.* Michelangelo was also an architect; patronized by the pope, he designed the dome of the new Saint Peter's Basilica in Rome. But perhaps his most stupendous work was the ceiling of the Sistine Chapel in the Vatican, commissioned by Pope Julius II. In four years, working with little assistance, Michelangelo covered the empty space with the most monumental sculpted pictures ever painted, pictures that summarize the Old Testament story. *The Creation of Adam* is the most famous of these superlative frescoes.

Raphael, the last of these three artistic giants, is especially famous for the sweetness of his Madonnas. But he was capable of painting other subjects and conveying other moods, as his portrait of his patron, *Pope Leo X with Two Cardinals,* reveals.

The Spread of the Renaissance

Aided by the invention of printing, the Renaissance spread to Germany, France, England, and Spain in the late fifteenth and sixteenth centuries. In its migration northward, Renaissance culture adapted itself to conditions different from those in Italy — particularly the strength of lay piety. For example, the Brethren of the Common Life was a lay movement emphasizing education and practical piety. Intensely Christian and at the same time anticlerical, the people in such lay movements found in Renaissance culture tools for sharpening their wits against the clergy — not to undermine the faith, but rather to restore it to its apostolic purity.

Thus, northern humanists, like those in Italy, were profoundly devoted to ancient learning. But nothing in northern humanism compares with the non-Christian trend of the Italian Renaissance. The northerners were chiefly interested in the question of what constituted original Christianity. They sought a model in the light of which they might reform the corrupted church of their own time.

Giovanni Arnolfini and His Bride by Jan van Eyck (c. 1390–1441). The painting uses the new technique of perspective and draws a careful, and idealized, portrait of a prosperous married couple in their bedroom. As such, it depicts a world that values privacy, sober prosperity, and intimacy of a certain kind: he stares out at us, while she looks deferentially at him. (*Reproduced by courtesy of the Trustees, The National Gallery, London*)

Humanism outside Italy was less concerned with the revival of classical values than with the reform of Christianity and society through a program of Christian humanism. The Christian humanists cultivated the new arts of rhetoric and history, as well as the classical languages — Latin, Greek, and Hebrew. But the ultimate purpose of these pursuits was more religious than it had been in Italy, where secular interests predominated. Northern humanists used humanist scholarship and language to satirize and vilify medieval scholastic Christianity and to build a purer, more scriptural Christianity. The discovery of accurate biblical texts, it was hoped, would lead to a great religious awakening. Protestant reformers, including Martin Luther, relied on humanist scholarship.

Erasmian Humanism

To Erasmus (c. 1466–1536) belongs the credit for making Renaissance humanism an international movement. He was educated in the Netherlands by the Brethren of the Common Life, which was one of the most advanced religious movements of the age, combining mystical piety with rigorous humanist pedagogy. Erasmus traveled throughout Europe as a humanist educator and biblical scholar. Like other Christian humanists, he trusted the power of words and used his pen to attack scholastic theology and clerical abuses and promote his philosophy of Christ. His weapon was satire, and his *Praise of Folly* and *Colloquies* won him a reputation for acid wit vented at the expense of conventional religion.

True religion, Erasmus argued, does not depend on dogma, ritual, or clerical power. Rather, it is revealed clearly and simply in the Bible and therefore is directly accessible to all people, from the wise and great to the poor and humble. Erasmian humanism stressed toleration, kindness, and respect for human rationality.

This clear but quiet voice was drowned out by the storms of the Reformation, and the Erasmian emphasis on the individual's natural capacities succumbed to a renewed emphasis on human sinfulness and dogmatic theology. Erasmus was caught in the middle and condemned on all sides; for him, the Reformation was both a personal and a historical tragedy. He had worked for peace and unity, only to experience a spectacle of war and fragmentation. Erasmian humanism, however, survived these horrors as an ideal, and during the next two centuries, whenever thinkers sought toleration and rational religion, they looked back to Erasmus for inspiration.

French and English Humanism

François Rabelais (c. 1494–c. 1553), a former monk, exemplified the humanist spirit in France. In response to religious dogmatism, he asserted the essential goodness of the individual and the right to enjoy the world rather than being bound by the fear of a punishing God. His folk-epic, *Gargantua and Pantagruel,* celebrates earthly life and earthly enjoyments, expresses an appreciation for secular learning and a confidence in human nature, and attacks monastic orders and clerical education for stifling the human spirit.

According to Rabelais, once freed from dogmatic theology, with its irrelevant concerns, and narrow-minded clergy, who deprived them of life's joys, people could, by virtue of their native goodness, build a paradise on earth and disregard the one dreamed up by theologians. In *Gargantua and Pantagruel,* Rabelais imagined a monastery where men and women spend their lives "not in laws, statutes, or rules, but according to their own free will and pleasure." They slept and ate when they desired and learned to "read, write, sing, play upon several musical instruments, and speak five or six...languages and compose in them all very quaintly." They observed only one rule: "do what thou wilt."[2]

The most influential humanist of the early English Renaissance was Sir Thomas More (1478–1535), who studied at Oxford. His impact came from both his writing and his career. Trained as a lawyer, he was a successful civil servant and member of Parliament. His most famous book is *Utopia,* the first major utopian treatise to be written in the West since Plato's *Republic* and one of the most original works of the entire Renaissance. Many humanists had attacked private wealth as the principal source of pride, greed, and human cruelty. However, only More carried this insight to its logical conclusion: in *Utopia*, he called for the elimination of private property. He had too keen a sense of human weakness to think that people could become perfect, but he used *Utopia* to call attention to contemporary abuses and to suggest radical reforms.

More succeeded Cardinal Wolsey as lord chancellor under Henry VIII. But when the king broke with the Roman Catholic church, More resigned, unable to reconcile his conscience with the king's rejection of papal supremacy. Three years later, in July 1535, More was executed for treason because he refused to swear an oath acknowledging the king's ecclesiastical supremacy.

William Shakespeare (1564–1616), widely considered the greatest playwright the world has ever produced, gave expression to conventional Renaissance values: honor, heroism, and the struggle against fate and fortune. But there is nothing conventional about Shakespeare's treatment of characters possessing these virtues. His greatest plays, the tragedies (*King Lear, Julius Caesar,* and others), explore a common theme: men, even heroic men, despite virtue, are able to overcome their human weaknesses only with the greatest difficulty, if at all. What fascinated Shakespeare was the contradiction between the Renaissance image of nobility, which is often the self-image of Shakespeare's heroes, and humans' capacity for evil and self-destruction. The plays are thus intensely human, but so much so that humanism fades into the background; art transcends doctrine to represent life itself.

The Renaissance and the Modern Age

The Renaissance, then, marks the birth of modernity — in art, in the idea of the individual's role in history and nature, and in society, politics, war, and diplomacy. Central to this birth was a bold new view of human nature that departed from the medieval view: individuals in all endeavors are not constrained by a destiny imposed by God from the outside but are free to make their own destiny, guided only by the example of the past, the force of present circumstances, and the drives of their own inner nature. Set free from theology, individuals were seen as the products, and in turn the shapers, of history; their future would be the work of their own free will.

Within the Italian city-states where the Renaissance was born, rich merchants were at least as important as the church hierarchy and the old nobility. Commercial wealth and a new politics produced a new culture that relied heavily on ancient Greece and Rome. This return to antiquity also entailed a rejection of the Middle Ages as dark, barbarous, and rude. The humanists clearly preferred the secular learning of ancient Greece and Rome to the clerical learning of the more recent past. The reason for this was obvious: the ancients had the same worldly concerns as the humanists; the scholastics did not.

The revival of antiquity by the humanists did not mean, however, that they identified completely with it. The revival itself was done too self-consciously for that. In the very act of looking back, the humanists differentiated themselves from the past and recognized that they were different. They were in this sense the first modern historians, because they could study and appreciate the past for its own sake and, to some degree, on its own terms.

In the works of Renaissance artists and thinkers, the world was, to a large extent, depicted and explained without reference to a higher supernatural realm of meaning and authority. This is clearly seen in Machiavelli's analysis of politics. Renaissance humanism exuded a deep confidence in the capacities of able people, instructed in the wisdom of the ancients, to understand and change the world.

This new confidence was closely related to another distinctive feature of the Renaissance: the cult of the individual. Both prince and painter were motivated in part by the desire to display their talents and to satisfy their ambitions. This individual striving was rewarded and encouraged by the larger society of rich patrons and calculating princes, which valued ability. Gone was the medieval Christian emphasis on the virtue of self-denial and the sin of pride. Instead, the Renaissance placed the highest value on self-expression and self-fulfillment — on the realization of individual potential, especially of the gifted few. The Renaissance fostered an atmosphere in which talent, even genius, was allowed to flourish.

To be sure, the Renaissance image of the individual and the world, bold and novel, was the exclusive prerogative of a small, well-educated urban elite and did not reach down to include the masses. Nevertheless, the Renaissance set an example of what people might achieve in art and architecture, taste and refinement, education and urban culture. In many fields, the Renaissance set the cultural standards of the modern age.

Background to the Reformation: The Medieval Church in Crisis

The Renaissance had revitalized European intellectual life and in the process discarded the medieval preoccupation with theology. Similarly, the Reformation marked the beginning of a new religious outlook. The Protestant Reformation, however, did not originate in the elite circles of humanistic scholars. Rather, it was sparked by Martin Luther (1483–1546), an obscure German monk and brilliant theologian. Luther started a rebellion against the church's authority that in less than one decade shattered the religious unity of Christendom. Begun in 1517, the Reformation dominated European history throughout much of the sixteenth century.

The Roman Catholic church, centered in Rome, was the one European institution that transcended geographic, ethnic, linguistic, and national boundaries. For centuries, it had extended its influence into every aspect of European society and culture. As a result, however, its massive wealth and power appeared to take precedence over its commitment to the search for holiness in this world and salvation in the next. Encumbered by wealth, addicted to international power, and protective of their own interests, the clergy, from the pope down, became the focus of a storm of criticism, starting in the Late Middle Ages.

In the fourteenth century, as kings increased their power and as urban centers with their sophisticated laity grew in size and number, people began to question the authority of the international church and its clergy. Political theorists rejected the pope's claim to supremacy over kings. The central idea of medieval Christendom — a Christian commonwealth led by the papacy — increasingly fell into disrepute. Theorists argued that the church was only a spiritual body, and therefore its power did not extend to the political realm. They said that the pope had no authority over kings, that the state needed no guidance from the papacy, and that the clergy were not above secular law. During the late fourteenth century, Latin Christendom witnessed the first systematic attacks ever launched against the church. Church corruption — such as the selling of indulgences (see page 229), nepotism (the practice of appointing one's relatives to offices), the pursuit of personal wealth by bishops, and the sexual indulgence of the clergy — was nothing new. What was new and startling was the willingness of both educated and uneducated Christians to attack these practices publicly.

Thus, the Englishman John Wycliffe and the Bohemian Jan Hus (see page 201), both learned theologians, denounced the wealth of the clergy as a violation of Christ's precepts and attacked the church's authority at its root by arguing that the church did not control an individual's destiny. They maintained that salvation depends not on participating in the church's rituals or receiving its sacraments, but on accepting God's gift of faith.

Wycliffe's and Hus's efforts to initiate reform coincided with a powerful resurgence of religious feeling in the form of mysticism. Late medieval mystics sought an immediate and personal communication with God, and such experiences inspired them to advocate concrete reforms aimed at renewing the church's spirituality. The church hierarchy inevitably regarded mysticism with some suspicion, for if individuals could experience God directly, they would seemingly have little need for the church and its rituals. In the fourteenth century, these mystical movements seldom became heretical. But in the sixteenth and seventeenth centuries, radical reformers often found in Christian mysticism a powerful alternative to institutional control and even to the need for a priesthood.

With the advent of Lutheranism, personal faith, rather than adherence to the practices of the church, became central to the religious life of European Protestants. Renaissance humanists had sought to reinstitute the wisdom of ancient times; Protestant reformers wanted to restore the spirit of early Christianity, in which faith seemed purer, believers more sincere, and clergy uncorrupted by luxury and power. By the 1540s, the Roman Catholic church had initiated its own internal reformation, but it came too late to stop the movement toward Protestantism in northern and Western Europe.

Martin Luther and the Wittenberg Reformers by Lucas Cranach the Younger, Sixteenth Century.   The central figure is Frederick, elector of Saxony, the patron and protector of Luther, who stands at the prince's right arm. Ulrich Zwingli, reformer of Zurich, is at his left. (*Toledo Art Museum, Gift of Edward Drummond Libbey*)

The Lutheran Revolt

Martin Luther, who had experienced the personal agony of doubting the church's power to give salvation, had the will and talent to convey that agony to all Christians and to win the support of powerful princes. In his youth, Luther at first fulfilled his father's wish and studied law, but at the age of twenty-one, he suddenly abandoned his legal studies to enter the Augustinian monastery at Erfurt. Luther began his search for spiritual and personal identity, and therefore for salvation, within the strict confinement and discipline of the monastery. He pursued his theological studies there and prepared for ordination.

The Break with Catholicism

As he studied and prayed, Luther grew increasingly terrified by the possibility of his damnation. As a monk, he sought union with God, and he understood the church's teaching that salvation depended on faith, works (meaning acts of charity, prayer, fasting, and so on), and grace — God's influence and favor, which sanctifies and regenerates human life. He participated in the sacraments of the church, which, according to its teaching, were intended to give grace. Indeed, after his ordination, Luther administered the sacraments. Yet he still felt the weight of his sins, and nothing the church could offer seemed to relieve that burden. Seeking solace and salvation, Luther increasingly turned to reading the Bible. Two passages seemed to speak directly to him: "For therein is the righteousness of God revealed from faith to faith: as it is written, 'He who through faith is righteous shall live'" (Romans 1:17); and "They are justified by his grace as a gift, through the redemption which is in Christ Jesus" (Romans 3:24). In these two passages, Luther found, for the first time in his adult life, some hope for his own salvation. Faith, freely given by God through Christ, enables the recipient to receive salvation.

The concept of salvation by faith alone provided an answer to Luther's spiritual quest. Practicing such good works as prayer, fasting, pilgrimages, and participation in the Mass and the other sacraments had never brought Luther peace of mind. He concluded that no amount of good works, however necessary for maintaining the Christian community, would bring salvation. Through reading the Bible and through faith alone, the Christian could find the meaning of earthly existence. For Luther, the true Christian was a courageous figure who faced the terrifying quest for salvation armed only with the hope that God had granted the gift of faith. The new Christian served others not to trade good works for salvation, but solely to fulfill the demands of Christian love.

The starting point for the Reformation was Luther's attack in 1517 on the church's practice of selling indulgences. The church taught that some individuals go directly to heaven or hell, while others go to heaven only after spending time in purgatory — a period of expiation necessary for those who have sinned excessively in this life but who have had the good fortune to repent before death. To die in a state of mortal sin meant to writhe in hell eternally. Naturally, people worried about how long they might have to suffer in purgatory. Indulgences were intended to remit portions of that time and were granted to individuals by the church for their prayers, attendance at Mass, and almost any acts of charity — including monetary offerings to the church. This last good work was the most controversial, since it could easily appear that people were buying their way into heaven.

In the autumn of 1517, a Dominican friar named John Tetzel was selling indulgences in the area near Wittenberg. Luther launched his attack on Tetzel and the selling of indulgences by tacking on the door of the Wittenberg castle church his Ninety-five Theses. Luther's theses (propositions) challenged the entire notion of selling indulgences not only as a corrupt practice, but also as a theologically unsound assumption — namely, that salvation can be earned by good works.

At the heart of Luther's argument in the Ninety-five Theses and in his later writings were the beliefs that the individual achieves salvation through inner religious feeling, a sense of contrition for sins, and a trust in God's mercy, and that church attendance, fasting, pilgrimages, charity, and other good works did not earn salvation. The church, in contrast, held that *both* faith and good works were necessary for salvation. Luther further insisted that every individual could discover the meaning of the Bible unaided by the clergy; the church, however, maintained that only the clergy could read and interpret the Bible properly. Luther argued that in matters of faith there was no difference between the clergy and the laity, for each person could receive faith directly and freely from God. But the church held that the clergy were intermediaries between individuals and God and that, in effect, Christians reached eternal salvation through the clergy. For Luther, no priest, no ceremony, and no sacrament could bridge the gulf between the Creator and his creatures. Hope lay only in a personal relationship between the individual and God, as expressed through faith in God's mercy and grace. By declaring that clergy and church rituals do not hold the key to salvation, Luther rejected the church's claim that it alone offered men and women the way to eternal life.

Recognizing that he might be in danger if he continued to preach without a protector, Luther appealed for support to the prince of his district, Frederick, the elector of Saxony. The elector was a powerful man in international politics — one of seven lay and ecclesiastical princes who chose the Holy Roman emperor. Frederick's support convinced church officials, including the pope, that this monk would have to be dealt with cautiously. When the pope finally acted against Luther in 1520, it was too late; Luther had been given the needed time to promote his views. He proclaimed that the pope was the Antichrist and that the church was the "most lawless den of robbers, the most shameless of all brothels, the very kingdom of sin, death and Hell."[3] When the papal bull excommunicating him was delivered, Luther burned it.

No longer members of the church, Luther and his followers established congregations for the purpose of Christian worship. Christians outside the church needed protection, and in 1520 Luther published the *Address to the Christian Nobility of the German Nation*. In it he appealed to the emperor and the German princes to reform the church and to cast off their allegiance to the pope, who, he argued, had used taxes and political power to exploit them for centuries. His appeal produced some success; the Reformation flourished on the resentment against foreign papal intervention that had long festered in Germany. In this and other treatises, Luther made it clear that he wanted to present no threat to legitimate political authority, that is, to the power of the German princes.

In 1521, Charles V, the Holy Roman emperor, who was a devout Catholic, summoned Luther to Worms, giving him a pass of safe conduct. There, Luther was to answer to the charge of heresy, both an ecclesiastical and a civil offense. When asked to recant, Luther replied: "Unless I am convinced of error by the testimony of Scripture or by clear reason . . . I cannot and will not recant anything, for it is neither safe nor honest to act against one's conscience. God help me. Amen." Shortly after this confrontation with the emperor, Luther went into hiding to escape arrest. During that one-year period, he translated the New Testament into German. His followers, or Lutherans, were eventually called *Protestants* — those who protested against the established church — and the term became generic for all followers of the Reformation.

The Appeal and Spread of Lutheranism

Rapidly disseminated by the new printing press, the tenets of Protestantism offered the hope of revitalization and renewal to Protestantism's adherents. Lutheranism appealed to the devout, who resented the worldliness and lack of piety of many clergy. But the movement found its greatest following among German townspeople, who objected to money flowing from their country to Rome in the form of church taxes and payment for church offices. In addition, the Reformation provided the nobility with an unprecedented opportunity to confiscate church lands, eliminate church taxes, and gain the support of their subjects by serving as leaders of a popular and dynamic religious movement. The Reformation also gave the nobles a way of resisting the Catholic Holy Roman emperor, Charles V, who wanted to extend his authority over the German princes. Resenting the Italian domination of the church, many other Germans who supported Martin Luther believed that they were freeing German Christians from foreign control.

Lutheranism drew support from the peasants as well, for they saw Luther as their champion against their oppressors — both lay and ecclesiastical lords and the townspeople. Indeed, in his writings and sermons, Luther often attacked the greed of the princes and bemoaned the plight of the poor. Undoubtedly, Luther's successful confrontation with the authorities served to inspire the peasants. In 1524, these long-suffering people openly rebelled against their lords. The Peasants' Revolt spread to over one-third of Germany; some 300,000 people took up arms against their masters.

Luther, however, had no wish to associate his movement with a peasant uprising and risk alienating the nobility who supported him. As a political conservative, he hesitated to challenge secular authority; to him, the good Christian was an obedient subject. Therefore, he virulently attacked the rebellious peasants, urging the nobility to become "both judge and executioner" and to "knock down, strangle, and stab" the insurgents. By 1525, the peasants had been put down by the sword. The failure of the Peasants' Revolt meant that the German peasantry remained among the most backward and oppressed until well into the nineteenth century.

Initially, the Holy Roman emperor, who was at war with France over parts of Italy and whose eastern territories were threatened by the Ottoman Turks, hesitated to intervene militarily in the strife between Lutheran and Catholic princes — a delay that proved crucial. Despite years of warfare, Charles V was unable to subdue the Lutheran princes. The religious conflict was settled by the Peace of Augsburg (1555), which decreed that each territorial prince should determine the religion of his subjects. Broadly speaking, northern Germany became largely Protestant, while Bavaria and other southern territories remained in the Roman Catholic church. The Holy Roman emperor, who had been successfully challenged by the Lutheran princes, saw his power diminished. The decentralization of the empire and its division into Catholic and Protestant regions would block German unity until the last part of the nineteenth century.

The Spread of the Reformation

Nothing better illustrates people's dissatisfaction with the church in the early sixteenth century than the rapid spread of Protestantism. There was a pattern to this phenomenon. Protestantism grew strong in northern Europe — northern Germany, Scandinavia, the Netherlands, and England. It failed in the Latin countries, although not without a struggle in France. In general, Protestantism was an urban phenomenon, and it prospered where local magistrates supported it and where the distance from Rome was greatest.

Calvinism

The success of the Reformation outside Germany and Scandinavia derived largely from the work of John Calvin (1509–1564), a French scholar and theologian. Sometime in 1533 or 1534, Calvin met French followers of Luther and became convinced of the truth of the new theology. He began to spread its beliefs immediately after his conversion, and within a year he and his friends were in trouble with the civil and ecclesiastical authorities.

Calvin soon abandoned his humanistic and literary studies to become a preacher of the Reformation. Even early in his religious experience, he emphasized the power of God over sinful and corrupt humanity. Calvin's God thundered and demanded obedience, and the terrible distance between God and the individual was mediated only by Christ. Calvin embraced a stern theology, holding that God's laws must be rigorously obeyed, that social and moral righteousness must be earnestly pursued, that political life must be carefully regulated, and that human emotions must be strictly controlled.

Even more than Luther, Calvin explained salvation in terms of uncertain predestination: that God, who grants grace for his own inscrutable reasons, knows in advance who will be saved and who will be condemned to hell. Calvin argued that although people are predestined to salvation or damnation, they can never know their fate with certainty in advance. This terrible decree could and did lead some people to despair. To others — in a paradox difficult for the modern mind to grasp — Calvinism gave a sense of self-assurance and righteousness that made the saint — that is, the truly predestined man or woman — into a new kind of European. Most of Calvin's followers seemed to believe that in having understood the fact of predestination, they had received a bold insight into their unique relationship with God.

Calvinists were individuals who assumed that only unfailing dedication to God's law could be seen as a sign of salvation; thus, Calvinism made for stern men and women, active in their congregations and willing to suppress vice in themselves and others. Calvinism could also produce revolutionaries willing to defy any temporal authorities perceived to be in violation of God's laws. For Calvinists, obedience to Christian law became the dominating principle of life. Forced to flee France, Calvin finally sought safety in Geneva, a small, prosperous Swiss city near the French border. There, he eventually established

John Calvin in His Study. According to Calvin, the Bible, the Word of God, was central to the life of all Protestants. Therefore, it was necessary to learn how to read. The Reformation also encouraged literacy, at least literacy in simple religious texts. (*Snark/Art Resource, NY*)

a Protestant church that closely regulated the citizens' personal and social lives. Elders of the Calvinist church governed the city and imposed strict discipline in dress, sexual mores, church attendance, and business affairs; they severely punished irreligious and sinful behavior. Prosperous merchants, as well as small shopkeepers, saw in Calvinism doctrines that justified the self-discipline they already exercised in their own lives and wished to impose on the unruly masses. They particularly approved of Calvin's economic views, for he saw nothing sinful in commercial activities, unlike many Catholic clergy.

Geneva became the center of international Protestantism. Calvin trained a new generation of Protestant reformers of many nationalities, who carried his message back to their homelands. Calvin's *Institutes of the Christian Religion* (1536), in its many editions, became (after the Bible) the leading textbook of the new theology. In the second half of the sixteenth century, Calvin's theology of predestination spread into France, England, the Netherlands, and parts of the Holy Roman Empire.

Calvin always opposed any recourse to violence and supported the authority of magistrates. Yet when monarchy became their persecutor, his followers felt compelled to resist. Calvinist theologians became the first political theoreticians of modern times to publish cogent arguments for opposition to monarchy, and eventually for political revolution. In France and later in the Netherlands, Calvinism became a revolutionary ideology, complete with an underground organization, composed of dedicated followers who challenged monarchical authority. In the seventeenth century, the English version of Calvinism — Puritanism — performed the same function. Thus, in certain circumstances, Calvinism possessed the moral force to undermine the claims of the monarchical state on the individual.

France

Although Protestantism was illegal in France after 1534, the Protestant minority, the Huguenots, grew, becoming a well-organized underground movement. Huguenot churches, often under the protection of powerful nobles, assumed an increasingly political character in response to monarchy-sponsored persecution. French Protestants became sufficiently organized and militant to challenge their persecutors, King Henry II and the Guise, one of the foremost Catholic families in Europe, and in 1562 civil war erupted between Catholics and Protestants. What followed was one of the most brutal religious wars in the history of Europe. In 1572, on Saint Bartholomew's Day, the gruesome slaughter of thousands of Protestant men, women, and children stained the streets with blood. So intense was the religious hatred at the time that the massacre inspired the pope to have a Mass said in thanksgiving for a Catholic "victory."

After nearly thirty years of brutal fighting throughout France, victory went to the Catholic side — but barely. Henry of Navarre, a Protestant leader, became King Henry IV, though only after he agreed to reconvert to Catholicism. Henry established a tentative peace by granting Protestants limited toleration. In 1598, he issued the Edict of Nantes, the first document in any national state that attempted to institutionalize a degree of religious toleration. In the seventeenth century, the successors of Henry IV (who was assassinated in 1610) gradually weakened and then in 1685 revoked the edict. The theoretical foundations of toleration, as well as its practice, remained tenuous in early modern Europe.

England

The king himself rather than religious reformers initiated the Reformation in England. Henry VIII (1509–1547) removed the English church from the jurisdiction of the papacy because the pope refused to grant him an annulment of his marriage to his first wife. The English Reformation thus began as a political act on the part of a self-confident Renaissance monarch. But the Reformation's origins stretched back into the Middle Ages, for England had a long tradition of heresy, as well as anticlericalism, rooted in Wycliffe's actions in the fourteenth century.

When Henry VIII decided that he wanted a divorce from the Spanish princess Catherine of Aragon, in 1527–28, the pope ignored his request. As the pope stalled, Henry grew more desperate: he needed a male heir and presumed that the failure to produce one lay with his wife. At the same time, he desired the shrewd and tempting Anne Boleyn. Henry VIII arranged to grant himself a divorce by severing England from the church. In 1534, with Parliament's approval, he had himself declared supreme head of the Church of England. In 1536, he dissolved the monasteries and seized their property, which was distributed or sold to his loyal supporters. In most cases, it went to the lesser nobility and landed gentry. By involving Parliament and the gentry, Henry VIII turned the Reformation into a national movement. Political considerations, not profound theological differences, were at the root of the English Reformation.

Henry VIII was succeeded by his son, Edward VI (1547–1553), a Protestant, who in turn was succeeded by Mary (1553–1558), the daughter of Henry VIII and Catherine of Aragon. A devout Catholic, Mary severely persecuted Protestants. With the succession of Elizabeth I, Henry's second daughter (by Anne Boleyn), in 1558, England again became a Protestant country. Elizabeth's reign, which lasted until 1603, was characterized by a heightened sense of national identity and the persecution of Catholics, who were deemed a threat to national security. Fear of invasion by Spain, which was bent on returning England to the papacy, contributed to English anti-Catholicism.

In its customs and ceremonies, the English, or Anglican, church as it developed in the sixteenth century differed to only a limited degree from the Roman Catholicism it replaced. The exact nature of England's Protestantism became a subject of growing dispute. Was the Anglican church to be truly Protestant? Were its services and churches to be simple, lacking in "popish" rites and rituals and centered on Scripture and sermon? Obviously, the powerful Anglican bishops would accept no form of Protestantism that might limit their privileges, ceremonial functions, and power. These issues contributed to the English Revolution of the seventeenth century (see Chapter 9).

The Radical Reformation

The leading Protestant reformers generally supported established political authorities, whether they were territorial princes or urban magistrates. For the reformers, human freedom was a spiritual, not a social, concept. Yet the Reformation did help trigger revolts among the artisan and peasant classes of central and then Western Europe. By the 1520s, several radical reformers arose, often from the lower classes of European society. They attempted to channel popular religion and folk beliefs into a new version of reformed Christianity that spoke directly to the temporal and spiritual needs of the oppressed.

Radical reformers proclaimed that God's will was known by his saints — those predestined for salvation. They said that the poor would inherit the

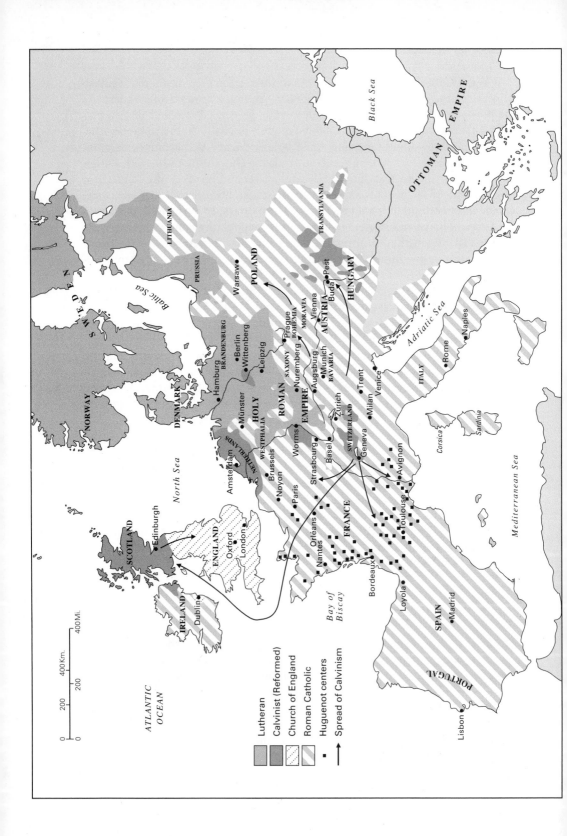

Black Sea

OTTOMAN EMPIRE

LITHUANIA

SWEDEN

PRUSSIA

Baltic Sea

•Warsaw

POLAND

TRANSYLVANIA

•Pest

Buda•

HUNGARY

BRANDENBURG

•Berlin

•Wittenberg

•Leipzig

Prague•

BOHEMIA

MORAVIA

Vienna•

AUSTRIA

Adriatic Sea

NORWAY

•Hamburg

DENMARK

•Münster

WESTPHALIA

HOLY

ROMAN

SAXONY

Nuremberg•

EMPIRE

Augsburg•

Munich•

BAVARIA

•Trent

Milan•

•Venice

ITALY

•Rome

•Naples

Sardinia

North Sea

•Amsterdam

NETHERLANDS

Brussels•

•Worms

Strasbourg•

Basel•

Zurich•

SWITZERLAND

Geneva•

Corsica

Mediterranean Sea

Edinburgh•

SCOTLAND

ENGLAND

Oxford•

London•

•Noyon

•Paris

•Orléans

•Nantes

FRANCE

•Avignon

•Toulouse

•Bordeaux

Bay of Biscay

•Loyola

SPAIN

•Madrid

PORTUGAL

•Lisbon

IRELAND

Dublin•

ATLANTIC OCEAN

400 Mi.
200
0

400 Km.
200
0

Lutheran

Calvinist (Reformed)

Church of England

Roman Catholic

Huguenot centers

Spread of Calvinism

earth, which at present was ruled by the Antichrist; the saint's task was to purge this earth of evil and thus make it ready for Christ's Second Coming. For the radicals, the Scriptures, which spoke of God's love for the wretched and lowly, became an inspiration for social revolution. Luther, Calvin, and other reformers vigorously condemned the social doctrines preached by the radical reformers.

The largest group in the Radical Reformation before 1550 has the general name of *Anabaptists*. Having received the inner light — the message of salvation — Anabaptists felt born anew and yearned to be rebaptized. Anabaptists were new Christians, new persons led by the light of conscience to seek reform and renewal of all institutions in preparation for Christ's Second Coming.

In 1534, Anabaptists captured the city of Münster in Westphalia, near the western border of Germany. They seized the property of nonbelievers, burned all books except the Bible, and, in a mood of jubilation and sexual excess, openly practiced polygamy. All the while, the Anabaptists proclaimed that the Day of Judgment was close at hand. Provoked by their actions, Lutheran Prince Philip of Hesse and his army crushed the Anabaptists.

In early modern Europe, *Münster* became a byword for dangerous revolution. Determined to prevent these wild enthusiasts from gaining strength in their own territories, princes attacked them with ferocity. In Münster today, the cages still hang from the church steeple where the Anabaptist leaders were tortured and left to die as a warning to all would-be imitators.

By the late sixteenth century, many radical movements had either gone underground or grown quiet. But a century later, during the English Revolution (1640–1660), the beliefs and political goals of the Radical Reformation surfaced again, threatening to push the revolution in a direction that its gentry leaders desperately feared. Although the radicals failed in England, too, they left a tradition of democratic and antihierarchical thought. The radical assertion that saints, who have received the inner light, are the equal of anyone, regardless of social status, helped shape modern democratic thought.

The Catholic Response

The Protestant threat impelled the Roman Catholic church to institute reforms. At first, the energy for reform came from ordinary clergy, as well as laypeople such as Ignatius Loyola (1491–1556). Trained as a soldier, this pious Spanish reformer sought to create a new religious order, fusing the intellectual excellence of humanism with a reformed Catholicism that would appeal to powerful economic and political groups. Founded in 1534, the Society of Jesus, more commonly known as the Jesuits, became the backbone of

◀   **Map 8.1**   The Protestant and the Catholic Reformations the Catholic Reformation in southern and Western Europe. The Jesuits combined traditional monastic discipline with a dedication to teaching and an emphasis on the power of preaching. They sought to use both to win converts back to the church.

The Jesuits brought hope: a religious revival based on ceremony, tradition, and the power of the priest to offer forgiveness. In addition, they opened some of the finest schools in Europe. Just as the Lutherans in Germany sought to bring literacy to the masses so that they might read the Bible, the Jesuits sought to bring intellectual enhancement to the laity, especially to the rich and powerful. The Jesuits pursued positions as confessors to princes and urged them to intensify their efforts to strengthen the church in their territories.

By the 1540s, the Counter Reformation was well under way. The leaders of this Catholic movement attacked many of the same abuses that had impelled Luther to speak out, but they avoided a break with the doctrinal and spiritual authority of the clergy. The Counter Reformation also took aggressive and hostile measures against Protestantism. The church tried to counter the popular appeal of Protestantism by emphasizing spiritual renewal through faith, prayer, and religious ceremony. It also resorted to sterner means. The Inquisition — the church court dealing with heretics — expanded its activities, and wherever Catholic jurisdiction prevailed, unrepentant Protestant heretics were subject to death or imprisonment. Catholics did not hold a monopoly on persecution: wherever Protestantism obtained official status — in England, Scotland, and Geneva, for instance — Catholics or religious radicals at times faced persecution.

One of the Catholic church's main tools was censorship. By the 1520s, the impulse to censor and burn dangerous books intensified dramatically as the church tried to prevent the spread of Protestant ideas. In the rush to eliminate heretical literature, the church condemned the works of reforming Catholic humanists as well as those of Protestants. The Index of Prohibited Books became an institutional part of the church's life. Over the centuries, the works of many leading thinkers were placed on the Index, which was not abolished until 1966.

The Counter Reformation policies of education, vigorous preaching, church building, persecution, and censorship did succeed in bringing thousands of people, Germans and Bohemians in particular, back into the church. Furthermore, the church implemented some concrete changes in policy and doctrine. In 1545, the Council of Trent met to reform the church and strengthen it for confronting the Protestant challenge. Over the many years that it was convened (until 1563), the council modified and unified church doctrine; abolished many corrupt practices, such as the selling of indulgences; and vested final authority in the papacy, thereby ending the long and bitter struggle within the church over papal authority. The Council of Trent purged the church and gave it doctrinal clarity on such matters as the roles of faith and good works in attaining salvation. It passed a decree that the church shall be the final arbiter of the Bible. All compromise with Protestantism was re-

The Council of Trent. When they met, the representatives to Trent were an angry lot, distressed by the long delay in calling them. The Pope resisted councils because they threatened his authority, but at Trent a great deal was accomplished that put the Church back on the offensive against the Protestants. (*John Freeman*)

jected (not that Protestants were eager for it). The Reformation had split Western Christendom irrevocably.

The Reformation and the Modern Age

The Renaissance broke with medieval artistic and literary forms and ushered in a vibrant secularism and individualism. Like the Renaissance, the Reformation drew its inspiration from the ancient world. Renaissance humanists and artists sought to imitate and revive classical art and literary forms; Reformation thinkers aspired to restore the spiritual purity of early Christianity, before the growth of a powerful clergy and a dogmatic theology. They used the Gospels in order to undermine the authority of the Church.

At first glance, the Reformation would seem to have renewed the medieval stress on otherworldliness and reversed the direction toward secularism taken by the Renaissance. Attracted to the ancient Stoic doctrine of the autonomous will, Renaissance humanists had broken with Augustine's stern view of original sin — a corrupt human nature and the person's inability to achieve salvation through his or her own efforts. Both Luther and Calvin, however, saw human beings as essentially depraved and corrupt and rejected completely the notion that individuals can do something for their own salvation; such an assertion of human will, they held, revealed a dangerous self-confidence in human beings. Whereas the humanists fostered freer discussion and criticism, the Reformation, at times, degenerated into narrow-mindedness and intolerance.

Yet in several important ways, the Reformation contributed to the shaping of modernity. By dividing Christendom into Catholic and Protestant, the Reformation destroyed the religious unity of Europe, the distinguishing feature of the Middle Ages, and weakened the church, the chief institution of medieval society. By strengthening monarchs at the expense of church bodies, the Reformation furthered the growth of the modern secular and centralized state. Protestant rulers repudiated all papal claims to temporal authority and extended their power over the newly established Protestant churches in their lands. In Catholic lands, the weakened church was reluctant to challenge monarchs whose support it now needed more than ever. This subordination of clerical authority to the throne permitted kings to build strong centralized states, a characteristic of political life of the modern West.

While absolute monarchy was the immediate beneficiary of the Reformation, indirectly Protestantism contributed to the growth of political liberty — another feature of the modern West. To be sure, neither Luther nor Calvin championed political freedom. For Luther, a good Christian was an obedient subject. Thus, he declared that subjects should obey their rulers' commands: "It is no wise proper for anyone who would be a Christian to set himself up against his government, whether it act justly or unjustly."[4] And again, "Those who sit in the office of magistrate sit in the place of God, and their judgment is as if God judged from heaven. . . . if the emperor calls me, God calls me."[5] Calvinists created a theocracy in Geneva that closely regulated the citizens' private lives, and Calvin strongly condemned resistance to political authority as wicked. He held that rulers were selected by God and that punishment of bad rulers belonged only to God and not to the ruler's subjects.

Nevertheless, the Reformation also provided a basis for challenging monarchs. Some Protestant theorists, mainly Calvinists, supported resistance to political authorities whose edicts, they believed, contravened God's law as expressed in the Bible. This religious justification for revolution against tyrannical rule helped fuel the resistance of English Calvinists, or Puritans, to the English monarchy in the seventeenth century.

The Reformation advanced the idea of equality. Equality is rooted in the Judeo-Christian belief that all people are the creatures of a single God. In two important ways, however, medieval society contravened the principle of equality. First, feudalism stressed hereditary distinctions between nobles and commoners. Medieval society was hierarchical, arranged in an ascending order of legal ranks, or estates: commoners, nobles, and clergy. Second, the medieval church taught that only the clergy could administer the sacraments, which provided people with the means of attaining salvation; for this reason, they were superior to the laity. Luther, in contrast, held that there was no spiritual distinction between the laity and the clergy. There was a spiritual equality of all believers: all were equally Christian; all were equally priests.

The Reformation also contributed to the creation of an individualistic ethic, which characterizes the modern world. Since Protestants, unlike Catholics, had no official interpreter of Scripture, the individual bore the awesome responsibility of interpreting the Bible according to the dictates of his or her conscience. Protestants confronted the prospect of salvation or damnation entirely on their own. No church provided them with security or certainty, and no priesthood interceded between them and God. Piety was not determined by the church, but by the autonomous individual, whose conscience, illuminated by God, was the source of judgment and authority.

For the Protestant, faith was personal and inward. This new arrangement called for a personal relationship between each individual and God and called attention to the individual's inner religious capacities. Certain that God had chosen them for salvation, many Protestants developed the inner self-assurance and assertiveness that marks the modern individual. Thus, the Protestant emphasis on private judgment in religious matters and on an inner personal conviction accentuated the importance of the individual and helped to mold a new and distinctly modern European.

The Reformation's stress on individual conscience may have contributed to the development of the capitalist spirit, which underlies modern economic life. So argued German sociologist Max Weber in *The Protestant Ethic and the Spirit of Capitalism* (1904). Weber acknowledged that capitalism had existed in Europe before the Reformation; merchant bankers in medieval Italian and German towns, for example, engaged in capitalistic activities. But, he contended, Protestantism (particularly Calvinism) made capitalism more dynamic; it produced a new type of individual who confidently set out to master himself and his environment. Protestant businesspeople believed that they had a religious obligation to make money, and their faith gave them the self-discipline to do so. Convinced that prosperity was God's blessing and poverty his curse, Calvinists had a spiritual inducement to labor industriously and to avoid laziness.

According to Calvin's doctrine of predestination, God had already determined in advance who would be saved; salvation could not be attained through any worldly actions. Although there was no definite way of discovering who had received God's grace, Calvin's followers came to believe that certain activities were signs that God was working through them, that they had indeed been elected. Thus, Calvinists viewed hard work, diligence, dutifulness, efficiency, frugality, and a disdain for pleasurable pursuits — all virtues that contribute to rational and orderly business procedures and to business success — as signs of election. In effect, Weber argued, Protestantism — unlike Catholicism — gave religious approval to moneymaking and the businesspeople's way of life. Moreover, Calvin's followers seemed to believe that they had attained a special insight into their relationship with God; this conviction fostered a sense of self-assurance and righteousness. Protestantism, therefore, produced a highly individualistic attitude that valued inner strength, self-discipline, and methodical and sober behavior — necessary traits for a middle class seeking business success in a highly competitive world.

Notes

1. Giovanni Pico della Mirandola, *Oration on the Dignity of Man*, trans. A. Robert Caponigri (Chicago: Henry Regnery, 1956), p. 7.
2. François Rabelais, *Gargantua and Pantagruel*, trans. Sir Thomas Urquhart (1883), bk. 1, chap. 57.
3. John Dillenberger, ed., *Martin Luther: Selections from His Writings* (Garden City, N.Y.: Doubleday, 1961), p. 46, taken from *The Freedom of a Christian* (1520).
4. Quoted in George H. Sabine, *A History of Political Thought* (New York: Holt, Rinehart & Winston, 1961), p. 361.
5. Quoted in Roland Bainton, *Here I Stand* (New York: Abingdon Press, 1950), p. 238.

Suggested Reading

Brucker, Gene A., *Renaissance Florence*, rev. ed. (1983). An excellent analysis of the city's physical character, its economic and social structure, its political and religious life, and its cultural achievements.

Burckhardt, Jacob, *The Civilization of the Renaissance in Italy* (1860), 2 vols. (1958). The first major interpretative synthesis of the Renaissance; still an essential resource.

Burke, Peter, *Popular Culture in Early Modern Europe* (1978). A fascinating account of the social underside from the Renaissance to the French Revolution.

Grimm, Harold J., *The Reformation Era, 1500–1650*, 2nd ed. (1973). The best and most complete narrative available.

Kelley, Donald R., *Renaissance Humanism* (1991). A recent synthesis.

King, Margaret L., *Women of the Renaissance* (1991). A useful survey of a burgeoning field of scholarship.

Marrus, Richard, *Martin Luther* (1999). A new biography.

Ozment, Steven E., *Protestants* (1992). The rise of Protestantism.

Ozment, Steven E., *The Reformation in the Cities* (1975). A good survey of the Reformation in Germany.

Pullan, Brian S., *A History of Early Renaissance Italy* (1973). A solid, brief account.

Reardon, Bernard M. G., *Religious Thought in the Reformation* (1981). Doctrinal issues and disputes.

Skinner, Quentin, *The Foundations of Modern Political Thought*, 2 vols. (1978). The first volume covers the Renaissance; highly informed.

Stephens, John, *The Italian Renaissance* (1990). A recent survey.

Review Questions

1. What is the connection between the Renaissance and the Middle Ages? What special conditions gave rise to the Italian Renaissance?
2. What is humanism and how did it begin? What did the humanists contribute to education and the writing of history?
3. How can it be said that Machiavelli invented a new politics?
4. What are the general features of Renaissance art?

5. What factors encouraged the spread of the Renaissance into other lands?
6. Why is the Renaissance considered a departure from the Middle Ages and the beginning of modernity?
7. What were the medieval roots of the Reformation?
8. How did Luther's theology mark a break with the church? Why did many Germans become followers of Luther?
9. In what ways did the radical reformers differ from the other Protestants?
10. What role did the Jesuits and the Inquisition play in the Counter Reformation? What did the Counter Reformation accomplish?
11. How did the Reformation contribute to the shaping of the modern world?

❖ CHAPTER 9

Political and Economic Transformation: National States, Overseas Expansion, Commercial Revolution

$\mathcal{F}$rom the thirteenth to the seventeenth century, a new and unique form of political organization emerged in the West: the dynastic, or national, state. It harnessed the material resources of its territory, directed the energies of the nobility into national service, and increasingly centralized political authority. The national state, a product of dynastic consolidation, is the essential political institution of the modern West.

The disintegration of medieval political forms and the emergence of the modern state coincided with the gradual breakdown of the medieval socioeconomic system, which was based on tradition, hierarchy, and orders or estates. In the medieval system, every group — clergy, lords, serfs, guild members — occupied a particular place and performed a specific function. Society functioned best when each person fulfilled the role allotted to him or her by God and tradition. Early modern times saw the growth of a capitalist market economy whose central focus was the self-sufficient individual, striving, assertive, and motivated by self-interest. This nascent market economy, greatly boosted by the voyages of discovery and the conquest and colonization of other parts of the world, subverted the hierarchically arranged and tradition-bound medieval community. Seeking to enrich their treasuries and extend their power, states promoted commercial growth and overseas expansion. The extension of European hegemony over much of the world was well under way by the eighteenth century. ❖

Toward the Modern State

During the Middle Ages, some kings began to forge national states. However, medieval political forms differed considerably from those that developed later, in the early modern period. In the Middle Ages, kings had to share

244

political power with feudal lords, the clergy, free cities, and representative assemblies. Central authority was tempered by overlapping jurisdictions and numerous and competing allegiances. People saw themselves as members of an estate — clergy, aristocracy, or commoners — rather than as subjects or citizens of a state. Church theorists envisioned Christian Europe as a unitary commonwealth, in which spiritual concerns prevailed over secular authority. According to this view, kings, who received their power from God, must never forget their religious obligation to rule in accordance with God's commands as interpreted by the clergy.

In the sixteenth and seventeenth centuries, kings successfully asserted their authority over competing powers, continuing a trend that had begun in the Late Middle Ages. Strong monarchs dominated or crushed the parliaments that had acted as a brake on royal power during the Middle Ages. Increasingly, too, these monarchs subjected lords and ecclesiastical authorities to royal control. They created a bureaucracy to coordinate the activities of the central government. The old medieval political order — characterized on the one hand by feudal particularism and the strength of local authorities, and on the other by the supranational claims and goals of a universal church — dissolved. Gradually, the national, territorial state, the hallmark of the modern world, became the essential political unit. Kings were the central figures in the creation of the national state. Strong dynastic states were formed wherever monarchs succeeded in subduing local aristocratic and ecclesiastical power systems. In their struggle to subdue the aristocracy, kings were aided by artillery; the lords' castles quickly became obsolete in the face of royal siege weapons. Where the monarchs failed, as they did in Germany and Italy, no viable states evolved until well into the nineteenth century.

By the early seventeenth century, Europeans had developed the concept of the state: an autonomous political entity to which its subjects owed duties and obligations. The essential prerequisite for the Western concept of the state, as it emerged in the early modern period, was the idea of *sovereignty*. Within its borders, the state was supreme; all other institutions, both secular and religious, had to recognize the state's authority. The art of governing entailed molding the ambitions and strength of the powerful and wealthy so that they could be harnessed to serve the state. Its power growing through war and taxation, the state had become the basic unit of political authority in the West.

Historically, the modern state has been characterized by a devotion to the nation and by feelings of national pride. A national language is used throughout the land, and the people have a sense of sharing a common culture and history, of being distinct from other peoples. There were some signs of growing national feeling during the sixteenth and seventeenth centuries, but this feature of the modern state did not become a major part of European political life until the nineteenth century. During the early modern period, devotion was largely given to a town, a province, or a noble or to the person of the king rather than to the nation, the people as a whole.

Chronology 9.1 ❖ Economic and Political Transformations

1394–1460	Henry the Navigator, prince of Portugal, encourages expansion into Africa for gold and his anti-Muslim crusade
1469	Ferdinand and Isabella begin their rule of Castile and Aragon
1485	Henry VII begins the reign of the Tudor dynasty in England
1488	Bartholomeu Dias reaches the tip of Africa
1492	Christopher Columbus reaches the Caribbean island of Española on his first voyage; the Jews are expelled from Spain; Granada, the last Muslim kingdom in Spain, is conquered, completing the Reconquest
1497	Vasco da Gama sails around the Cape of Good Hope (Africa) to India
1519	Charles V of Spain becomes Hapsburg emperor of the Holy Roman Empire
1519–1521	Hernando Cortés conquers the Aztecs in Mexico
1531–1533	Francisco Pizarro conquers the Incas in Peru
1552	Silver from the New World flows into Europe via Spain, contributing to a price revolution
1556–1598	Philip II of Spain persecutes Jews and Muslims
1562–1598	Religious wars in France

In the sixteenth and seventeenth centuries, the idea of liberty, now so basic to Western political life and thought, was only rarely discussed, and then chiefly by Calvinist opponents of absolutism. Not until the mid-seventeenth century in England was there a body of political thought contending that human liberty was compatible with the new modern state. In general, despite the English (and Dutch) developments, absolutism dominated the political structure of early modern Europe. It was not until the late eighteenth and nineteenth centuries that absolutism was widely challenged by advocates of liberty.

The principle of the balance of power, an integral part of modern international relations, also emerged during early modern times. When one state threatened to dominate Europe, as did Spain under Philip II and France under Louis XIV, other states joined forces and resisted. The fear that one state would upset the balance of power and achieve European domination pervaded international relations in later centuries.

Chronology 9.1 ❖ Continued	
1572	Saint Bartholomew's Day Massacre — Queen Catherine of France orders thousands of Protestants executed
1588	English fleet defeats the Spanish Armada
1598	French Protestants are granted religious toleration by the Edict of Nantes
1624–1642	Cardinal Richelieu, Louis XIII's chief minister, determines royal policies
1640–1660	English Revolution
1648	Treaty of Westphalia ends the Thirty Years' War
1649	Charles I, Stuart king of England, is executed by an act of Parliament
1649–1660	England is co-ruled by Parliament and the army under Oliver Cromwell
1660	Charles II returns from exile and becomes king of England
1685	Louis XIV of France revokes the Edict of Nantes
1688–1689	Revolution in England: end of absolutism
1694	The Bank of England is founded
1701	Louis XIV tries to bring Spain under French control

Hapsburg Spain

The Spanish political experience of the sixteenth century was one of the most extraordinary in the history of modern Europe. Spanish kings built a dynastic state that burst through its frontiers and encompassed Portugal, part of Italy, the Netherlands, and enormous areas in the New World. Spain became an intercontinental empire — the first in the West since Roman times.

In the eighth and ninth centuries, the Muslims controlled all of Spain except some tiny Christian kingdoms in the far north. In the ninth century, these Christian states began a five-hundred-year struggle, the Reconquest, to drive the Muslims from the Iberian Peninsula. By the middle of the thirteenth century, Granada in the south was all that remained of Muslim lands in Spain. This long struggle for Christian hegemony in the Iberian Peninsula left the Spanish fiercely religious and strongly suspicious of foreigners. Despite centuries of intermarriage with non-Christians, by the early sixteenth century purity of blood and orthodoxy of faith became necessary for, and synonymous with, Spanish identity.

Ferdinand and Isabella

In 1469, Ferdinand, heir to the throne of Aragon, married Isabella, heir to the throne of Castile. Although Ferdinand and Isabella did not give Spain a single legal and tax system or a common currency, their policies did contribute decisively to Spanish unity and might. They broke the power of aristocrats, who had operated from their fortified castles like kings, waging their private wars at will; they brought the Spanish church into alliance with the state; and in 1492, they drove the Muslims from Granada, the Muslims' last territory in Spain. The crusade against the Muslim infidels accorded with the aims of the militant Spanish church. With a superior army, with the great aristocrats pacified, and with the church and the Inquisition under monarchical control, the Catholic kings expanded their interests and embarked on an imperialist foreign policy that made Spain dominant in the New World.

The Spanish state and church persecuted both Muslims and Jews, who for centuries had contributed substantially to Spanish cultural and economic life. In 1391, thousands of Jews were massacred when anti-Jewish sentiments, fanned by popular preachers, turned to violence in major cities. Under threat of death, many Jews submitted to baptism. In succeeding years, other attacks on Jews led to more conversions. A number of these *conversos,* or new Christians, continued to practice the religion of their fathers in secret, a situation that appalled clerical authorities and the devout Ferdinand and Isabella.

In 1492, in a move to enforce religious uniformity, the crown expelled from Spain Jews who were unwilling to accept baptism. About 150,000 Jews (some estimates are considerably higher) were driven out, including many conversos, who opted to stay with their people. The thousands of Jews who underwent conversion and the conversos who remained were watched by the Inquisition — the church tribunal that dealt with insincere converts — for signs of backsliding. Death by fire, sometimes in elaborate public ceremonies, was the ultimate penalty for those of the conversos and their descendants who were suspected of practicing Judaism. Muslims also bore the pain of forced conversions and investigations, torture, and executions conducted by the Inquisition. Finally, in 1609–1614, Spain expelled them.

The Reign of Charles V: King of Spain and Holy Roman Emperor

Dynastic marriage constituted another crucial part of Ferdinand and Isabella's foreign policy. They strengthened their ties with the Austrian Hapsburg kings by marrying one of their children, Juana (called "the Mad" for her insanity), to Philip the Fair, son of Maximilian of Austria, the head of the ruling Haps-

Allegory of the Abdication of Charles V by Frans Francken II, 1556.   Emperor
Charles V, who ruled half of Europe and most of the Americas, abdicated in 1555,
giving his German imperial crown to his brother Ferdinand, archduke of Austria, and
the kingdoms of Spain and the Netherlands to his son Philip II. The Hapsburg dynasty
ruled Spain until the eighteenth century and Austria and Hungary until the early twentieth century. (*Rijksmuseum, Amsterdam*)

burg family. Philip and Juana's son Charles inherited the kingdom of Ferdinand and Isabella in 1516 and reigned until 1556. Through his other grand-
parents, he also inherited the Netherlands, Austria, Sardinia, Sicily, the
kingdom of Naples, and Franche Comté. In 1519, he was elected Holy
Roman emperor, Charles V. Charles became the most powerful ruler in Europe. But his reign saw the emergence of political, economic, and social problems that eventually led to Spain's decline.

The Charles's inheritance was simply too vast to be governed effectively, but
that was only dimly perceived at the time. The Lutheran Reformation
proved to be the first successful challenge to Hapsburg power. It was the
first phase of a religious and political struggle between Catholic Spain and
Protestant Europe, a struggle that would dominate the last half of the sixteenth century.

The achievements of Charles V's reign rested on the twin instruments of
army and bureaucracy. The Hapsburg Empire in the New World was vastly

extended but, on the whole, effectively administered and policed. Out of this sprawling empire, with its exploited native populations, came the greatest flow of gold and silver ever witnessed by Europeans. Constant warfare in Europe, coupled with the immensity of the Spanish administrative network, required a steady intake of capital. In the long run, however, this easy access to capital seems to have hurt the Spanish economy. There was no incentive for the development of domestic industry, bourgeois entrepreneurship, or international commerce.

Moreover, constant war engendered and perpetuated a social order geared to the aggrandizement of a military class rather than the development of a commercial class. Although war expanded Spain's power in the sixteenth century, it sowed the seeds for the financial crises of the 1590s and beyond and for the eventual decline of Spain as a world power.

Philip II

Philip II inherited the throne from his father, Charles V, who abdicated in 1556. Charles left his son with a vast empire in both the Old World and the New. Although this empire had been administered competently enough, it was facing the specters of bankruptcy and heresy. A zeal for Catholicism ruled Philip's private conduct and infused his foreign policy. In the 1560s, Philip sent the largest land army ever assembled in Europe into the Netherlands with the intention of crushing Protestant-inspired opposition to Spanish authority. The ensuing revolt of the Netherlands lasted until 1609, and the Spanish lost their industrial heartland as a result of it.

The Dutch established a republic governed by the prosperous and progressive bourgeoisie. Rich from the fruits of manufacture and trade in everything from tulip bulbs to ships and slaves, the Dutch merchants ruled their cities and provinces with fierce pride. In the early seventeenth century, this new nation of only 1.5 million people already practiced the most innovative commercial and financial techniques in Europe.

Philip's disastrous attempt to invade England was also born of religious zeal. Philip regarded an assault on England, the main Protestant power, as a holy crusade against the "heretic and bastard," Queen Elizabeth; he particularly resented English assistance to the Protestant Dutch rebels. Sailing from Lisbon in May 1588, the Spanish Armada, carrying twenty-two thousand seamen and soldiers, met with defeat. More than half of the Spanish ships were destroyed or put out of commission. Many ships were wrecked by storms as they tried to return to Spain by rounding the coasts of Scotland and Ireland. The defeat had an enormous psychological effect on the Spanish, who saw it as divine punishment and openly pondered what they had done to incur God's displeasure.

The End of the Spanish Hapsburgs

After the defeat of the Armada, Spain gradually and reluctantly abandoned its imperial ambitions in northern Europe. The administrative structure built by

Charles V and Philip II remained strong throughout the seventeenth century; nevertheless, by the first quarter of the century, enormous weaknesses in Spanish economic and social life had surfaced. In 1596, Philip II was bankrupt, his vast wealth depleted by the cost of foreign wars. Bankruptcy reappeared at various times in the seventeenth century, while the agricultural economy, at the heart of any early modern nation, stagnated. The Spanish in their golden age had never paid enough heed to increasing domestic production.

Despite these setbacks, Spain was still capable of taking a very aggressive posture during the Thirty Years' War (1618–1648). The Austrian branch of the Hapsburg family joined forces with their Spanish cousins, and neither the Swedes and Germans nor the Dutch could stop them. Only French participation in the Thirty Years' War on the Protestant side tipped the balance decisively against the Hapsburgs. Spanish aggression brought no victories, and with the Peace of Westphalia (1648), Spain officially recognized the independence of the Netherlands and severed its diplomatic ties with the Austrian branch of the family.

By 1660, the imperial age of the Spanish Hapsburgs had ended. The rule of the Protestant princes had been secured in the Holy Roman Empire; the largely Protestant Dutch Republic flourished; Portugal and its colony of Brazil were independent of Spain; and dominance over European affairs had passed to France. The quality of material life in Spain deteriorated rapidly, and the ever-present gap between the rich and the poor widened even more drastically. The traditional aristocracy and the church retained their land and power but failed to produce effective leadership.

The Spanish experience illustrates two aspects of the history of the European state. First, the state as empire could survive and prosper only if the domestic economic base remained sound. The Spanish reliance on bullion from its colonies and the failure to cultivate industry and reform the taxation system spelled disaster. Second, states with a vital and aggressive bourgeoisie flourished at the expense of the regions where the aristocracy and the church dominated and controlled society and its mores — Spain's situation. The latter social groups tended to despise manual labor, profit taking, and technological progress. Even though they had been created by kings and dynastic families, after 1700 the major dynastic states were increasingly nurtured by the economic activities of merchants and traders — the bourgeoisie. Yet the bureaucracy of the dynastic states continued to be dominated by men drawn from the lesser aristocracy.

The Growth of French Power

Although both England and France effectively consolidated the power of their central governments, each became a model of a different form of statehood. The English model was a constitutional monarchy, in which the king's power was limited by Parliament and the rights of the English people were protected by law and tradition. The French model emphasized at every turn the glory of the king and, by implication, the sovereignty of the state and its right to stand above the interests of its subjects. France's monarchy became absolute, and French kings claimed that they had been selected by God to rule, a theory known as the divine right of kings. This theory gave monarchy a sanctity that various French kings exploited to enforce their commands on the population, including rebellious feudal lords.

The evolution of the French state was a very gradual process, completed only in the late seventeenth century. In the Middle Ages, the French monarchs recognized the rights of representative assemblies — the Estates — and consulted with them. These assemblies (whether regional or national) were composed of deputies drawn from the various elites: the clergy, the nobility, and, significantly, the leaders of cities and towns in a given region. Early modern French kings increasingly wrested power from the nobility, reduced the significance of the Estates, and eliminated interference from the church.

Religion and the French State

In every emergent state, tension existed between the monarch and the papacy. At issue was control over the church within that territory — over its personnel, its wealth, and, of course, its pulpits, from which an illiterate majority learned what their leaders wanted them to know, not only about religious issues, but also about submission to civil authority. The monarch's power to make church appointments could ensure a complacent church — a church willing to preach obedience to royal authority and to comply on matters of taxes.

For the French monarchs, centuries of tough bargaining with the papacy paid off in 1516, when Francis I (1515–1547) concluded the Concordat of Bologna. Under this agreement, Pope Leo X permitted the French king to nominate, and so in effect appoint, men of his choice to all the highest offices in the French church. The Concordat of Bologna laid the foundation for what became known as the *Gallican church* — a term signifying that the Catholic church in France was sanctioned and overseen by the French kings. Thus, in the early sixteenth century, the central government had been strengthened at the expense of papal authority and of traditional privileges enjoyed by local aristocracy.

The Protestant Reformation, however, challenged royal authority and threatened the very survival of France as a unified state. Fearful that Protestantism would undermine his power, Francis I declared Protestant beliefs and practices illegal and punishable by fines, imprisonment, and even execution. But the Protestant minority (the Huguenots) grew in strength. From 1562 to 1598, France experienced waves of religious wars, which cost the king control over vast areas of the kingdom. The great aristocratic families, the Guise for the Catholics and the Bourbons for the Protestants, drew up armies that

Map 9.1   Europe, 1648 ▶

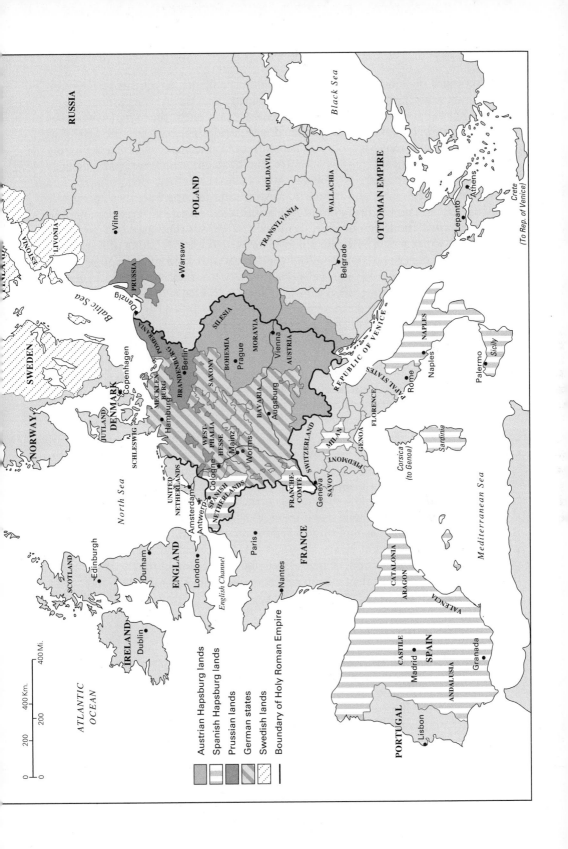

RUSSIA

Black Sea

Crete
(To Rep. of Venice)

Athens

Lepanto

OTTOMAN EMPIRE

WALLACHIA

MOLDAVIA

Belgrade

TRANSYLVANIA

POLAND

Vilna

Warsaw

PRUSSIA

Danzig

SILESIA

BOHEMIA

MORAVIA

Prague

Vienna

AUSTRIA

REPUBLIC OF VENICE

PAPAL STATES

NAPLES

Rome

Naples

Sicily

Palermo

Sardinia

Corsica
(to Genoa)

Baltic Sea

SWEDEN

NORWAY

POMERANIA

BRANDENBURG

Berlin

SAXONY

BAVARIA

Augsburg

FLORENCE

GENOA

MILAN

PIEDMONT

SAVOY

SWITZERLAND

FRANCHE-
COMTÉ

Geneva

MECKLEN
BURG

Copenhagen

DENMARK

JUTLAND

SCHLESWIG

Hamburg

WEST-
PHALIA

HESSE

Mainz

Worms

Cologne

SPANISH
NETHERLANDS

Antwerp

UNITED
NETHERLANDS

Amsterdam

North Sea

SCOTLAND

Edinburgh

IRELAND

Dublin

ENGLAND

London

Durham

English Channel

Paris

FRANCE

Nantes

ATLANTIC
OCEAN

PORTUGAL

Lisbon

SPAIN

Madrid

CASTILE

ANDALUSIA

Granada

VALENCIA

ARAGON

CATALONIA

Mediterranean Sea

LIVONIA

ESTONIA

FINLAND

400 Mi.

400 Km.

200

200

0

0

Austrian Hapsburg lands

Spanish Hapsburg lands

Prussian lands

German states

Swedish lands

Boundary of Holy Roman Empire

scourged the land, killing and maiming their religious opponents and dismantling the authority of the central government.

In 1579, extreme Huguenot theorists published the *Vindiciae contra Tyrannos.* This statement, combined with a call to action, was the first of its kind in early modern times. It justified rebellion against, and even the execution of, an unjust king. European monarchs might claim power and divinely sanctioned authority, but by the late sixteenth century, their subjects had available the moral and theoretical justification for opposing their monarch's will, by force, if necessary, and this justification rested on Scripture and religious conviction. Significantly, this same treatise was translated into English in 1648, a year before Parliament publicly executed Charles I, king of England.

The Valois kings floundered in the face of this kind of political and religious opposition. The era of royal supremacy instituted by Francis I came to an abrupt end during the reign of his successor, Henry II (1547–1559). Wed to Catherine de' Medici, a member of the powerful Italian banking family, Henry occupied himself not with the concerns of government, but with the pleasures of the hunt. The sons who succeeded Henry — Francis II (1559–1560), Charles IX (1560–1574), and Henry III (1574–1589) — were uniformly weak. Their mother, Catherine, who was the virtual ruler, ordered the execution of thousands of Protestants by royal troops in Paris — the beginning of the infamous Saint Bartholomew's Day Massacre (1572), which, with the bloodbath that followed, became a symbol of the excesses of religious zeal.

The civil wars begun in 1562 were renewed in the massacre's aftermath. They dragged on until the death of the last Valois king in 1589. The Valois failure to produce a male heir to the throne placed Henry, duke of Bourbon and a Protestant, in line to succeed to the French throne. Realizing that the overwhelmingly Catholic population would not accept a Protestant king, Henry (apparently without much regret) renounced his adopted religion and embraced the church. Henry IV (1589–1610) granted his Protestant subjects and former followers a degree of religious toleration through the Edict of Nantes (1598), but they were never welcomed into the royal bureaucracy in significant numbers. Throughout the seventeenth century, every French king attempted to undermine the Protestants' regional power bases and ultimately to destroy their religious liberties.

The Consolidation of French Monarchical Power

The defeat of Protestantism as a national force set the stage for the final consolidation of the French state in the seventeenth century under the great Bourbon kings, Louis XIII and Louis XIV. Louis XIII (1610–1643) realized that his rule depended on an efficient and trustworthy bureaucracy, a replenishable treasury, and constant vigilance against the localized claims to power by the great aristocracy and Protestant cities and towns. Cardinal Richelieu, who served as Louis XIII's chief minister from 1624 to 1642, became the great architect of French absolutism.

Richelieu's morality rested on one absolute principle, embodied in a phrase he invented: *raison d'état,* reason of state. Richelieu sought to serve the state by bringing under the king's control the disruptive and antimonarchical elements within French society. He increased the power of the central bureaucracy, attacked the power of independent, and often Protestant, towns and cities, and persecuted the Huguenots. Above all, he humbled the great nobles by limiting their effectiveness as councilors to the king and prohibiting their traditional privileges, such as settling grievances through a duel rather than through court action. Reason of state also guided Richelieu's foreign policy. It required that France turn against Catholic Spain and enter the war that was raging at the time in the Holy Roman Empire on the Protestant — and hence anti-Spanish — side. France's entry into the Thirty Years' War produced a decisive victory for French power on the Continent.

Richelieu died in 1642, and Louis XIII the following year. Cardinal Mazarin, who took charge during the minority of Louis XIV (he was five years old when Louis XIII died), continued Richelieu's policies. Mazarin's heavy-handed actions produced a rebellious reaction, the *Fronde,* a series of street riots that lasted from 1648 to 1653, eventually cost the government control over Paris. Centered in Paris and supported by the great aristocracy, the courts, and the city's poorer classes, the Fronde threatened to develop into a full-scale uprising. It might have done so, but for one crucial factor: its leadership was divided. Court judges (lesser nobles who had often just risen from the ranks of the bourgeoisie) deeply distrusted the great aristocrats and refused in the end to make common cause with them. And both groups feared disorders among the urban masses.

When Louis XIV finally assumed responsibility for governing in 1661, he vowed that the events he had witnessed as a child during the Fronde would never be repeated. In the course of his reign, he achieved the greatest degree of monarchical power held during the early modern period. No absolute monarch in Western Europe, before or at that time, had so much personal authority or commanded such a vast and effective military and administrative machine. Louis XIV's reign represents the culmination of the process of increasing monarchical authority that had been under way for centuries. Intelligent, cunning, and possessing a unique understanding of the requirements of his office, Louis XIV worked long hours at being king, and he never undertook a venture without an eye to his personal grandeur. The sumptuous royal palace at Versailles was built for that reason; similarly, etiquette and style were cultivated there on a scale never before seen in any European court.

When Mazarin died, Louis XIV did away with the office of first minister; he would rule France alone. The great nobles, "princes of the blood," enjoyed great social prestige but exercised decreasing political influence. Louis XIV treated the aristocrats to elaborate rituals, feasts, processions, displays, and banquets; amid all the clamor, however, their political power dwindled.

Louis XIV's domestic policies centered on his incessant search for new revenues. Not only the building of Versailles but also wars cost money, and

The Royal Palace at Versailles.   Versailles was the wonder of the age. Immense and grand, it too, like the person of the king, said to his subjects: I am grandeur incarnate. Even by today's standards, it is an impressive building, both inside and out. (*C. L. Chrysun/The Image Bank*)

Louis XIV waged them to excess. To raise capital, he used the services of Jean Baptiste Colbert, a brilliant administrator who improved the methods of tax collecting, promoted new industries, and encouraged international trade. Operating with a total bureaucracy of about a thousand officials and no longer bothering even to consult the parlements or Estates, Louis XIV ruled absolutely in accordance with the principle of divine right — that the monarch is selected to rule by God.

Yet Louis XIV's system was fatally flawed. Without any effective check on his power and on his dreams of international conquest, no limit was imposed on the state's capacity to make war or on the ensuing national debt. Louis XIV coveted vast sections of the Holy Roman Empire; he also sought to curb Dutch commercial prosperity and had designs on the Spanish Netherlands. By the 1680s, his domestic and foreign policies turned violently aggressive. In 1685, he revoked the Edict of Nantes, forcing many of the country's remaining Protestants to flee. In 1689, he embarked on a military campaign to secure territory from the Holy Roman Empire. And in 1701, he tried to bring Spain under the control of the Bourbon dynasty. Louis XIV, however, underestimated the power of his northern rivals, England and the Netherlands. Their combined power, in alliance with the Holy Roman Empire and the Austrians, defeated his ambitions.

Louis XIV's participation in these long wars emptied the royal treasury. By the late seventeenth century, taxes had risen intolerably, and they were levied mostly on those least able to pay — the peasants. Absolutism also meant increased surveillance of the population. Royal authorities censored books, spied on suspected heretics, Protestants, and freethinkers, and tortured and executed opponents of state policy.

In the France of Louis XIV, the dynastic state had reached maturity and had begun to display some of its classic characteristics: centralized bureaucracy, royal patronage to enforce allegiance, a system of taxation universally but inequitably applied, and suppression of political opposition either through the use of patronage or, if necessary, through force. Another important feature was the state's cultivation of the arts and sciences as a means of increasing national power and prestige. Together, these policies enabled the French monarchy to achieve political stability, enforce a uniform system of law, and channel the country's wealth and resources into the service of the state as a whole.

Yet at his death in 1715, Louis XIV left his successors a system of bureaucracy and taxation that was vastly in need of overhaul but was still locked into the traditional social privileges of the church and nobility to an extent that made reform virtually impossible. The pattern of war, excessive taxation of the lower classes, and expenditures that surpassed revenues had severely damaged French finances. Failure to reform the system led to the French Revolution of 1789.

The Growth of Limited Monarchy and Constitutionalism in England

In 1066, William, duke of Normandy and vassal to the French king, had invaded and conquered England, acquiring at a stroke the entire kingdom. In succeeding centuries, English monarchs continued to strengthen central authority and to tighten the bonds of national unity. At the same time, however, certain institutions and traditions evolved — common law, Magna Carta, and Parliament — that checked royal power and protected the rights of the English people.

Central government in England was threatened after the Hundred Years' War (1337–1453), when English aristocrats brought back from France a taste for warfare. In the ensuing civil war — the War of the Roses (1455–1485) — gangs of noblemen with retainers roamed the English countryside, and lawlessness prevailed for a generation. Only in 1485 did the Tudor family emerge triumphant.

The Tudor Achievement

Victory in the civil war allowed Henry VII (1485–1509) to begin the Tudor dynasty. Henry VII's goal was to check the unruly nobility. To this end, he brought commoners into the government. These commoners, unlike the great magnates, could be channeled into royal service because they craved what the king offered: financial rewards and elevated social status. Although they did not fully displace the aristocracy, commoners were brought into Henry VII's inner circle, into the Privy Council, and into the courts. The strength and efficiency of Tudor government were shown during the Reformation, when Henry VIII (1509–1547) made himself head of the English church.

The Protestant Reformation in England was a revolution in royal, as well as ecclesiastical, government. It attacked and defeated the main obstacle to monarchical authority: the power of the papacy. However, no change in religious practice could be instituted by the monarchy alone. Parliament's participation in the Reformation gave it a greater role and sense of importance than it had ever possessed in the past.

At Henry VIII's death, the Tudor bureaucracy and centralized government were strained to the utmost, yet they survived. The government weathered the reign of Henry's sickly son Edward VI (1547–1553) and the extreme Protestantism of some of his advisers; it also survived the brief and deeply troubled reign of Henry's first daughter, Mary (1553–1558), who attempted to return England to Catholicism. At Mary's death, England had come dangerously close to the religious instability and sectarian tension that undermined the French kings during the final decades of the sixteenth century.

Henry's second daughter, Elizabeth I, became queen in 1558 and reigned until her death in 1603. The Elizabethan period was characterized by a heightened sense of national identity. The English Reformation enhanced that sense, as did the increasing fear of foreign invasion by Spain. That fear was abated only by the defeat of the Spanish Armada in 1588. In the seventeenth century, the English would look back on Elizabeth's reign as a golden age. It was the calm before the storm: a time when a new commercial class was formed that, in the seventeenth century, would demand a greater say in government operations.

Religion played a vital role in this realignment of political interests and forces. Many of the old aristocracy clung to the Anglicanism of the Henrican Reformation and in some cases to Catholicism. The newly risen gentry found in the Protestant Reformation of Switzerland and Germany a form of religious worship more suited to their independent and entrepreneurial spirit. Many of them embraced Puritanism, the English version of Calvinism.

The English Revolution, 1640–1660 and 1688–1689

The forces threatening established authority were dealt with ineffectively by the first two Stuart kings, James I (1603–1625) and Charles I (1625–1649). Like their Continental counterparts, both believed in royal absolutism, and

Henry VIII.   Henry VIII sought to impress upon his subjects that he was a new and powerful monarch. He sought to compete in style, if not in power, with the French and the Spanish kings. (*Sudley Castle, Gloucestershire, England*)

both preached, through the established church, the doctrine of the divine right of kings. James I angered Parliament by conducting foreign policy without consulting it. The conflict between Parliament and Charles I centered on taxes and religion.

Badly needing funds in order to wage war, Charles I exacted "forced loans" from subjects and imprisoned without a specific charge those who would not pay. Fearing that such arbitrary behavior threatened everyone's property and person, Parliament struck back. In 1628, it refused to grant Charles I tax revenues unless he agreed to the Petition of Right, which stated that the king could not collect taxes without Parliament's consent or imprison people without a specific charge. Thus, the monarch had to acknowledge formally the long-established traditions protecting the rights of the English people.

Nevertheless, tensions between the throne and Parliament persisted, and in 1629 Charles I dissolved Parliament, which would not meet again for eleven years. What forced him to reconvene Parliament in 1640 was his need for funds to defend the realm against an invasion from Scotland. The conflict stemmed from Archbishop William Laud's attempt, approved by Charles I, to impose a common prayer book on Scottish Calvinists, or Presbyterians. Infuriated by this effort to impose Anglican liturgy on them, Scottish Presbyterians took up arms. The Long Parliament — so called because it was not disbanded until 1660 — abolished the extralegal courts and commissions that had been used by the king to try opponents, provided for regular meetings of Parliament, and strengthened Parliament's control over taxation. When Puritan members pressed to reduce royal authority even more and to strike at the power of the Anglican church, a deep split occurred in Parliament's ranks: Puritans and all-out supporters of parliamentary supremacy were opposed by Anglicans and supporters of the king. The ensuing civil war was directed by Parliament, financed by taxes and the merchants, and fought by the New Model Army led by Oliver Cromwell (1599–1658), a Puritan squire who gradually realized his potential for leadership.

Parliament's rich supporters financed the New Model Army, gentlemen farmers led it, and religious zealots filled its ranks, along with the usual cross section of poor artisans and day laborers. This army brought defeat to the king, his aristocratic followers, and the Anglican church's hierarchy. In January 1649, Charles I was publicly executed by order of Parliament. During the interregnum (time between kings), which lasted eleven years, one Parliament after another joined with the army to govern the country as a republic. In the distribution of power between the army and Parliament, Cromwell proved to be a key element. He had the support of the army's officers and some of its rank and file, and he had been a member of Parliament for many years. His control over the army was secured, however, only after its rank and file was purged of radicals, drawn largely from the poor. Some of these radicals wanted to level society, that is, to redistribute property and to give the vote to all male citizens.

Cromwell's death left the country without effective leadership. Parliament, having secured the interests of its constituency (gentry, merchants, and some small landowners), chose to restore court and crown and invited the exiled son of the executed king to return to the kingship. Having learned the lesson his father had spurned, Charles II (1660–1685) never instituted royal absolutism.

But Charles's brother, James II (1685–1688), was a foolishly fearless Catholic and admirer of French absolutism. He gathered at his court a coterie of Catholic advisers and supporters of royal prerogative and attempted to bend Parliament and local government to the royal will. James II's Catholicism was the crucial element in his failure. The Anglican church would not back him, and political forces similar to those that in 1640 had rallied against his father, Charles I, descended on him. The ruling elites, however, had learned their lesson back in the 1650s: Civil war would produce social discontent among the masses. The upper classes wanted to avoid open warfare and preserve the monarchy as a constitutional authority, but not as an absolute one. Puritanism, with its sectarian fervor and its dangerous association with republicanism, was allowed to play no part in this second and last phase of the English Revolution.

In early 1688, Anglicans, some aristocrats, and opponents of royal prerogative formed a conspiracy against James II. Their purpose was to invite his son-in-law, William of Orange, stadholder (head) of the Netherlands and husband of James's Protestant daughter Mary, to invade England and rescue its government from James's control. Having lost the loyalty of key men in the army, powerful gentlemen in the counties, and the Anglican church, James II fled the country, and William and Mary were declared king and queen by act of Parliament.

This bloodless revolution — sometimes called the Glorious Revolution — created a new political and constitutional reality. Parliament secured its rights to assemble regularly and to vote on all matters of taxation; the rights of habeas corpus and trial by jury (for men of property and social status) were also secured. These rights were in turn legitimated in a constitutionally binding document, the Bill of Rights (1689). All Protestants, regardless of their sectarian bias, were granted toleration.

The English Revolution, in both its 1640 and its 1688 phases, secured English parliamentary government and the rule of law. Eventually, the monarchical element in that system would yield to the power and authority of parliamentary ministers and state officials. The Revolution of 1688–89 was England's last revolution. In the nineteenth and twentieth centuries, parliamentary institutions would be gradually and peacefully reformed to express a more democratic social reality. The events of 1688–89 have rightly been described as "the year one," for they fashioned a system of government that operated effectively in Britain and could also be transplanted elsewhere with modification. The British system became a model for other forms of representative government, adopted in France and in the former British colonies, beginning with the United States.

The Holy Roman Empire: The Failure to Unify Germany

In contrast to the experience of the French, English, Spanish, and Dutch in the early modern period, the Germans failed to achieve national unity. This failure is tied to the history of the Holy Roman Empire. That union of various distinct central European territories was created in the tenth century when Otto I, in a deliberate attempt to revive Charlemagne's empire, was crowned emperor of the Romans. Later, the title was changed to Holy Roman emperor, with the kingdom consisting mainly of German-speaking principalities.

Most medieval Holy Roman emperors busied themselves not with administering their territories, but with attempting to gain control of the rich Italian peninsula and with challenging the rival authority of various popes. In the meantime, the German nobility extended and consolidated their rule over their peasants and over various towns and cities. The feudal aristocracy's power remained a constant obstacle to German unity.

In the medieval and early modern periods, the Holy Roman emperors were dependent on their most powerful noble lords — including an archbishop or two — because the office of emperor was elective rather than hereditary. German princes, some of whom were electors — for instance, the archbishops of Cologne and Mainz, the Hohenzollern elector of Brandenburg, the landgrave of Hesse, and the duke of Saxony — were fiercely independent. All belonged to the empire, yet all regarded themselves as autonomous powers. These decentralizing tendencies were highly developed by the fifteenth century. The Hapsburgs had maneuvered themselves into a position from which they could monopolize the imperial elections.

The centralizing efforts of the Hapsburg Holy Roman emperors Maximilian I (1493–1519) and Charles V (1519–1556) were impeded by the Reformation, which bolstered the Germans' already strong propensity for local independence. The German nobility were all too ready to use the Reformation as a vindication of their local power, and indeed Luther made just such an appeal to their interests. War raged in Germany between the Hapsburgs and the Protestant princes, united for mutual protection in the Schmalkaldic League. The Treaty of Augsburg (1555) conferred on every German prince the right to determine the religion of his subjects. The princes retained their power, and a unified German state was never constructed by the Hapsburgs. Religious disunity and the particularism and provinciality of the German nobility prevented its creation.

When an exhausted Emperor Charles V abdicated in 1556, he gave his kingdom to his son Philip and his brother Ferdinand. Philip inherited Spain and its colonies, as well as the Netherlands, and Ferdinand acquired the Austrian territories; two branches of the Hapsburg family were thus formed. Throughout the sixteenth century, the Austrian Hapsburgs barely managed to control the sprawling and deeply divided German territories. However, they never missed an opportunity to further the cause of Catholicism and to strike at the power of the German nobility.

No Hapsburg was ever more fervid in that regard than the Jesuit-trained Archduke Ferdinand II, who ascended the throne in Vienna in 1619. His policies provoked a war within the empire that engulfed the whole of Europe: the Thirty Years' War. It began when the Bohemians, whose anti-Catholic tendencies could be traced back to Jan Hus, tried to put a Protestant king on their throne. The Austrian and Spanish Hapsburgs reacted by sending an army into the kingdom of Bohemia, and suddenly the whole empire was forced to take sides along religious lines. Bohemia suffered an almost unimaginable devastation; the ravaging Hapsburg army sacked and burned three-fourths of the kingdom's towns and practically exterminated its aristocracy.

Until the 1630s, it looked as if the Hapsburgs would be able to use the war to enhance their power and promote centralization. But the intervention of Protestant Sweden, led by Gustavus Adolphus and encouraged by France, wrecked Hapsburg ambitions. The ensuing military conflict devastated vast areas of northern and central Europe. The civilian population suffered untold hardships. Partly because the French finally intervened directly, the Spanish Hapsburgs emerged from the Thirty Years' War with no benefits. The Treaty of Westphalia gave the Austrian Hapsburgs firm control of the eastern states of the kingdom, with Vienna as their capital. Austria took shape as a dynastic state, while the German territories in the empire remained fragmented by the independent interests of the feudal nobility.

European Expansion

The emergence of the modern state coincided with the gradual breakdown of a medieval socioeconomic system based on tradition, hierarchy, and estates. In the medieval system, every group — clergy, lords, serfs, guildsmen — occupied a particular place and had a unique function. Society functioned best when each person fulfilled the role allotted to him or her by God and tradition. Early modern times saw the growth of a capitalist market economy whose central focus was the self-sufficient individual, striving, assertive, and motivated by self-interest. This nascent market economy, greatly boosted by the voyages of discovery and the conquest and colonization of other parts of the world, subverted the hierarchically arranged and tradition-bound medieval community.

During the period from 1450 to 1750, Western Europe entered an era of overseas exploration and economic expansion that transformed society. European adventurers discovered a new way to reach the rich trading centers of India by sailing around Africa. They also conquered, colonized, and exploited a new world across the Atlantic. These discoveries and conquests brought about an extraordinary increase in business activity and the supply of money, which stimulated the growth of capitalism. People's values changed in ways that were alien and hostile to the medieval outlook. By 1750, the model Christian in northwestern Europe was no longer the selfless saint but the enterprising businessman. The era of secluded manors and walled towns was drawing to a close. A world economy was emerging, in which European economic life depended on the market in Eastern spices, African slaves, and American silver. During this age of exploration and commercial expansion, Europe generated a peculiar dynamism unmatched by any other civilization. A process was initiated that by 1900 would give Europe mastery over most of the globe and wide-ranging influence over other civilizations.

Forces Behind the Expansion

A combination of forces propelled Europeans outward and enabled them to dominate Asians, Africans, and American Indians. European monarchs, merchants, and aristocrats fostered expansion for power and profit. As the numbers of the landed classes exceeded the supply of available land, the sons of the aristocracy looked beyond Europe for the lands and fortunes denied them at home. Nor was it unnatural for them to try to gain these things by plunder and conquest; their ancestors had done the same thing for centuries.

Merchants and shippers also had reason to look abroad. Trade between Europe, Africa, and the Orient had gone on for centuries, but always through

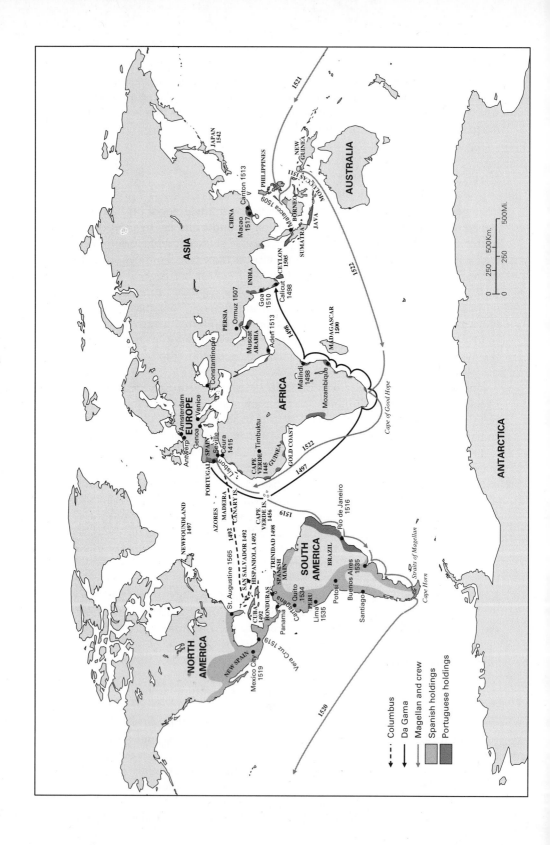

NORTH AMERICA

SOUTH AMERICA

NEW SPAIN

SPANISH MAIN

BRAZIL

PERU

St. Augustine 1565

Mexico City 1519

Vera Cruz 1519

Honduras

Panama

Cape

Quito 1534

Lima 1535

Potosí

Santiago

Buenos Aires 1535

Rio de Janeiro 1516

Straits of Magellan

Cape Horn

CUBA 1492

HISPANIOLA 1492

SAN SALVADOR 1492

TRINIDAD 1498

CAPE VERDE IS. 1498

CANARY IS.

MADEIRA

AZORES

NEWFOUNDLAND 1497

1519

1520

EUROPE

Amsterdam

Antwerp

Genoa

Venice

Seville

SPAIN

PORTUGAL

Lisbon

Ceuta 1415

Timbuktu

CAPE VERDE 1445

GUINEA

GOLD COAST

Constantinople

PERSIA

ARABIA

Musqat

Aden 1513

Ormuz 1507

AFRICA

Malindi 1498

Mozambique

MADAGASCAR 1500

Cape of Good Hope

1497

1522

1498

ASIA

JAPAN 1542

CHINA

Macao 1517

Canton 1513

INDIA

Goa 1510

Calicut 1498

CEYLON 1505

SUMATRA

BORNEO

JAVA

Malacca 1509

MOLUCCAS 1511

PHILIPPINES

NEW GUINEA

AUSTRALIA

ANTARCTICA

1521

1522

500 Km.

500 Mi.

250

250

0

0

- - - → Columbus
———→ Da Gama
———→ Magellan and crew
          Spanish holdings
          Portuguese holdings

intermediaries, who increased the costs and decreased the profits on the European end. Gold from the riverbeds of West Africa had been transported across the Sahara by Arab nomads. Spices had been shipped from India and the East Indies by way of Muslim and Venetian merchants. Western European merchants now sought to break those monopolies by going directly to the source: to West Africa for gold, slaves, and pepper, and to India for pepper, spices, and silks.

The centralizing monarchical state was an important factor in the expansion. Monarchs who had successfully established royal hegemony at home, like Ferdinand and Isabella of Spain, sought opportunities to extend their control overseas. From overseas empires came gold, silver, and commerce, which paid for ever more expensive royal government at home and for war against rival dynasties abroad.

Religion helped in the expansion because the crusading tradition was well established — especially on the Iberian Peninsula, where a five-hundred-year struggle, known as the Reconquest, to drive out the Muslims had taken place. Cortés, the Spanish conqueror of Mexico, for example, saw himself as following in the footsteps of Paladin Roland, the great medieval military hero who had fought to drive back Muslims and pagans. Prince Henry the Navigator (see below) hoped that the Portuguese expansion into Africa would serve two purposes: the discovery of gold and the extension of Christianity at the expense of Islam.

Not only did the West have the will to expand, it also possessed the technology needed for successful expansion, the armed sailing vessels. This asset distinguished the West from China and the lands of Islam and helps explain why the West, rather than Eastern civilizations, launched an age of conquest resulting in global mastery. Not only were sailing ships more maneuverable and faster in the open seas than galleys (ships propelled by oars), but the addition of guns below deck that could fire on and cripple or sink distant enemy ships gave them another tactical advantage. The galleys of the Arabs in the Indian Ocean and the junks of the Chinese were not armed with such guns. In battle, they relied instead on the ancient tactic of coming up alongside the enemy vessel, shearing off its oars, and boarding to fight on deck.

The gunned ship gave the West naval superiority from the beginning. The Portuguese, for example, made short work of the Muslim fleet sent to drive them out of the Indian Ocean in 1509. That victory at Diu, off the western coast of India, indicated that the West not only had found an all-water route to the Orient, but was there to stay.

The Portuguese Empire

In the first half of the fifteenth century, a younger son of the king of Portugal, named Prince Henry the Navigator (1394–1460) by English writers, sponsored voyages of exploration and the nautical studies needed to undertake

◀ **Map 9.2**   Overseas Exploration and Conquest, c. 1400–1600

them. The Portuguese first expanded into islands in the Atlantic Ocean. In 1420, they began to settle Madeira and farm there, and in the 1430s, they pushed into the Canaries and the Azores in search of new farmlands and slaves for their colonies. In the middle decades of the century, they moved down the West African coast to the mouth of the Congo River and beyond, establishing trading posts as they went.

By the end of the fifteenth century, the Portuguese had developed a viable imperial economy among the ports of West Africa, their Atlantic islands, and Western Europe — an economy based on sugar, black slaves, and gold. Africans panned gold in the riverbeds of central and Western Africa, and the Portuguese purchased it at its source.

The Portuguese did not stop in Western Africa. By 1488, Bartholomeu Dias had reached the southern tip of the African continent; a decade later, Vasco da Gama sailed around the Cape of Good Hope and across the Indian Ocean to India. By discovering an all-water route to the Orient, Portugal broke the commercial monopoly on Eastern goods that Genoa and Venice had enjoyed. With this route to India and the East Indies, the Portuguese found the source of the spices needed to make dried and tough meat palatable. As they had done along the African coast, they established fortified trading posts — most notably at Goa on the western coast of India (Malabar) and at Malacca, on the Malay Peninsula.

The Spanish Empire

Spain stumbled onto its overseas empire, and it proved to be the biggest and richest of any until the eighteenth century. Christopher Columbus, who believed that he could reach India by sailing west, won the support of Isabella, queen of Castile. But on his first voyage (1492), he landed on a large Caribbean island, which he named Española (Little Spain). Within decades, two events revealed that Columbus had discovered not a new route to the East, but new continents: Vasco Nuñez de Balboa's discovery of the Pacific Ocean at the Isthmus of Panama in 1513, and the circumnavigation of the globe (1519–1521) by the expedition led by Ferdinand Magellan, which sailed through the strait at the tip of South America that now bears Magellan's name.

Stories of the existence of large quantities of gold and silver to the west lured the Spaniards from their initial settlements in the Caribbean to Mexico. In 1519, Hernando Cortés landed on the Mexican coast with a small army; during two years of campaigning, he managed to defeat the native rulers, the Aztecs, and to conquer Mexico for the Spanish crown. A decade later, Francisco Pizarro achieved a similar victory over the mountain empire of the Incas in Peru.

For good reasons, the Mexican and Peruvian conquests became the centers of the Spanish overseas empire. First, there were the gold hoards accumulated over the centuries by the indigenous rulers for religious and ceremonial purposes. When these supplies were exhausted, the Spanish discovered silver at

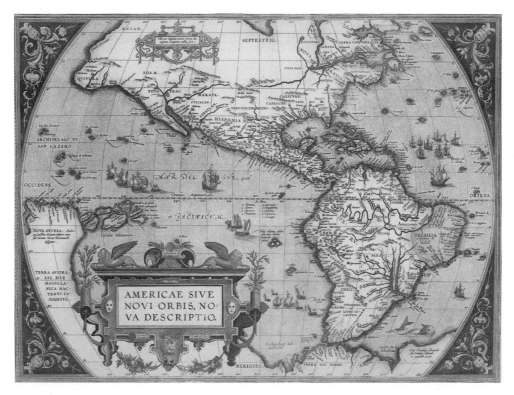

Map of the New World, Seventeenth Century.   Voyages of exploration and the exploitation of new commercial markets continued throughout the sixteenth and seventeenth centuries. The French, Dutch, and English followed the Portuguese and Spanish in planting colonies in the New World. European trading posts were established in Africa, India, and the Far East. The modern worldwide economy was being born. (*Fotomas Index, London*)

Potosí in Upper Peru in 1545 and at Zacatecas in Mexico a few years later. From the middle of the century, the annual treasure fleets sailing to Spain became the financial bedrock of Philip II's war against the Muslim Turks and the Protestant Dutch and English.

Not only gold and silver lured Spaniards to the New World. The crusading spirit spurred them on as well. The will to conquer and convert the pagan peoples of the New World stemmed from the crusading tradition developed during the five previous centuries of Spanish history, in campaigns against the Muslims. The rewards were what they had always been: the propagation of the true faith, service to the crown, and handsome land grants. The land was especially attractive in the sixteenth century, for the number of *hidalgos* (lesser nobility) was increasing with the general rise in population; as a result, the amount of land available to them at home was shrinking.

In the New World, power and land gradually became concentrated in fewer and fewer hands. In particular, royal officials, their associates, and the church gained substantially in wealth and privilege. As recurrent depressions ruined smaller landowners, they were forced to sell out to their bigger neighbors. Upon their conversion to Christianity, the Indians were persuaded to give more and more land to the church. Thus, Spanish America became permanently divided between the privileged elite and the impoverished masses.

The effects of conquest were severe in other ways. Between 1500 and 1600, the number of Indians shrank from about twenty million to little more than two million. The major cause of this catastrophe, however, was not forced labor but the diseases introduced from Europe — dysentery, malaria, hookworm, and smallpox — against which the Indians had little or no natural resistance. Beginning in the 1540s, the position of the natives gradually improved as the crown withdrew grants that gave authority over the native population and took increasing responsibility for controlling the Indians.

Black Slavery and the Slave Trade

One group suffered even more than the Indians: the black slaves originally brought over from West Africa. During the long period of their dominance in North Africa and the Middle East (from the seventh to the nineteenth century), the Muslim states relied on slave labor and slave soldiers from black Africa south of the Sahara. Blacks were captured and transported across the Sahara to be sold in the slave markets of North Africa. At its height in the eighteenth century, this trans-Saharan trade may have risen to some ten thousand slaves a year.

But this annual traffic was eventually dwarfed by the slave trade between West Africa and the European colonies in the New World, which began in earnest in the early sixteenth century. As Roland Oliver notes, "By the end of the seventeenth century, stimulated by the growth of plantation agriculture in Brazil and the West Indies, Atlantic shipments had increased to about thirty thousand a year, and by the end of the eighteenth century they were nearly eighty thousand."[1]

Captured in raids by African slavers, the victims were herded into specially built prisons on the West African coast. Those accepted for sale were "marked on the breast with a red-hot iron, imprinting the mark of the French, English or Dutch companies so that each nation may distinguish their own property."[2] Across the centuries, some eleven or twelve million blacks in all were exported to the New World. Of these, some 600,000 ended up in the thirteen colonies of British North America, forming the basis of the slave population of the new United States at the end of the American Revolution.

The conditions of the voyage from Africa, the so-called middle passage, were brutal. Crammed into the holds of ships, some 13 to 30 percent of blacks died on board. Upon arrival in the New World, slaves were greased with palm oil to improve their appearance and paraded naked into the auction hall for the benefit of prospective buyers, who paid top prices for "the strongest, youthfullest, and most beautiful."[3] The standard workload for slaves everywhere was ten or eleven hours a day six days a week. But some distinction must be made between slavery in the American South and elsewhere in the New World. In Brazil and the West Indies, slaves were worked to exhaustion and death and then replaced. Slaves formed a large majority there and were concentrated on very large plantations. Revolts were frequent but were always crushed and savagely punished. In the American South, by contrast, slaves were a minority dispersed over relatively small holdings; large plantations were few. As a result, revolts and deadly epidemics were rare. After 1808, when the United States abolished the external slave trade, slaveholders could not ruthlessly exploit their slaves if they were to meet the growing need for workers caused by the increasing industrial demand for raw cotton. By 1830, the slave population of the southern states rose through natural increase to more than two million, which represented over one-third of all slaves in the New World.

The Price Revolution

Linked to overseas expansion was another phenomenon: an unprecedented inflation during the sixteenth century, known as the price revolution. For example, cereal prices multiplied by eight times or more in certain regions in the course of that century, and they continued to rise, although more slowly, during the first half of the seventeenth century. Economic historians have generally assumed that the prices of goods other than cereals increased by half as much as grain prices.

The main cause of the price revolution was the population growth during the late fifteenth and sixteenth centuries. The population of Europe almost doubled between 1460 and 1620. Until the middle of the seventeenth century, the number of mouths to feed outran the capacity of agriculture to supply basic foodstuffs, causing the vast majority of people to live close to subsistence. Until food production could catch up with the increasing population, prices, especially those of the staple food, bread, continued to rise.

The other principal cause of the price revolution was probably the silver that flowed into Europe from the New World via Spain, beginning in 1552. At some point, the influx of silver may have exceeded the necessary expansion of the money supply and may have begun contributing to the inflation. A key factor in the price revolution, then, was too many people with too much money chasing too few goods. The effects of the price revolution were momentous.

The Expansion of Agriculture

The price revolution had its greatest effect on farming. Food prices, which rose roughly twice as much as the prices of other goods, spurred ambitious farmers to take advantage of the situation and to produce for the expanding

Summer Harvest (c. 1615–1620) by Peter Brueghel the Younger (1564–1637).
England and the Netherlands underwent major agricultural changes in the early modern period. Enclosure of common fields by landlords and the abandonment of subsistence farming for specialized commercial farming transformed the agricultural economy of many parts of Europe. (*Oil on wood panel, 17¼″ × 23¼″, The Nelson-Atkins Museum of Art, Kansas City, Missouri: Purchase: Nelson Trust*)

market. The opportunity for profit drove some farmers to work harder and manage their land better.

All over Europe, landlords held their properties in the form of manors. A particular type of rural society and economy had evolved on these manors in the Late Middle Ages. By the fifteenth century, much manor land was held by peasant tenants according to the terms of a tenure known in England as *copyhold*. The tenants had certain hereditary rights to the land in return for the performance of certain services and the payment of certain fees to the landlord. Principal among these rights was the use of the commons — the pasture, woods, and pond. For the copyholder, access to the commons often made the difference between subsistence and real want because the land tilled on the manor might not produce enough to keep a family. Arable land was worked according to ancient custom. The land was divided into strips, and each peasant of the manor was traditionally assigned a certain number of strips. This whole pattern of peasant tillage and rights in the commons was known as the *open-field system*. After changing little for centuries, it was met head-on by the incentives generated by the price revolution.

In England, landlords aggressively pursued the possibilities for profit resulting from the inflation of farm prices. This pursuit required far-reaching changes in ancient manorial agriculture, changes that are called *enclosure*. The open-field system was geared to providing subsistence for the local village and, as such, prevented large-scale farming for a distant market. In the open-field system, the commons could not be diverted to the production of crops for sale. Moreover, the division of the arable land into strips reserved for each peasant made it difficult to engage in profitable commercial agriculture.

English landlords in the sixteenth century launched a two-pronged attack against the open-field system in an effort to transform their holdings into market-oriented, commercial ventures. First they deprived their tenant peasantry of the use of the commons, depriving poor tenants of critically needed produce; then they changed the conditions of tenure from copyhold to leasehold. Whereas copyhold was heritable and fixed, leasehold was not. When a lease came up for renewal, the landlord could raise the rent beyond the tenant's capacity to pay. Both acts of the landlord forced peasants off the manor or into the landlord's employ as farm laborers. With tenants gone, fields could be incorporated into larger, more productive units. Landlords could hire labor at bargain prices because of the swelling population and the large supply of peasants forced off the land by enclosure. Subsistence farming gave way to commercial agriculture: the growing of a surplus for the marketplace. But rural poverty increased because of the mass evictions of tenant farmers.

In the fifteenth and sixteenth centuries, the Dutch developed a new kind of farming known as *convertible husbandry* that also expanded production. This farming system employed a series of innovations, including the use of soil-restoring legumes, that replaced the old three-field system of crop rotation, which had left one-third of the land unused at any given time. The new techniques used all the land every year and provided a more diversified agriculture.

The Expansion of Trade and Industry

The conditions of the price revolution also caused trade and industry to expand. Population growth that exceeded the capacity of local food supplies stimulated commerce in basic foodstuffs — for example, the Baltic trade with Western Europe. Equally important as a stimulus to trade and industry was the growing income of landlords, merchants, and, in some instances, peasants. This income created a rising demand for consumer goods. Another factor in commercial and industrial expansion was the growth of the state. With increasing amounts of tax revenue to spend, the expanding monarchies of the sixteenth and seventeenth centuries bought more and more supplies — ships, weapons, uniforms, paper — and so spurred economic expansion.

Innovations in Business

Markets tended to shift from local to regional or even to international — a condition that gave rise to the merchant capitalist. The merchant capitalists' operations, unlike those of local producers, extended across local and national boundaries. An essential feature of merchant capitalism was the *putting-out system* of production. The manufacture of woolen textiles is a good example of how the system worked. The merchant capitalist would buy the raw wool from English landlords, who had enclosed their manors to take advantage of the rising price of wool. The merchant's agents collected the wool and took it (put it out) to nearby villages for spinning, dyeing, and weaving. The work was done in the cottages of peasants, many of whom had been evicted from the surrounding manors as a result of enclosure and therefore had to take what work they could get at very low wages. When the wool had been processed into cloth, it was picked up and shipped to market.

A cluster of other innovations in business life accompanied the emergence of the merchant capitalist and the putting-out system. Some of these innovations had roots in the Middle Ages and were important in the evolution of the modern capitalist economy. Banking operations grew more sophisticated, making it possible for depositors to pay their debts by issuing written orders to their banks to make transfers to their creditors' accounts — the origins of the modern check. Accounting methods also improved. The widespread use of double-entry bookkeeping made errors immediately evident and gave a clear picture of the financial position of a commercial enterprise. Very important to overseas expansion was a new form of business enterprise known as the joint-stock company, which allowed small investors to buy shares in a venture. These companies made possible the accumulation of the large amounts of capital needed for large-scale operations, like the building and deployment of merchant fleets, that were quite beyond the resources of one person.

Different Patterns of Commercial Development

England and the Netherlands   In both England and the United Provinces (the Netherlands), the favorable conditions led to large-scale commercial expansion. In the 1590s, the Dutch devised a new ship, the *fluit,* or flyboat, to handle bulky grain shipments at the lowest possible cost. This innovation allowed them to capture the Baltic trade, which became a principal source of their phenomenal commercial expansion between 1560 and 1660.

Equally dramatic was their commercial penetration of the Orient. Profits from the European carrying trade built the ships that allowed the Dutch first to challenge and then to displace the Portuguese in the spice trade with the East Indies during the early seventeenth century. The Dutch chartered the United East India Company in 1602 and established trading posts in the islands, which were the beginnings of a Dutch empire that lasted until World War II.

The English traded throughout Europe in the sixteenth and seventeenth centuries, especially with Spain and the Netherlands. The seventeenth century saw the foundation of a British colonial empire along the Atlantic seaboard in North America, from Maine to the Carolinas, and in the West Indies, where the English managed to dislodge the Spanish in some places.

In both England and the Netherlands, government promoted the interests of business. Political power in the Netherlands passed increasingly into the hands of an urban patriciate of merchants and manufacturers, based in cities like Delft, Haarlem, and especially Amsterdam. There, urban interests pursued public policies that served their pocketbooks. In England, because of the revolutionary transfer of power from the king to Parliament, economic policies also reflected the interests of big business, whether agricultural or commercial. Enclosure, for example, was abetted by parliamentary enactment. The Bank of England, founded in 1694, expanded credit and increased business confidence. The Navigation Acts, which proved troublesome to American colonists, placed restrictions on colonial trade and manufacturing in order to prevent competition with English merchants and manufacturers.

France and Spain   France benefited from commercial and industrial expansion, but not to the same degree as England, mainly owing to the aristocratic structure of French society. Family ties and social intercourse between the aristocracy and the merchants, like those that developed in England, were largely absent in France. Consequently, the French aristocracy remained contemptuous of commerce. Also inhibiting economic expansion were the guilds — remnants of the Middle Ages that restricted competition and production. In France, there was relatively less room than in England for the merchant capitalist operating outside the guild structures.

Spain presents an even clearer example of the failure to grasp the opportunities afforded by the price revolution. By the third quarter of the sixteenth century, Spain possessed the makings of economic expansion: unrivaled amounts of capital in the form of silver, a large and growing population, rising consumer demand, and a vast overseas empire. These factors did not bear fruit because the Spanish value system regarded business as social heresy. The Spanish held in high esteem gentlemen who possessed land gained through military service and crusading ardor, which enabled them to live on rents and privileges. Commerce and industry remained contemptible pursuits.

Numerous wars in the sixteenth century (with France, the Lutheran princes, the Ottoman Turks, the Dutch, and the English) put an increasing strain on the Spanish treasury, despite the annual shipments of silver from the New World. Spain spent its resources on maintaining and extending its imperial power and Catholicism, rather than on investing in economic expansion. In the end, the wars cost more than Spain could handle. The Dutch for a time and the English and the French for a much longer period displaced Spain as the great power. The English and the Dutch had taken advantage of the opportunities presented by the price revolution; the Spanish had not.

View of a Sixteenth-Century Marketplace.   Market towns were growing all over Western Europe after 1500. The increasing population made for brisk business in the marketplace. Note the ships in the harbor, the churches, and the variety of products available to those who could afford them. (*Private Collection/Bridgeman Art Library*)

The Fostering of Mercantile Capitalism

The changes described — especially in England and the Netherlands — represent a crucial stage in the development of the modern economic system known as *capitalism.* This is a system of *private enterprise:* the main economic decisions (what, how much, where, and at what price to produce, buy, and sell) are made by private individuals in their capacity as owners, workers, or consumers.

From 1450 to 1600, several conditions sustained the incentive to invest and reinvest — a basic factor in the emergence of modern capitalism. One was the price revolution stemming from a supply of basic commodities that could not keep pace with rising demand. Prices continued to climb, creating the most powerful incentive of all to invest rather than to consume. Why spend now, those with surplus wealth must have asked, when investment in commercial farming, mining, shipping, and publishing (to name a few important outlets) is almost certain to yield greater wealth in the future?

Additional stimuli for investment came from governments. Governments acted as giant consumers, and throughout the early modern period their appetites were expanding. Merchants who supplied governments with everything from guns to frescoes not only prospered, but reinvested as well, because of the constancy and growth of government demand. Governments also sponsored new forms of investment, whether to supply the debauched taste for new luxuries at the king's court or to meet the requirements of the military. Moreover, private investors reaped incalculable advantages from overseas empires. Colonies supplied cheap raw materials and cheap (slave) labor and served as markets for exports. They greatly stimulated the construction of both ships and harbor facilities and the sale of insurance.

State policies, known as *mercantilism,* were also aimed at augmenting national wealth and power. According to mercantilist theory, wealth from trade was measured in gold and silver, of which there was believed to be a more or less fixed quantity. The state's goal in international trade became to sell more abroad than it bought, that is, to establish a favorable balance of payments. When the amount received for sales abroad was greater than that spent for purchases, the difference would be an influx of precious metal into the state. By this logic, mercantilists were led to argue for the goal of national sufficiency: a country should try to supply most of its own needs to keep imports to a minimum.

To fuel the national economy, governments subsidized new industries, chartered companies to engage in overseas trade, and broke down local trade barriers, such as guild regulations and internal tariffs. The price revolution, the concentration of wealth in private hands, and government activity combined to provide the foundation for sustained investment and for the emergence of mercantile capitalism. This new force in the world should not be confused with industrial capitalism. The latter evolved with the Industrial Revolution in eighteenth-century England, but mercantile capitalism paved the way for it.

Toward a Global Economy

The transformations considered in this chapter were among the most momentous in the world's history. In an unprecedented development, one small part of the world, Western Europe, had become the lord of the sea-lanes, the master of many lands throughout the globe, and the banker and profit taker in an emerging world economy. Western Europe's global hegemony was to last well into the twentieth century. In conquering and settling new lands, Europeans exported Western culture around the globe, a process that accelerated in the twentieth century.

The effects of overseas expansion were profound. The native populations of the New World were decimated. As a result of the labor shortage, millions of blacks were imported from Africa to work as slaves on plantations and in mines. Black slavery would produce large-scale effects on culture, politics, and society that have lasted to the present day.

The widespread circulation of plant and animal life also had great consequences. Horses and cattle were introduced into the New World. (So amazed were the Aztecs to see men on horseback that at first they thought horse and rider were one demonic creature.) In return, the Old World acquired such novelties as corn, the tomato, and, most important, the potato, which was to become a staple of the northern European diet. Manioc, from which tapioca is made, was transplanted from the New World to Africa, where it helped sustain the population.

Western Europe was wrenched out of the subsistence economy of the Middle Ages and launched on a course of sustained economic growth. This transformation resulted from the grafting of traditional forms, such as primogeniture and holy war, onto new forces, such as global exploration, price revolution, and convertible husbandry. Out of this change emerged the beginnings of a new economic system, mercantile capitalism. This system, in large measure, paved the way for the Industrial Revolution of the eighteenth and nineteenth centuries and provided the economic thrust for European world predominance.

Notes

1. Roland Oliver, *The African Experience* (New York: HarperCollins, 1991), p. 123.
2. Quoted in Basil Davidson, *Africa in History* (New York: Collier Books, 1991), p. 215.
3. Quoted in Richard S. Dunn, *Sugar and Slaves* (Chapel Hill: University of North Carolina Press, 1972), p. 248.

Suggested Reading

Anderson, Perry, *Lineages of the Absolutist State* (1974). A useful survey, written from a Marxist perspective.

Cipolla, Carlo M., *Guns, Sails and Empires* (1965). Connections between technological innovation and overseas expansion, 1400 to 1700.

Davis, David Brion, *The Problem of Slavery in Western Culture* (1966). An authoritative study.

Davis, Ralph, *The Rise of the Atlantic Economies* (1973). A reliable survey of early modern economic history.

Dor Ner, Zvi, *Columbus and the Age of Discovery* (1991). Companion volume to the seven-part PBS series; lavishly illustrated.

Elliott, J. H., *Imperial Spain, 1469–1716* (1963). An excellent survey of the major European power of the early modern period.

Koenigsberger, H. G., *Early Modern Europe, 1500–1789* (1987). A valuable survey of the period.

Kolchin, Peter, *American Slavery: 1619–1877* (1993). An informed synthesis.

Parry, J. H., *The Age of Reconnaissance* (1963). A short survey of exploration.

Plumb, J. H., *The Growth of Political Stability in England, 1675–1725* (1967). A basic book, clear and readable.

Shennan, J. H., *The Origins of the Modern European State* (1974). An excellent brief introduction.

Review Questions

1. In what ways did early modern kings increase their power? What relationship did they have with the commercial bourgeoisie in their countries?
2. What were the strengths and weaknesses of the Spanish state?
3. Why did England move in the direction of parliamentary government, while most countries on the Continent embraced absolutism? Describe the main factors.
4. What were the new forces for expansion operating in early modern Europe?
5. Discuss the connection between the price revolution and overseas expansion. What was the principal cause of the price revolution? Why?
6. What was enclosure? How did the price revolution encourage it?
7. What is mercantile capitalism? What fostered its development?
8. European expansion gave rise to an emerging world economy. Discuss this statement.

❖ CHAPTER 10

Intellectual Transformation: The Scientific Revolution and the Age of Enlightenment

*T*he movement toward modernity initiated by the Renaissance was greatly advanced by the Scientific Revolution of the seventeenth century. The Scientific Revolution destroyed the medieval view of the universe and established the scientific method — rigorous and systematic observation and experimentation — as the essential means of unlocking nature's secrets. Increasingly, Western thinkers maintained that nature was a mechanical system, governed by laws that could be expressed mathematically. The new discoveries electrified the imagination. Science displaced theology as the queen of knowledge, and reason, which had been subordinate to religion in the Middle Ages, asserted its autonomy. The great confidence in reason inspired by the Scientific Revolution helped give rise to the Enlightenment, which explicitly rejected the ideas and institutions of the medieval past and articulated the essential norms of modernity. ❖

The Medieval View of the Universe*

Medieval thinkers had constructed a coherent picture of the universe that blended the theories of two ancient Greeks, Aristotle and Ptolemy of Alexandria, with Christian teachings. To the medieval mind, the cosmos was a giant ladder, a qualitative order, ascending toward heaven. God was at the summit of this hierarchical universe, and the earth, base and vile, was at the bottom, just above hell. It was also the center of the universe. In the medieval view, the earth's central location meant that the universe centered on human beings, that by God's design, human beings — the only creatures on whom God had bestowed reason and the promise of salvation — were lords of the earth. Around the stationary earth revolved seven transparent spheres, each of which carried one of the "planets" — the moon, Mercury, Venus, the sun, Mars, Jupiter, and Saturn. (Since the earth did not move, it was not considered a planet.) The eighth sphere, in which the stars were embedded, also re-

*See also Chapter 7.

278

volved about the earth. Beyond the stars was a heavenly sphere, the prime mover, that imparted motion to the planets and the stars, so that in one day the entire celestial system turned around the stationary earth. Enclosing the entire system was another heavenly sphere, the Empyrean, where God sat on his throne, attended by angels.

Medieval thinkers inherited Aristotle's view of a qualitative universe. Earthly objects were composed of earth, water, air, and fire, whereas celestial objects, belonging to a higher world, were composed of ether or quintessence — an element too pure and perfect to be found on earth, which consisted of base matter. In contrast to earthly objects, heavenly bodies were incorruptible, that is, they experienced no change. Since the quintessential heavens differed totally from earth, the paths of planets could not follow the same laws that governed the motion of earthly objects. This two-world orientation blended well with the Christian outlook.

Like Aristotle, Ptolemy held that planets moved around the earth in perfect circular orbits and at uniform speeds. However, in reality the path of planets is not a circle but an ellipse, and planets do not move at uniform speed but accelerate as they approach the sun. Therefore, problems arose that required Ptolemy to incorporate into his system certain ingenious devices that earlier Greek astronomers had employed. For example, to save the appearance of circular orbits, Ptolemy made use of epicycles, small circles attached to the rims of larger circles. A planet revolved uniformly around the small circle, the epicycle, which in turn revolved about the earth in a larger circle. If one ascribed a sufficient number of epicycles to a planet, the planet could seem to move in a perfectly circular orbit.

The Aristotelian-Ptolemaic model of the cosmos did appear to accord with common sense and raw perception: the earth does indeed seem and feel to be at rest. And the validity of this view seemed to be confirmed by evidence, for the model enabled thinkers to predict with considerable accuracy the movement and location of celestial bodies and the passage of time. This geocentric model and the division of the universe into higher and lower worlds also accorded with passages in Scripture. Scholastic philosophers harmonized Aristotelian and Ptolemaic science with Christian theology, producing an intellectually and emotionally satisfying picture of the universe in which everything was arranged according to a divine plan.

A New View of Nature

In several ways, the Renaissance contributed to the Scientific Revolution. The revival of interest in antiquity during the Renaissance led to the rediscovery of some ancient scientific texts, including the works of Archimedes (287–212 B.C.), which fostered new ideas in mechanics, and to improved translations of the medical works of Galen, a contemporary of Ptolemy, which stimulated the study of anatomy. Renaissance art, too, was a factor in the rise of modern science, for it linked an exact representation of the human body to

---

Chronology 10.1 ❖ The Scientific Revolution and the Enlightenment

1543	Publication of Copernicus's *On the Revolutions of the Heavenly Spheres* marks the beginning of modern astronomy
1605	Publication of Bacon's *Advancement of Learning*
1610	Publication of Galileo's *The Starry Messenger,* asserting the uniformity of nature
1632	Galileo's teachings are condemned by the church, and he is placed under house arrest
1687	Publication of Newton's *Principia Mathematica*
1690	Publication of Locke's *Two Treatises of Government*
1733	Publication of Voltaire's *Letters Concerning the English Nation*
1751–1765	Publication of the *Encyclopedia* edited by Diderot
1776	Declaration of Independence
1789	French Revolution begins

---

mathematical proportions and demanded accurate observation of natural phenomena. By defining visual space and the relationship between the object and the observer in mathematical terms and by delineating the natural world with unprecedented scientific precision, Renaissance art helped to promote a new view of nature, which later found expression in the astronomy of Copernicus and Kepler and the physics of Galileo.

The Renaissance revival of ancient Pythagorean and Platonic ideas, which stressed mathematics as the key to comprehending reality, also contributed to the Scientific Revolution. Extending the mathematical harmony found in music to the universe at large, Pythagoras (c. 580–507 B.C.) and his followers believed that all things have form, which can be expressed numerically, and that reality consists fundamentally of number relations, which the mind can grasp. Plato maintained that beyond the world of everyday objects made known to us through the senses lies a higher reality, the world of Forms, which contains an inherent mathematical order apprehended only by thought. The great thinkers of the Scientific Revolution were influenced by these ancient ideas of nature as a harmonious mathematical system knowable to the mind.

Nicolaus Copernicus: The Dethronement of the Earth

Modern astronomy begins with Nicolaus Copernicus (1473–1543), a Polish astronomer, mathematician, and church canon. He proclaimed that earth is a planet that orbits a centrally located sun together with the other planets. This heliocentric theory served as the kernel of a new world picture that eventually supplanted the medieval view of the universe. Copernicus did not base his heliocentric theory on new observations and new data. What led him to remove the earth from the center of the universe was the complexity and cumbersomeness of the Ptolemaic system, which offended his sense of mathematical order. To Copernicus, the numerous epicycles (the number had been increased since Ptolemy, making the model even more cumbersome) violated the Platonic vision of the mathematical symmetry of the universe.

Concerned that his theories would spark a controversy, Copernicus refused to publish his work, but, persuaded by his friends, he finally relented. His masterpiece, *On the Revolutions of the Heavenly Spheres,* appeared in 1543. As Copernicus had feared, his views did stir up controversy, but the new astronomy did not become a passionate issue until the early seventeenth century, more than fifty years after the publication of *On the Revolutions.* The Copernican theory frightened clerical authorities, who controlled the universities as well as the pulpits, for it seemed to conflict with Scripture. For example, Psalm 93 says: "Yea, the world is established, that it cannot be moved." And Psalm 103 says that God "fixed the earth upon its foundation not to be moved forever." In 1616, the church placed *On the Revolutions* and all other works that ascribed motion to the earth on the Index of Prohibited Books.

Galileo: Uniformity of Nature and Experimental Physics

Galileo Galilei (1564–1642) is the principal reason that the seventeenth century has been called "the century of genius." A Pisan by birth, Galileo was a talented musician and artist and a cultivated humanist; he knew and loved the Latin classics and Italian poetry. He was also an astronomer and physicist who helped shatter the medieval conception of the cosmos and shape the modern scientific outlook. Galileo was indebted to the Platonic tradition, which tried to grasp the mathematical harmony of the universe, and to Archimedes, the Hellenistic mathematician-engineer who had sought a geometric understanding of space and motion.

Galileo rejected the medieval division of the universe into higher and lower realms and proclaimed the modern idea of nature's uniformity. Learning that a telescope had been invented in Holland, Galileo built one for himself and used it to investigate the heavens — the first person to do so. From his observations of the moon, Galileo concluded

> *that the surface of the moon is not smooth, uniform, and precisely spherical as a great number of philosophers believe it (and the other heavenly bodies) to be, but is uneven, rough, and full of cavities and prominences, being not unlike the face of the earth, relieved by chains of mountains and deep valleys.*[1]

This discovery of the moon's craters and mountains and of spots on the supposedly unblemished sun led Galileo to break with the Aristotelian notion that celestial bodies were pure, perfect, and unchangeable. For Galileo, there

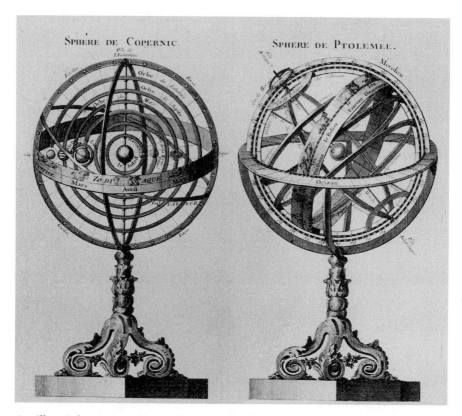

Armillary Spheres According to Copernicus and Ptolemy. The spheres reflect the opposing views of the nature of the cosmos that confronted scholars in the sixteenth and early seventeenth centuries. Gradually, Copernicus's heliocentric viewpoint, supported by the discoveries of Kepler, Galileo, and Newton, overturned the Ptolemaic system. (*Smithsonian Institution Libraries*)

was no difference in quality between celestial and terrestrial bodies. Nature was not a hierarchical order, in which physical entities were ranked according to their possession or lack of quality; rather, it was a homogeneous system, the same throughout.

With his telescope, Galileo discovered the four moons that orbit Jupiter, an observation that overcame a principal objection to the Copernican system. Galileo showed that a celestial body could indeed move around a center other than the earth, that the earth was not the common center for all celestial bodies, and that a celestial body (the earth's moon or Jupiter's moons) could orbit a planet at the same time that the planet revolved around another body (the sun).

Galileo pioneered in experimental physics and advanced the modern idea that knowledge of motion should be derived from direct observation and from mathematics. In dealing with problems of motion, he insisted on applying mathematics to the study of moving bodies and did in fact study acceleration by performing experiments, which required careful mathematical measurement. For Aristotelian scholastics, a rock fell because it was striving to reach its proper place in the universe, thereby fulfilling its nature; it was acting in accordance with the purpose God had assigned it. Galileo completely rejected the view that motion is due to a quality inherent in an object. Rather, he said, motion is the relationship of bodies to time and distance. By holding that bodies fall according to uniform and quantifiable laws, Galileo posited an entirely different conceptual system. This system requires that we study angles and distances and search for mathematical ratios but avoid inquiring into an object's quality and purpose — the role God assigned it in a hierarchical universe.

For Galileo, the universe was a "grand book which . . . is written in the language of mathematics and its characters are triangles, circles, and other geometric figures without which it is humanly impossible to understand a single word of it."[2] In the tradition of Plato, Galileo sought to grasp the mathematical principles governing reality — reality was physical nature itself, not Plato's higher realm, of which nature was only a poor copy — and ascribed to mathematics absolute authority. Like Copernicus and Kepler, he believed that mathematics expresses the harmony and beauty of God's creation.

Attack on Authority

Insisting that physical truth is arrived at through observation, experimentation, and reason, Galileo strongly denounced reliance on authority. Scholastic thinkers regarded Aristotle as the supreme authority on questions concerning nature, and university education was based on his works. These doctrinaire Aristotelians angered Galileo, who protested that they sought truth not by opening their eyes to nature and new knowledge, but by slavishly relying on ancient texts. In *Dialogue Concerning the Two Chief World Systems — Ptolemaic and Copernican* (1632), Galileo upheld the Copernican view and attacked the unquestioning acceptance of Aristotle's teachings.

Galileo also criticized Roman Catholic authorities for attempting to suppress the Copernican theory. He argued that passages from the Bible had no authority in questions involving nature.

A sincere Christian, Galileo never intended to use the new science to undermine faith. What he desired was to separate science from faith so that reason and experience alone would be the deciding factors on questions involving nature. He could not believe that "God who has endowed us with senses, reason and intellect,"[3] did not wish us to use these faculties in order to acquire knowledge. He was certain that science was compatible with Scripture rightly understood, that is, allowing for the metaphorical language of Scripture and its disinterest in conveying scientific knowledge. For Galileo, the aim of Scripture was to teach people the truths necessary for salvation, not to instruct them in the operations of nature, which is the task of science.

Galileo's support of Copernicus aroused the ire of both scholastic philosophers and the clergy, who feared that the brash scientist threatened a world

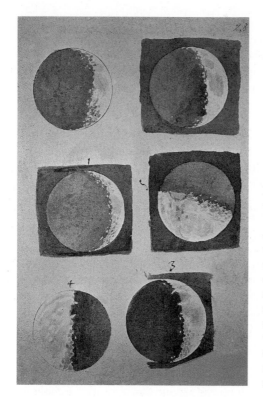

Notebook Sketches of the Phases of the Moon by Galileo Galilei, 1609–1610.   Galileo saw only shadows when he looked into his telescope. But because he was trained as an artist in the principles of light and dark coloring to emphasize or shorten distance, he knew that what he saw represented real objects, in this case mountains and valleys. Somewhat satirically, he compared the moon to Bohemia. (*Biblioteca Nazionale Centrale, Florence*)

picture that had the support of venerable ancient authorities, Holy Writ, and scholastic tradition. Already traumatized by the Protestant threat, Catholic officials cringed at ideas that might undermine traditional belief and authority.

In 1616, the Congregation of the Index, the church's censorship organ, condemned the teaching of Copernicanism. In 1633, the aging and infirm Galileo was summoned to Rome. Tried and condemned by the Inquisition, he was ordered to abjure the Copernican theory. Not wishing to bring harm to himself and certain that the truth would eventually prevail, Galileo bowed to the Inquisition. He was sentenced to life imprisonment — mostly house arrest at his own villa near Florence — the *Dialogue* was banned, and he was forbidden to write on Copernicanism. Not until 1820 did the church lift the ban on Copernicanism.

Johannes Kepler: Laws of Planetary Motion

Johannes Kepler (1571–1630), a German mathematician and astronomer, combined the Pythagorean-Platonic quest to comprehend the mathematical harmony within nature with a deep commitment to Lutheran Christianity. He contended that God gave human beings the ability to understand the laws of harmony and proportion.

As a true Pythagorean, Kepler yearned to discover the geometric harmony of the planets — what he called the "music of the spheres." Such knowledge, he believed, would provide supreme insight into God's mind. No doubt this mystical quality sparked the creative potential of the imagination, but to be harnessed for science, it had to be disciplined by the rational faculties.

Kepler discovered the three basic laws of planetary motion, which shattered the Ptolemaic cosmology. In doing so, he utilized the data collected by Tycho Brahe, a Danish astronomer, who for twenty years had systematically observed the planets and stars and recorded their positions with far greater accuracy than had ever been done. Kepler sought to fit Tycho's observations into Copernicus's heliocentric model.

Kepler's first law demonstrated that planets move in elliptical orbits — not circular ones, as Aristotle and Ptolemy (and Copernicus) had believed — and that the sun is one focus of the ellipse. This discovery that a planet's path was one simple oval eliminated all the epicycles that had been used to preserve the appearance of circular motion. Kepler's second law showed that planets do not move at uniform speed, as had been believed, but accelerate as they near the sun, and he provided the rule for deciphering a planet's speed at each point in its orbit. His third law drew a mathematical relationship between the time it takes a planet to complete its orbit of the sun and its average distance from the sun. On the basis of these laws, one could calculate accurately a planet's position and velocity at a particular time — another indication that the planets were linked together in a unified mathematical system.

Derived from carefully observed facts, Kepler's laws of planetary motion buttressed Copernicanism, for they made sense only in a heliocentric universe. But why did the planets move in elliptical orbits? Why did they not fly off into space or crash into the sun? To these questions Kepler had no satisfactory answers. It was Isaac Newton (1642–1727), the great British mathematician-scientist, who arrived at a celestial mechanics that linked the astronomy of Copernicus and Kepler with the physics of Galileo and accounted for the behavior of planets.

The Newtonian Synthesis

The publication in 1687 of Isaac Newton's *Mathematical Principles of Natural Philosophy* marks the climax of the Scientific Revolution. Newton postulated three laws of motion that joined all celestial and terrestrial objects into a vast mechanical system, whose parts worked in perfect harmony and whose connections could be expressed in mathematical terms, and he invented the calculus, which facilitated the expression of physical laws in mathematical equations. Since Copernican astronomy was essential to his all-encompassing theory of the universe, Newton provided mathematical proof for the heliocentric system, and opposition to it dissipated.

Newton's first law is the principle of inertia: that a body at rest remains at rest unless acted on by a force and that a body in rectilinear motion continues to move in a straight line at the same velocity unless a force acts on it. A moving body does not require a force to keep it in motion, as ancient and medieval thinkers had believed. Once started, bodies continue to move; motion is as natural a condition as rest. Newton's second law states that a given force produces a measurable change in a body's velocity; a body's change of velocity is proportional to the force acting on it. Newton's third law holds that for every action or force there is an equal and opposite reaction or force. The sun pulls the earth with the same force that the earth exercises on the sun. An apple falling to the ground is being pulled by the earth, but the apple is also pulling the earth toward it. (However, since the mass of the apple is so small in comparison with that of the earth, the force that the apple exercises on the earth causes no visible change in the earth's motion.)

Newton asserted that the same laws of motion and gravitation that operate in the celestial world also govern the movement of earthly bodies. Ordinary mechanical laws explain both why apples fall to the ground and why planets orbit the sun. Both the planet and the apple are subject to the same force, and the very same mathematical formula describes the sun's action on a planet and the earth's pull on an apple. Newtonian physics ended the medieval division of the cosmos into higher and lower worlds, with different laws operating in each realm. The universe is an integrated, harmonious mechanical system held together by the force of gravity. By demonstrating that the universe contains an inherent mathematical order, Newton realized the Pythagorean and Platonic visions. To his contemporaries, it seemed that Newton had unraveled all of nature's mysteries: the universe was fully explicable. It was as if Newton had penetrated God's mind.

Deeply committed to Anglican Christianity, Newton retained a central place for God in his world system. God for him was the grand architect whose wisdom and skill accounted for nature's magnificent clockwork design. Newton also believed that God periodically intervened in his creation to restore energy to the cosmic system and that there was no conflict between divine miracles and a mechanical universe. However, in future generations, thinkers called deists (see page 293) came to regard miracles as incompatible with a universe governed by impersonal mechanical principles.

With his discovery of the composition of light, Newton also laid the foundation of the science of optics. He was a cautious experimentalist who valued experimental procedures, including drawing appropriate conclusions from accumulated data. Both Newton's mechanical universe and his championing of the experimental method were foundation blocks of the Age of Enlightenment.

Prophets of Modern Science

The accomplishments of the Scientific Revolution extended beyond the creation of a new model of the universe. They also included the formulation of a new method of inquiry into nature and the recognition that science could serve humanity. Two thinkers instrumental in articulating the implications of the Scientific Revolution were Francis Bacon and René Descartes. Both repudiated the authority of Aristotle and other ancients in scientific matters and urged the adoption of new methods for seeking and evaluating truth.

Francis Bacon: The Inductive Method

Sir Francis Bacon (1561–1626), an English statesman and philosopher, vigorously supported the advancement of science and the scientific method. Although he himself had no laboratory and made no discoveries, his advocacy of the scientific method has earned him renown as a prophet of modern science. Bacon attributed the limited progress of science over the ages to the interference of scholastic philosophers, who sought to bend theories of nature to the requirements of Scripture. Bacon also denounced scholastic thinkers for their slavish attachment to Aristotelian doctrines, which prevented independent thinking and the acquisition of new information about nature. To acquire new knowledge and improve the quality of human life, said Bacon, we should not depend on ancient texts; old authorities must be discarded. Knowledge must be pursued and organized in a new way.

The method that Bacon advocated as the way to truth and useful knowledge was the inductive approach: careful observation of nature and the systematic accumulation of data, drawing general laws from the knowledge of particulars, and testing these laws through constant experimentation. People committed to such a method would never subscribe to inherited fables and myths about nature or invent new ones. Rather, they would investigate nature directly and base their conclusions on observable facts. In his discovery of the circulation of blood, Bacon's contemporary, British physician William Harvey (1578–1657), successfully employed the inductive method championed by Bacon. Grasping the essential approach of modern natural science, Bacon attacked practitioners of astrology, magic, and alchemy for their errors, secretiveness, and enigmatic writings and urged instead the pursuit of cooperative and methodical scientific research that could be publicly criticized.

Bacon was among the first to appreciate the value of the new science for human life. Knowledge, he said, should help us utilize nature for human advantage; it should improve the quality of human life by advancing commerce, industry, and agriculture. Holding that knowledge is power, Bacon urged the state to found scientific institutions and praised progress in technology and the mechanical arts. In Bacon's transvaluation of values, the artisan, mechanic, and engineer advanced knowledge more and contributed more to human betterment than did philosopher-theologians who constructed castles in the air.

René Descartes: The Deductive Method

The scientific method encompasses two approaches to knowledge that usually complement each other: the empirical (inductive) and the rational (deductive). In the inductive approach, which is employed in such descriptive sciences as

Engraving of René Descartes (1596–1650) Tutoring Queen Christina of Sweden. Descartes was rare among major scientists in that he believed passionately in the intelligence of his female followers and correspondents. Rejecting authority, he asserted confidence in the human mind's ability to arrive at truth through its own capacities. *(Jean-Loup Charmet)*

biology, anatomy, and geology, general principles are derived from the analysis of data collected through observation and experiment. The essential features of the inductive method, as we have seen, were championed by Bacon, who regarded sense data as the foundation of knowledge. In the deductive approach, which is employed in mathematics and theoretical physics, truths are derived in successive steps from first principles, indubitable axioms. In the seventeenth century, the deductive method was formulated by René Descartes (1596–1650), a French mathematician and philosopher, who is also regarded as the founder of modern philosophy.

In the *Discourse on Method* (1637), Descartes expressed his disenchantment with the learning of his day. Since much of what he had believed on the basis of authority had been shown to be untrue, Descartes resolved to seek no knowledge other than that which he might find within himself or within nature. Rejecting as absolutely false anything about which he could have the least doubt, Descartes searched for an incontrovertible truth that could serve as the first principle of knowledge, the basis of an all-encompassing philosophical system.

Descartes found one truth to be certain and unshakable: that it was he who was doing the doubting and thinking. In his dictum "I think therefore I am," Descartes had his starting point of knowledge. Descartes is viewed as the founder of modern philosophy because he called for the individual to question and if necessary to overthrow all traditional beliefs, and he proclaimed the mind's inviolable autonomy and importance, its ability and right to understand truth. His assertions about the power of thought made people aware of their capacity to comprehend the world through their own mental powers.

Descartes saw the method used in mathematics as the most reliable avenue to certain knowledge. By applying mathematical reasoning to philosophical problems, we can achieve the same certainty and clarity evidenced in geometry. Mathematics is the key to understanding both the truths of nature and the moral order underlying human existence. The mathematical, or deductive, approach favored by Descartes consists of finding a self-evident principle, an irrefutable premise, such as a geometric axiom, and then deducing other truths from it through a chain of logical reasoning. The Cartesian deductive method, with its mathematical emphasis, perfectly complements Bacon's inductive approach, which stresses observation and experimentation. The scientific achievements of modern times have stemmed from the skillful synchronization of induction and deduction.

The Meaning of the Scientific Revolution

The radical transformation of our conception of the physical universe produced by the Scientific Revolution ultimately transformed our understanding of the individual, society, and the purpose of life. The Scientific Revolution, therefore, was a decisive factor in the shaping of the modern world. It destroyed the medieval world-view, in which the earth occupied the central position, heaven lay just beyond the fixed stars, and every object had its place in a hierarchical and qualitative order. It replaced this view with the modern conception of a homogeneous universe of unbounded space and an infinite number of celestial bodies. Gone were the barriers that separated the heavens and the earth. The glory of the heavens was diminished by the new view that celestial objects were composed of the same stuff and subject to the same laws as all other natural objects. Gone also was the medieval notion that God had assigned an ultimate purpose to all natural objects and to all plant and animal life, that in God's plan everything had an assigned role: we have eyes because God wants us to see and rain because God wants crops to grow. Eschewing ultimate purposes, modern science examines physical nature for mathematical relationships and chemical composition.

In later centuries, further implications of the new cosmology caused great anguish. The conviction that God had created the universe for them, that the earth was fixed beneath their feet, and that God had given the earth the central position in his creation had brought medieval people a profound sense of security. They knew why they were here, and they never doubted that heaven was the final resting place for the faithful. Copernican astronomy dethroned the earth, expelled human beings from their central position, and implied an infinite universe. In the sixteenth and seventeenth centuries, few thinkers grasped the full significance of this displacement. However, in succeeding centuries, this radical cosmological transformation proved as traumatic for the modern mind as did Adam and Eve's expulsion from the Garden of Eden for the medieval mind. Today we know that the earth is one of billions and billions of celestial bodies, a tiny speck in an endless cosmic ocean, and that the universe is some twelve billion years old. Could such a universe have been created just for human beings? Could it contain a heaven that assures eternal life for the faithful and a hell with eternal fires and torments for sinners?

Few people at the time were aware of the full implications of the new cosmology. One who did understand was Blaise Pascal (1623–1662), a French scientist and mathematician. A devout Catholic, Pascal was frightened by what he called "the eternal silence of these infinite spaces" and realized that the new science could feed doubt, uncertainty, and anxiety, which threatened belief.

The conception of reason advanced by Galileo and other thinkers of the period differed fundamentally from that of medieval scholastics. Scholastic thinkers viewed reason as a useful aid for contemplating divine truth; as such, reason always had to serve theology. Influenced by the new scientific spirit, thinkers now saw the investigation of nature as reason's principal concern. What is more, they viewed this activity as autonomous and not subject to theological authority.

The Scientific Revolution fostered a rational and critical spirit among the intellectual elite. Descartes's methodical doubt, rejection of authority, and insistence on the clarity, precision, and accuracy of an idea and Francis Bacon's insistence on verification pervaded the outlook of the eighteenth-century Enlightenment thinkers; they denounced magic, spells, demons, witchcraft, alchemy, and astrology as vulgar superstitions. Phenomena attributed to occult forces, they argued, could be explained by reference to natural forces. A wide breach opened up between the intellectual elite and the masses, who remained steeped in popular superstitions and committed to traditional Christian dogma.

The creators of modern science had seen no essential conflict between traditional Christianity and the new view of the physical universe and made no war on the churches. Indeed, they believed that they were unveiling the laws of nature instituted by God at the Creation — that at last the human mind could comprehend God's magnificent handiwork. But the new cosmology and new scientific outlook ultimately weakened traditional Christianity, for it dispensed with miracles and the need for God's presence.

The new critical spirit led the thinkers of the Enlightenment to doubt the literal truth of the Bible and to dismiss miracles as incompatible with what science teaches about the regularity of nature. So brilliantly had God crafted the universe, they said, so exquisite a mechanism was nature, that its operations did not require God's intervention. In the generations after the Scientific Revolution, theology, long considered the highest form of contemplation, was denounced as a barrier to understanding or even dismissed as irrelevant, and the clergy rapidly lost their position as the arbiters of knowledge. To many intellectuals, theology seemed sterile and profitless in comparison with the new science. Whereas science promised the certitude of mathematics, theologians seemed to quibble endlessly over unfathomable and, even worse, inconsequential issues. That much blood had been spilled over these questions discredited theology still more. In scientific academies, in salons, and in coffee houses, educated men and some women met to discuss the new ideas, and journals published the new knowledge for eager readers. European culture was undergoing a great transformation, marked by the triumph of a scientific and secular spirit among the intellectual elite.

The Scientific Revolution repudiated reliance on Aristotle, Ptolemy, and other ancient authorities in matters concerning nature and substituted in their place knowledge derived from observation, experimentation, and mathematical thinking. Citing an ancient authority was no longer sufficient to prove a point or win an argument. The new standard of knowledge derived from experience with the world, not from ancient texts or inherited views. This new outlook had far-reaching implications for the Age of Enlightenment. If the authority of ancient thinkers regarding the universe could be challenged, could not inherited political beliefs be challenged as well — for example, the divine right of kings to rule? Impressed with the achievements of science, many intellectuals started to urge the application of the scientific method to all fields of knowledge.

The new outlook generated by the Scientific Revolution served as the foundation of the Enlightenment. The Scientific Revolution gave thinkers great confidence in the power of the mind, which had discovered nature's laws, reinforcing the confidence in human abilities expressed by Renaissance humanists. In time, it was believed, the scientific method would unlock all nature's secrets, and humanity, gaining ever greater knowledge and control of nature, would progress rapidly.

The Age of Enlightenment: Affirmation of Reason and Freedom

The Enlightenment of the eighteenth century was the culmination of the movement toward modernity initiated by the Renaissance. The thinkers of the Enlightenment, called *philosophes,* aspired to create a more rational and humane society. To attain this goal, they attacked medieval otherworldliness, rejected theology as an avenue to truth, denounced the Christian idea of people's inherent depravity, and sought to understand nature and society through reason alone, unaided by revelation or priestly authority. Adopting Descartes's method of systematic doubt, they questioned all inherited opinions and traditions. "We think that the greatest service to be done to men," said Denis Diderot, "is to teach them to use their reason, only to hold for truth what they have verified and proved."[4] The philosophes believed that they were inaugurating an enlightened age. Through the power of reason, humanity was at last liberating itself from the fetters of ignorance, superstition, and despotism with which tyrants and priests had bound it in past ages. Paris was the center of the Enlightenment, but there were philosophes and adherents of their views in virtually every leading city in Western Europe and North America.

In many ways, the Enlightenment grew directly out of the Scientific Revolution. The philosophes sought to expand knowledge of nature and to apply the scientific method to the human world in order to uncover society's defects and to achieve appropriate reforms. Newton had discovered universal laws that explained the physical phenomena. Are there not general rules that also apply to human behavior and social institutions, asked the philosophes? Could a "science of man" be created that would correspond to and complement Newton's science of nature — that would provide clear and certain answers to the problems of the social world in the same way that Newtonian science had solved the mysteries of the physical world?

By relying on the same methodology that Newton had employed to establish certain knowledge of the physical universe, the philosophes hoped to arrive at the irrefutable laws that operated in the realm of human society. They aspired to shape religion, government, law, morality, and economics in accordance with these natural laws. They believed that all things should be reevaluated to see if they accorded with nature and promoted human well-being.

In championing the methodology of science, the philosophes affirmed respect for the mind's capacities and for human autonomy. Individuals are self-governing, they insisted. The mind is self-sufficient; rejecting appeals to clerical or princely authority, it relies on its own ability to think, and it trusts the evidence of its own experience. Rejecting the authority of tradition, the philosophes wanted people to have the courage to break with beliefs and institutions that did not meet the test of reason and common sense and to seek new guideposts derived from experience and reason unhindered by passion, superstition, dogma, and authority. The numerous examples of injustice, inhumanity, and superstition in society outraged the philosophes. Behind their devotion to reason and worldly knowledge lay an impassioned moral indignation against institutions and beliefs that degraded human beings.

Christianity Assailed: The Search for a Natural Religion

The philosophes waged an unremitting assault on traditional Christianity, denouncing it for harboring superstition, promulgating unreason, and fostering fanaticism and persecution. Relying on the facts of experience, as Bacon had taught, the philosophes dismissed miracles, angels, and devils as violations of nature's laws and figments of the imagination, which could not be substantiated by the norms of evidence. Applying the Cartesian spirit of careful reasoning to the Bible, they pointed out flagrant discrepancies between various biblical passages and rejected as preposterous the theologians' attempts to resolve these contradictions. With science as an ally, the philosophes challenged Christianity's claim that it possessed infallible truths, and they ridiculed theologians for wrangling over pointless issues and for compelling obedience to doctrines that defied reason.

Moreover, the philosophes assailed Christianity for viewing human nature as evil and human beings as helpless without God's assistance, for focusing on heaven at the expense of human happiness on earth, and for impeding the acquisition of useful knowledge by proclaiming the higher authority of dogma and revelation. Frightened and confused by religion, people have been held in subjection by clergy and tyrants, the philosophes argued. To establish an enlightened society, clerical power must be broken, Christian dogmas repudiated, and the fanaticism that produced the horrors of the Crusades, the Inquisition, and the wars of the Reformation purged from the European soul. The philosophes broke with the Christian past, even if they retained the essential elements of Christian morality.

François Marie Arouet (1694–1778), known to the world as Voltaire, was the recognized leader of the French Enlightenment. Few of the philosophes had a better mind, and none had a sharper wit. Living in exile in Britain in the late 1720s, Voltaire acquired a great admiration for English liberty, commerce, science, and religious toleration. Voltaire's angriest words were directed against established Christianity, to which he attributed many of the ills of French society. He regarded Christianity as "the Christ-worshiping superstition," which someday would be destroyed "by the weapons of reason."[5] Many Christian dogmas are incomprehensible, said Voltaire, yet Christians have slaughtered one another to enforce obedience to these doctrines.

While some philosophes were atheists, most were deists, including Voltaire and Thomas Paine (1737–1809), the English-American radical. Deists sought to fashion a natural religion that accorded with reason and science, and they tried to adapt the Christian tradition to the requirements of the new science. They denied that the Bible was God's revelation, rejected clerical authority, and dismissed Christian mysteries, prophecies, and miracles — the virgin birth, Jesus walking on water, the Resurrection, and others — as violations of a lawful natural order. They did consider it reasonable that this magnificently structured universe, operating with clockwork precision, was designed and created at a point in time by an all-wise Creator. But in their view, once God had set the universe in motion, he refrained from interfering with its operations. Thus, deists were at odds with Newton, who allowed for divine intervention in the world.

For deists, the essence of religion was morality — a commitment to justice and humanity — and not adherence to rituals, doctrines, or clerical authority. In *The Age of Reason* (1794–95), Paine declared: "I believe in the equality of man; and I believe that religious duties consist in doing justice, loving mercy, and endeavoring to make our fellow-creatures happy."[6] Deists deemed it entirely reasonable that after death those who had fulfilled God's moral law would be rewarded, while those who had not would be punished.

Political Thought

Besides established religion, the philosophes identified another source of the evil that beset humanity: despotism. If human beings were to achieve happiness, they had to extirpate revealed religion and check the power of their rulers. "Every age has its dominant idea," wrote Diderot; "that of our age seems to be Liberty."[7] Eighteenth-century political thought is characterized by a thoroughgoing secularism; an indictment of despotism, the divine right of kings, and the special privileges of the aristocracy and the clergy; a respect for English constitutionalism because it enshrined the rule of law; and an affirmation of John Locke's theory that government had an obligation to protect the natural rights of its citizens. Central to the political outlook of the philosophes was the conviction that political solutions could be found for the ills that afflicted society.

In general, the philosophes favored constitutional government that protected citizens from the abuse of power. With the notable exception of Rousseau, the philosophes' concern for liberty did not lead them to embrace democracy, for they put little trust in the masses. Several philosophes, notably Voltaire, placed their confidence in reforming despots, like Frederick II of Prussia, who were sympathetic to enlightened ideas. However, the philosophes were less concerned with the form of government — monarchy or republic — than with preventing the authorities from abusing their power.

Seventeenth-Century Antecedents: Hobbes and Locke

The political thought of the Enlightenment was greatly affected by the writings of two seventeenth-century philosophers: Thomas Hobbes (1588–1679) and John Locke (1632–1704). Hobbes witnessed the agonies of the English civil war, including the execution of Charles I in 1649. These developments fortified his conviction that absolutism was the most desirable and logical form of government. Only the unlimited power of a sovereign, Hobbes wrote in his major work, *Leviathan* (1651), could contain the human passions that disrupt the social order and threaten civilized life; only absolute rule could provide an environment secure enough for people to pursue their individual interests.

Influenced by the new scientific thought that saw mathematical knowledge as the avenue to truth, Hobbes aimed at constructing political philosophy on a scientific foundation and rejected the authority of tradition and religion as inconsistent with a science of politics. Thus, although Hobbes supported absolutism, he dismissed the idea advanced by other theorists of absolutism that the monarch's power derived from God. He also rejected the idea that the state should not be obeyed when it violated God's law. Like Machiavelli, Hobbes made no attempt to fashion the earthly city in accordance with Christian teachings. *Leviathan* is a rational and secular political statement; its significance lies in its modern approach, rather than in Hobbes's justification of absolutism.

Hobbes had a pessimistic view of human nature. Believing that people are innately selfish and grasping, he maintained that competition and dissension, rather than cooperation, characterize human relations. Without a stringent authority to make and enforce law, life would be miserable, a war of every man against every man, he said. Therefore, he prescribed a state with unlimited power, since only in this way could people be protected from one another and civilized life preserved. Although the philosophes generally rejected Hobbes's gloomy view of human nature, they embraced his secular approach to politics, particularly his denunciation of the theory of the divine right of kings. Hobbes's concern with protecting the social order from human antisocial tendencies is still a central consideration of modern political life.

In contrast to Hobbes, John Locke saw people as essentially good and humane and developed a conception of the state that was fundamentally different from Hobbes's. In the *Two Treatises of Government* (1690), Locke maintained that human beings are born with natural rights to life, liberty, and property, and they establish the state to protect these rights. Consequently, neither executive nor legislature — neither king nor assembly — has the authority to deprive individuals of their natural rights. Whereas Hobbes justified absolute monarchy, Locke explicitly endorsed constitutional government, in which the power to govern derives from the consent of the governed and the state's authority is limited by agreement. Rulers hold their authority under the law; when they act outside the law, they forfeit their right to govern. Thus, if government fails to fulfill the end for which it was established — the preservation of the individual's right to life, liberty, and property — the people have a right to dissolve that government.

Both Hobbes and Locke agreed that the state exists in order to ensure the tranquillity, security, and well-being of its citizens. However, they proposed radically different ways of attaining this end. Unlike Hobbes, Locke believed that social well-being encompassed personal freedom. Rejecting Hobbes's view that absolute power can remedy the defects of the state of nature, Locke stated the case for limited government, the rule of law, the protection of fundamental human rights, and the right of resistance to arbitrary power. Underlying Locke's conception of the state is the conviction that people have the capacity for reason and freedom: "We are born Free as we are born Rational."

The value that Locke gave to reason and freedom and his theories of natural rights, the rule of law, and the right to resist despotic authority had a profound effect on the Enlightenment and the liberal revolutions of the late eighteenth and early nineteenth centuries. Thus, in the Declaration of Independence, Thomas Jefferson restated Locke's principles to justify the American Revolution. Locke's tenets that property is a natural right and that state interference with personal property leads to the destruction of liberty also became core principles of modern liberalism.

Montesquieu

The contribution of Charles Louis de Secondat, baron de la Brède et de Montesquieu (1689–1755), to political theory rests essentially on his *The Spirit of the Laws* (1748), a work of immense erudition covering many topics. Montesquieu held that the study of political and social behavior is not an exercise in abstract thought, but must be undertaken in relation to geographic, economic, and historic conditions. To this end, Montesquieu accumulated and classified a wide diversity of facts, from which he tried to draw general rules governing society. He concluded that different climatic and geographic conditions and different national customs, habits, religions, and institutions give each nation a particular character; each society requires constitutional forms and laws that pay heed to the character of its people. Montesquieu's effort to explain social and political behavior empirically — to found a science of society based on the model of natural science — makes him a forerunner of modern sociology.

Montesquieu regarded despotism as a pernicious form of government, corrupt by its very nature. Ruling as he wishes and unchecked by law, the despot knows nothing of moderation and institutionalizes cruelty and violence. The slavelike subjects, wrote Montesquieu, know only servitude, fear, and misery. Driven by predatory instincts, the despotic ruler involves his state in wars of conquest, caring not at all about the suffering this causes his people. In a despotic society, economic activity stagnates, for merchants, fearful that their goods will be confiscated by the state, lose their initiative. Reformers used Montesquieu's characterization of despotism to show the limitations of absolute monarchy.

To safeguard liberty from despotism, Montesquieu advocated the principle of separation of powers. In every government, said Montesquieu, there are three sorts of powers: legislative, executive, and judiciary. When one person or one body exercises all three powers — if the same body both prosecutes and judges, for example — liberty cannot be preserved. Where sovereignty is monopolized by one person or body, power is abused and political liberty is denied. In a good government, one power balances and checks another power, an argument that impressed the framers of the U.S. Constitution.

Several of Montesquieu's ideals were absorbed into the liberal tradition — constitutional government and the rule of law, separation of powers, freedom of thought, religious toleration, and protection of individual liberty. The conservative tradition drew on Montesquieu's respect for traditional ways of life and his opposition to sudden reforms that ignored a people's history and culture.

Voltaire

Unlike Hobbes and Locke, Voltaire was not a systematic political theorist, but a propagandist and polemicist, who hurled pointed barbs at all the abuses of the Old Regime. Nevertheless, Voltaire's writings do contain ideas that

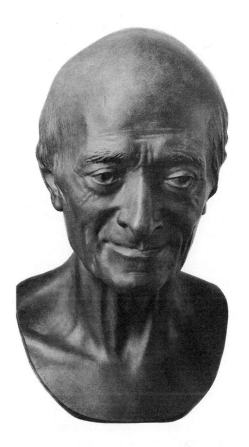

Marble Bust of Voltaire by Jean Antoine Houdon, 1781. François Marie Arouet (1694–1778), better known as Voltaire, was the most celebrated mind and wit in Europe. A relentless critic of religious dogmatism and intolerance, he denounced censorship and advised and urged the enlightened despots of Russia and Prussia to use their absolute power to reform society. He attacked his own country's institutions and praised those of England. His literary brilliance was acknowledged even by his enemies; he was the single most effective leader of the French philosophes. (*Musée Fabre, Montpellier*)

form a coherent political theory that in many ways expresses the outlook of the Enlightenment.

Voltaire disdained arbitrary power, since it is based on human whim rather than on established law. He described a prince who imprisons or executes his subjects unjustly and without due process as "nothing but a highway robber who is called 'Your Majesty.'" For Voltaire, freedom consisted in being governed by an established and standard code of law that applies equally to all. Without the rule of law, wrote Voltaire, there is no liberty of person, no freedom of thought or of religion, no protection of personal property, no impartial judiciary, and no protection from arbitrary arrest. Underlying Voltaire's commitment to the rule of law was his conviction that power should be used rationally and beneficially.

Voltaire's respect for the rule of law was strengthened by his stay in England between 1726 and 1729, which led to the publication of *The English Letters* in 1733. In this work, Voltaire presents an idealized and, at times, inaccurate picture of English politics and society. More important, however, is the fact that his experience with English liberty gave him hope that a just and tolerant society was not a utopian dream, thereby strengthening his resolve to attack the abuses of French society.

As noted earlier, Voltaire was no democrat. He had little confidence in the capacities of the common people, whom he saw as prone to superstition and fanaticism. Nor did he advocate revolution. What he did favor was reforming society through the advancement of reason and the promotion of science and technology. Voltaire himself fought to introduce several reforms into France, including freedom of the press, religious toleration, a fair system of criminal justice, proportional taxation, and curtailment of the privileges of the clergy and nobility.

Rousseau

"Man is born free and everywhere he is in chains."[8] With these stirring words, the Geneva-born French thinker Jean Jacques Rousseau (1712–1778) began *The Social Contract* (1762). Rousseau considered the state as it was then constituted to be unjust and corrupt. It was dominated by the rich and the powerful, who used it to further their interests, whereas the weak knew only oppression and misery. In Rousseau's view, the modern state deprived human beings of their natural freedom and fostered a selfish individualism, which undermined feelings of mutuality and concern for the common good.

Rousseau wanted the state to be a genuine democracy, a moral association that bound people together in freedom, equality, and civic devotion. For Rousseau, individuals fulfilled their moral potential not in isolation, but as committed members of the community; human character was ennobled when people cooperated with one another and cared for one another. Rousseau admired the ancient Greek city-state, the polis, for it was an organic community in which citizens set aside private interests in order to attain the common good. In *The Social Contract,* he sought to recreate the community spirit and the political freedom that characterized the Greek city-state.

What Rousseau proposed was that each person surrender unconditionally all his rights to the community as a whole and submit to its authority. To prevent the assertion of private interests over the common good, Rousseau wanted the state to be governed in accordance with the general will — an underlying principle that expressed what was best for the community. He did not conceive of the general will as a majority or even a unanimous vote, both of which could be wrong. Rather, it was a plainly visible truth, easily discerned by common sense and by reason and by listening to our hearts. In Rousseau's view, just and enlightened citizens imbued with public spirit would have the good sense and moral awareness to legislate in accordance with the general will.

Like ancient Athens, the state that Rousseau envisioned was a direct democracy, in which the citizens themselves, not their representatives, constituted the lawmaking body. Consequently, the governed and the government were one and the same. Rousseau condemned arbitrary and despotic monarchy, the divine-right theory of kingship, and the traditional view that people should be governed by their betters, lords and clergy, who were entitled to special privileges. He granted sovereignty to the people as a whole and affirmed the principle of equality.

Rousseau remains a leading theorist of democratic thought. His critics assert that his political thought, whose goal is a body of citizens who think alike, buttresses a dangerous collectivism and even totalitarianism. These critics argue that Rousseau did not place constitutional limitations on sovereignty or erect safeguards to protect individual and minority rights from a potentially tyrannical majority. They note, too, that Rousseau rejected entirely the Lockean principle that citizens possess rights independently of the state, as well as the right to act against the state.

Social and Economic Thought

The philosophes rejected the Christian belief that human beings are endowed with a sinful nature, a consequence of Adam and Eve's disobedience of God. They knew from experience, of course, that human beings behave wickedly and seem hopelessly attached to nonrational modes of thinking. While they retained a certain pessimism about human nature, however, the philosophes generally believed in individuals' essential goodness and in their capacity for moral improvement. "Nature has not made us evil," wrote Diderot, "it is bad education, bad models, bad legislation that corrupt us."[9] And Voltaire declared that a person is "born neither good nor wicked; education, example, the government into which he is thrown — in short, occasion of every kind — determines him to virtue or vice."[10] The philosophes' conception of human nature rested heavily on John Locke's epistemology, or theory of knowledge. To the philosophes, it seemed that Locke had discovered the fundamental principles governing the human mind, an achievement comparable to Newton's discovery of the laws governing physical bodies.

Epistemology, Psychology, and Education

In his *Essay Concerning Human Understanding* (1690), a work of immense significance in the history of philosophy, Locke argued that human beings are not born with innate ideas (the idea of God, principles of good and evil, and rules of logic, for example) divinely implanted in their minds, as Descartes had maintained. Rather, said Locke, the human mind is a blank slate upon which are imprinted sensations derived from contact with the phenomenal world. Knowledge is derived from experience.

Locke's theory of knowledge had profound implications. If there are no innate ideas, said the philosophes, then human beings, contrary to Christian doctrine, are not born with original sin, are not depraved by nature. All that individuals are derives from their particular experiences. If people are provided with a proper environment and education, they will behave morally; they will become intelligent and productive citizens. By the proper use of their reason, people could bring their beliefs, their conduct, and their institutions into harmony with natural law. This was how the reform-minded philosophes interpreted Locke. They preferred to believe that evil stemmed from faulty institutions and poor education, both of which could be remedied, rather than from a defective human nature.

The most important work of Enlightenment educational thought was Rousseau's *Émile* (1762), in which he suggested educational reforms that would instill in children self-confidence, self-reliance, and emotional security — necessary qualities if they were to become productive adults and responsible citizens. If the young are taught to think for themselves, said Rousseau, they will learn to cherish personal freedom. A strong faith in the essential goodness of human nature underlay Rousseau's educational philosophy. He also assumed that youngsters have an equal capacity to learn and that differences in intelligence are due largely to environmental factors.

Rousseau understood that children should not be treated like little adults, for children have their own ways of thinking and feeling. He railed against those who robbed children of the joys and innocence of childhood by chaining them to desks, ordering them about, and filling their heads with rote learning. Instead, he urged that children experience direct contact with the world to develop their body and senses and their curiosity, ingenuity, resourcefulness, and imagination. It is the whole child that concerns Rousseau.

Freedom of Conscience and Thought

The philosophes regarded religious persecution — whose long and blood-stained history included the burning of heretics in the Middle Ages, the slaughter of Jews and Muslims during the First Crusade, and the massacres of the wars of the Reformation — as humanity's most depraved offense against reason. While the worst excesses of religious fanaticism had dissipated by the eighteenth century, examples of religious persecution still abounded, particularly in Catholic lands. In his pleas for tolerance, Voltaire spoke for all the philosophes:

> *I shall never cease . . . to preach tolerance from the housetops . . . until persecution is no more. The progress of reason is slow, the roots of prejudice lie deep. Doubtless, I shall never see the fruits of my efforts, but they are seeds which may one day germinate.*[11]

Censorship was a serious and ever-present problem for the philosophes. After the publication of Voltaire's *English Letters*, his printer was arrested and the book confiscated and publicly burned as irreligious. On another occasion, when Voltaire was harassed by the authorities, he commented that "It is easier for me to write books than to get them published."[12] Denounced by ecclesiastical and ministerial authorities as a threat to religion and constituted authority, *On the Mind* (1758), by Claude-Adrien Helvetius (1715–1771), was burned by the public executioner. Denis Diderot (1713–1784), the principal editor of the thirty-eight-volume *Encyclopedia*, whose 150 or more contributors included the leading Enlightenment thinkers, had to contend with

French authorities, who at times suspended publication. After the first two volumes appeared, the authorities condemned the work for containing "maxims that would tend to destroy royal authority, foment a spirit of independence and revolt . . . and lay the foundations for the corruption of morals and religion."[13] In 1759, Pope Clement XIII condemned the *Encyclopedia* for having "scandalous doctrines [and] inducing scorn for religion."[14] It required careful diplomacy and clever ruses to finish the project and still incorporate ideas considered dangerous by religious and governmental authorities. The *Encyclopedia* had been undertaken in Paris during the 1740s as a monumental effort to bring together all human knowledge and to propagate Enlightenment ideas. Its numerous articles on science and technology and its limited coverage of theological questions attest to the new interests of eighteenth-century intellectuals. With the project's completion in 1772, Diderot and Enlightenment opinion triumphed over clerical, royal, and aristocratic censors.

An article in the *Encyclopedia,* "The Press,"conveys the philosophes' yearning for freedom of thought and expression. For them, the term *press* designated more than newspapers and journals; it encompassed everything in print, particularly books.

> *People ask if freedom of the* press *is advantageous or prejudicial to a state. The answer is not difficult. It is of the greatest importance to conserve this practice in all states founded on liberty. I would even say that the disadvantages of this liberty are so inconsiderable compared to the advantages that this ought to be the common right of the universe, and it is certainly advisable to authorize its practices in all governments.*[15]

Humanitarianism

A humanitarian spirit, which no doubt owed something to Christian compassion, pervaded the outlook of the philosophes. It expressed itself in attacks on torture, which was commonly used to obtain confessions in many European lands, on cruel punishments for criminals, on slavery, and on war. The philosophes' humanitarianism rested on the conviction that human nature was essentially virtuous and that human beings were capable of benevolent feelings toward one another.

In *On Crimes and Punishments* (1764), Cesare Beccaria (1738–1794), an Italian economist and criminologist inspired in part by Montesquieu, condemned torture as inhuman, "a criterion fit for a cannibal."[16] He saw it as an irrational way of determining guilt or innocence, for an innocent person unable to withstand the agonies of torture will confess to anything and a criminal with a high threshold for pain will be exonerated. Influenced by Beccaria's work, reform-minded jurists, legislators, and ministers called for the elimination of torture from codes of criminal justice, and several European lands abolished torture in the eighteenth century.

Engraving, Newgate Prison, Eighteenth Century.   Prison conditions during the Age of Enlightenment were appalling. Here, a manacled man struggles with a wheelbarrow, and two others are led off to the gallows. Meanwhile, a guard watches over the dungeon filled with bound prisoners, who were as often debtors as criminals.

Though not pacifists, the philosophes denounced war as barbaric and an affront to reason. They deemed it to be a scourge promoted by power-hungry monarchs and supported by fanatical clergy, wicked army leaders, and ignorant commoners. In his literary masterpiece, *Candide* (1759), Voltaire ridiculed the rituals of war.

> *Nothing could be smarter, more splendid, more brilliant, better drawn up than the two armies. Trumpets, fifes, hautboys [oboes], drums, cannons, formed a harmony such as has never been heard even in hell. The cannons first of all laid flat about six thousand men on each side; then the musketry removed from the best of worlds some nine or ten thousand blackguards who infested its surface. The bayonet also was the sufficient reason for the death of some thousands of men. The whole might amount to thirty thousand souls.*[17]

Voltaire was particularly outraged by the belief that the outcome of this "heroic butchery" was ordained by God. The article "Peace" in the *Encyclopedia* described war as

> *the fruit of man's depravity; it is a convulsive and violent sickness of the body politic. . . . [It] depopulates the nation, causes the reign of disorder. . . . makes the freedom and property of citizens uncertain . . . disturbs and causes the neglect of commerce; land becomes uncultivated and abandoned. . . . If reason governed men and had the influence over the heads of nations that it deserves, we would never see them inconsiderately surrender themselves to the fury of war; they would not show that ferocity that characterizes wild beasts.*[18]

Montesquieu, Voltaire, Hume, Benjamin Franklin, Thomas Paine, and other philosophes condemned slavery and the slave trade. In Book 15 of *The Spirit of the Laws,* Montesquieu scornfully refuted all justifications for slavery. Ultimately, he said, slavery, which violates the fundamental principle of justice underlying the universe, derived from base human desires to dominate and exploit other human beings. Adam Smith (see next section), the Enlightenment's leading economic theorist, demonstrated that slave labor was inefficient and wasteful. In 1780, Paine helped draft the act abolishing slavery in Pennsylvania. An article in the *Encyclopedia,* "The Slave Trade," denounced slavery as a violation of the individual's natural rights:

> *If commerce of this kind can be justified by a moral principle, there is no crime, however atrocious it may be, that cannot be made legitimate. . . . Men and their liberty are not objects of commerce; they can be neither sold nor bought. . . . There is not, therefore, a single one of these unfortunate people regarded only as slaves who does not have the right to be declared free.*[19]

The philosophes, although they often enjoyed the company of intelligent and sophisticated women in the famous salons, continued to view women as intellectually and morally inferior to men. Although some philosophes, notably Condorcet (see p. 305), who wrote *Plea for the Citizenship of Women* (1791), did argue for female emancipation, they were the exception. Most concurred with David Hume (1711–1776), a Scottish sceptic, who held that "nature has subjected" women to men and that their "inferiority and infirmities are absolutely incurable."[20] Rousseau, who also believed that nature had granted men power over women, regarded traditional domesticity as a woman's proper role.

> *I would a thousand times rather have a homely girl, simply brought up, than a learned lady and a wit who would make a literary circle of my house and install herself as its president. A female wit is a scourge to her husband, her children, her friends, her servants, to everybody. From the lofty height of her genius, she scorns every womanly duty, and she is always trying to make a man of herself.*[21]

Nevertheless, by clearly articulating the ideals of liberty and equality, the philosophes made a women's movement possible. The growing popularity of these ideals could not escape women, who measured their own position by them. Moreover, by their very nature, these ideals were expansive. Denying them to women would ultimately be seen as an indefensible contradiction.

Thus, Mary Wollstonecraft's *Vindication of the Rights of Woman,* written under the influence of the French Revolution, protested against the prevailing subordination and submissiveness of women and the limited opportunities afforded them to cultivate their minds. If women were also endowed with reason, why should men alone determine the standards and ground rules, she asked pungently. She reminded enlightened thinkers that the same arbitrary power that they objected to when wielded by monarchs and slave owners they condoned when exercised by husbands in domestic life. She considered it an act of tyranny for women "to be excluded from a participation of the natural rights of mankind."[22]

Laissez-Faire Economics

In *An Inquiry into the Nature and Causes of the Wealth of Nations* (1776), Adam Smith (1732–1790), professor of moral philosophy in Scotland, attacked the theory of mercantilism, which held that a state's wealth was determined by the amount of gold and silver it possessed. According to this theory, to build up its reserves of precious metals, the state should promote domestic industries, encourage exports, and discourage imports. Mercantilist theory called for government regulation of the economy so that the state could compete successfully with other nations for a share of the world's scarce resources. Smith argued that the real basis of a country's wealth was measured by the quantity and quality of its goods and services, not by its storehouse of precious metals. Government intervention, he said, retards economic progress; it reduces the real value of the annual produce of the nation's land and labor. On the other hand, when people pursue their own interests — when they seek to better their condition — they foster economic expansion, which benefits the whole society.

Smith limited the state's authority to maintaining law and order, administering justice, and defending the nation. The concept of *laissez faire* — that government should not interfere with the market — became a core principle of nineteenth-century liberal thought.

The Idea of Progress

The philosophes were generally optimistic about humanity's future progress. Two main assumptions contributed to this optimism. First, accepting Locke's theory of knowledge, the philosophes attributed evil to a flawed but remediable environment, not to an inherently wicked human nature. Hopeful that a reformed environment would bring out the best in people, they looked forward to a day when reason would prevail over superstition, prejudice, intolerance, and tyranny. Second, the philosophes' veneration of science led them to believe that the progressive advancement of knowledge would promote material and moral progress.

A work written near the end of the century epitomized the philosophes' vision of the future: *Sketch for a Historical Picture of the Progress of the Human Mind* (1794) by Marie Jean Antoine Nicolas Caritat, marquis de Condorcet (1743–1794). A mathematician and historian of science and a contributor to the *Encyclopedia,* Condorcet campaigned for religious toleration and the abolition of slavery. During the French Revolution, he attracted the enmity of the dominant Jacobin party and in 1793 was forced to go into hiding. Secluded in Paris, he wrote *Sketch.* Arrested in 1794, Condorcet died during his first night in prison, either from exhaustion or from self-administered poison. In *Sketch*, Condorcet lauded recent advances in knowledge that enabled reason to "lift her chains (and) shake herself free"[23] from superstition and tyranny. Passionately affirming the Enlightenment's confidence in reason and science, Condorcet expounded a theory of continuous and indefinite human improvement. He pointed toward a future golden age, characterized by the triumph of reason and freedom.

> *Our hopes for the future condition of the human race can be subsumed under three important heads: the abolition of inequality between nations, the progress of equality within each nation, and the true perfection of mankind. . . .*
>
> *The time will therefore come when the sun will shine only on free men who know no other master but their reason; when tyrants and slaves, priests and their stupid or hypocritical instruments will exist only in works of history and on the stage; and we shall think of them only to pity their victims and their dupes; to maintain ourselves in a state of vigilance by thinking on their excesses; and to learn how to recognize and so to destroy, by force of reason, the first seeds of tyranny and superstition, should they ever dare to reappear amongst us.*[24]

But the philosophes were not starry-eyed dreamers. They knew that progress was painful, slow, and reversible. Voltaire's *Candide* was a protest against a naive optimism that ignored the granite might of human meanness, ignorance, and irrationality. "Let us weep and wail over the lot of philosophy," wrote Diderot. "We preach wisdom to the deaf and we are still far indeed from the age of reason."[25]

War, Revolution, and Politics

The major conflicts of the eighteenth century were between Britain and France for control of territory in the New World and between Austria and Prussia for dominance in central Europe. Then, in the late 1700s, the

The Signing of the Declaration of Independence, Philadelphia, July 4, 1776, by John Trumbull (Detail).   The success of the American Revolution was hailed as a victory of liberty over tyranny. French military and financial support of the Americans led to the bankruptcy of the French monarchy by 1788, a factor that contributed to the French Revolution. The American Founding Fathers were familiar with the ideas of the Enlightenment, particularly John Locke's theory of natural rights. (*Copyright Yale University Art Gallery*)

American and French Revolutions broke out; they helped shape the liberal-democratic tradition.

Warfare and Revolution

In 1740, Prussia, ruled by the aggressive Frederick the Great, launched a successful war against Austria and was rewarded with Silesia, which increased the Prussian population by 50 percent. Maria Theresa, the Austrian queen, never forgave Frederick and in 1756 formed an alliance with France against Prussia. The ensuing Seven Years' War (1756–1763), which involved every major European power, did not significantly change Europe, but it did reveal Prussia's growing might.

At the same time, the French and the English fought over their claims in the New World. England's victory in the conflict (known in American history as the French and Indian War) deprived France of virtually all of its North American possessions and set in motion a train of events that culminated in the American Revolution. The war drained the British treasury, and now Britain had the additional expense of paying for troops to guard the new North American territories that it had gained in the war. As strapped British taxpayers could not shoulder the whole burden, the members of Parliament thought it quite reasonable that the American colonists should help pay the bill; after all, Britain had protected the colonists from the French and was still protecting them in their conflicts with Indians. New colonial taxes and import duties imposed by Parliament produced vigorous protests from the Americans.

The quarrel turned to bloodshed in April and June 1775, and on July 4, 1776, delegates from the various colonies adopted the Declaration of Independence, written mainly by Thomas Jefferson. Applying Locke's theory of natural rights, this document declared that government derives its power from the consent of the governed, that it is the duty of a government to protect the rights of its citizens, and that people have the right to "alter or abolish" a government that deprives them of their "unalienable rights."

Why were the American colonists so ready to revolt? For one thing, they had brought with them a highly idealized understanding of English liberties; long before 1776, they had extended representative institutions to include small property owners, who probably could not have voted in England. The colonists had come to expect representative government, trial by jury, and protection from unlawful imprisonment. Each of the thirteen colonies had an elected assembly, which acted like a miniature parliament. In these assemblies, Americans gained political experience and quickly learned to be self-governing.

Familiarity with the thought of the Enlightenment and the republican writers of the English Revolution also contributed to the Americans' awareness of liberty. The ideas of the philosophes traversed the Atlantic and influenced educated Americans, particularly Thomas Jefferson and Benjamin Franklin. Like the philosophes, American thinkers expressed a growing confidence in reason, valued freedom of religion and of thought, and championed the principle of natural rights.

Another source of hostility toward established authority among the American colonists was their religious traditions, particularly those of the Puritans, who believed that the Bible was infallible and its teachings a higher law than the law of the state. Like their counterparts in England, American Puritans challenged political and religious authorities who, in their view, contravened God's law. Thus, Puritans acquired two habits that were crucial to the development of political liberty: dissent and resistance. When transferred to the realm of politics, these Puritan tendencies led Americans to resist authority that they considered unjust.

American victory came about in 1783 as a result of several factors. George Washington proved to be a superior leader, able to organize and retain the loyalty of his troops. France, seeking to avenge its defeat in the Seven Years' War, helped the Americans with money and provisions and then, in 1778, entered the conflict. Britain had difficulty shipping supplies across three thousand miles of ocean, was fighting the French in the West Indies and elsewhere at the same time, and ultimately lacked commitment to the struggle.

Reformers in other lands quickly interpreted the American victory as a successful struggle of liberty against tyranny. During the Revolution, the various American states drew up constitutions based on the principle of popular sovereignty and included bills of rights that protected individual liberty. They also managed, somewhat reluctantly, to forge a nation. Rejecting both monarchy and hereditary aristocracy, the Constitution of the United States created a republic in which power derived from the people. A system of separation of powers and checks and balances set safeguards against the abuse of power, and the Bill of Rights provided for protection of individual rights. To be sure, the ideals of liberty and equality were not extended to all people — slaves knew nothing of the freedom that white Americans cherished, and women were denied the vote and equal opportunity. But to reform-minded Europeans, it seemed that Americans were fulfilling the promise of the Enlightenment; they were creating a freer and better society.

Enlightened Despotism

The philosophes used the term *enlightened despotism* to refer to an ideal shared by many of them: rule by a strong monarch who would implement rational reforms and remove obstacles to freedom. Some eighteenth-century monarchs and their ministers — Frederick the Great in Prussia, Catherine the Great in Russia, Charles III in Spain, Maria Theresa and, to a greater extent, her son Joseph II in Austria, and Louis XV in France — did institute educational, commercial, and religious reforms.

Behind the reforms of enlightened despots lay the realization that the struggle for power in Europe called for efficient government administration and ample funds. Enlightened despots appointed capable officials to oversee the administration of their kingdoms, eliminate costly corruption, and collect taxes properly. Rulers strengthened the economy by encouraging the expansion of commerce through reduced taxes on goods and through agricultural reforms. In central and Eastern Europe, some rulers moved toward abolishing serfdom, or at least improving conditions for serfs. (In Western Europe, serfdom had virtually died out.) Provisions were made to care for widows, orphans, and invalids. Censorship was eased, greater religious freedom was granted to minorities, criminal codes were made less harsh, and there were some attempts at prison reform. By these measures, enlightened despots hoped to inspire greater popular support for the state, an important factor in the European power struggle.

The Enlightenment and the Modern Mentality

The philosophes articulated core principles of the modern outlook. Asserting that human beings are capable of thinking independently of authority, they insisted on a thoroughgoing rational and secular interpretation of nature and society. They critically scrutinized authority and tradition and valued science and technology as a means for promoting human betterment. Above all, they sought to emancipate the mind from the bonds of ignorance and superstition and to rescue people from intolerance, cruelty, and oppression. Because of their efforts, torture (which states and Christian churches had endorsed and practiced) was eventually abolished in Western lands, and religious toleration and freedom of speech and of the press became the accepted norms. The arguments that the philosophes marshaled against slavery were utilized by those who fought against the slave trade and called for emancipation. Enlightenment economic thought, particularly Adam Smith's *Wealth of Nations,* gave theoretical support to a market economy based on supply and demand — an outlook that fostered commercial and industrial expansion. The separation of church and state, a basic principle of modern political life, owes much to the philosophes, who frequently cited the dangers of politics inflamed by religious passions. The philosophes' denunciation of despotism and championing of natural rights, equality under the law, and constitutional government are the chief foundations of modern liberal government.

The ideals of the Enlightenment spread from Europe to America and helped shape the political thought of the Founding Fathers. The Declaration of Independence clearly articulated Locke's basic principles: that government derives its authority from the governed; that human beings are born with natural rights, which government has a responsibility to protect; and that citizens have the right to resist a government that deprives them of these rights. The Constitution asserted that the people are sovereign: "We the People of the United States . . . do ordain and establish this Constitution for the United States of America." And it contained several safeguards against despotic power, including Montesquieu's principle of separation of powers, which was also written into several state constitutions. Both the bills of rights drawn up by the various states and the federal Bill of Rights gave recognition to the individual's inherent rights and explicitly barred government from tampering with them — a principal concern of the philosophes.

The philosophes broke with the traditional Christian view of human nature and the purpose of life. In that view, men and women were born in sin; suffering and misery were divinely ordained, and relief could come only from God; social inequality was instituted by God; and for many, eternal damnation was a deserved final consequence. In contrast, the philosophes saw injustice and suffering as man-made problems that could be solved through reason; they expressed confidence in people's ability to attain happiness by improving the conditions of their earthly existence and articulated a theory of human progress that did not require divine assistance.

To be sure, the promise of the Enlightenment has not been achieved. More education for more people and the spread of constitutional government have not eliminated fanaticism and superstition, violence and war, or evil and injustice. In the light of twentieth-century events, it is difficult to subscribe to Condorcet's belief in linear progress. As Peter Gay observes:

> *The world has not turned out the way the philosophes wished and half expected that it would. Old fanaticisms have been more intractable, irrational forces more inventive than the philosophes were ready to conjecture in their darkest moments. Problems of race, of class, of nationalism, of boredom and despair in the midst of plenty have emerged almost in defiance of the philosophes' philosophy. We have known horrors, and may know horrors, that the men of the Enlightenment did not see in their nightmares.*[26]

Nevertheless, the philosophes' achievement should not be diminished. Their ideals became an intrinsic part of the liberal-democratic tradition and inspired nineteenth- and twentieth-century reformers. The spirit of the Enlightenment will always remain indispensable to all those who cherish the traditions of reason and freedom.

Notes

1. Galileo Galilei, *The Starry Messenger,* in *Discoveries and Opinions of Galileo,* trans. and ed. Stillman Drake (Garden City, N.Y.: Doubleday Anchor Books, 1957), p. 31.
2. Galileo Galilei, *The Assayer,* in *Discoveries and Opinions,* pp. 237–238.
3. Galileo Galilei, "Letter to the Grand Duchess Christina," in *Discoveries and Opinions,* p. 183.
4. Quoted in Frank E. Manuel, *Age of Reason* (Ithaca, N.Y.: Cornell University Press, 1951), p. 28.
5. Quoted in Ben Ray Redman, ed., *The Portable Voltaire* (New York: Viking Press, 1949), p. 26.
6. Thomas Paine, *The Age of Reason* (New York: Eckler, 1892), p. 5.
7. Quoted in Paul Hazard, *European Thought in the Eighteenth Century* (New Haven: Yale University Press, 1954), p 174.
8. Jean Jacques Rousseau, *The Social Contract,* in *The Social Contract and Discourses,* ed. and trans.

G. D. H. Cole (New York: Dutton, 1950), bk. 1, chap. 1, p. 3.
9. Quoted in Peter Gay, *The Enlightenment: An Interpretation,* vol. 2, *The Science of Freedom* (New York: Vintage Books, 1966), p. 170.
10. Quoted in Steven Seidman, *Liberalism and the Origins of European Social Theory* (Berkeley: University of California Press, 1983), p. 30.
11. Voltaire, "Letter to M. Bertrand," in *Candide and Other Writings,* ed. Haskell M. Block (New York: Modern Library, 1956), p. 525.
12. Quoted in Peter Gay, *Voltaire's Politics* (New York: Random House, Vintage Books, 1965), p. 71.
13. Quoted in Stephen J. Gendzier, ed. and trans., *Denis Diderot's The Encyclopedia Selections* (New York: Harper Torchbooks, 1967), p. xxv.
14. Ibid., p. xxvi.
15. Excerpted in Gendzier, *Diderot's Encyclopedia Selections,* p. 199.

16. Cesare Beccaria, *On Crimes and Punishments,* trans. Henry Paolucci (Indianapolis: Library of Liberal Arts, 1963), p. 32.

17. Voltaire, *Candide,* in *The Portable Voltaire,* ed. Ben Ray Redman (New York: Viking, 1949), p. 234.

18. Excerpted in Gendzier, *Diderot's Encyclopedia Selections,* pp. 183–184.

19. Excerpted in ibid., pp. 229–230.

20. Quoted in Bonnie S. Anderson and Judith P. Zinsser, *A History of Their Own* (New York: Harper & Row, 1988), 2:113.

21. Jean Jacques Rousseau, *Emile,* trans. Barbara Foxley (London: Dent, Everyman's Library, 1974), p. 370.

22. Mary Wollstonecraft, *Vindication of the Rights of Woman* (London: Dent, 1929), pp. 11–12.

23. Antoine Nicolas de Condorcet, *Sketch for a Historical Picture of the Progress of the Human Mind,* trans. June Barraclough (London: Weidenfeld & Nicholas, 1955), p. 124.

24. Ibid., pp. 173–179.

25. Quoted in Gay, *The Enlightenment,* vol. 1, *The Rise of Modern Paganism,* 1:20.

26. Ibid., 2:567.

Suggested Reading

Anchor, Robert, *The Enlightenment Tradition* (1967). A useful survey.

Andrade, da C. E. N., *Sir Isaac Newton* (1954). Brief and clear.

Armitage, Angus, *The World of Copernicus* (1951). Good discussion of the old astronomy and the birth of the new.

Brumfit, J. H., *The French Enlightenment* (1972). A useful survey.

Cohen, I. B., *The Birth of a New Physics* (1960). A classic study.

Commager, Henry Steele, *The Empire of Reason* (1977). The Enlightenment in the United States.

Drake, Stillman, *Galileo* (1980). By a leading authority.

Einaudi, Mario, *The Early Rousseau* (1967). Good discussions of some key works.

Gay, Peter, *The Enlightenment: An Interpretation,* 2 vols. (1966). An exhaustive study.

Hampson, Norman, *The Enlightenment* (1968). A useful survey.

McMullen, Ernan, ed., *Galileo Man of Science* (1967). Contains many thoughtful essays on Galileo's life and achievement.

Outram, Dorinda, *The Enlightenment* (1995). An accessible recent synthesis.

Rosen, Edward, *Copernicus and the Scientific Revolution* (1984). By a recognized authority.

Yolton, John W., ed., *The Blackwell Companion to the Enlightenment* (1991). An excellent reference work for all phases of the Enlightenment.

Review Questions

1. How did the Scientific Revolution transform the medieval view of the universe?

2. Describe the major achievements of Copernicus, Kepler, Galileo, and Newton.

3. How did the Scientific Revolution contribute to the shaping of the modern mentality?

4. Why is the eighteenth century referred to as the Age of

Enlightenment? What are the antecedents of the Enlightenment?

5. Why did the philosophes attack Christianity?

6. How did Voltaire exemplify the philosophes?

7. Compare and contrast the political thought of Hobbes and Locke. Why is Locke considered a forerunner of liberalism?

8. Why is Rousseau considered a theorist of democracy? Why has his political thought come under attack?

9. What was the significance of Locke's theory of knowledge for the Enlightenment?

10. How did the ideals of the Enlightenment contribute to feminism and the movement to abolish slavery?

11. What ideals of the Enlightenment found expression during the period of the American Revolution?

12. How did the Enlightenment contribute to the shaping of the modern mentality?

❖ Index